FORCE

ATSUSHI
OHKUBO

18

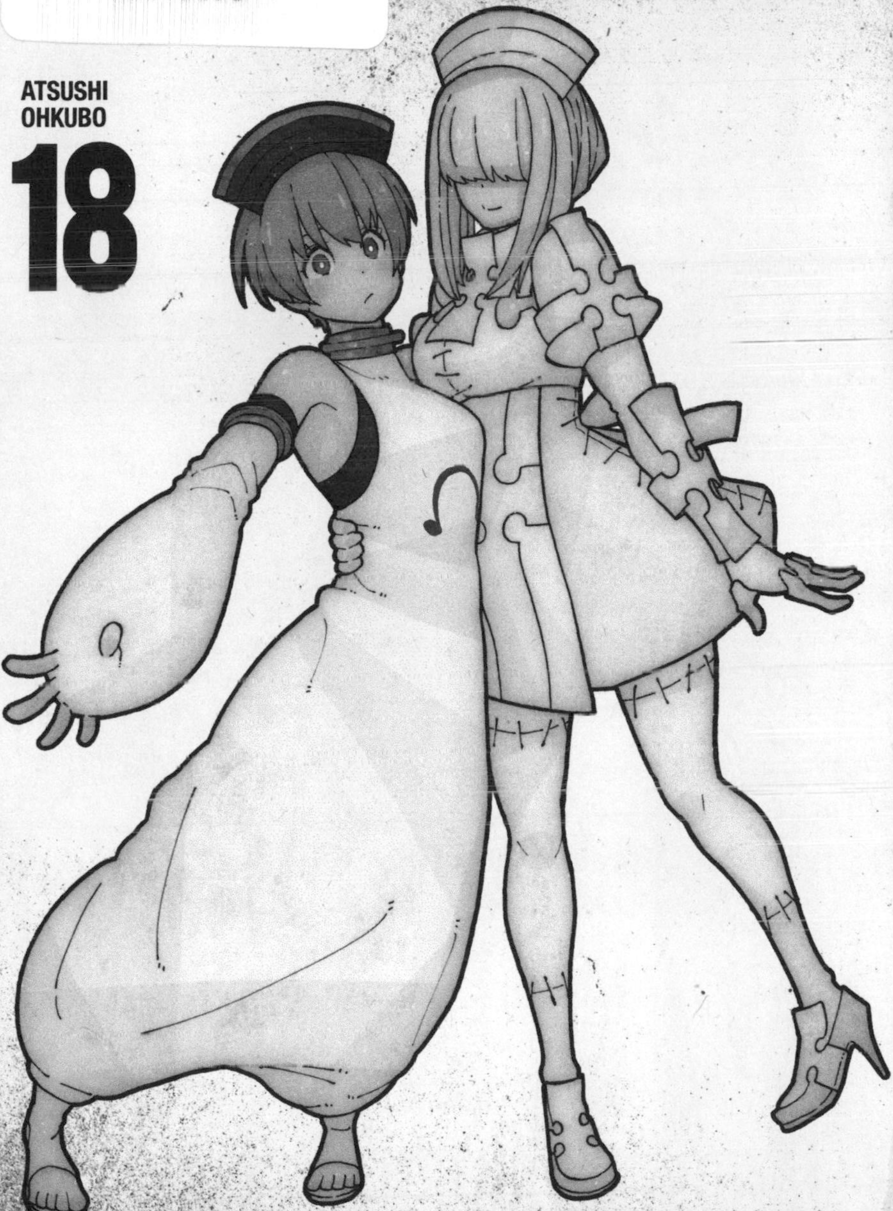

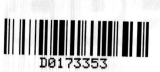

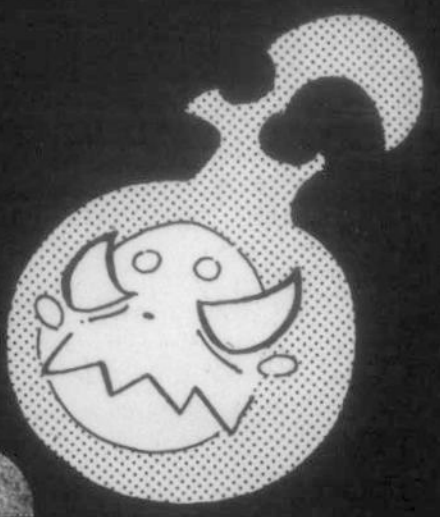

dive, dive...

burn, burn...

die, die...

VOL. 18

ATSUSHI OHKUBO

Dive,
Burn,
Die,

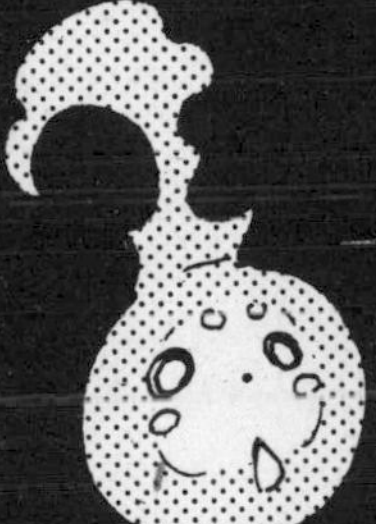

FIRE FORCE

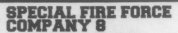

SPECIAL FIRE FORCE COMPANY 8

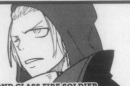

CAPTAIN
(NON-POWERED)
AKITARU ŌBI

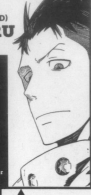

The caring leader of the newly established Company 8. His goal is to investigate the other companies and uncover the truth about spontaneous human combustion. He has no powers, but uses his finely honed muscles as a weapon in a battle style that makes him worthy of the Captain title. A man of character, respected even in other companies.

SECOND CLASS FIRE SOLDIER
(THIRD GENERATION PYROKINETIC)
ARTHUR BOYLE

Trained at the academy with Shinra. He follows his own personal code of chivalry as the self-proclaimed Knight King. He's a blockhead who is bad at mental exercise. But girls love him. He creates a fire sword with a blade that can cut through most anything. He's a weirdo who grows stronger the more delusional he gets.

WATCHES OUT FOR

TRUSTS

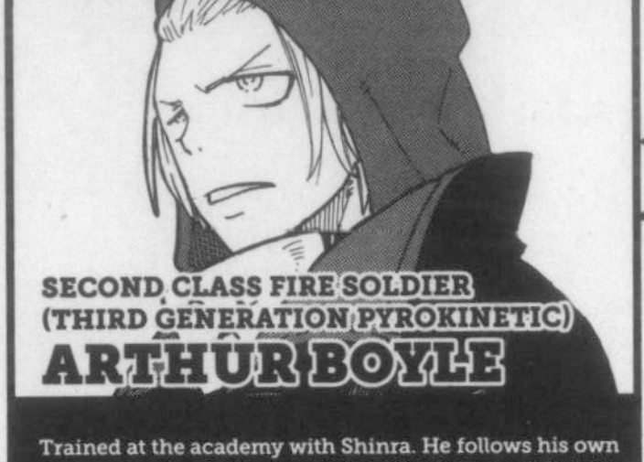

IDIOT!!

WATCHES OUT FOR

TRUSTS

STRONG BOND

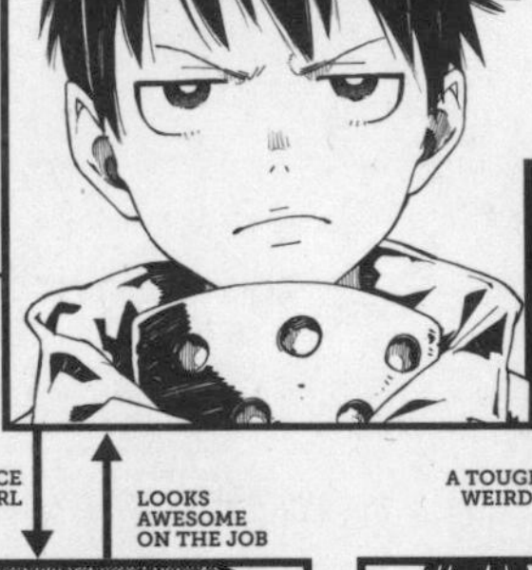

SECOND CLASS FIRE SOLDIER
(THIRD GENERATION PYROKINETIC)
SHINRA KUSAKABE

The bizarre smile that shows on his face when he gets nervous has earned him the derisive nickname of "devil," but he dreams of becoming a hero who saves people from spontaneous combustion! His weapon is a fiery kick. He wields a special flame called the Adolla Burst. Before entering the training academy, he was kept in the custody of Haijima Industries' Power Development Facility.

A NICE GIRL

LOOKS AWESOME ON THE JOB

A TOUGH BUT WEIRD LADY

HANG IN THERE, ROOKIE!

TERRIFIED

STRICT DISCIPLINARIAN

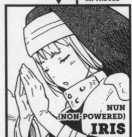

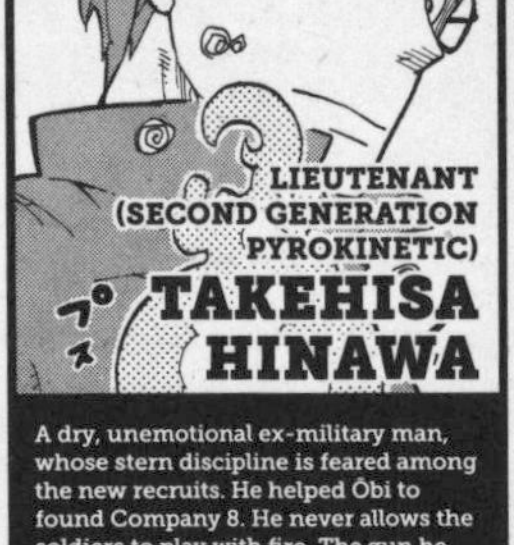

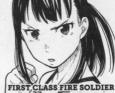

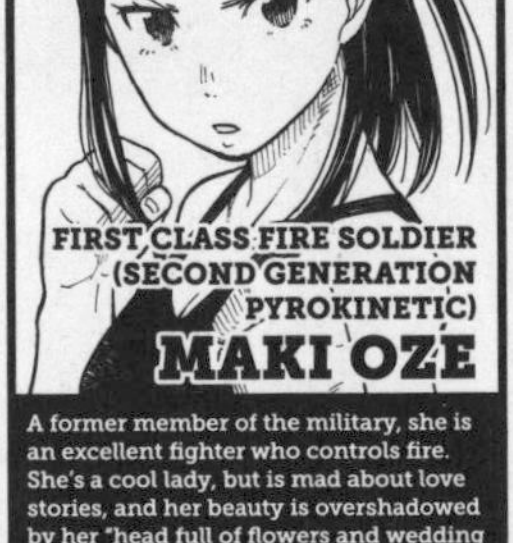

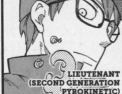

LIEUTENANT
(SECOND GENERATION PYROKINETIC)
TAKEHISA HINAWA

A dry, unemotional ex-military man, whose stern discipline is feared among the new recruits. He helped Ōbi to found Company 8. He never allows the soldiers to play with fire. The gun he uses is a cherished memento from his friend who became an Infernal.

FIRST CLASS FIRE SOLDIER
(SECOND GENERATION PYROKINETIC)
MAKI OZE

A former member of the military, she is an excellent fighter who controls fire. She's a cool lady, but is mad about love stories, and her beauty is overshadowed by her "head full of flowers and wedding bells." She's friendly, but goes berserk when anyone comments on her muscles. Her compatibility with Vulcan's invention, the Tekkyō, is superb.

NUN
(NON-POWERED)
IRIS

A sister of the Holy Sol Temple, her prayers are an indispensable part of extinguishing Infernals. Personality-wise, she is no less than an angel. Her boobs are big. Very big. She demonstrated incredible resilience in facing the Infernal hordes.

THE GIRLS' CLUB

RESPECTS

FOLLOWERS OF THE EVANGELIST

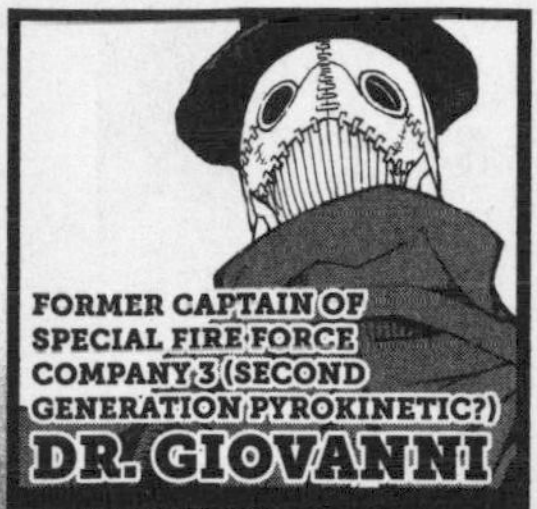

FORMER CAPTAIN OF SPECIAL FIRE FORCE COMPANY 3 (SECOND GENERATION PYROKINETIC?)

DR. GIOVANNI

A traitor who started working for the Evangelist despite being a captain in the Special Fire Force. Is performing experiments on using bugs to create artificial Infernals.

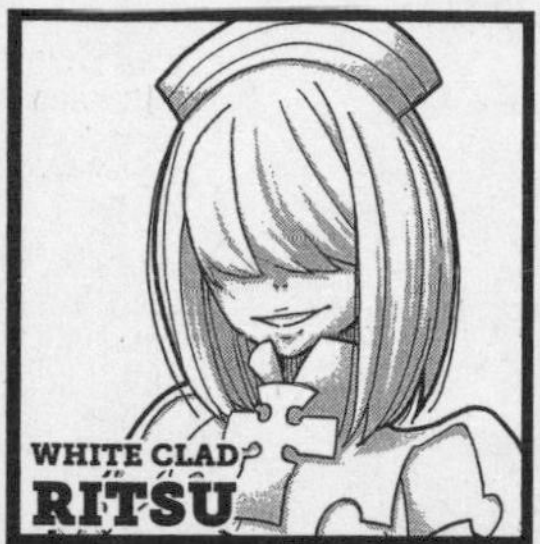

WHITE CLAD

RITSU

Guardian Maid of the Fifth Pillar, Inca. Has the power to animate the dead and create the giant Great Fiery Infernal.

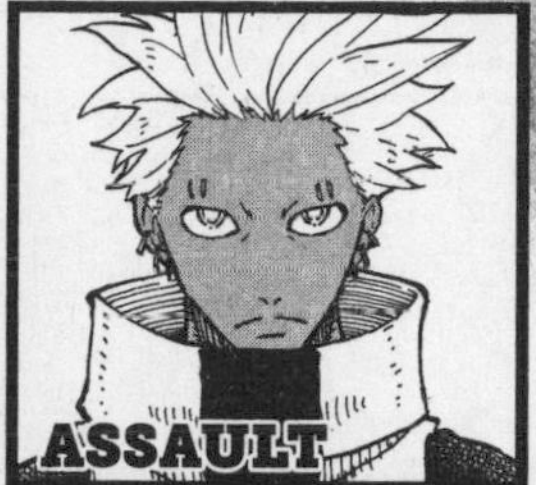

ASSAULT

Third Generation Pyrokinetic. His extreme skill has earned him various other names, but in the Nether he was defeated by Tamaki's Lucky Lecher Lure.

SPECIAL FIRE FORCE COMPANY 2

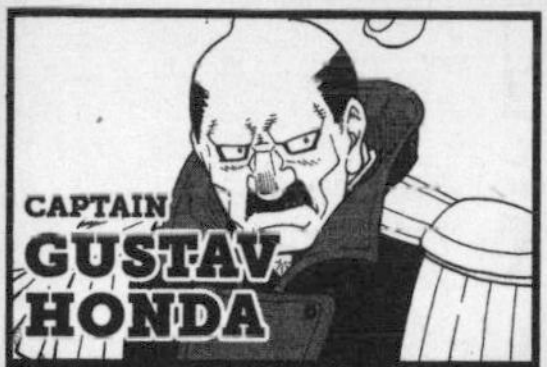

CAPTAIN

GUSTAV HONDA

Captain of Company 2, which is directly affiliated with the military.

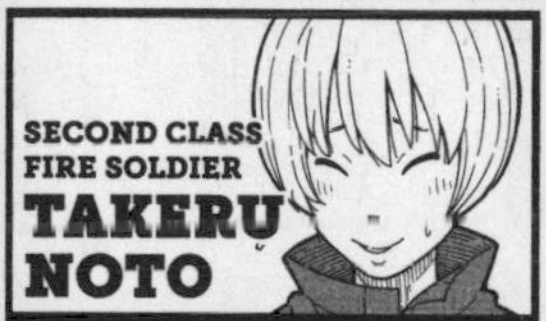

SECOND CLASS FIRE SOLDIER

TAKERU NOTO

A native of Xinqing Dao and a potato farmer nicknamed "Juggernaut." A quasi immortal character who keeps himself alive by bundling up in his turnout gear.

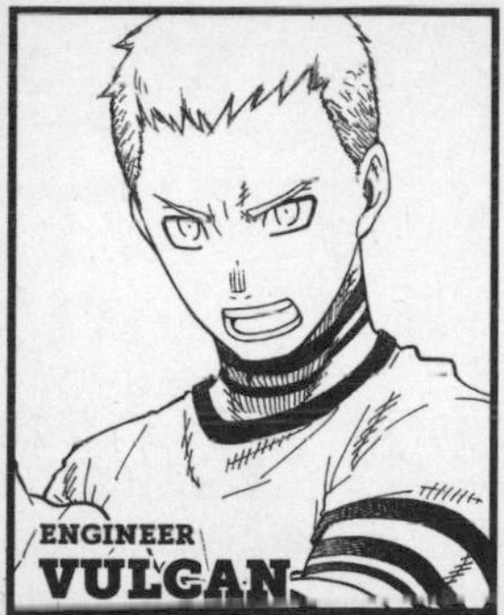

ENGINEER

VULCAN

The greatest contemporary engineer, renowned as the God of Fire and the Forge. The weapons he created have increased Company 8's powers immensely. Is determined to create a power generator that is better than Amaterasu and that won't require a sacrifice.

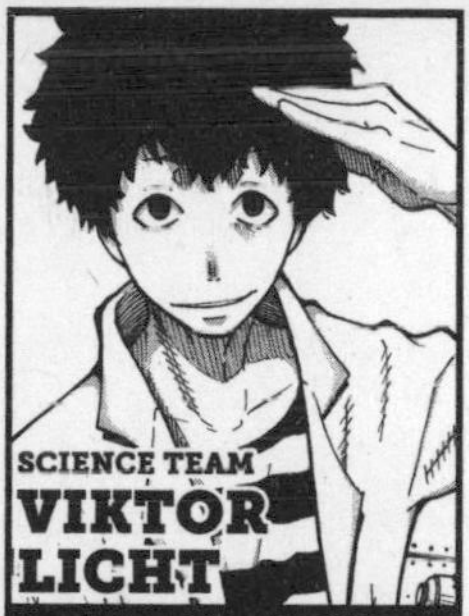

SCIENCE TEAM

VIKTOR LICHT

A suspicious genius deployed from Haijima Industries to fill the vacancy in Company 8's science department. He also analyzes fire scenes. Has confessed to being a Haijima spy.

SUMMARY...

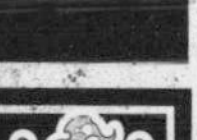
SPUTT
SPUTT

The fight over Nataku, who just awakened to his Adolla Burst powers, became a three-way battle when the Evangelist's goons got between Company 8 and Haijima Industries. Absorbed into the Great Firey Infernal created by Ritsu's magic, and with his mind taken over by a specter of Rekka, Nataku lost control. He emitted dangerous radiation and beams of light that could raze buildings. This escalated until Nataku almost wiped out all of Tokyo. However, the White Clad Charon deflected the attack onto the moon, and with Kurono's help, Nataku regains control of his former weaker state...

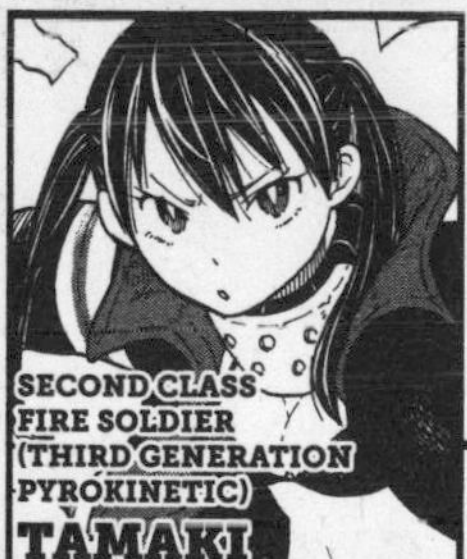

SECOND CLASS FIRE SOLDIER (THIRD GENERATION PYROKINETIC)

TAMAKI KOTATSU

HAS HIM ON HER MIND

A rookie from Company 1 currently in Company 8's care. Although she has a "Lucky Lecher Lure" condition, she nevertheless has a pure heart. Which, in a sense, makes her unbeatable.

FIRE FORCE 18

CONTENTS

HIS TRAINING IS COMPLETE?
THAT EPIC, INTENSE TRAINING? ALREADY?
THE TIME HAS COME.
THE FIERY BLAST RISES.
OR RATHER ...
WHOOOOOSH

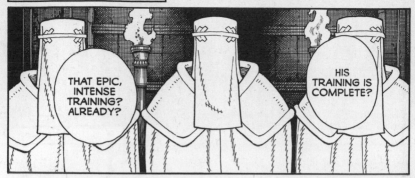

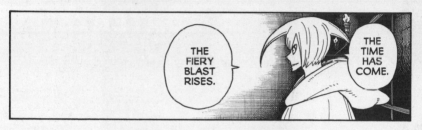

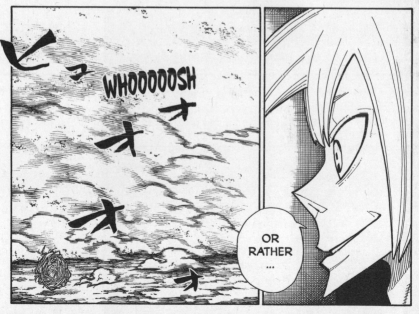

CHAPTER CLI:

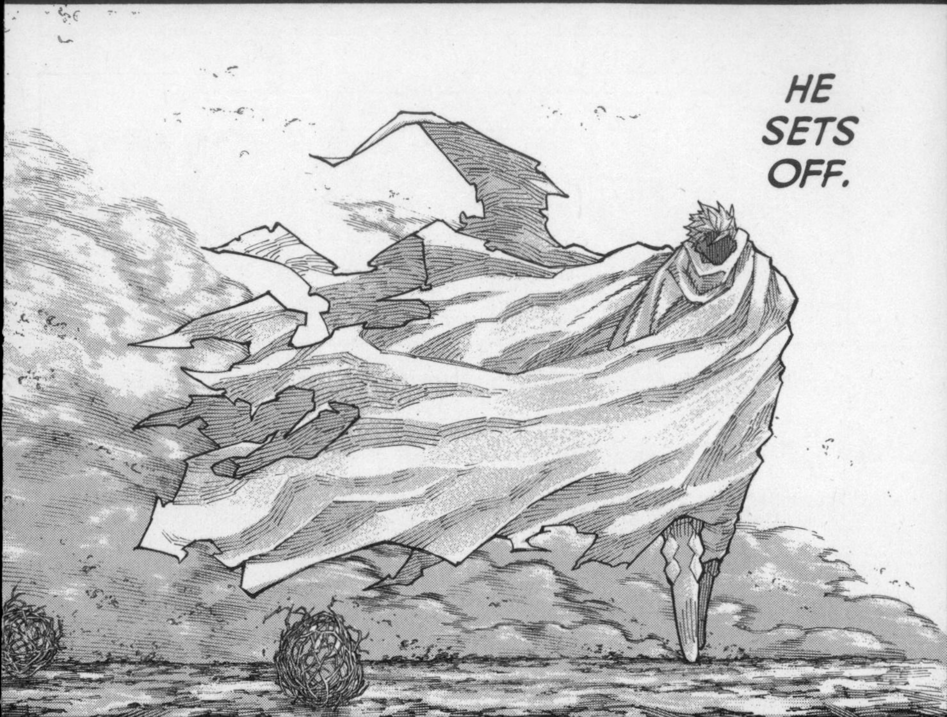
HE SETS OFF.

THE MAN, ASSAULT

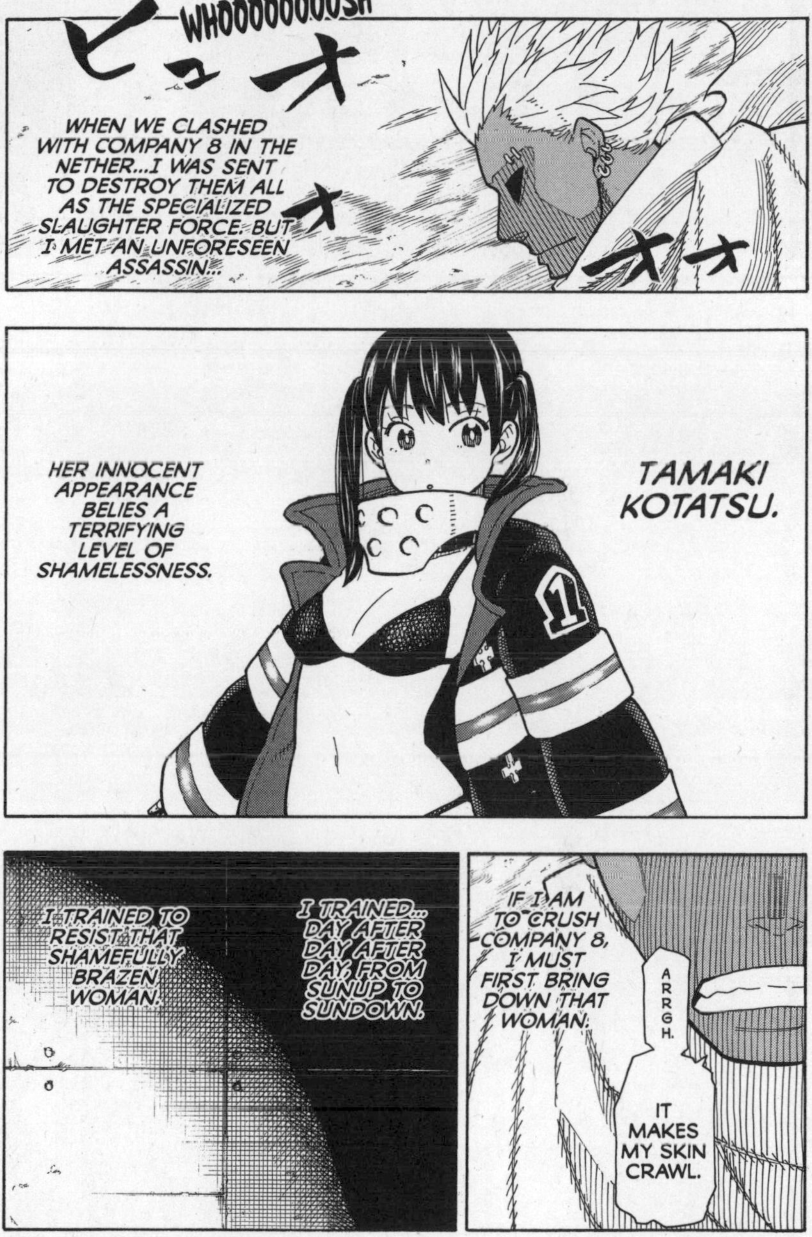
ヒュオ
WHOOOOOOOOSH
WHEN WE CLASHED WITH COMPANY 8 IN THE NETHER...I WAS SENT TO DESTROY THEM ALL AS THE SPECIALIZED SLAUGHTER FORCE. BUT I MET AN UNFORESEEN ASSASSIN...
オ
オオ
TAMAKI KOTATSU.
HER INNOCENT APPEARANCE BELIES A TERRIFYING LEVEL OF SHAMELESSNESS.
IF I AM TO CRUSH COMPANY 8, I MUST FIRST BRING DOWN THAT WOMAN.
ARRGH.
IT MAKES MY SKIN CRAWL.
I TRAINED... DAY AFTER DAY AFTER DAY, FROM SUNUP TO SUNDOWN.
I TRAINED TO RESIST THAT SHAMEFULLY BRAZEN WOMAN.

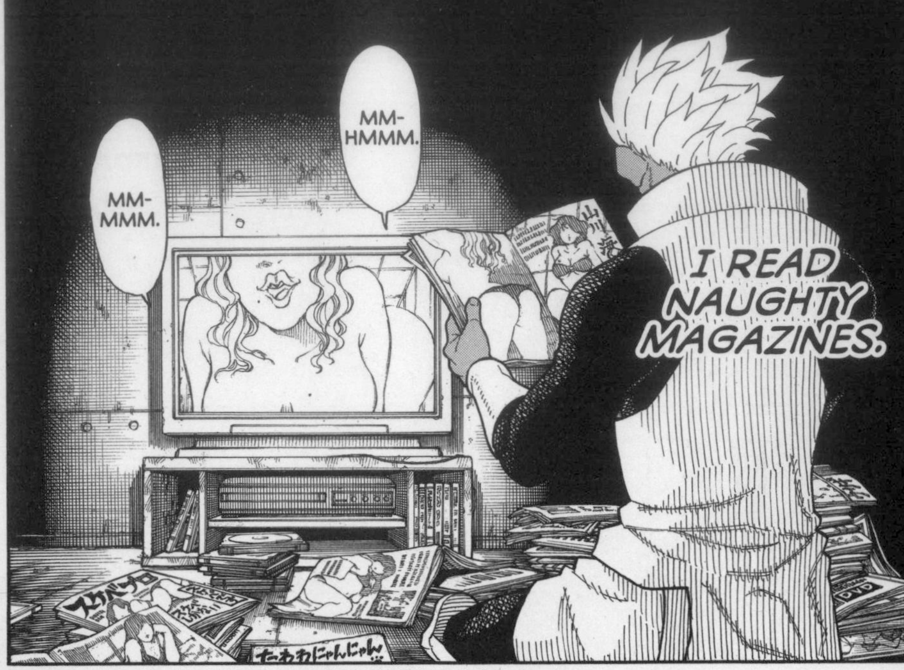
MM-HMMM.
MM-MMM.
I READ NAUGHTY MAGAZINES.

Magazine (R to L): Umi Yamakawa; Total Me-Yow Ow!; PERVS PRO We're Pervs! All-Perv Central

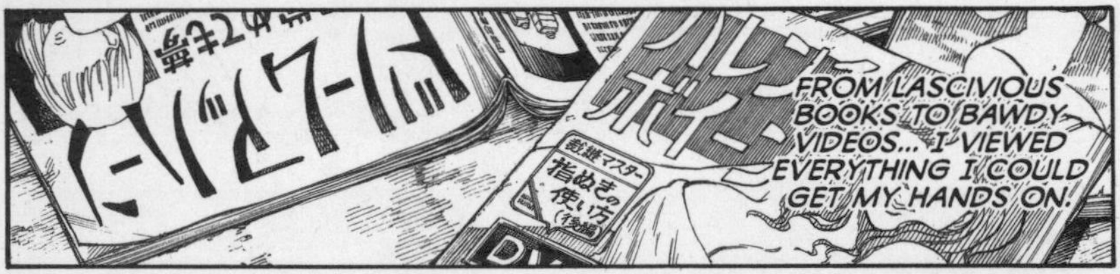
FROM LASCIVIOUS BOOKS TO BAWDY VIDEOS... I VIEWED EVERYTHING I COULD GET MY HANDS ON.

Magazines (R to L): BRAZEN BOING, Embroidery Master: How to Use a Thimble (Pt.2); OOH LA LA DREAM, Neverending Dream

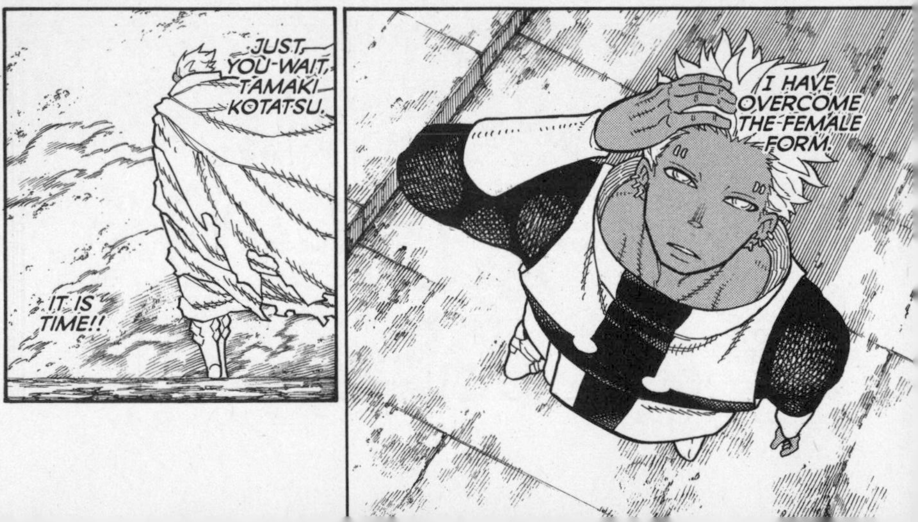
I HAVE OVERCOME THE FEMALE FORM.
JUST YOU WAIT, TAMAKI KOTATSU.
IT IS TIME!!

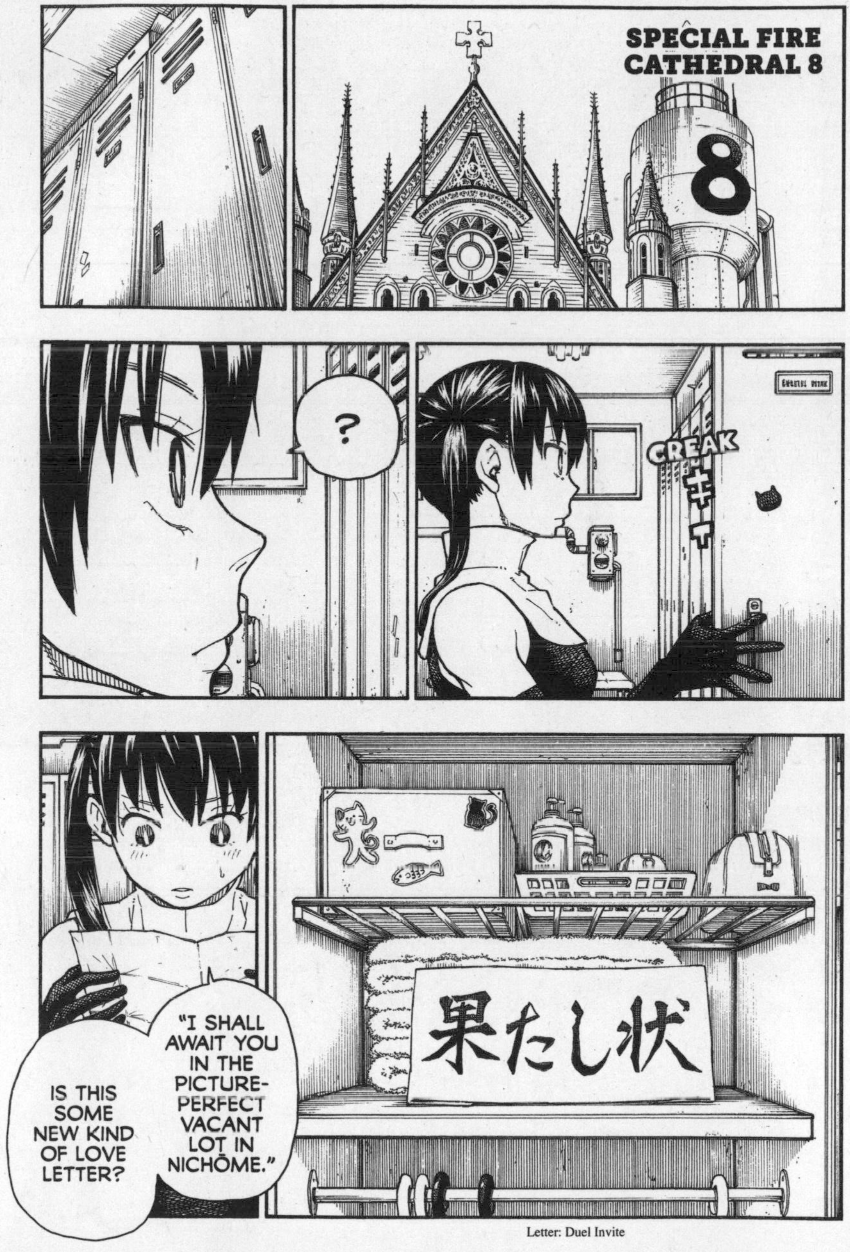
SPECIAL FIRE CATHEDRAL 8
8
CREAK
キィ
?
果たし状
"I SHALL AWAIT YOU IN THE PICTURE-PERFECT VACANT LOT IN NICHŌME."
IS THIS SOME NEW KIND OF LOVE LETTER?

Letter: Duel Invite

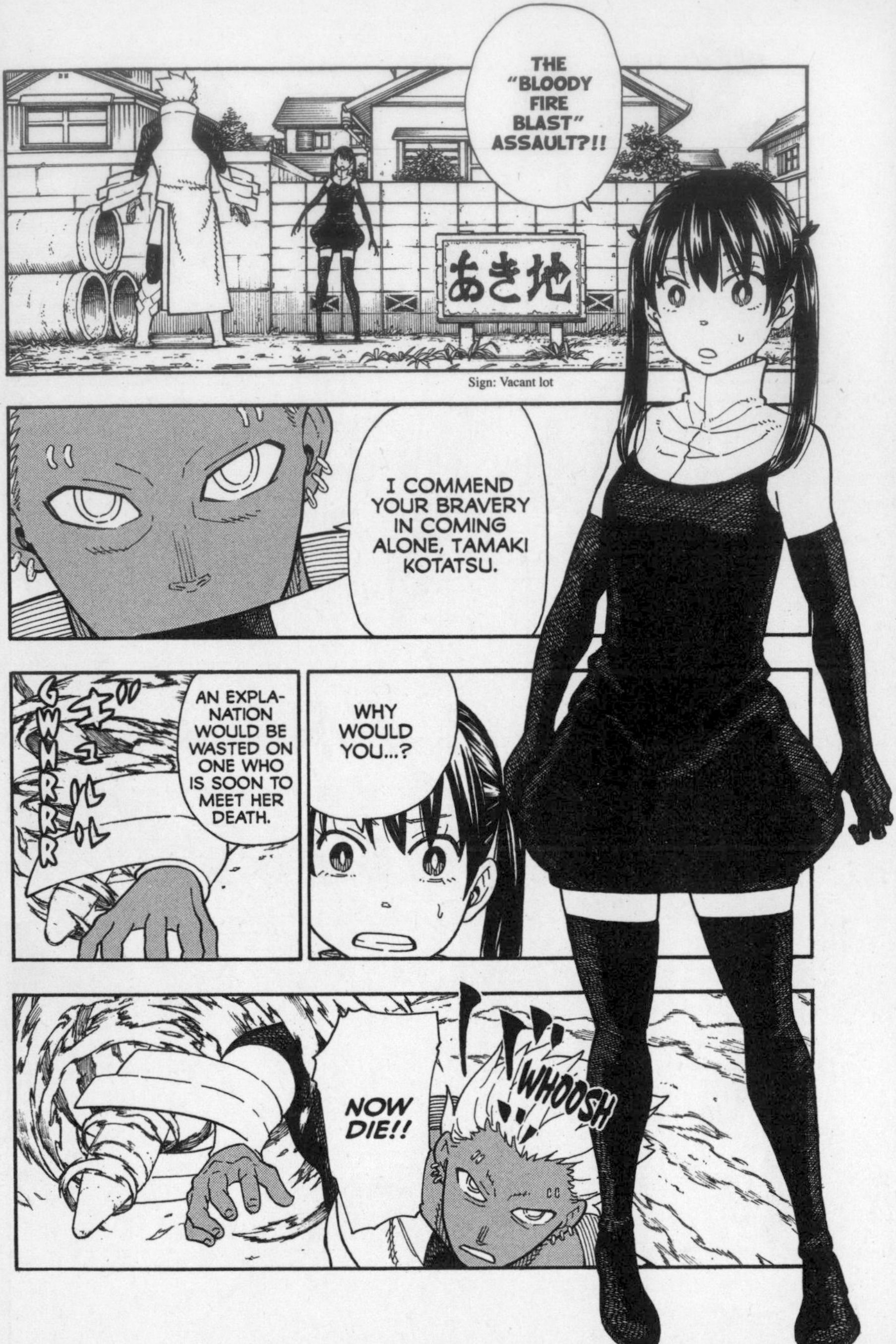
THE "BLOODY FIRE BLAST" ASSAULT?!!
あき地
Sign: Vacant lot
I COMMEND YOUR BRAVERY IN COMING ALONE, TAMAKI KOTATSU.
WHY WOULD YOU...?
AN EXPLANATION WOULD BE WASTED ON ONE WHO IS SOON TO MEET HER DEATH.
GWHRRR
WHOOSH
NOW DIE!!

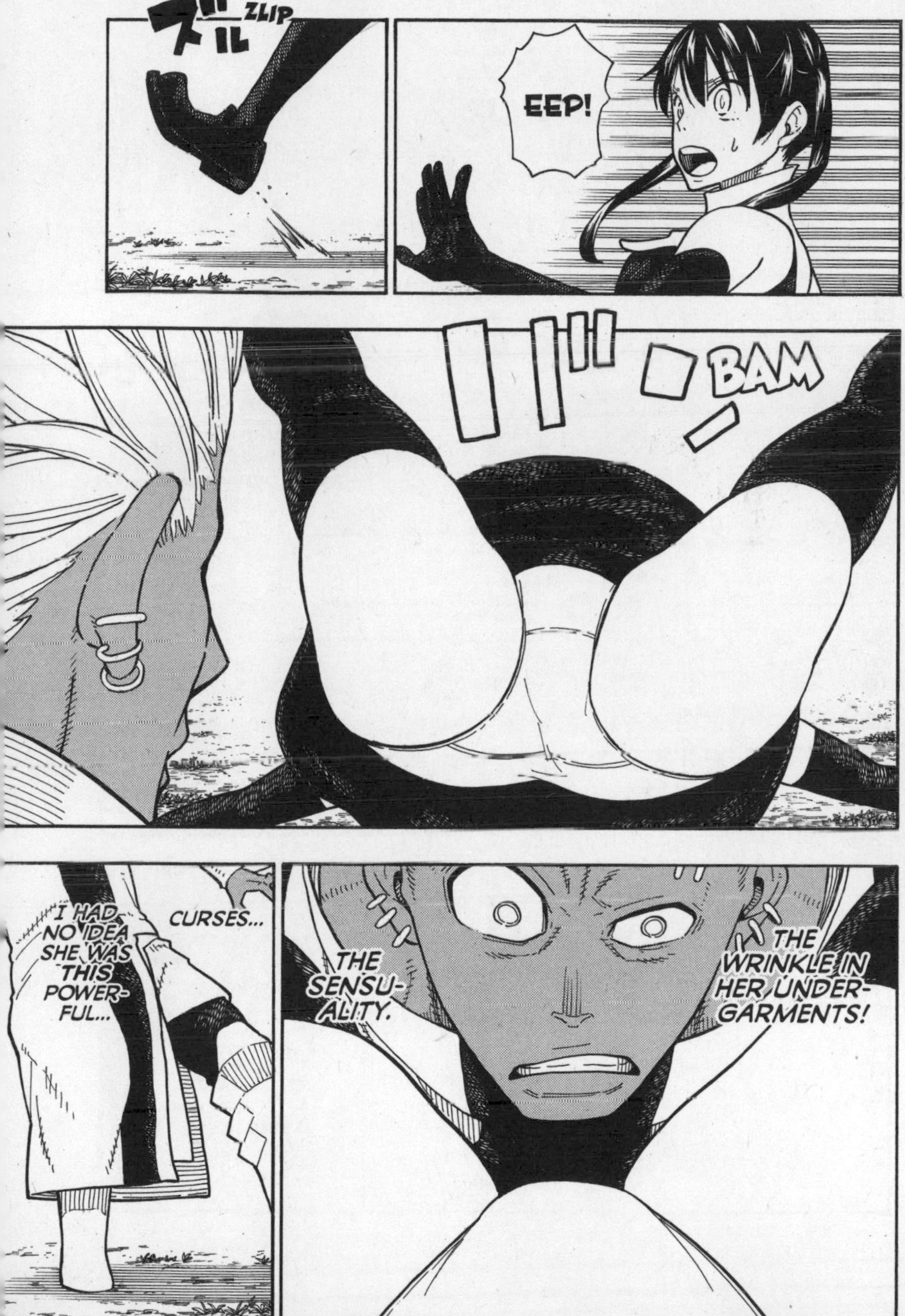
EEP!
ズル
ZLIP
BAM
THE WRINKLE IN HER UNDER-GARMENTS!
THE SENSU-ALITY.
CURSES...
I HAD NO IDEA SHE WAS THIS POWER-FUL...

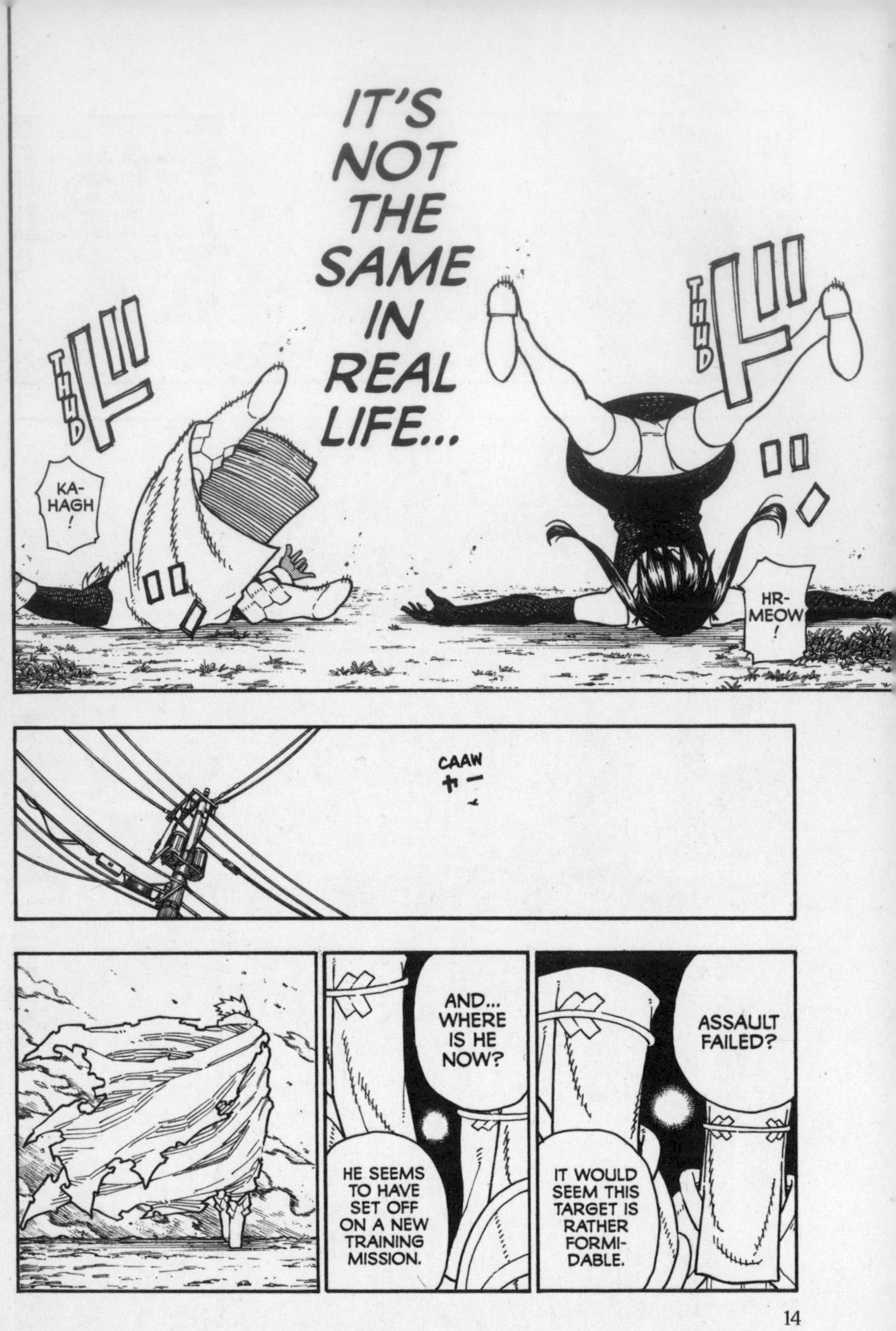
THUD
HR-MEOW!
IT'S NOT THE SAME IN REAL LIFE...
THUD
KA-HAGH!
CAAW
ASSAULT FAILED?
IT WOULD SEEM THIS TARGET IS RATHER FORMIDABLE.
AND... WHERE IS HE NOW?
HE SEEMS TO HAVE SET OFF ON A NEW TRAINING MISSION.

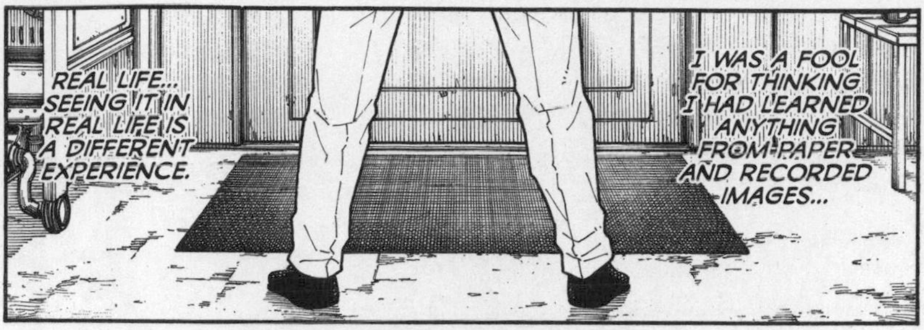
I WAS A FOOL FOR THINKING I HAD LEARNED ANYTHING FROM PAPER AND RECORDED IMAGES...
REAL LIFE... SEEING IT IN REAL LIFE IS A DIFFERENT EXPERIENCE.

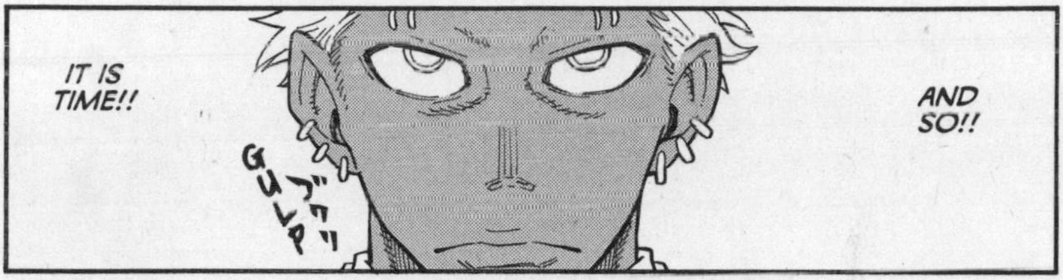
AND SO!!
ゴクッ
GULP
IT IS TIME!!

Sign and door: Club Chupa-Cabaret

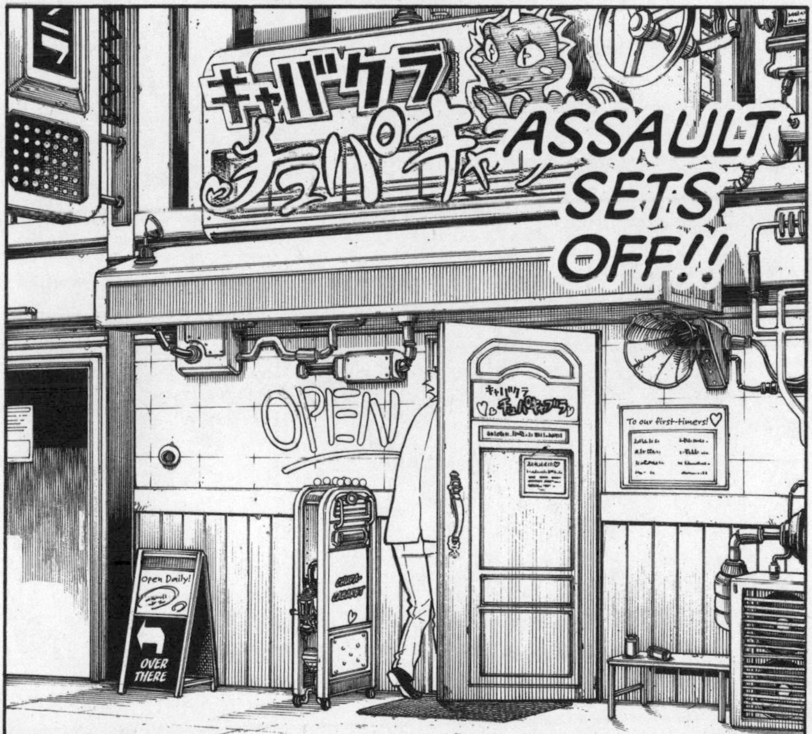
キャバクラ
チュパキャ
ASSAULT SETS OFF!!
To our first-timers!
OPEN
Open Daily!
OVER THERE

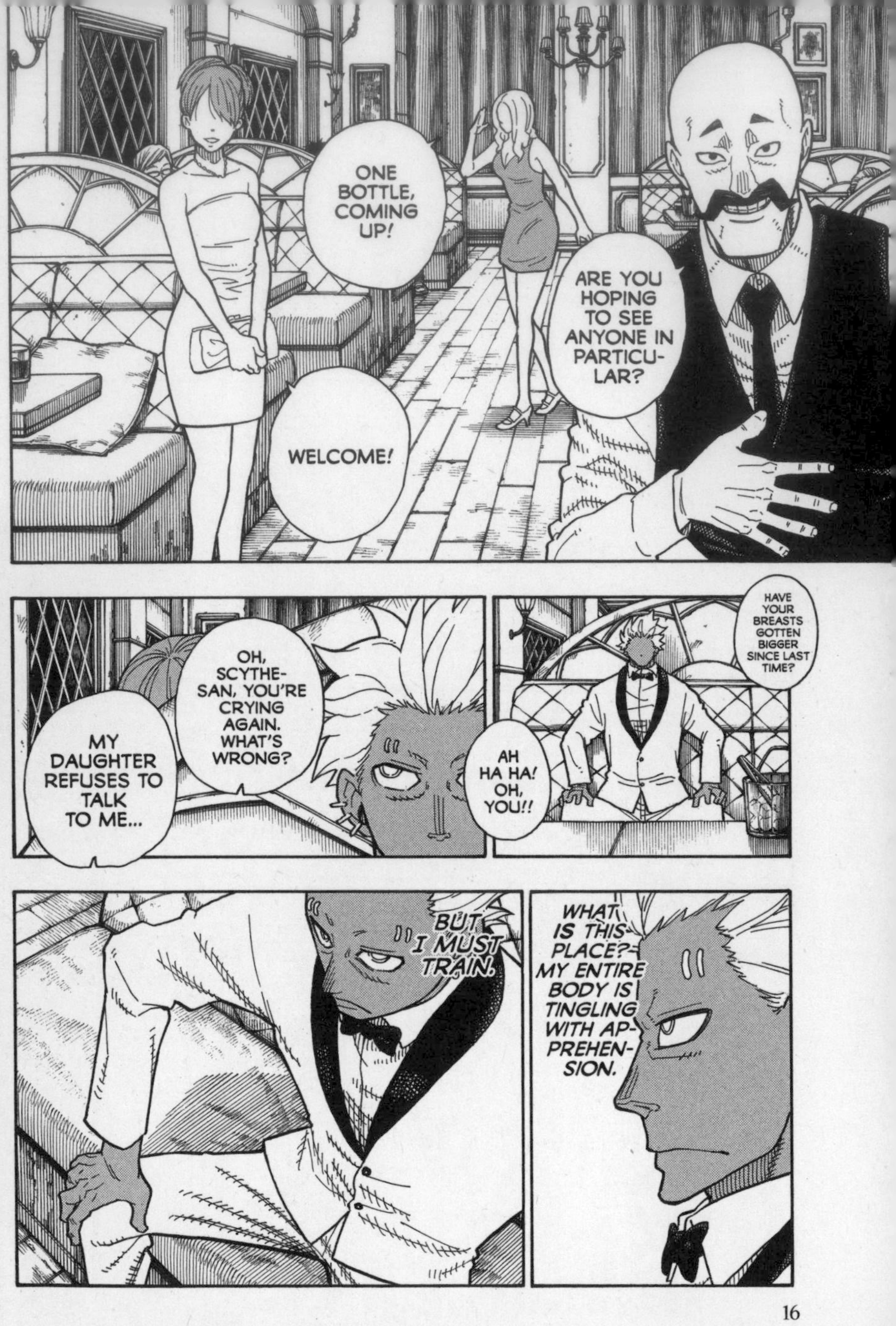
ARE YOU HOPING TO SEE ANYONE IN PARTICULAR?
ONE BOTTLE, COMING UP!
WELCOME!
HAVE YOUR BREASTS GOTTEN BIGGER SINCE LAST TIME?
AH HA HA! OH, YOU!!
OH, SCYTHE-SAN, YOU'RE CRYING AGAIN. WHAT'S WRONG?
MY DAUGHTER REFUSES TO TALK TO ME...
WHAT IS THIS PLACE? MY ENTIRE BODY IS TINGLING WITH APPREHENSION.
BUT I MUST TRAIN.

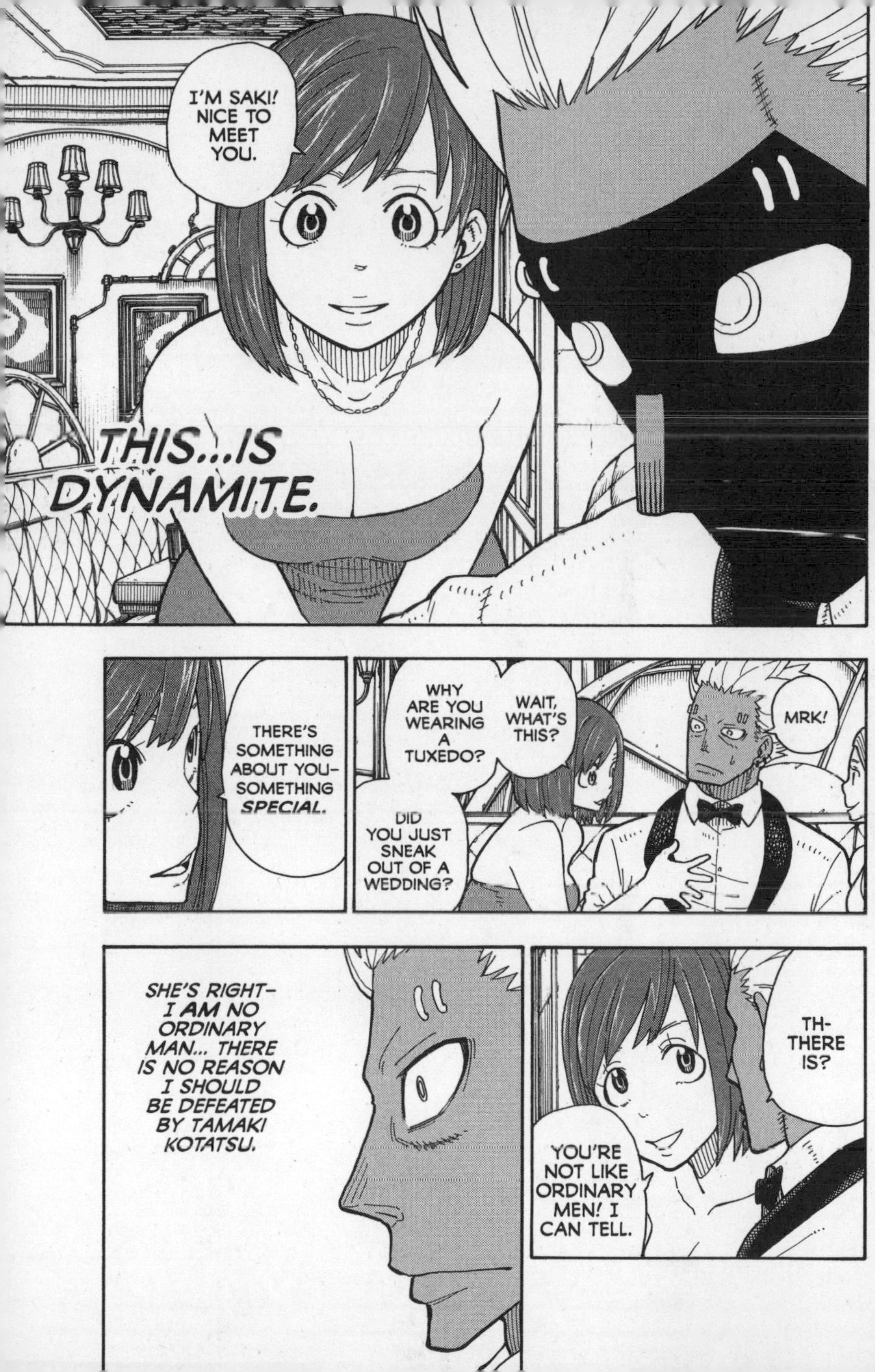
I'M SAKI! NICE TO MEET YOU.
THIS...IS DYNAMITE.
MRK!
WAIT, WHAT'S THIS?
WHY ARE YOU WEARING A TUXEDO?
DID YOU JUST SNEAK OUT OF A WEDDING?
THERE'S SOMETHING ABOUT YOU- SOMETHING *SPECIAL*.
TH- THERE IS?
YOU'RE NOT LIKE ORDINARY MEN! I CAN TELL.
*SHE'S RIGHT- I **AM** NO ORDINARY MAN... THERE IS NO REASON I SHOULD BE DEFEATED BY TAMAKI KOTATSU.*

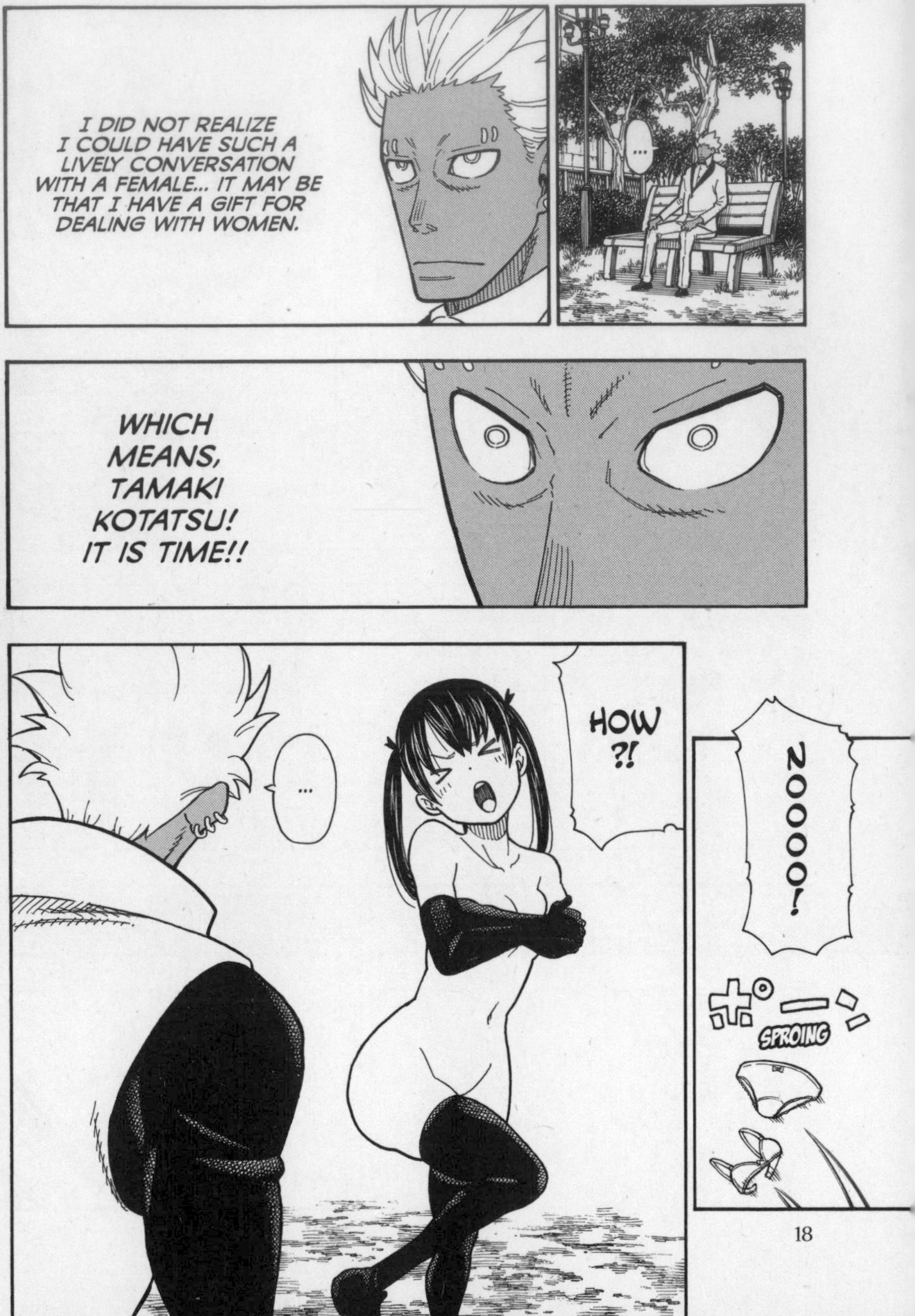
...
I DID NOT REALIZE I COULD HAVE SUCH A LIVELY CONVERSATION WITH A FEMALE... IT MAY BE THAT I HAVE A GIFT FOR DEALING WITH WOMEN.
WHICH MEANS, TAMAKI KOTATSU! IT IS TIME!!
NOOOOO!
ポーン
SPROING
HOW ?!
...

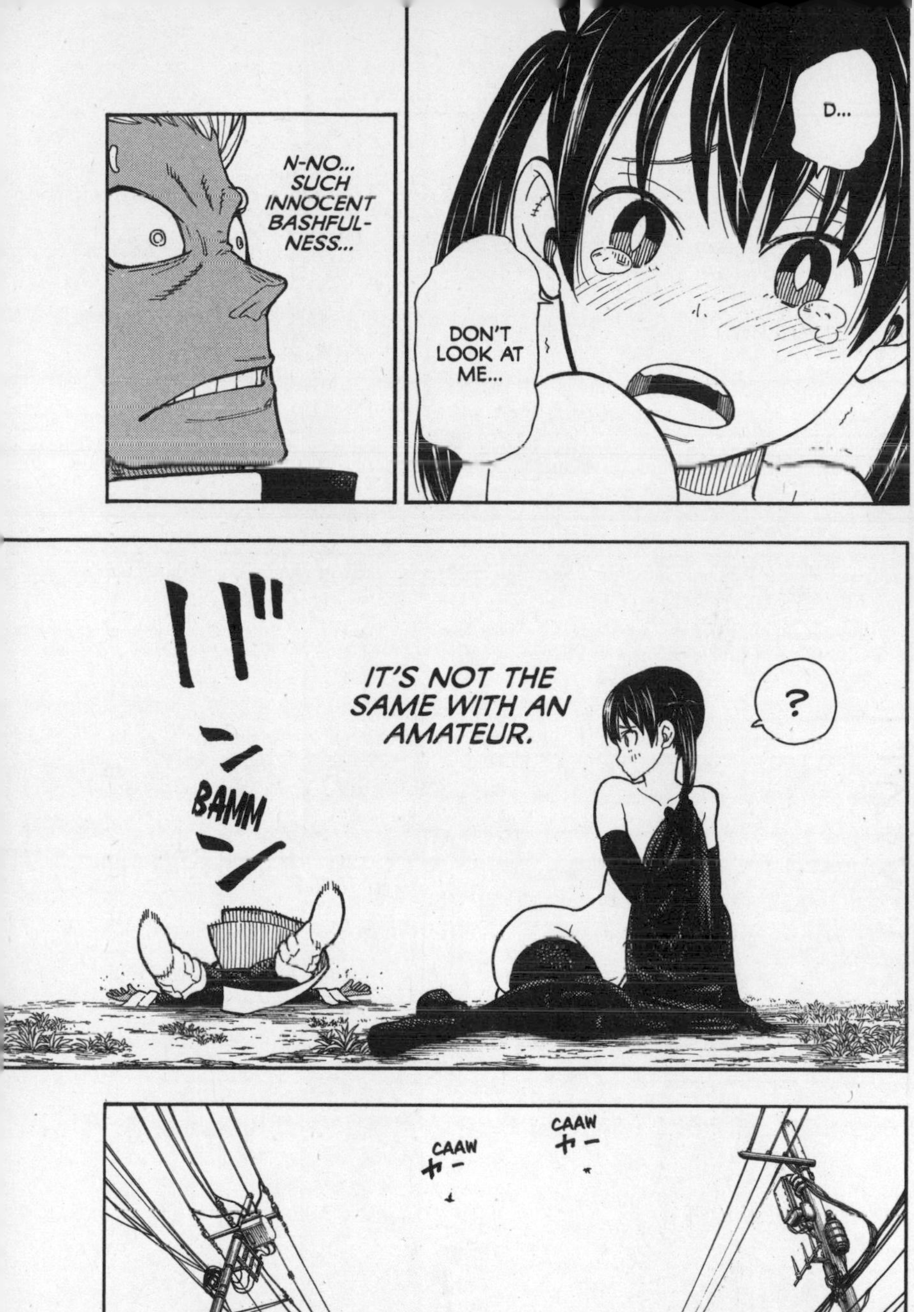
D...
DON'T LOOK AT ME...
N-NO... SUCH INNOCENT BASHFUL-NESS...
?
IT'S NOT THE SAME WITH AN AMATEUR.
BAMM
CAAW
CAAW

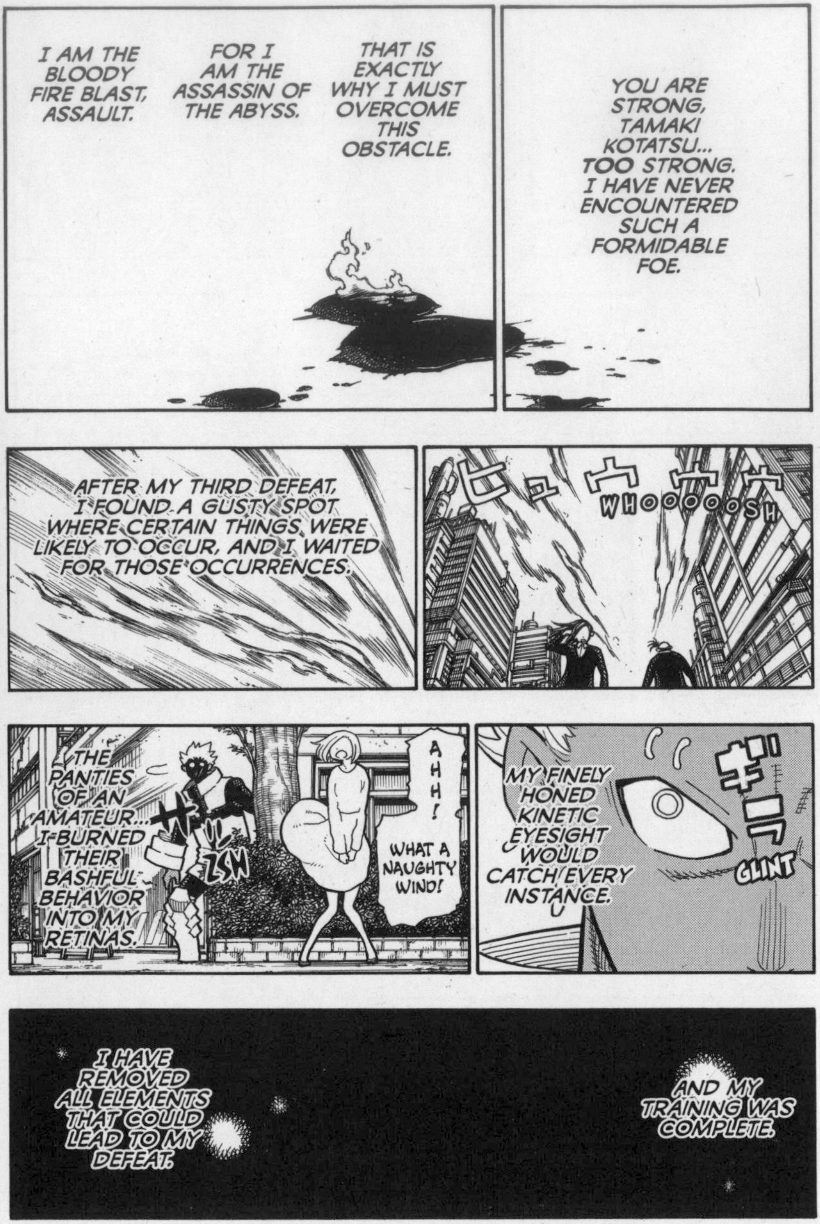
YOU ARE STRONG, TAMAKI KOTATSU... TOO STRONG. I HAVE NEVER ENCOUNTERED SUCH A FORMIDABLE FOE.
I AM THE BLOODY FIRE BLAST, ASSAULT.
FOR I AM THE ASSASSIN OF THE ABYSS.
THAT IS EXACTLY WHY I MUST OVERCOME THIS OBSTACLE.
ヒュウウウ
WHOOOOOOSH
AFTER MY THIRD DEFEAT, I FOUND A GUSTY SPOT WHERE CERTAIN THINGS WERE LIKELY TO OCCUR, AND I WAITED FOR THOSE OCCURRENCES.
ギラ
GLINT
MY FINELY HONED KINETIC EYESIGHT WOULD CATCH EVERY INSTANCE.
AHH!
WHAT A NAUGHTY WIND!
THE PANTIES OF AN AMATEUR... I BURNED THEIR BASHFUL BEHAVIOR INTO MY RETINAS.
ZSH
I HAVE REMOVED ALL ELEMENTS THAT COULD LEAD TO MY DEFEAT.
AND MY TRAINING WAS COMPLETE.

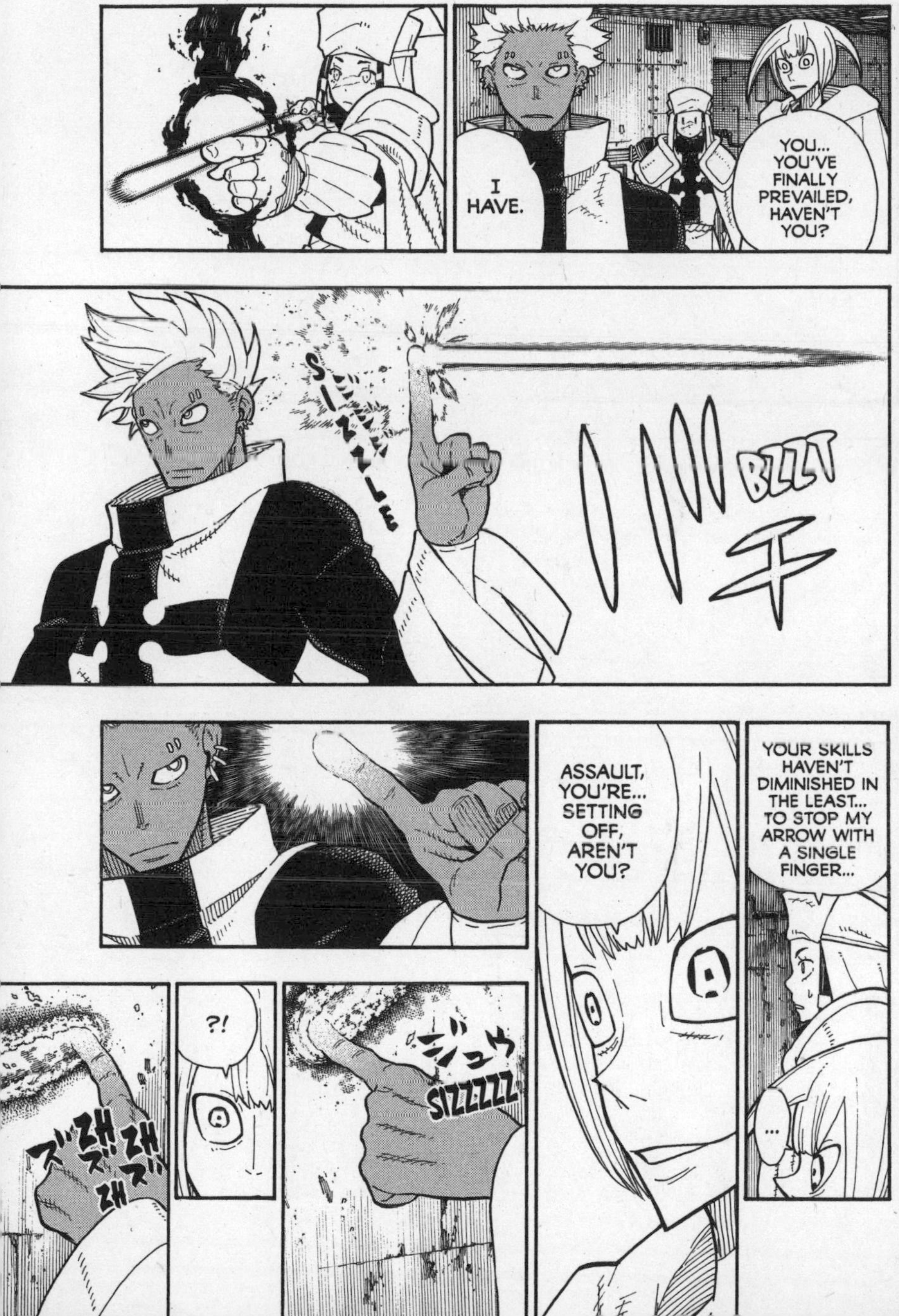
YOU... YOU'VE FINALLY PREVAILED, HAVEN'T YOU?
I HAVE.
BZZT
SIZZLE
YOUR SKILLS HAVEN'T DIMINISHED IN THE LEAST... TO STOP MY ARROW WITH A SINGLE FINGER...
...
ASSAULT, YOU'RE... SETTING OFF, AREN'T YOU?
SIZZZZZ
?!
ZH ZH ZH

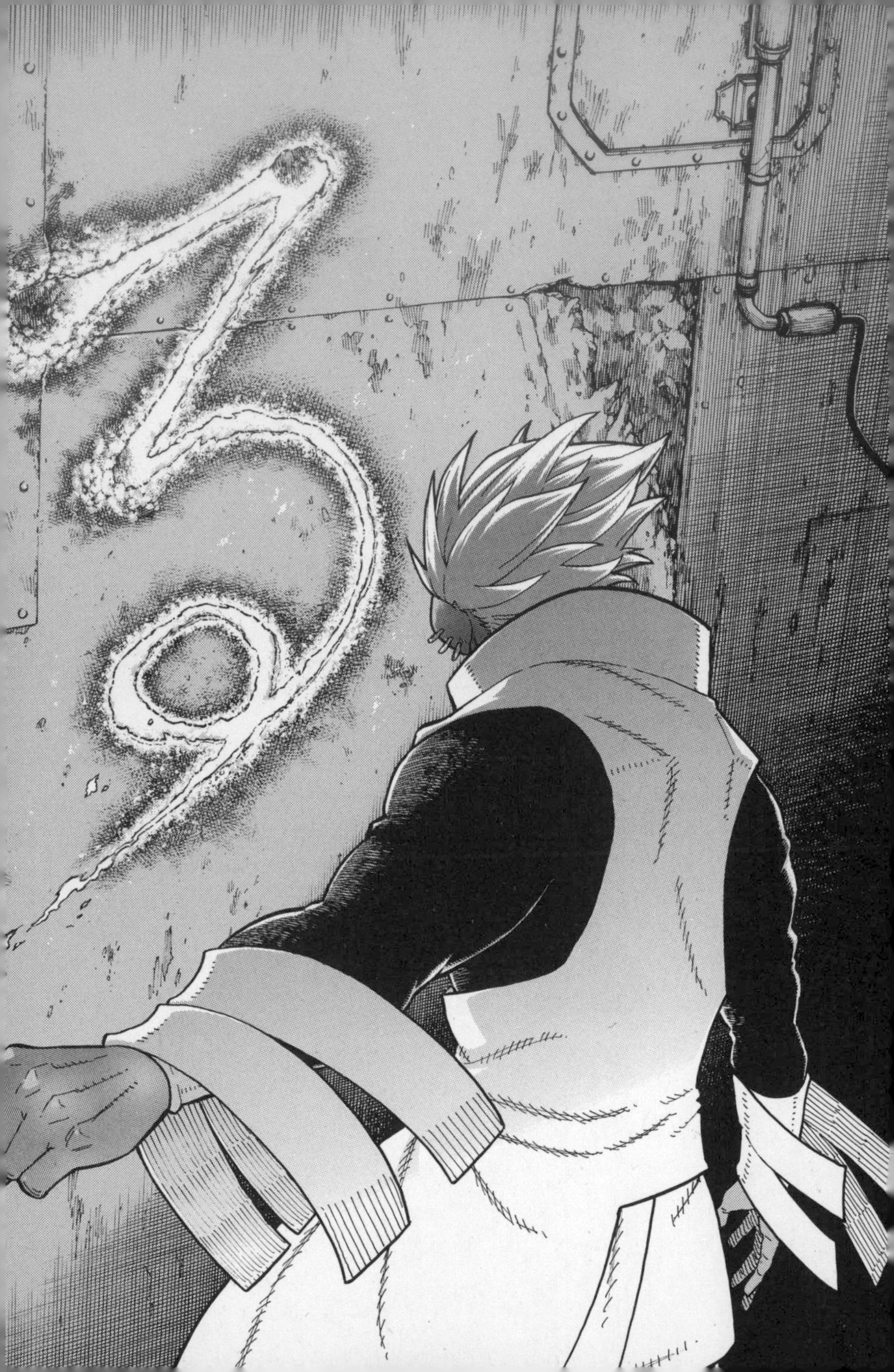

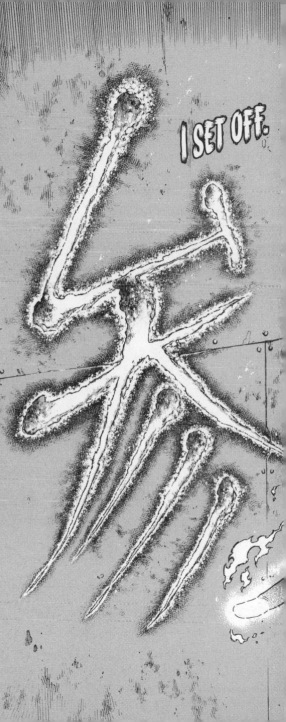

I SET OFF.

ASSAULT...

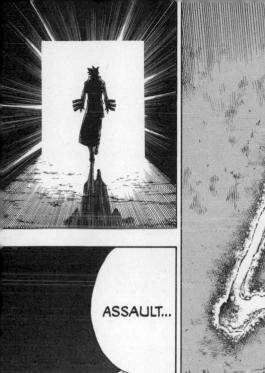

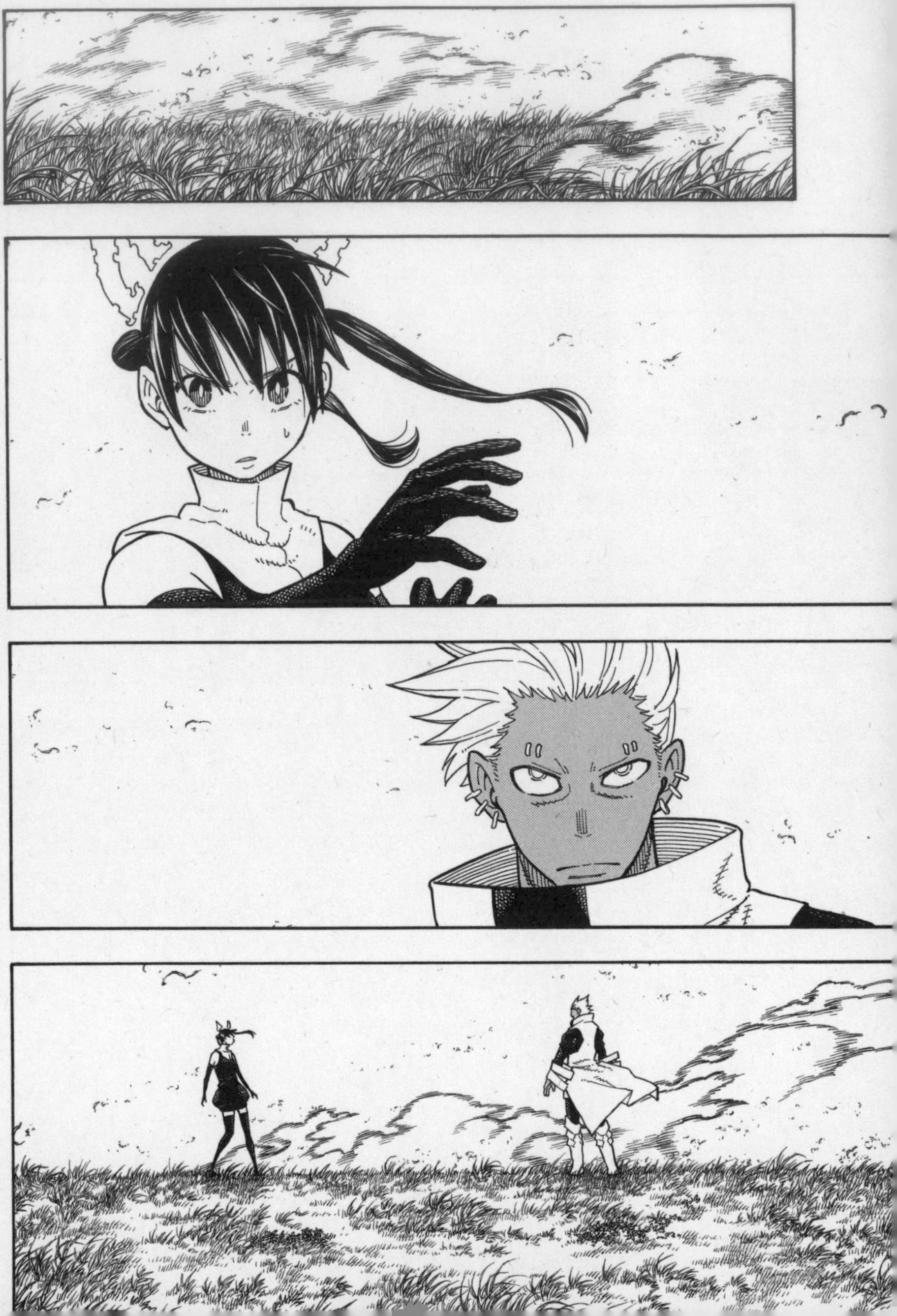

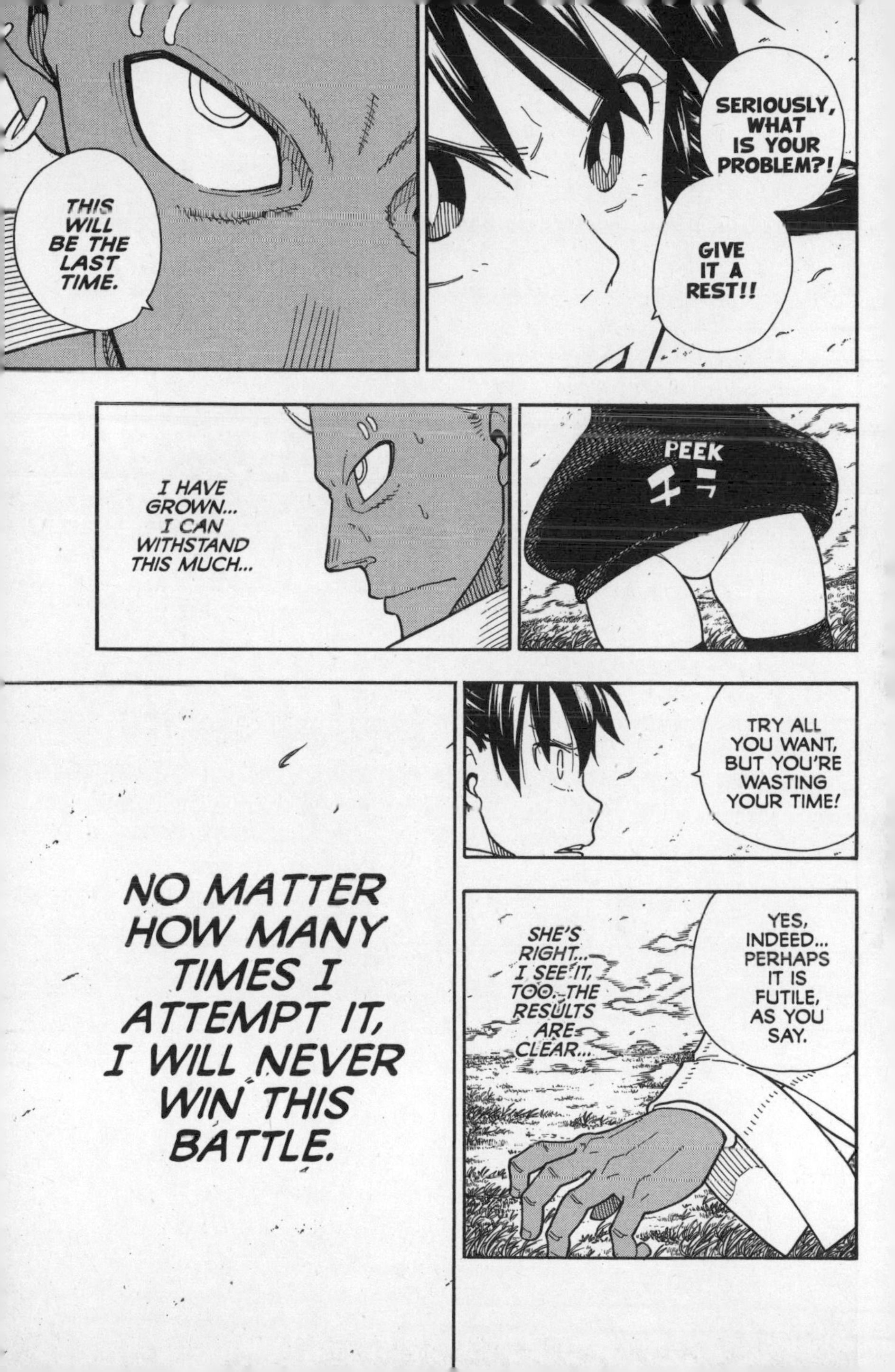
SERIOUSLY, WHAT IS YOUR PROBLEM?!
GIVE IT A REST!!
THIS WILL BE THE LAST TIME.
PEEK
チラ
I HAVE GROWN... I CAN WITHSTAND THIS MUCH...
TRY ALL YOU WANT, BUT YOU'RE WASTING YOUR TIME!
YES, INDEED... PERHAPS IT IS FUTILE, AS YOU SAY.
SHE'S RIGHT... I SEE IT, TOO. THE RESULTS ARE CLEAR...
NO MATTER HOW MANY TIMES I ATTEMPT IT, I WILL NEVER WIN THIS BATTLE.

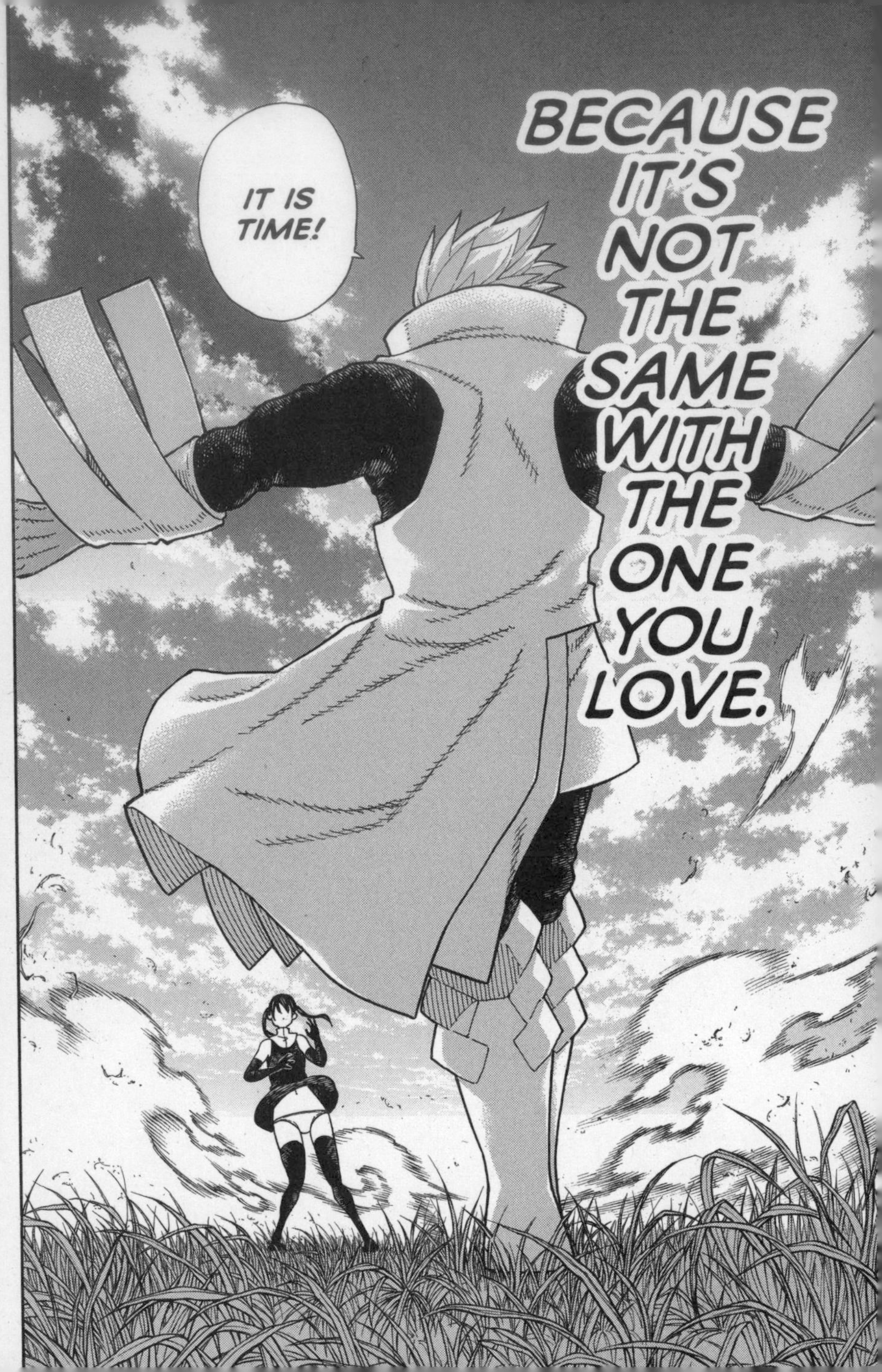
BECAUSE IT'S NOT THE SAME WITH THE ONE YOU LOVE.
IT IS TIME!

FIRE FORCE

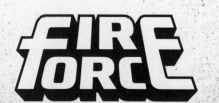

FIRE FORCE

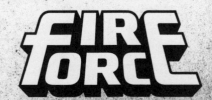

CHAPTER CLII:
THE OZE FAMILY

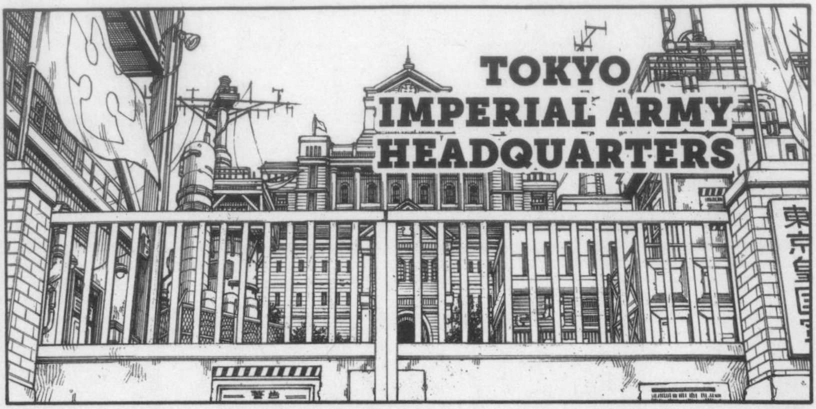
TOKYO IMPERIAL ARMY HEADQUARTERS

Sign: Warning

Sign: Tokyo Imperial Army

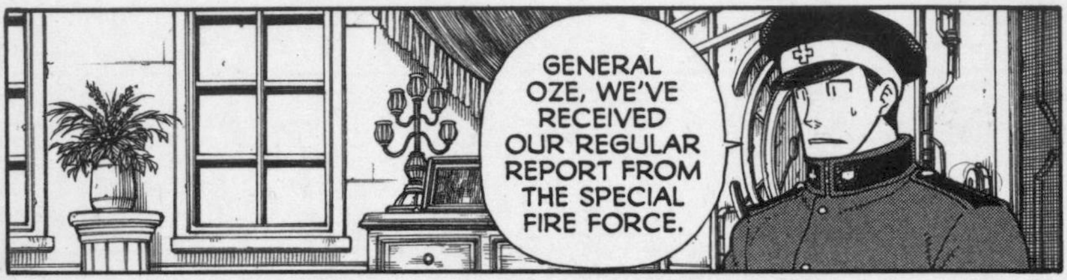
GENERAL OZE, WE'VE RECEIVED OUR REGULAR REPORT FROM THE SPECIAL FIRE FORCE.

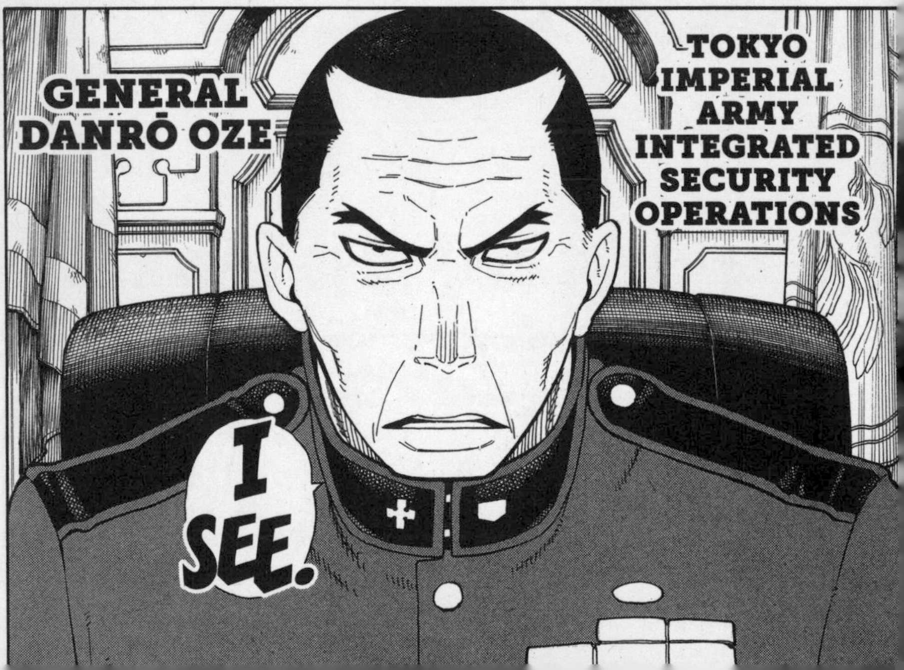
TOKYO IMPERIAL ARMY INTEGRATED SECURITY OPERATIONS
GENERAL DANRŌ OZE
I SEE.

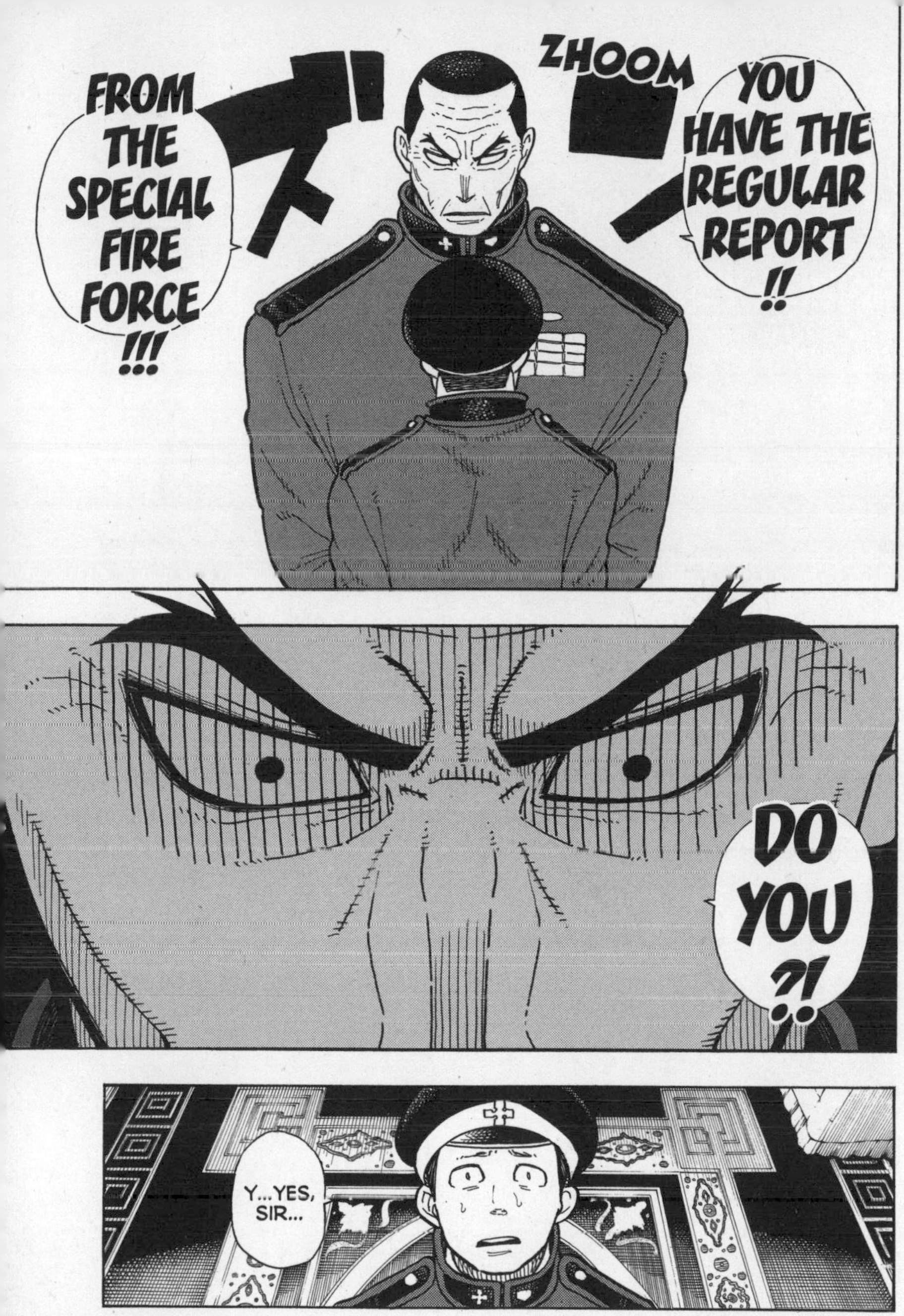
ZHOOM
YOU HAVE THE REGULAR REPORT!!
FROM THE SPECIAL FIRE FORCE!!!
DO YOU?!
Y...YES, SIR...

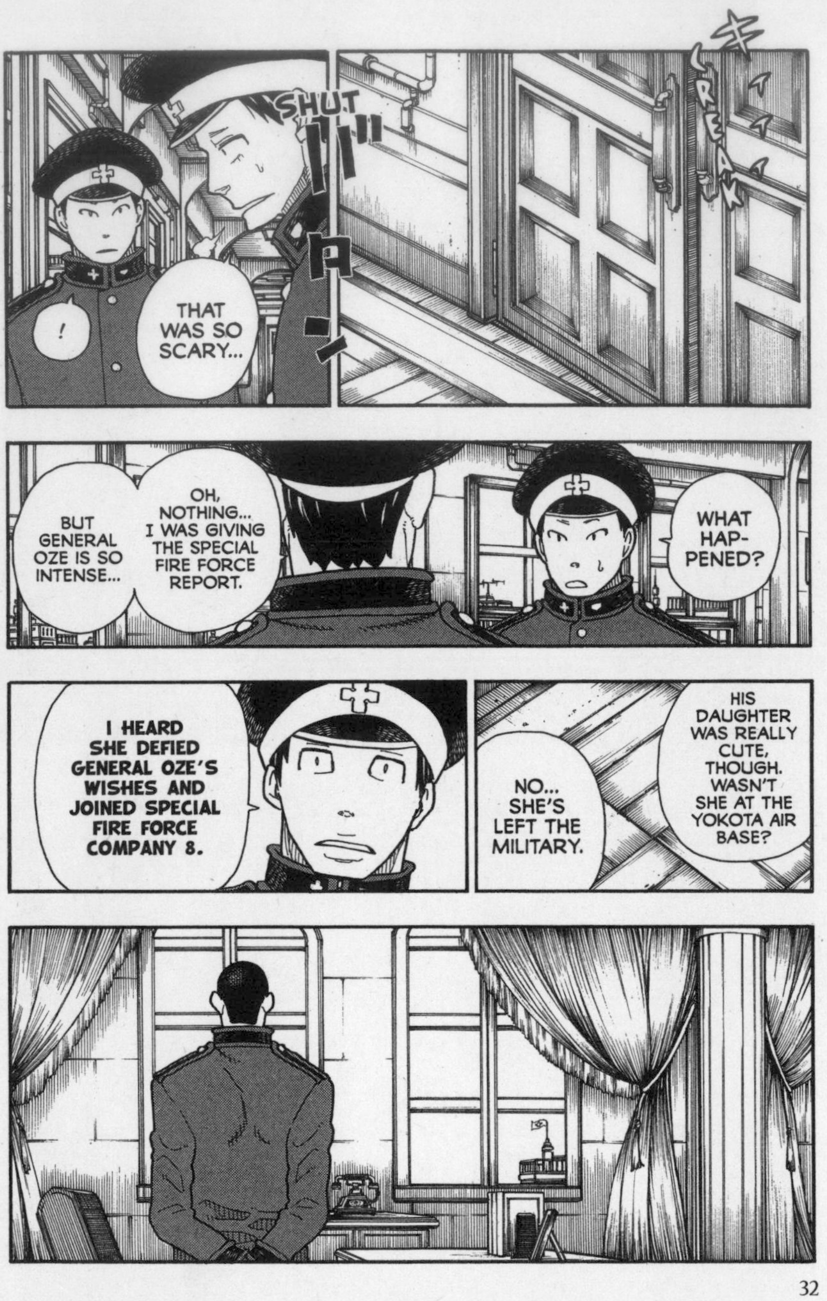
CREAK
SHUT
THAT WAS SO SCARY...
!
WHAT HAP-PENED?
OH, NOTHING... I WAS GIVING THE SPECIAL FIRE FORCE REPORT.
BUT GENERAL OZE IS SO INTENSE...
HIS DAUGHTER WAS REALLY CUTE, THOUGH. WASN'T SHE AT THE YOKOTA AIR BASE?
NO... SHE'S LEFT THE MILITARY.
I HEARD SHE DEFIED GENERAL OZE'S WISHES AND JOINED SPECIAL FIRE FORCE COMPANY 8.

HRRM
...

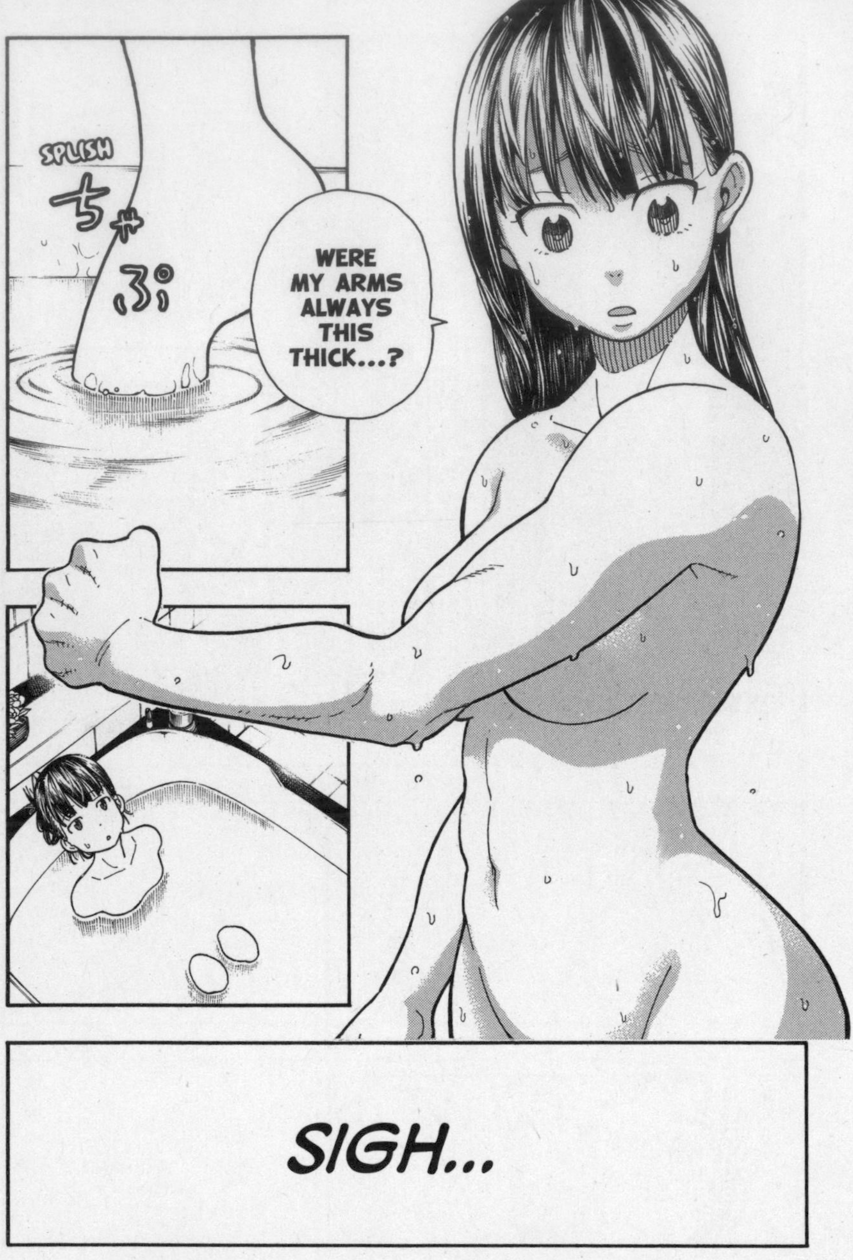
WERE MY ARMS ALWAYS THIS THICK...?
SPLISH
ちゃぷ
SIGH...

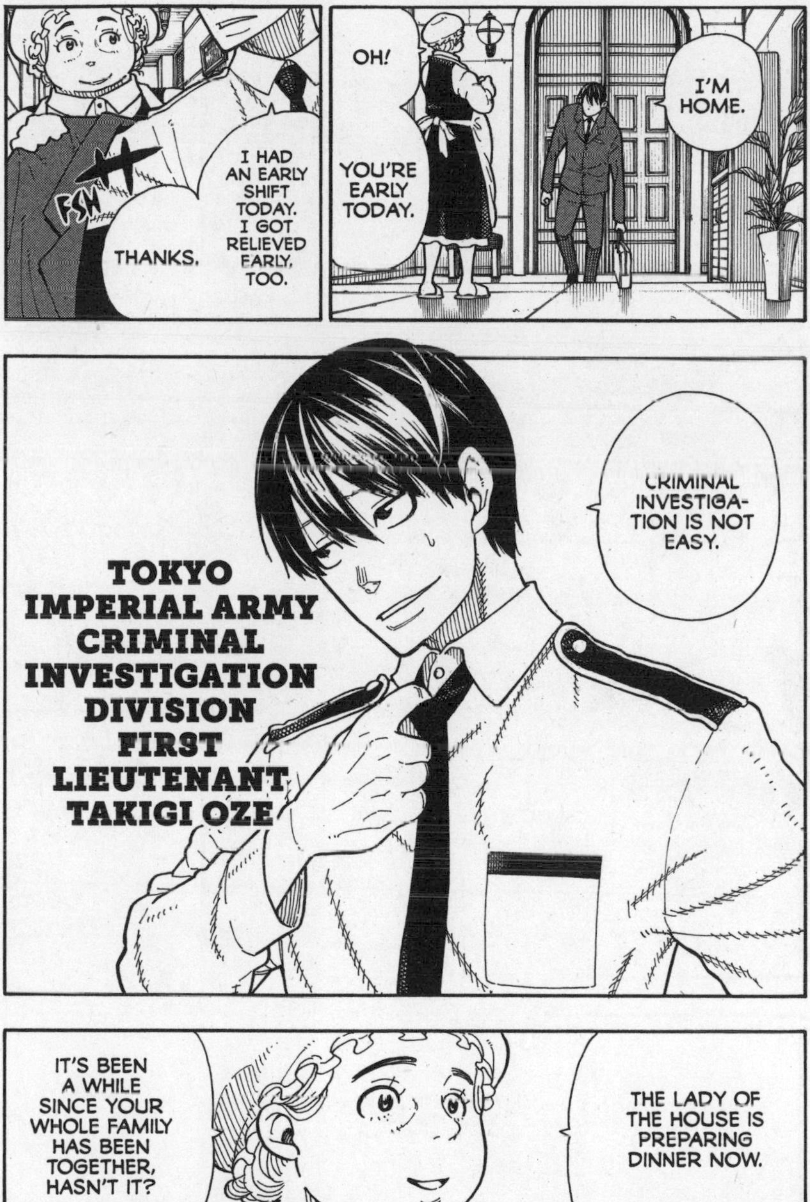
I'M HOME.
OH!
YOU'RE EARLY TODAY.
I HAD AN EARLY SHIFT TODAY. I GOT RELIEVED EARLY, TOO.
FSH
THANKS.
CRIMINAL INVESTIGATION IS NOT EASY.
TOKYO IMPERIAL ARMY CRIMINAL INVESTIGATION DIVISION FIRST LIEUTENANT TAKIGI OZE
THE LADY OF THE HOUSE IS PREPARING DINNER NOW.
IT'S BEEN A WHILE SINCE YOUR WHOLE FAMILY HAS BEEN TOGETHER, HASN'T IT?

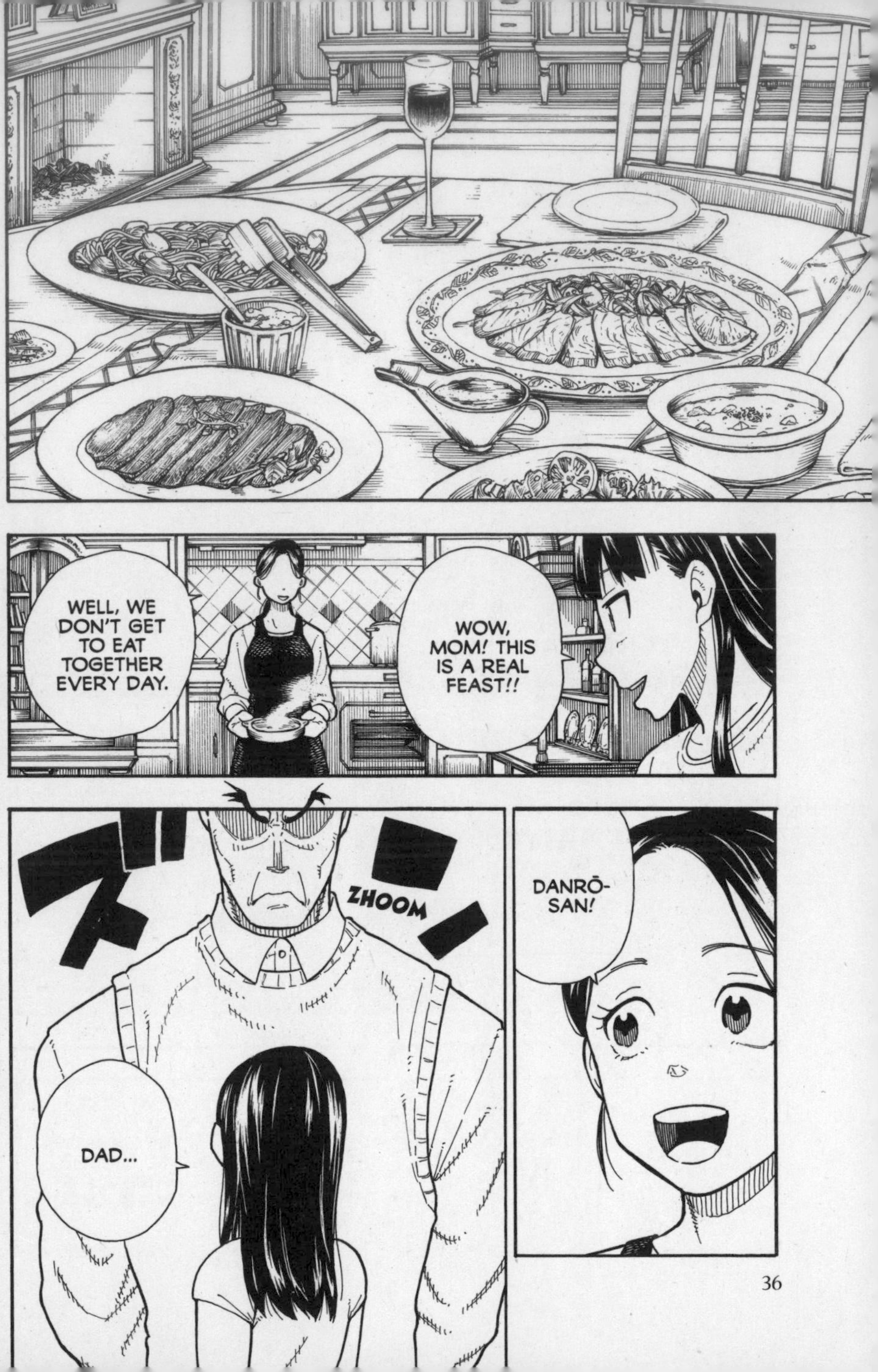
WOW, MOM! THIS IS A REAL FEAST!!
WELL, WE DON'T GET TO EAT TOGETHER EVERY DAY.
DANRŌ-SAN!
ZHOOM
DAD...

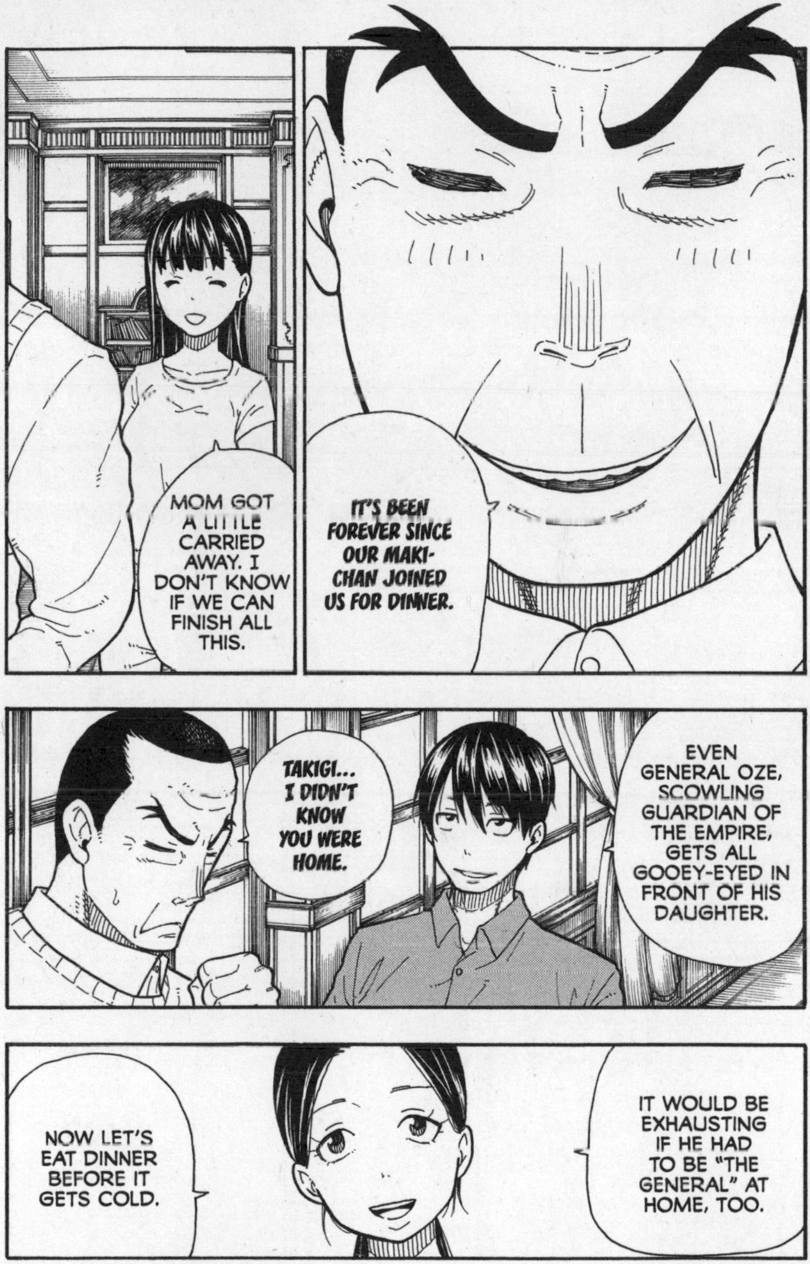
IT'S BEEN FOREVER SINCE OUR MAKI-CHAN JOINED US FOR DINNER.
MOM GOT A LITTLE CARRIED AWAY. I DON'T KNOW IF WE CAN FINISH ALL THIS.
EVEN GENERAL OZE, SCOWLING GUARDIAN OF THE EMPIRE, GETS ALL GOOEY-EYED IN FRONT OF HIS DAUGHTER.
TAKIGI... I DIDN'T KNOW YOU WERE HOME.
IT WOULD BE EXHAUSTING IF HE HAD TO BE "THE GENERAL" AT HOME, TOO.
NOW LET'S EAT DINNER BEFORE IT GETS COLD.

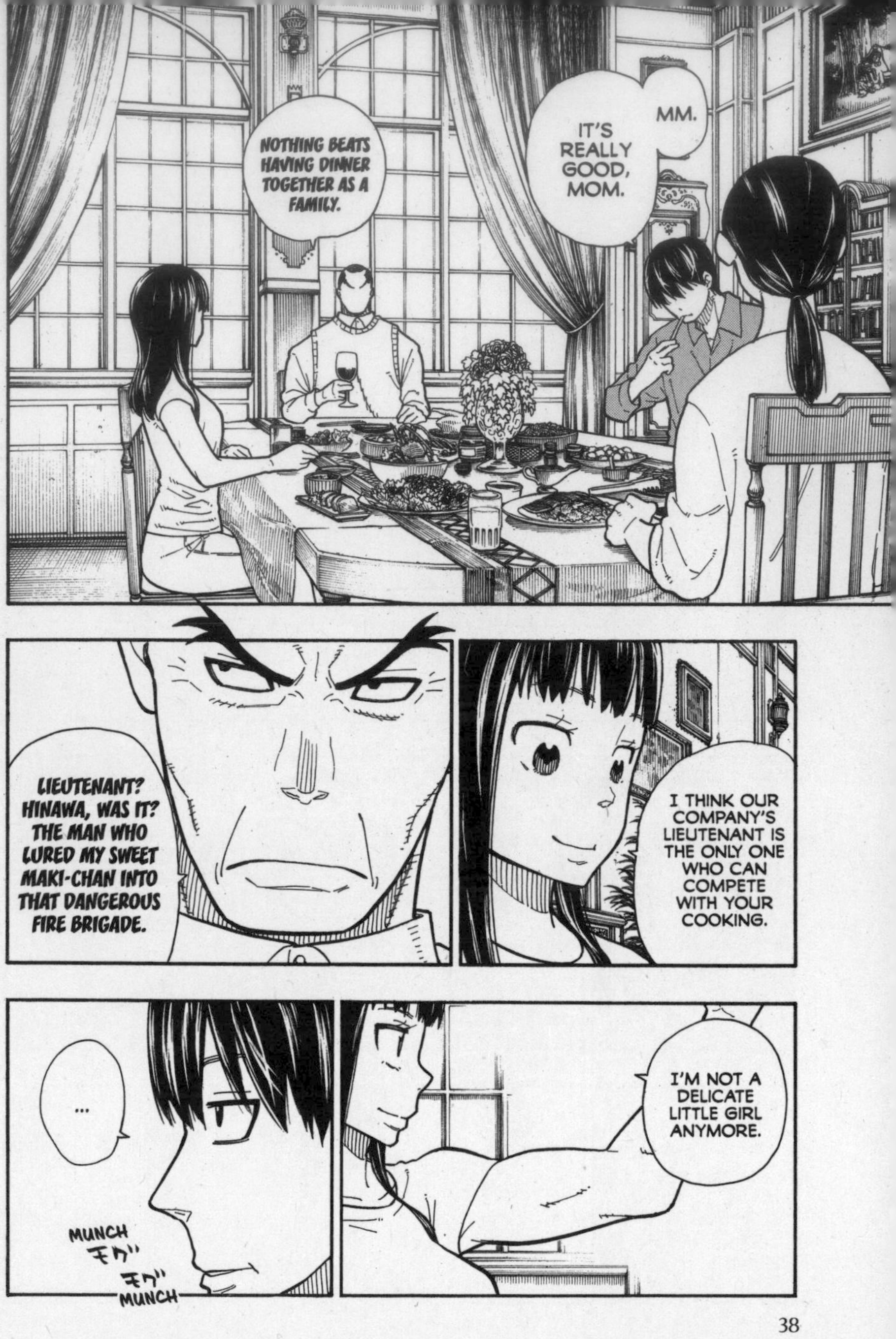
MM.
IT'S REALLY GOOD, MOM.
NOTHING BEATS HAVING DINNER TOGETHER AS A FAMILY.
I THINK OUR COMPANY'S LIEUTENANT IS THE ONLY ONE WHO CAN COMPETE WITH YOUR COOKING.
LIEUTENANT? HINAWA, WAS IT? THE MAN WHO LURED MY SWEET MAKI-CHAN INTO THAT DANGEROUS FIRE BRIGADE.
I'M NOT A DELICATE LITTLE GIRL ANYMORE.
...
MUNCH モグ
モグ MUNCH

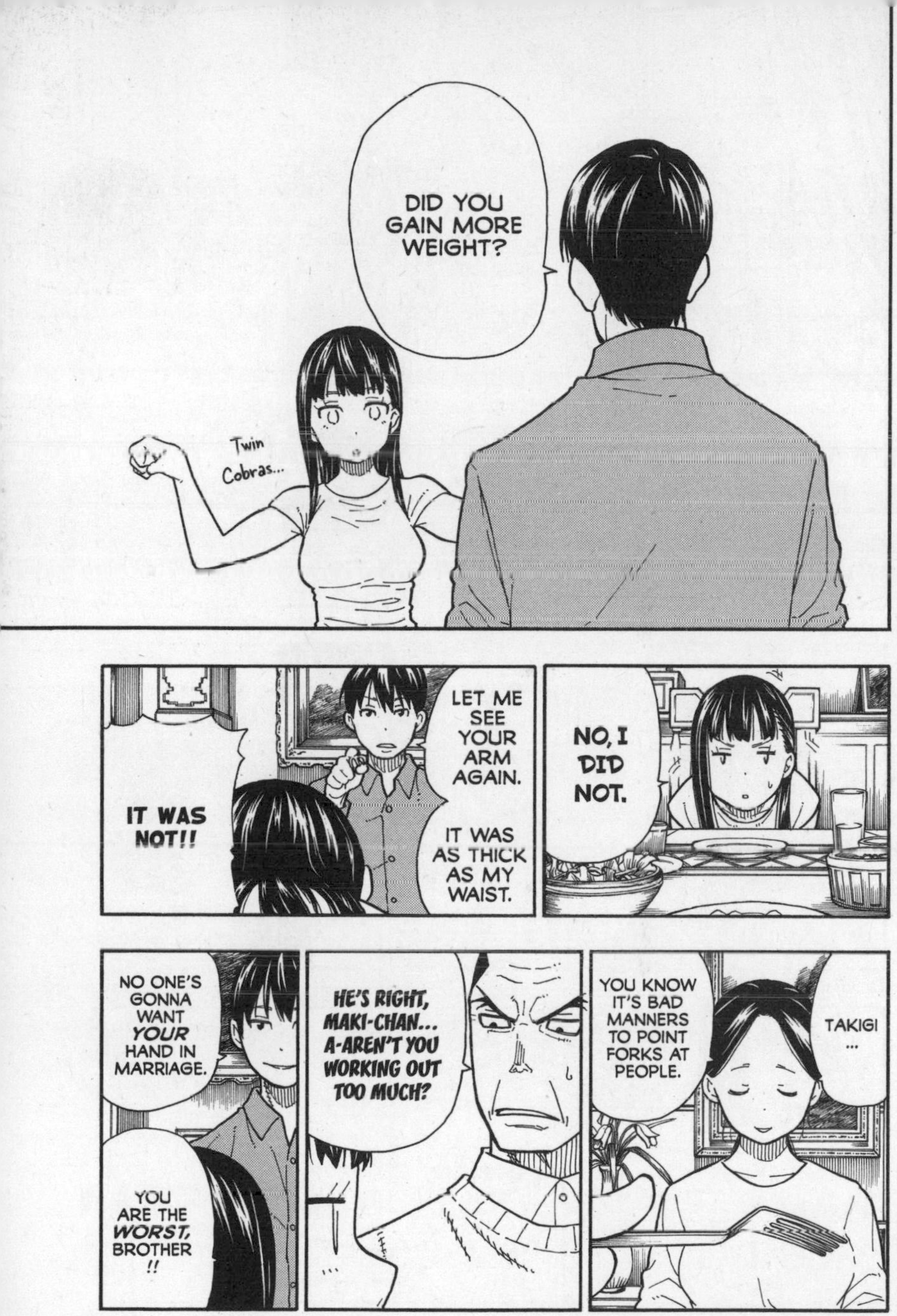

DID YOU GAIN MORE WEIGHT?
Twin Cobras...
NO, I DID NOT.
LET ME SEE YOUR ARM AGAIN.
IT WAS AS THICK AS MY WAIST.
IT WAS NOT!!
TAKIGI ...
YOU KNOW IT'S BAD MANNERS TO POINT FORKS AT PEOPLE.
HE'S RIGHT, MAKI-CHAN... A-AREN'T YOU WORKING OUT TOO MUCH?
...
NO ONE'S GONNA WANT YOUR HAND IN MARRIAGE.
YOU ARE THE WORST, BROTHER!!

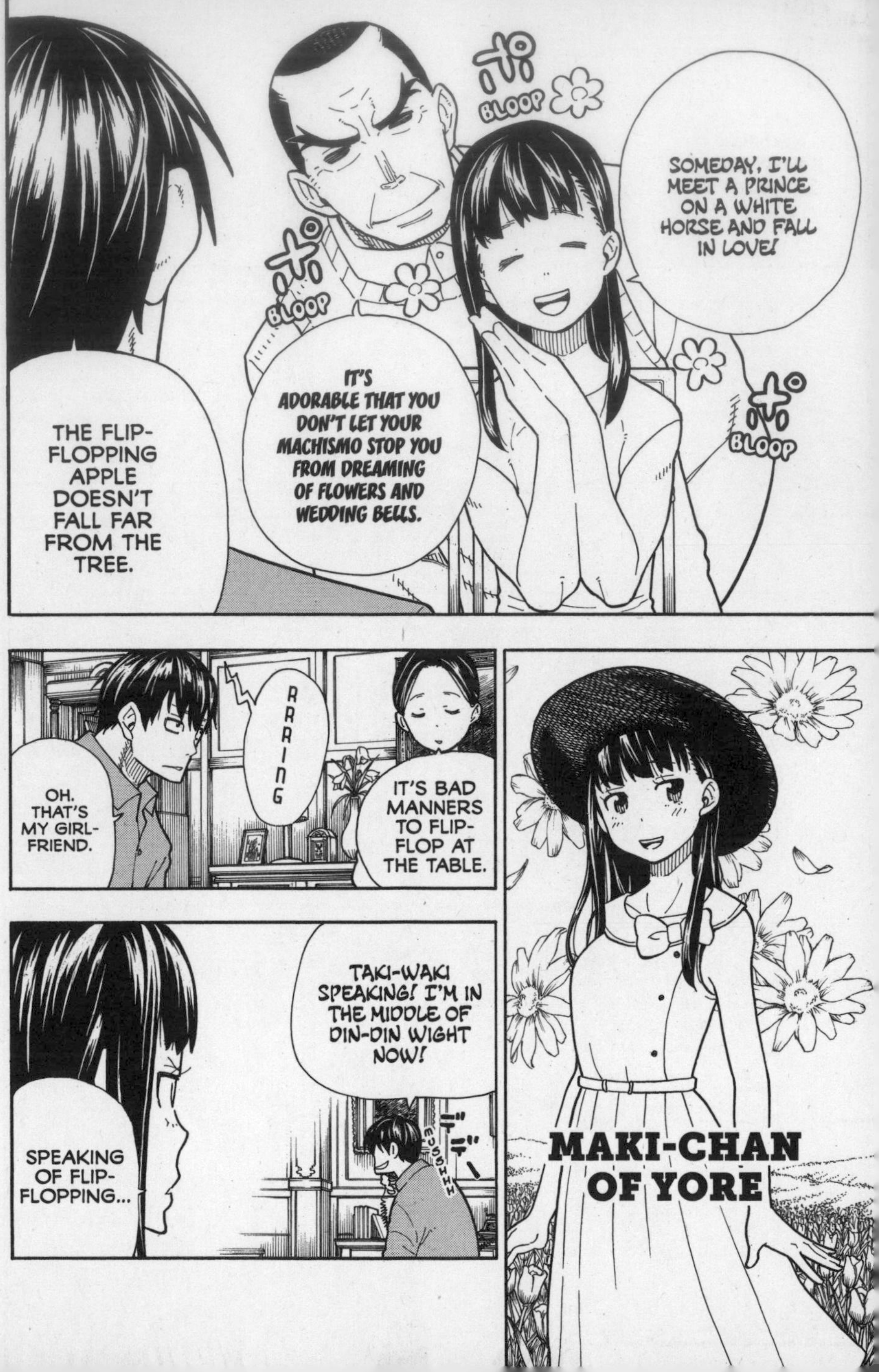
BLOOP
SOMEDAY, I'LL MEET A PRINCE ON A WHITE HORSE AND FALL IN LOVE!
BLOOP
IT'S ADORABLE THAT YOU DON'T LET YOUR MACHISMO STOP YOU FROM DREAMING OF FLOWERS AND WEDDING BELLS.
BLOOP
THE FLIP-FLOPPING APPLE DOESN'T FALL FAR FROM THE TREE.
MAKI-CHAN OF YORE
RRRING
IT'S BAD MANNERS TO FLIP-FLOP AT THE TABLE.
OH. THAT'S MY GIRL-FRIEND.
TAKI-WAKI SPEAKING! I'M IN THE MIDDLE OF DIN-DIN NIGHT NOW!
MUSSHHH
SPEAKING OF FLIP-FLOPPING...

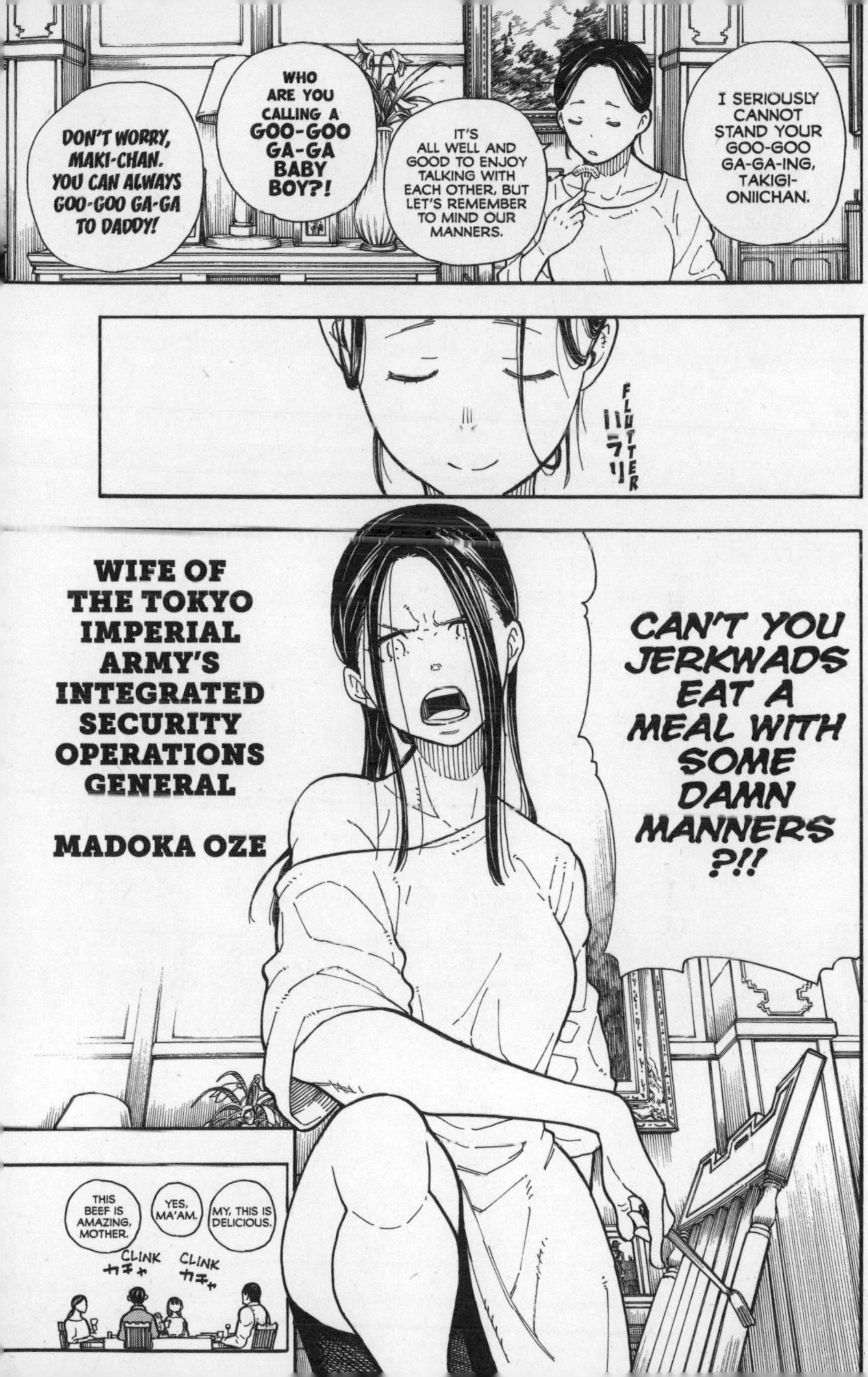
I SERIOUSLY CANNOT STAND YOUR GOO-GOO GA-GA-ING, TAKIGI-ONIICHAN.
IT'S ALL WELL AND GOOD TO ENJOY TALKING WITH EACH OTHER, BUT LET'S REMEMBER TO MIND OUR MANNERS.
WHO ARE YOU CALLING A GOO-GOO GA-GA BABY BOY?!
DON'T WORRY, MAKI-CHAN. YOU CAN ALWAYS GOO-GOO GA-GA TO DADDY!
ハラリ
FLUTTER
CAN'T YOU JERKWADS EAT A MEAL WITH SOME DAMN MANNERS?!!
WIFE OF THE TOKYO IMPERIAL ARMY'S INTEGRATED SECURITY OPERATIONS GENERAL
MADOKA OZE
MY, THIS IS DELICIOUS.
YES, MA'AM.
THIS BEEF IS AMAZING, MOTHER.
カチャ
CLINK
カチャ
CLINK

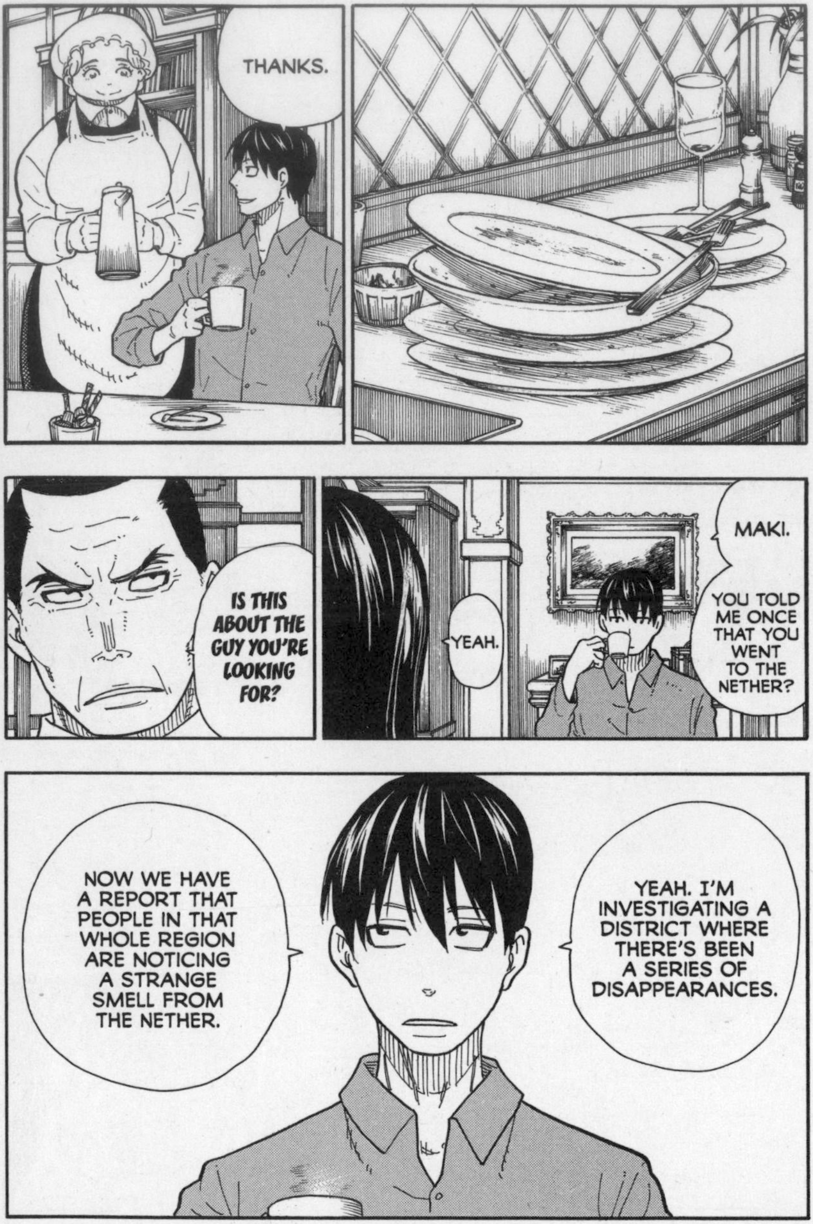
THANKS.
MAKI.
YOU TOLD ME ONCE THAT YOU WENT TO THE NETHER?
YEAH.
IS THIS ABOUT THE GUY YOU'RE LOOKING FOR?
YEAH. I'M INVESTIGATING A DISTRICT WHERE THERE'S BEEN A SERIES OF DISAPPEARANCES.
NOW WE HAVE A REPORT THAT PEOPLE IN THAT WHOLE REGION ARE NOTICING A STRANGE SMELL FROM THE NETHER.

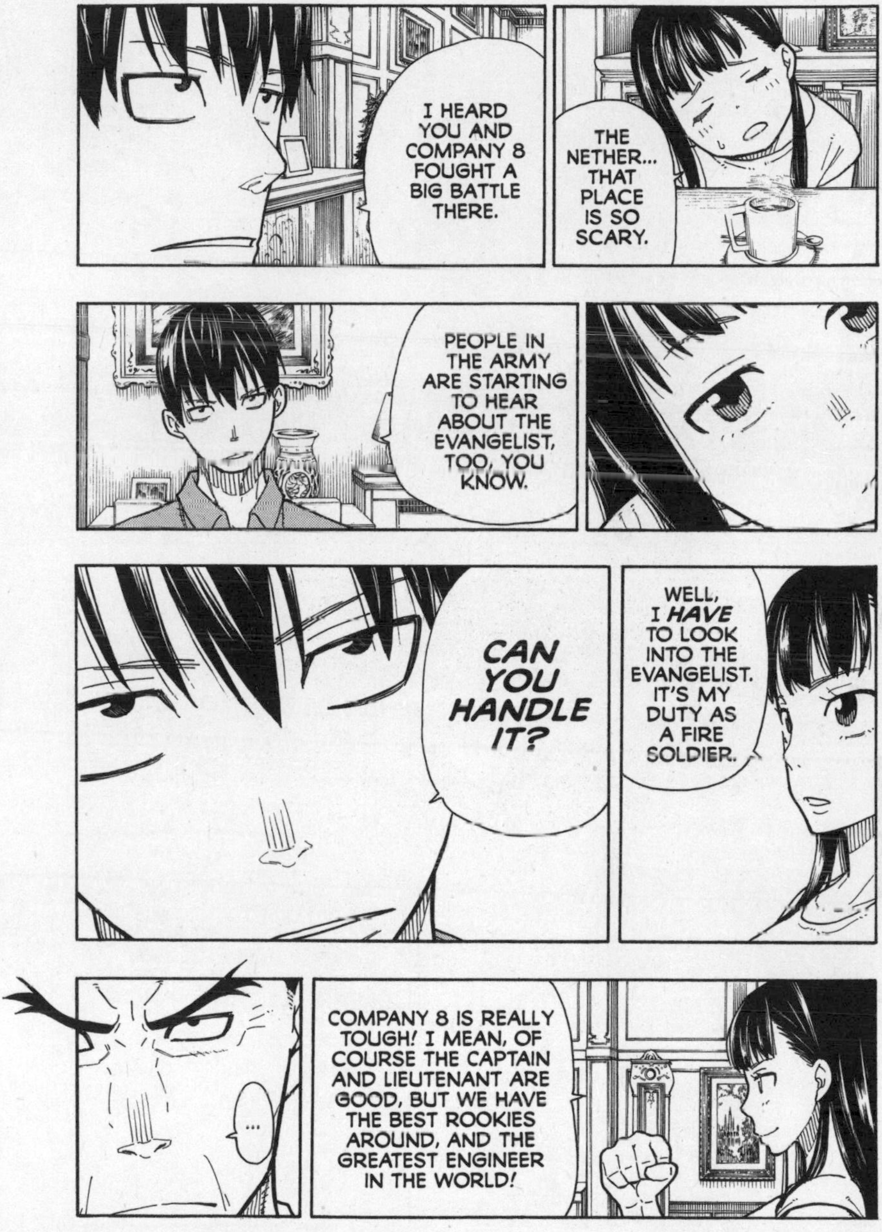
THE NETHER... THAT PLACE IS SO SCARY.
I HEARD YOU AND COMPANY 8 FOUGHT A BIG BATTLE THERE.
PEOPLE IN THE ARMY ARE STARTING TO HEAR ABOUT THE EVANGELIST, TOO, YOU KNOW.
WELL, I *HAVE* TO LOOK INTO THE EVANGELIST. IT'S MY DUTY AS A FIRE SOLDIER.
CAN YOU HANDLE IT?
COMPANY 8 IS REALLY TOUGH! I MEAN, OF COURSE THE CAPTAIN AND LIEUTENANT ARE GOOD, BUT WE HAVE THE BEST ROOKIES AROUND, AND THE GREATEST ENGINEER IN THE WORLD!
...

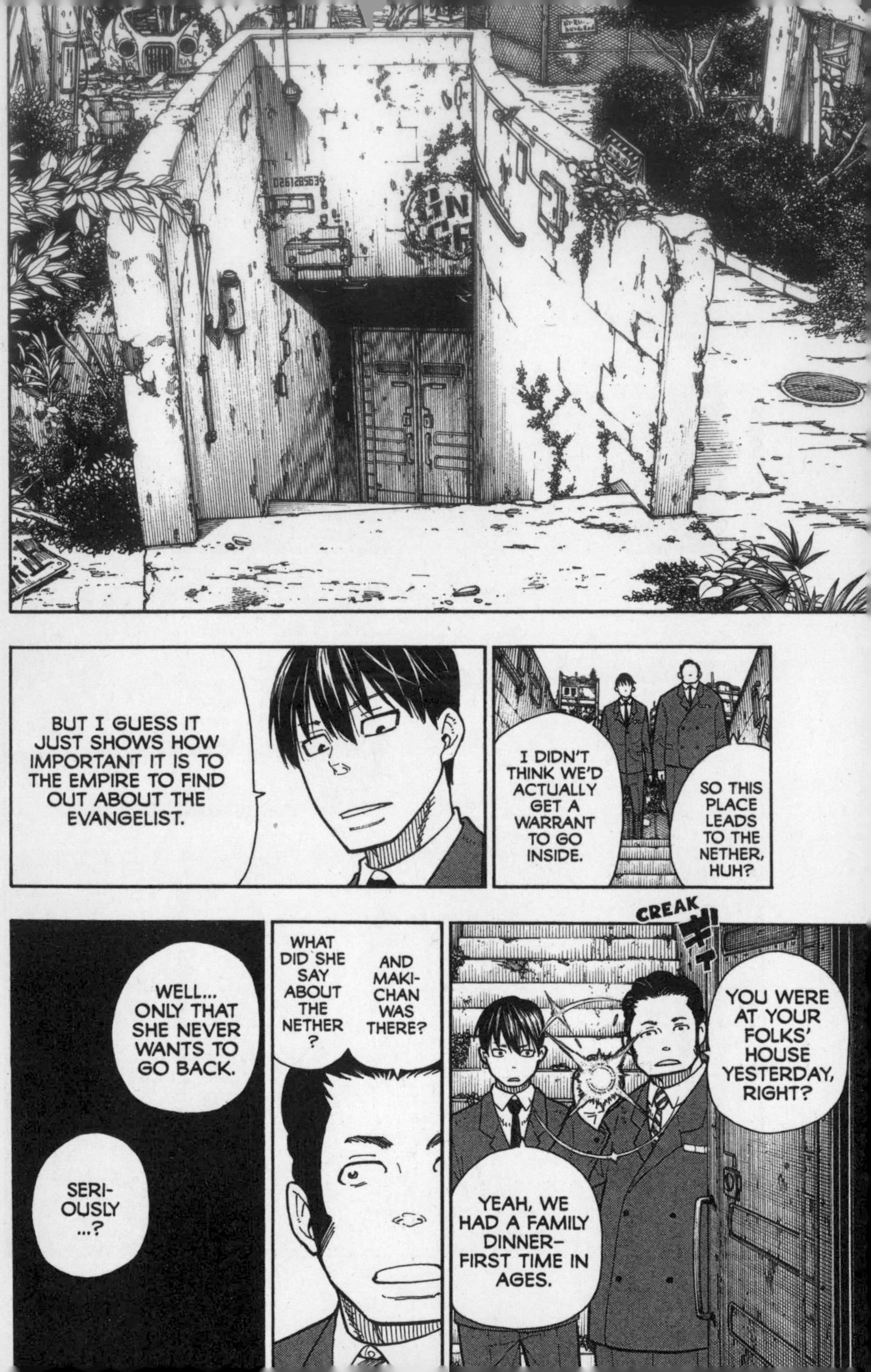
SO THIS PLACE LEADS TO THE NETHER, HUH?
I DIDN'T THINK WE'D ACTUALLY GET A WARRANT TO GO INSIDE.
BUT I GUESS IT JUST SHOWS HOW IMPORTANT IT IS TO THE EMPIRE TO FIND OUT ABOUT THE EVANGELIST.
CREAK
YOU WERE AT YOUR FOLKS' HOUSE YESTERDAY, RIGHT?
YEAH, WE HAD A FAMILY DINNER—FIRST TIME IN AGES.
AND MAKI-CHAN WAS THERE?
WHAT DID SHE SAY ABOUT THE NETHER?
WELL... ONLY THAT SHE NEVER WANTS TO GO BACK.
SERIOUSLY...?

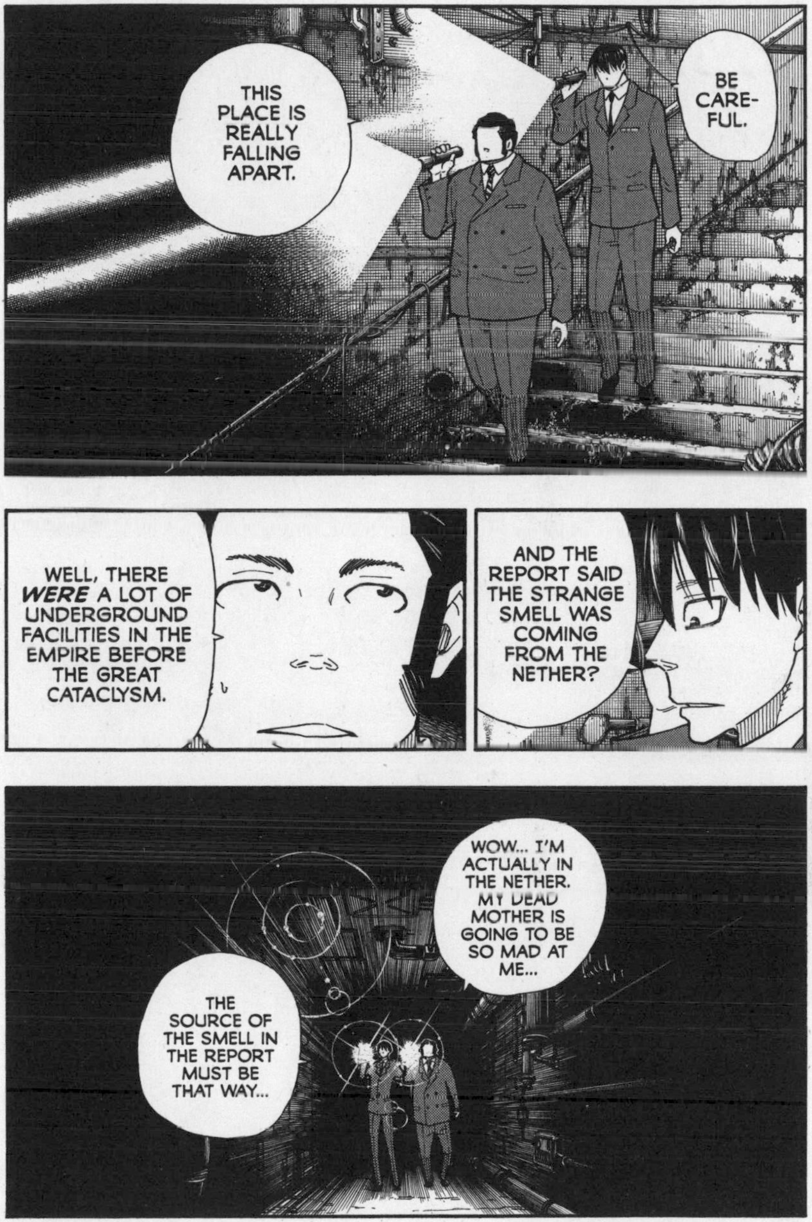
BE CARE-FUL.
THIS PLACE IS REALLY FALLING APART.
AND THE REPORT SAID THE STRANGE SMELL WAS COMING FROM THE NETHER?
WELL, THERE *WERE* A LOT OF UNDERGROUND FACILITIES IN THE EMPIRE BEFORE THE GREAT CATACLYSM.
WOW... I'M ACTUALLY IN THE NETHER. MY DEAD MOTHER IS GOING TO BE SO MAD AT ME...
THE SOURCE OF THE SMELL IN THE REPORT MUST BE THAT WAY...

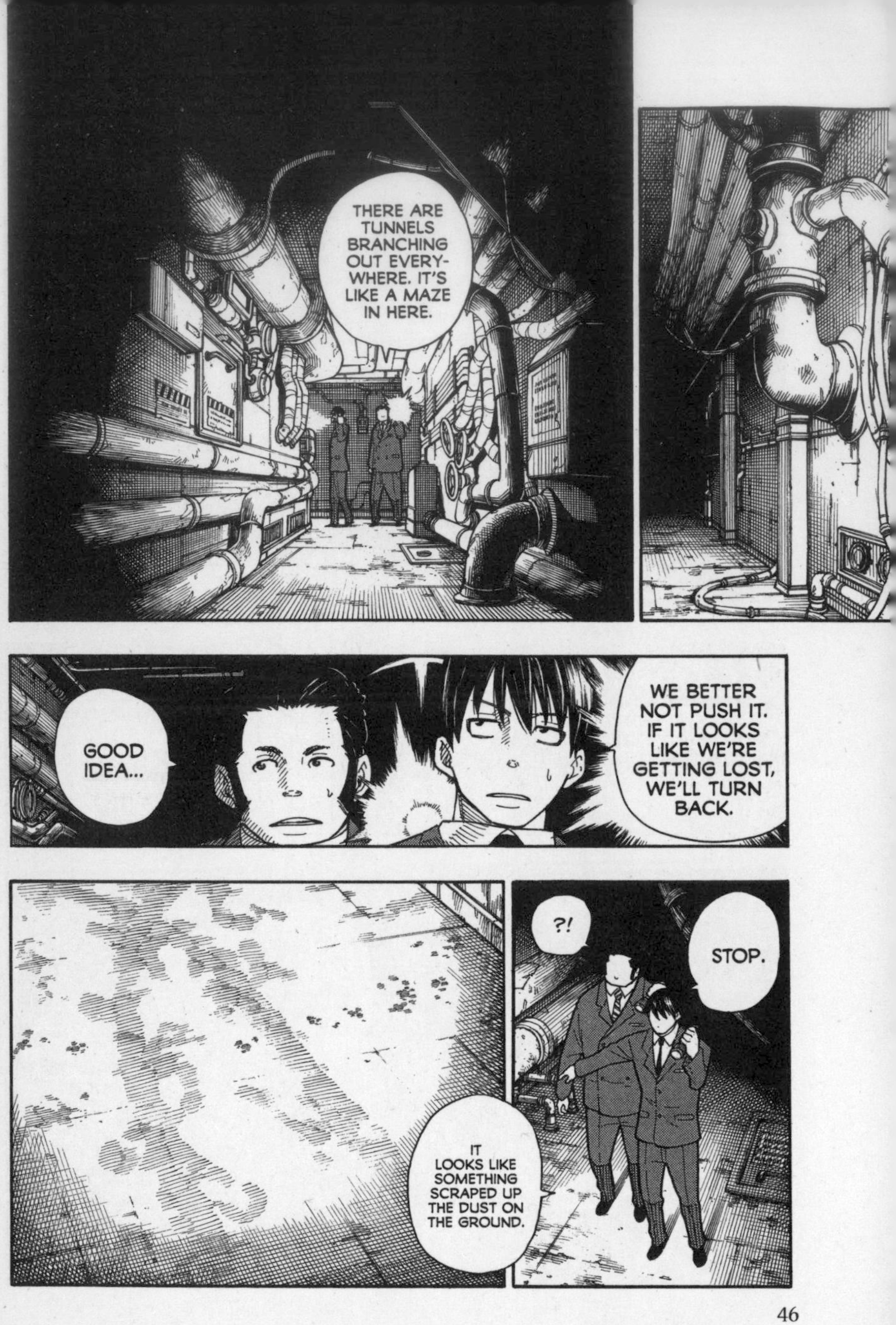
THERE ARE TUNNELS BRANCHING OUT EVERY-WHERE. IT'S LIKE A MAZE IN HERE.
WE BETTER NOT PUSH IT. IF IT LOOKS LIKE WE'RE GETTING LOST, WE'LL TURN BACK.
GOOD IDEA...
STOP.
?!
IT LOOKS LIKE SOMETHING SCRAPED UP THE DUST ON THE GROUND.

THE TRACKS ARE STILL FRESH.
THEY'RE GOING THAT WAY.
THE MACHINE ROOM... HERE IT IS.
...
I HEAR SOMETHING.
KA-CHAK
CRRREAK

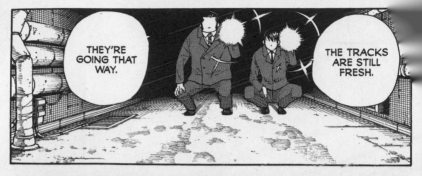

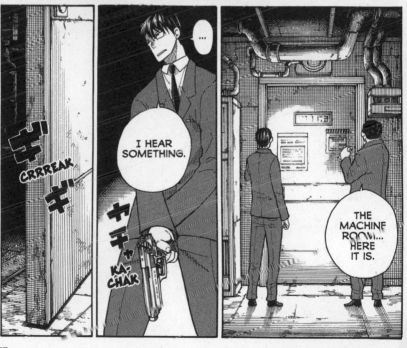

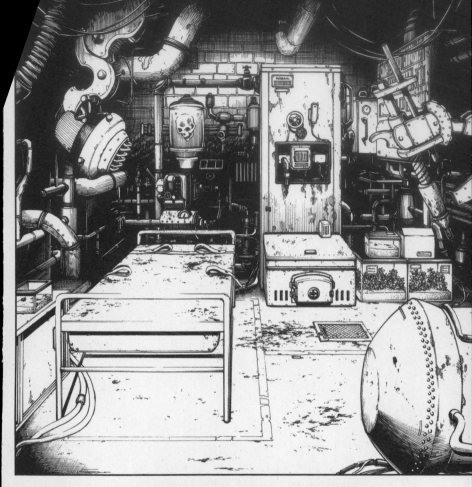

WHAT *IS* THIS PLACE?

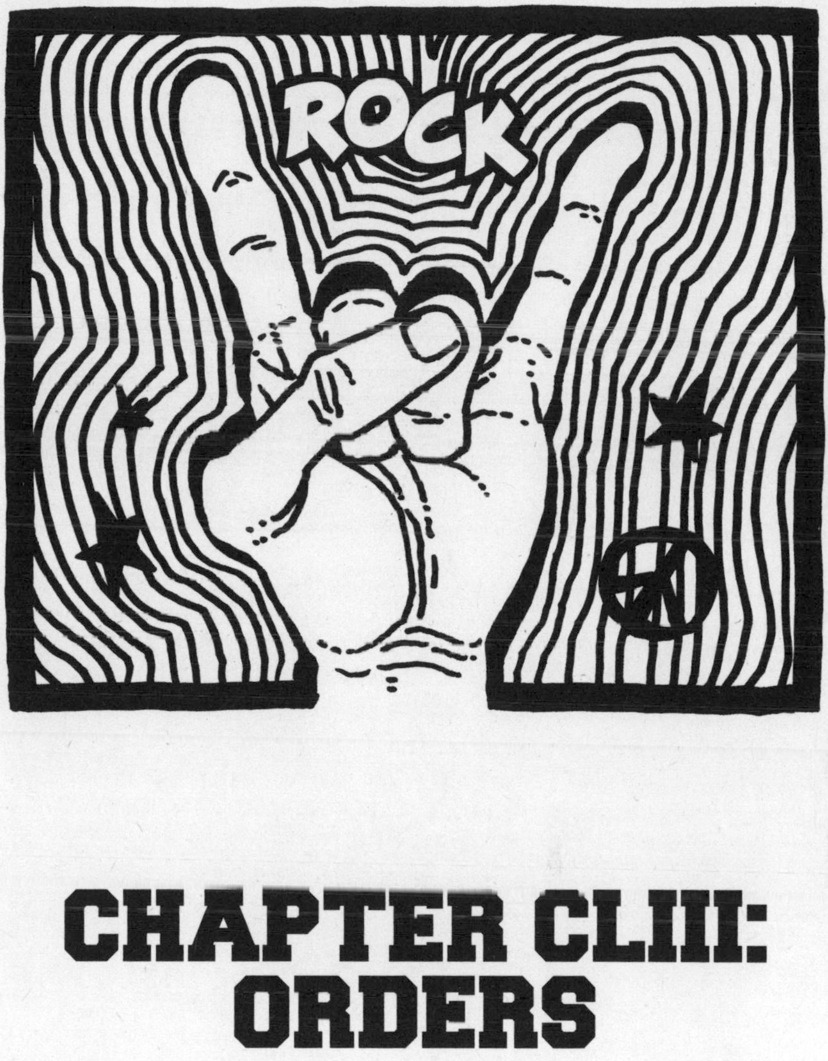
ROCK

CHAPTER CLIII: ORDERS

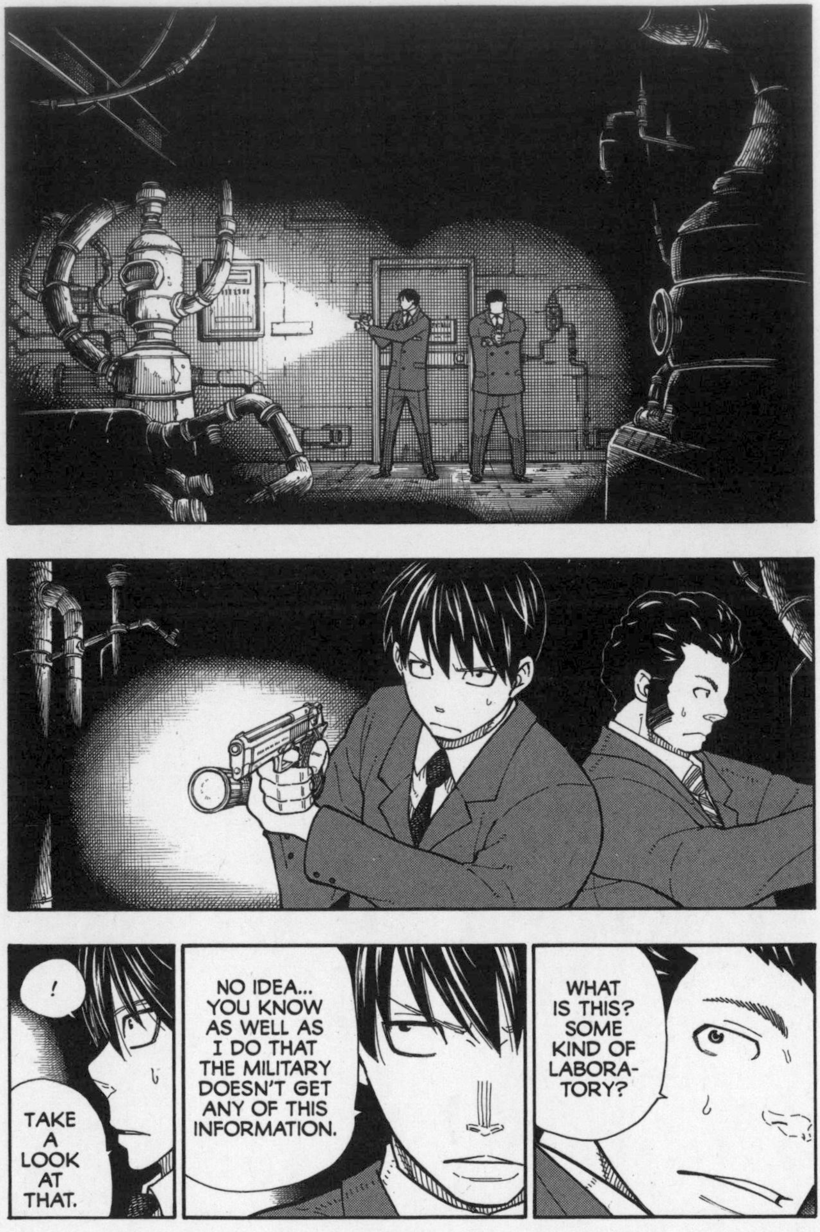
WHAT IS THIS? SOME KIND OF LABORA-TORY?
NO IDEA... YOU KNOW AS WELL AS I DO THAT THE MILITARY DOESN'T GET ANY OF THIS INFORMATION.
!
TAKE A LOOK AT THAT.

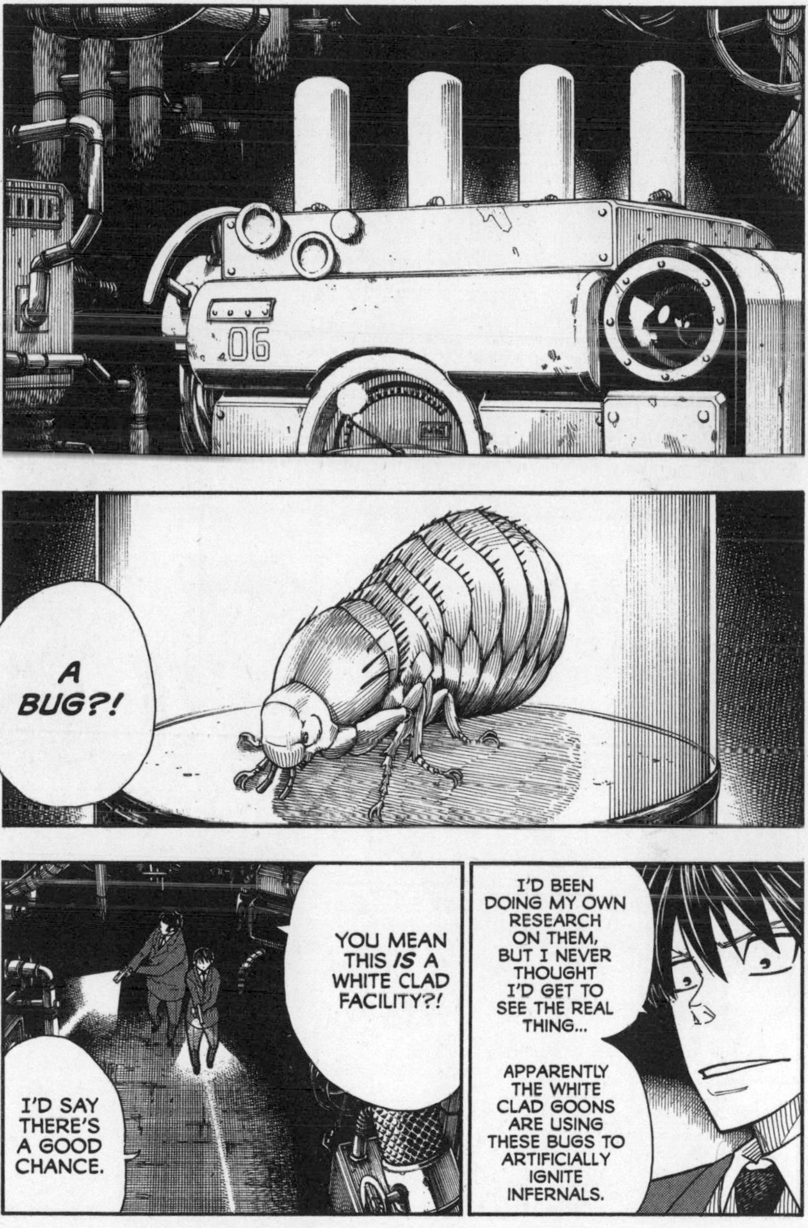
A BUG?!
I'D BEEN DOING MY OWN RESEARCH ON THEM, BUT I NEVER THOUGHT I'D GET TO SEE THE REAL THING...
APPARENTLY THE WHITE CLAD GOONS ARE USING THESE BUGS TO ARTIFICIALLY IGNITE INFERNALS.
YOU MEAN THIS *IS* A WHITE CLAD FACILITY?!
I'D SAY THERE'S A GOOD CHANCE.

SH-SNFF

LET ME SEE IF I CAN FIND SOMETHING.

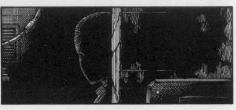

KA-CHAK ヤチャ

WHO'S THERE?!

GRUNCH

WATCH YOUR BACK. WE'RE NOT ALONE.

YEAH...

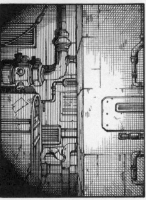

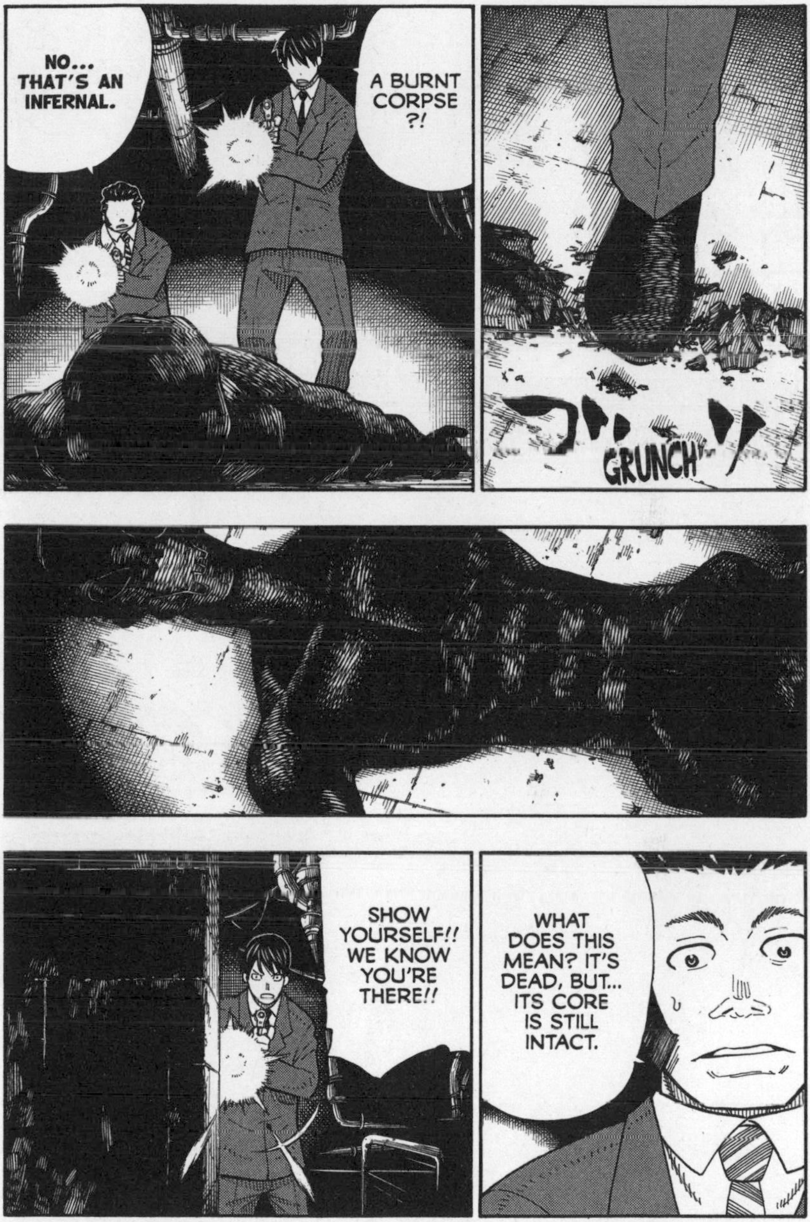
GRUNCH
A BURNT CORPSE ?!
NO... THAT'S AN INFERNAL.
WHAT DOES THIS MEAN? IT'S DEAD, BUT... ITS CORE IS STILL INTACT.
SHOW YOURSELF!! WE KNOW YOU'RE THERE!!

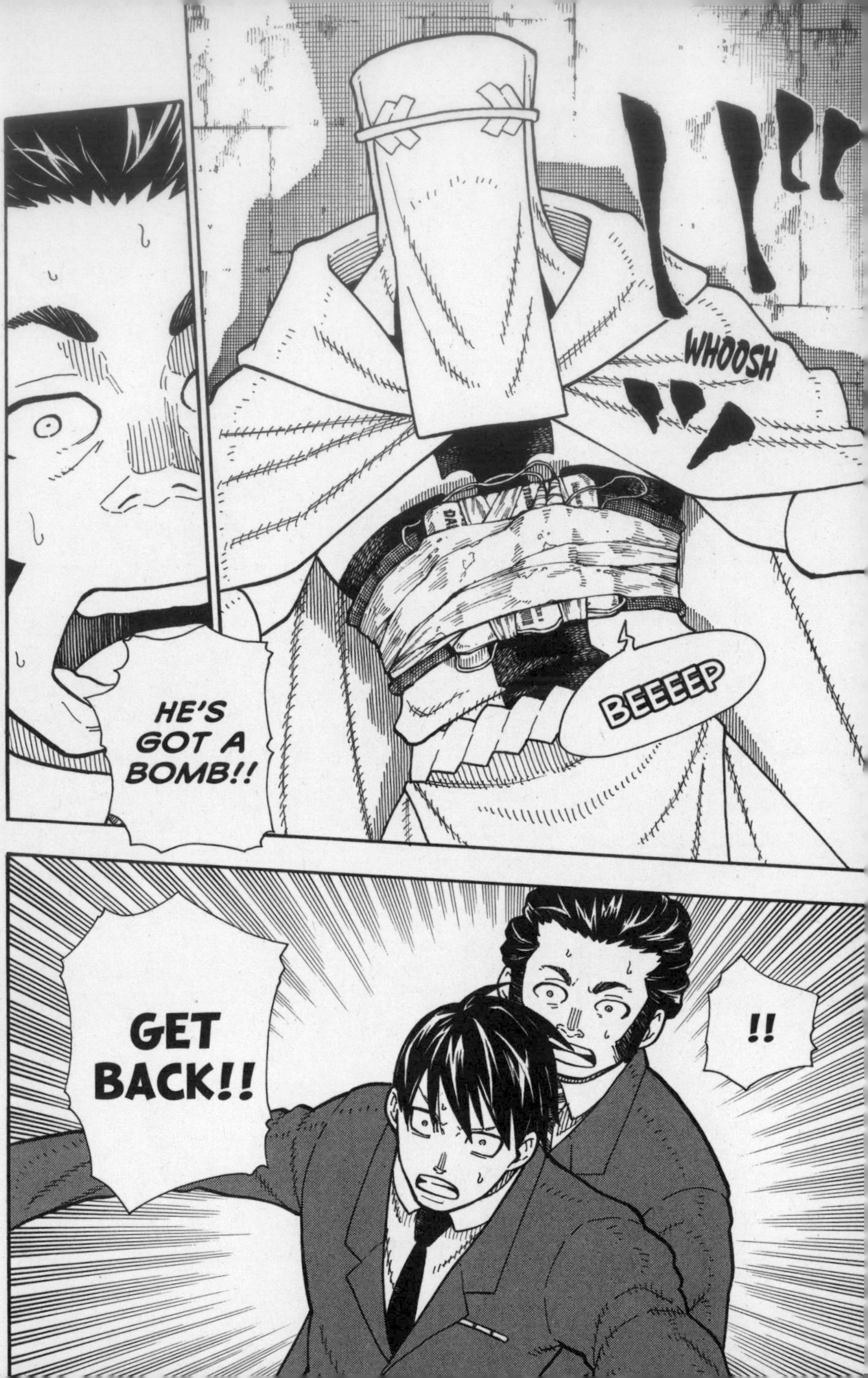
WHOOSH
BEEEEP
HE'S GOT A BOMB!!
!!
GET BACK!!

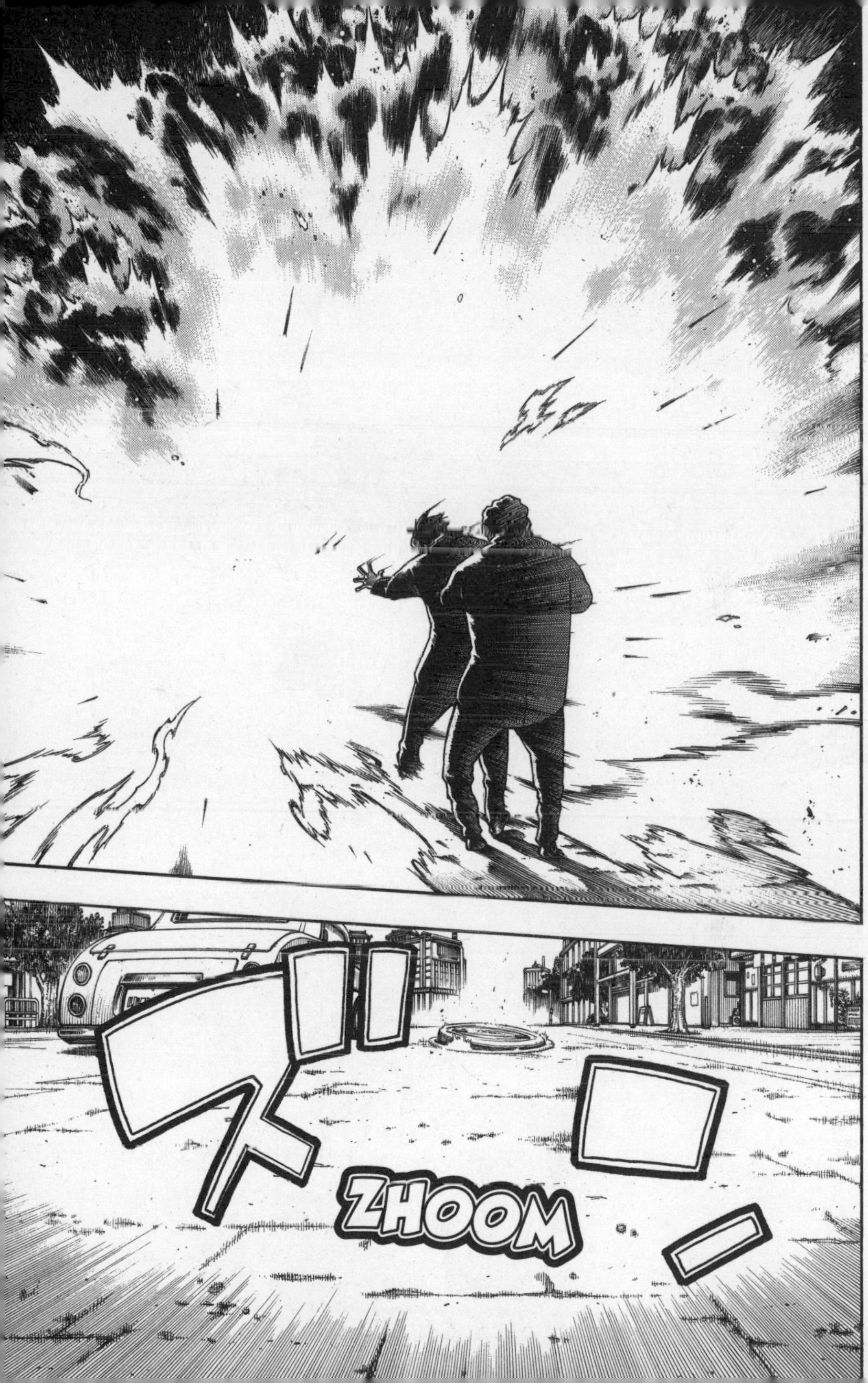
ZHOOM

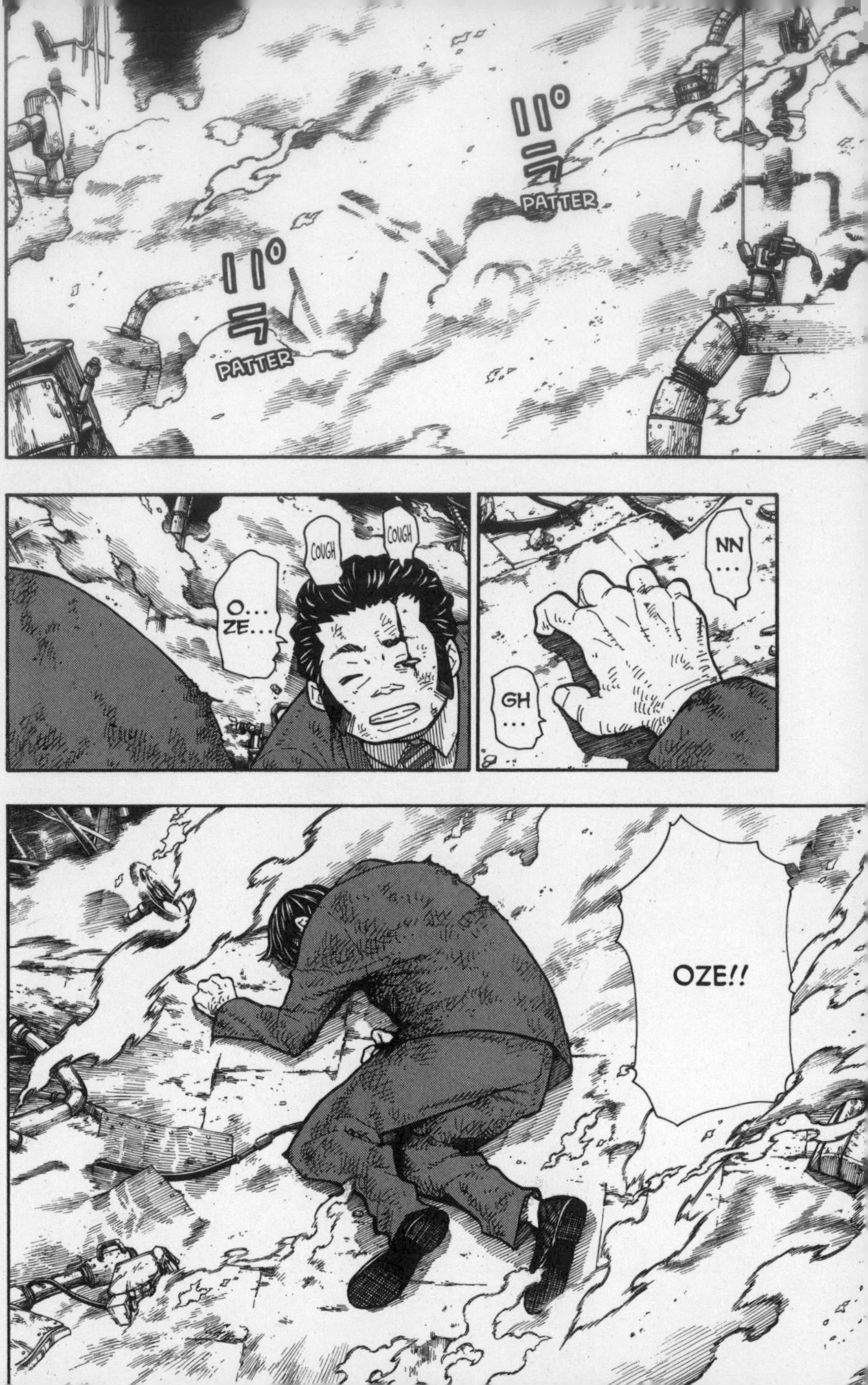

パラ
PATTER
パラ
PATTER
NN...
GH...
COUGH
COUGH
O... ZE...
OZE!!

Sign: No Running

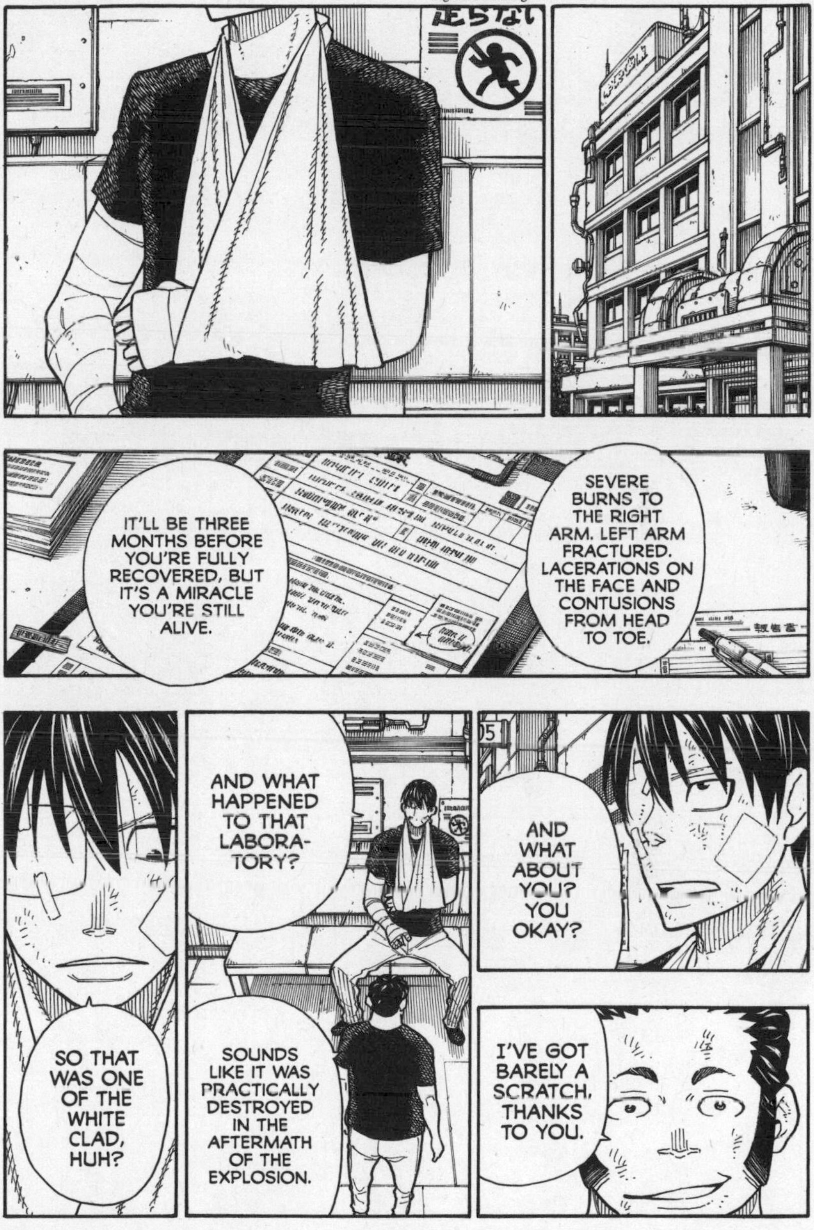
SEVERE BURNS TO THE RIGHT ARM. LEFT ARM FRACTURED. LACERATIONS ON THE FACE AND CONTUSIONS FROM HEAD TO TOE.
IT'LL BE THREE MONTHS BEFORE YOU'RE FULLY RECOVERED, BUT IT'S A MIRACLE YOU'RE STILL ALIVE.
AND WHAT ABOUT YOU? YOU OKAY?
I'VE GOT BARELY A SCRATCH, THANKS TO YOU.
AND WHAT HAPPENED TO THAT LABORA-TORY?
SOUNDS LIKE IT WAS PRACTICALLY DESTROYED IN THE AFTERMATH OF THE EXPLOSION.
SO THAT WAS ONE OF THE WHITE CLAD, HUH?

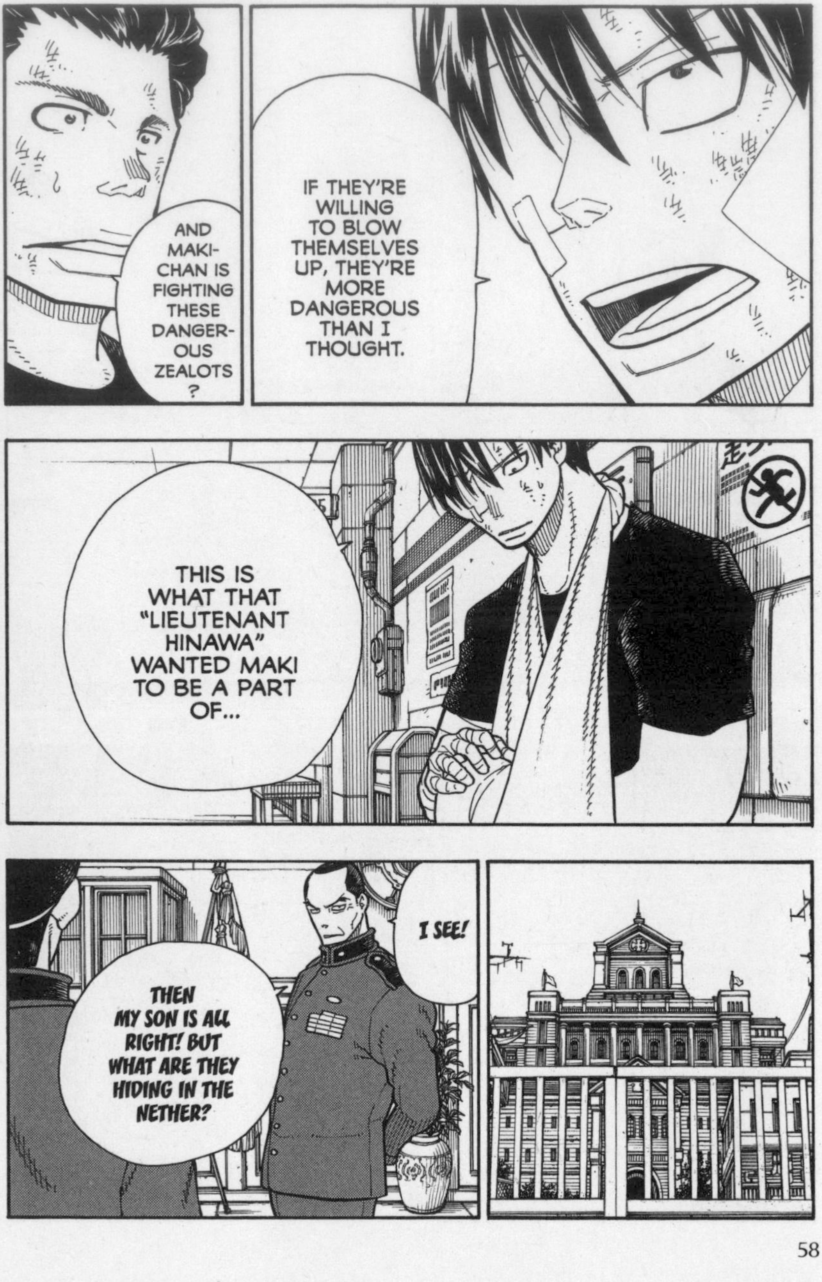
IF THEY'RE WILLING TO BLOW THEMSELVES UP, THEY'RE MORE DANGEROUS THAN I THOUGHT.
AND MAKI-CHAN IS FIGHTING THESE DANGER-OUS ZEALOTS?
THIS IS WHAT THAT "LIEUTENANT HINAWA" WANTED MAKI TO BE A PART OF...
I SEE!
THEN MY SON IS ALL RIGHT! BUT WHAT ARE THEY HIDING IN THE NETHER?

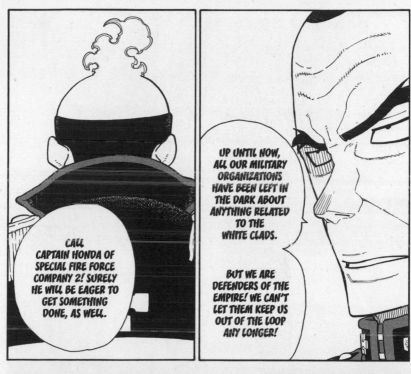

UP UNTIL NOW, ALL OUR MILITARY ORGANIZATIONS HAVE BEEN LEFT IN THE DARK ABOUT ANYTHING RELATED TO THE WHITE CLADS.
BUT WE ARE DEFENDERS OF THE EMPIRE! WE CAN'T LET THEM KEEP US OUT OF THE LOOP ANY LONGER!
CALL CAPTAIN HONDA OF SPECIAL FIRE FORCE COMPANY 2! SURELY HE WILL BE EAGER TO GET SOMETHING DONE, AS WELL.
I WILL GIVE COMPANY 2 A MISSION— TO INVESTIGATE THE NETHER!

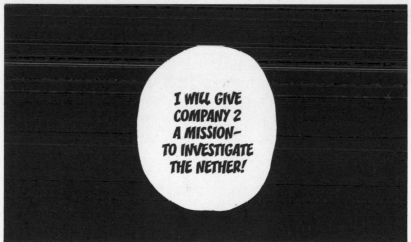

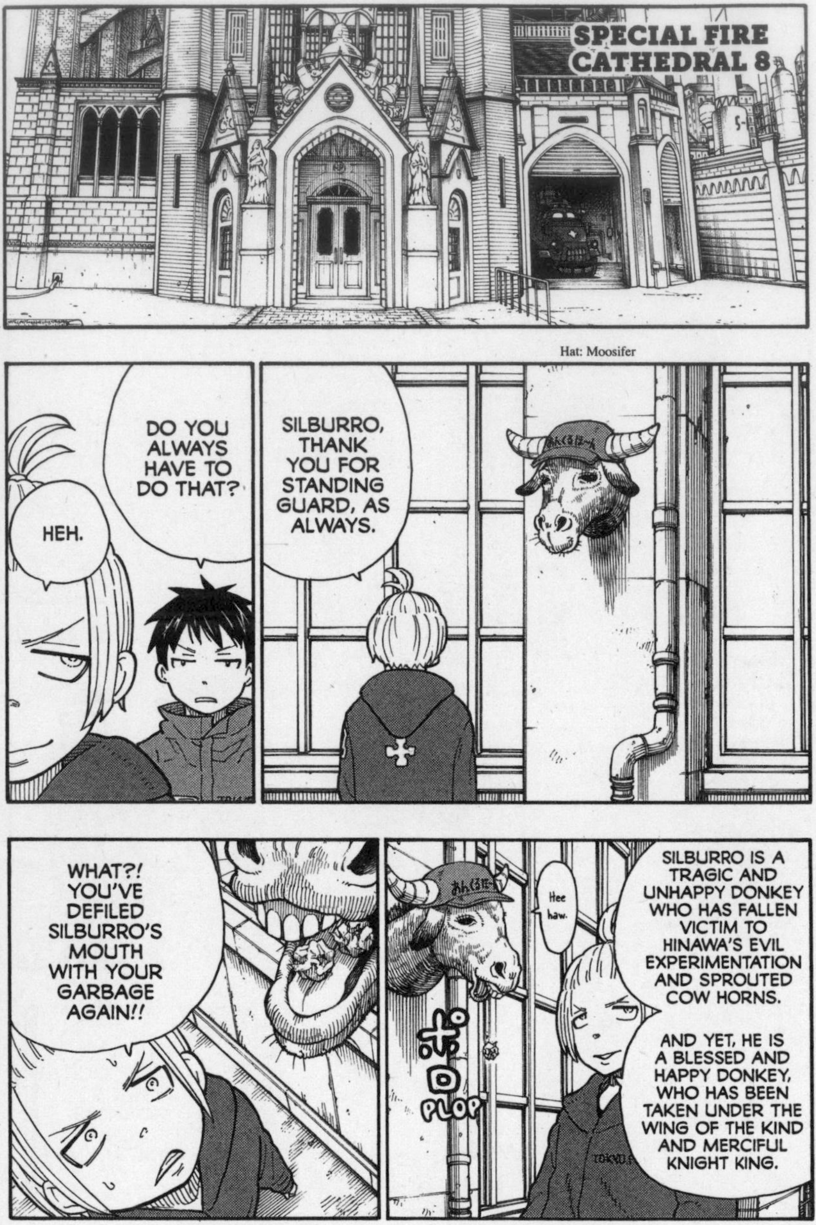
SPECIAL FIRE CATHEDRAL 8
Hat: Moosifer
SILBURRO, THANK YOU FOR STANDING GUARD, AS ALWAYS.
DO YOU ALWAYS HAVE TO DO THAT?
HEH.
SILBURRO IS A TRAGIC AND UNHAPPY DONKEY WHO HAS FALLEN VICTIM TO HINAWA'S EVIL EXPERIMENTATION AND SPROUTED COW HORNS.
Hee haw.
AND YET, HE IS A BLESSED AND HAPPY DONKEY, WHO HAS BEEN TAKEN UNDER THE WING OF THE KIND AND MERCIFUL KNIGHT KING.
PLOP
WHAT?! YOU'VE DEFILED SILBURRO'S MOUTH WITH YOUR GARBAGE AGAIN!!

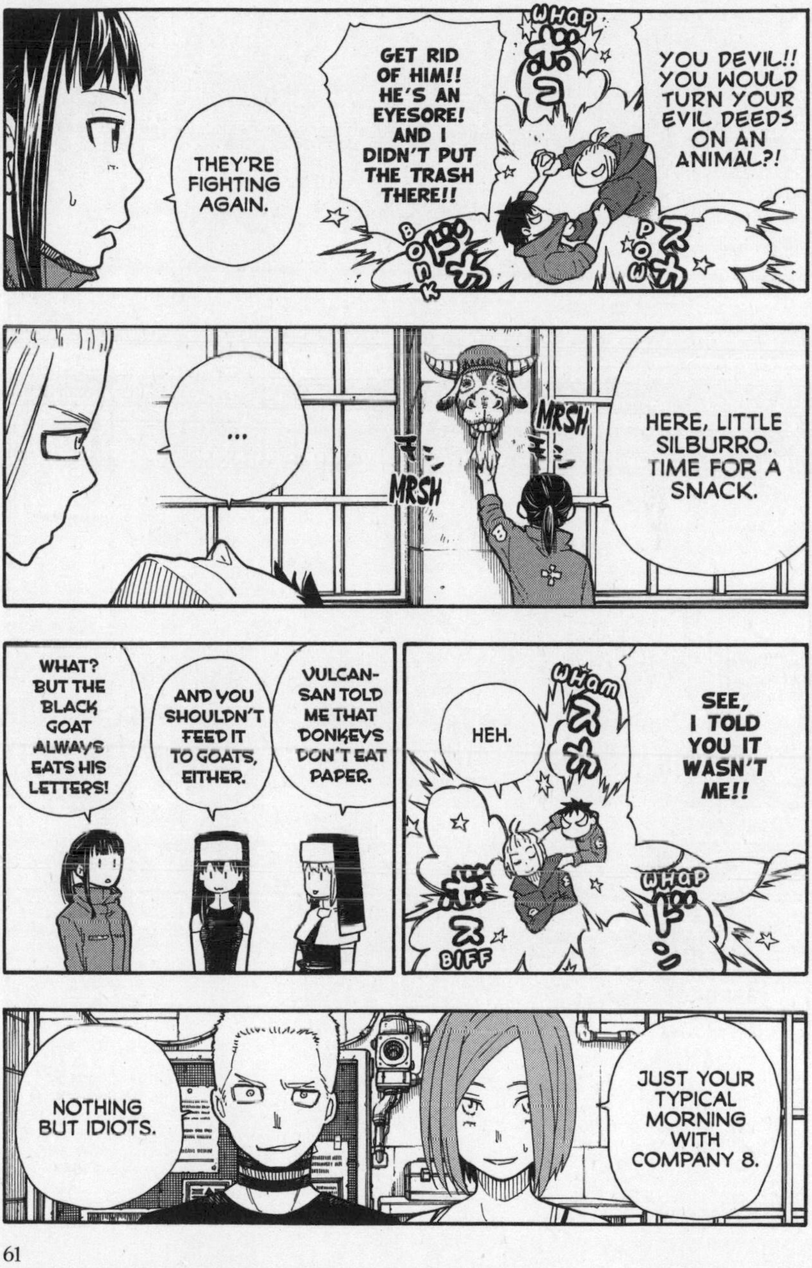
YOU DEVIL!! YOU WOULD TURN YOUR EVIL DEEDS ON AN ANIMAL?!
WHAP
GET RID OF HIM!! HE'S AN EYESORE! AND I DIDN'T PUT THE TRASH THERE!!
POW
BONK
THEY'RE FIGHTING AGAIN.
HERE, LITTLE SILBURRO. TIME FOR A SNACK.
MRSH
MRSH
...
SEE, I TOLD YOU IT WASN'T ME!!
WHAM
HEH.
WHAP
BIFF
VULCAN-SAN TOLD ME THAT DONKEYS DON'T EAT PAPER.
AND YOU SHOULDN'T FEED IT TO GOATS, EITHER.
WHAT? BUT THE BLACK GOAT ALWAYS EATS HIS LETTERS!
JUST YOUR TYPICAL MORNING WITH COMPANY 8.
NOTHING BUT IDIOTS.

Hat: Head Spa

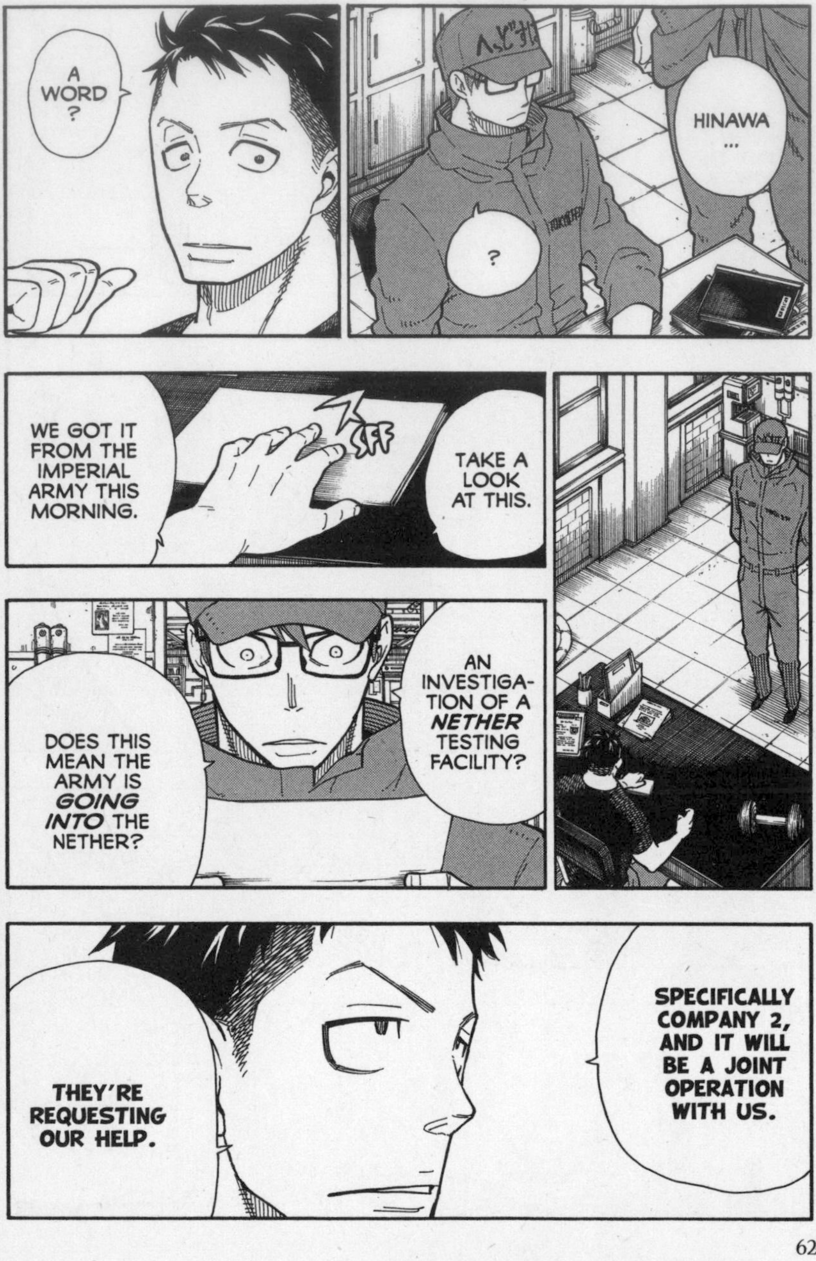
HINAWA ...
?
A WORD ?
TAKE A LOOK AT THIS.
SFF
WE GOT IT FROM THE IMPERIAL ARMY THIS MORNING.
AN INVESTIGA-TION OF A *NETHER* TESTING FACILITY?
DOES THIS MEAN THE ARMY IS *GOING INTO* THE NETHER?
SPECIFICALLY COMPANY 2, AND IT WILL BE A JOINT OPERATION WITH US.
THEY'RE REQUESTING OUR HELP.

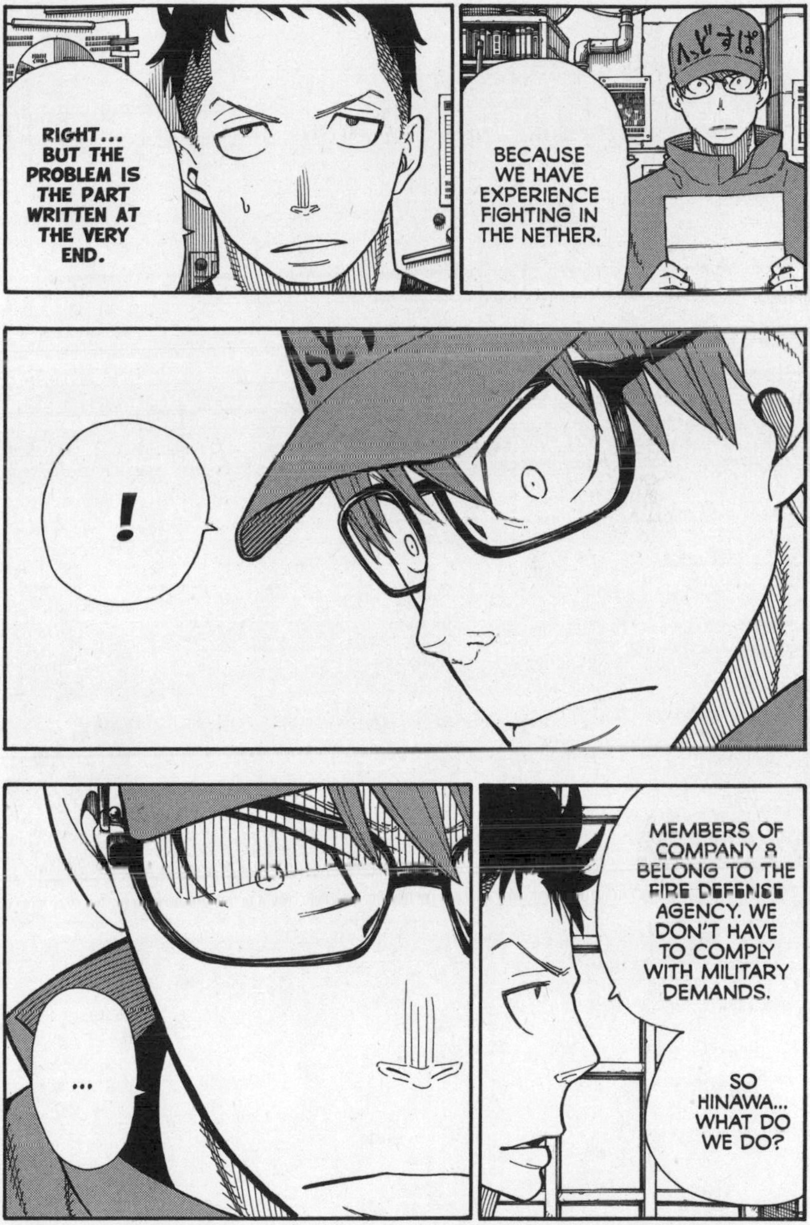
BECAUSE WE HAVE EXPERIENCE FIGHTING IN THE NETHER.
RIGHT... BUT THE PROBLEM IS THE PART WRITTEN AT THE VERY END.
!
MEMBERS OF COMPANY 8 BELONG TO THE FIRE DEFENSE AGENCY. WE DON'T HAVE TO COMPLY WITH MILITARY DEMANDS.
SO HINAWA... WHAT DO WE DO?
...

?

...

WHAT
IS IT,
SIR?

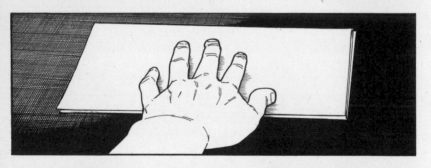

FROM THE
TOKYO
IMPERIAL
ARMY...

ALL
RIGHT.

REQUESTING ASSISTANCE
MAKI OZE'S RETURN
IN THIS OPERATION

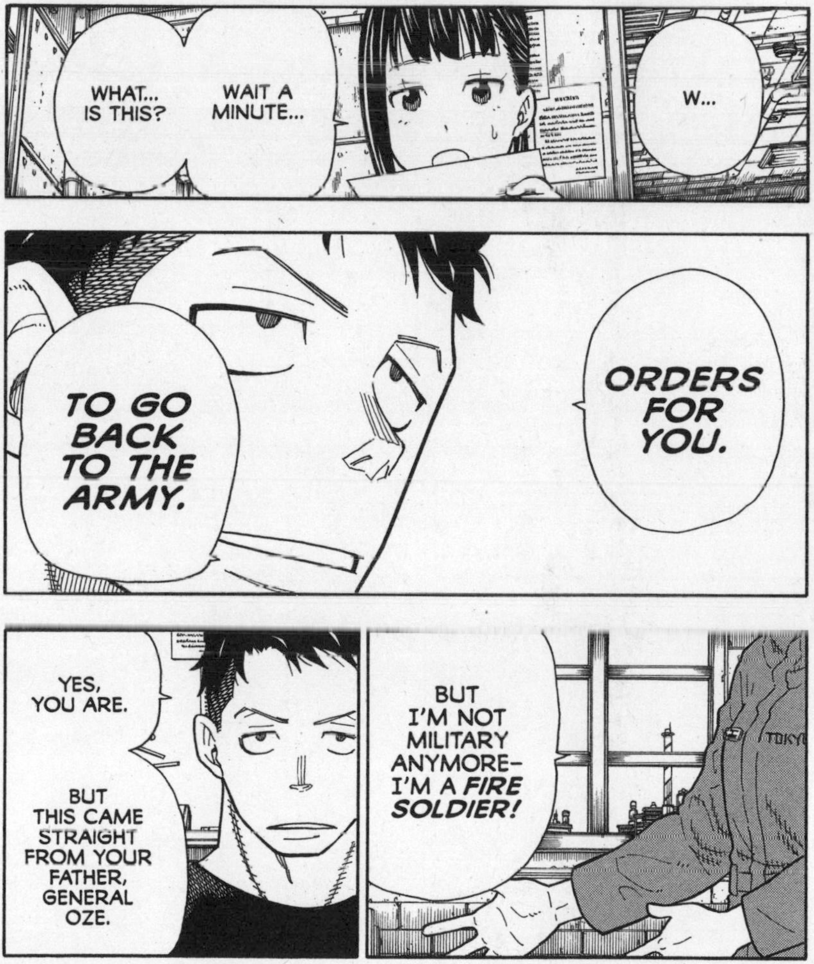
W...
WAIT A MINUTE...
WHAT... IS THIS?
ORDERS FOR YOU.
TO GO BACK TO THE ARMY.
BUT I'M NOT MILITARY ANYMORE— I'M A FIRE SOLDIER!
YES, YOU ARE.
BUT THIS CAME STRAIGHT FROM YOUR FATHER, GENERAL OZE.

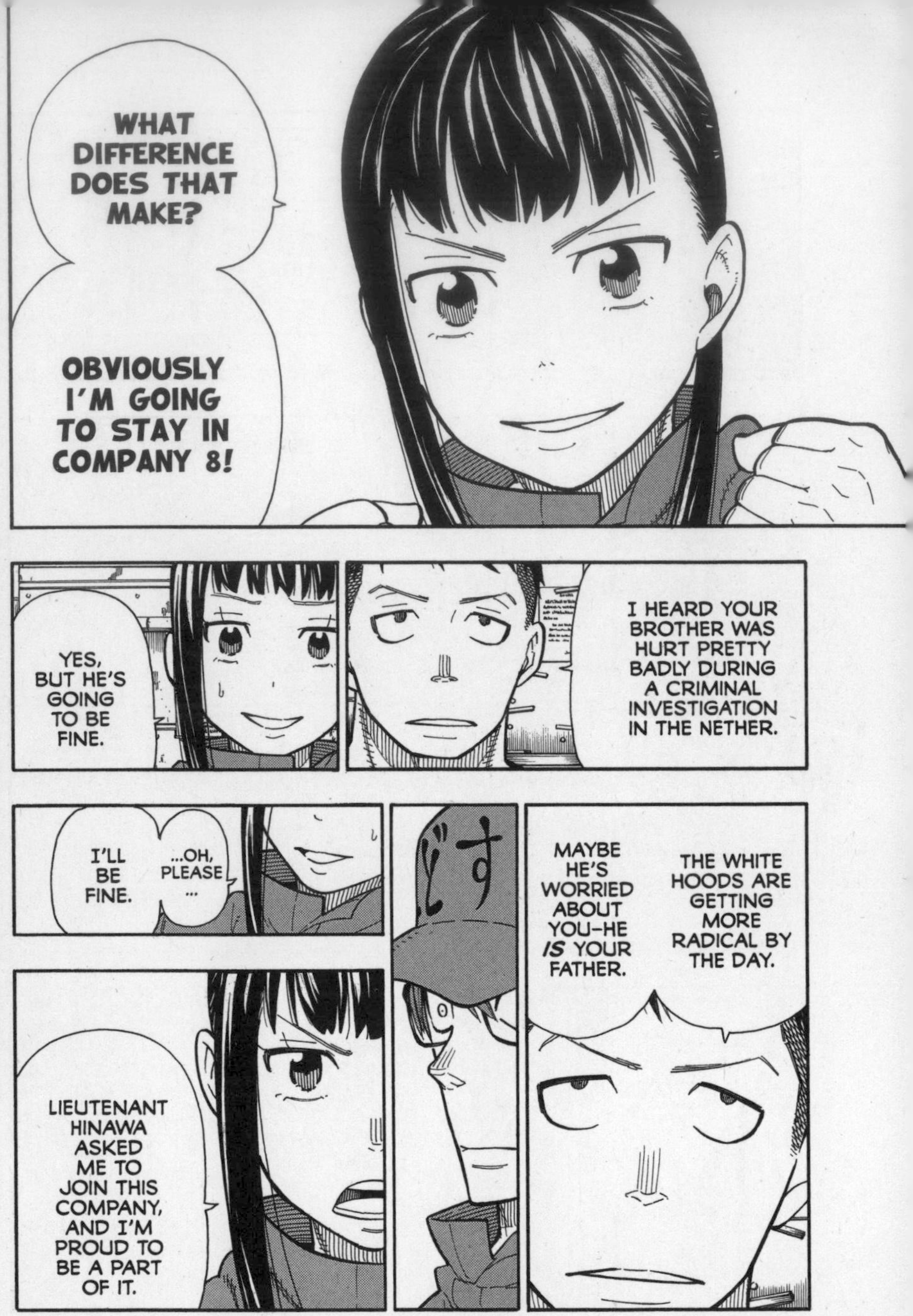
WHAT DIFFERENCE DOES THAT MAKE?
OBVIOUSLY I'M GOING TO STAY IN COMPANY 8!
I HEARD YOUR BROTHER WAS HURT PRETTY BADLY DURING A CRIMINAL INVESTIGATION IN THE NETHER.
YES, BUT HE'S GOING TO BE FINE.
THE WHITE HOODS ARE GETTING MORE RADICAL BY THE DAY.
MAYBE HE'S WORRIED ABOUT YOU–HE *IS* YOUR FATHER.
...OH, PLEASE...
I'LL BE FINE.
LIEUTENANT HINAWA ASKED ME TO JOIN THIS COMPANY, AND I'M PROUD TO BE A PART OF IT.

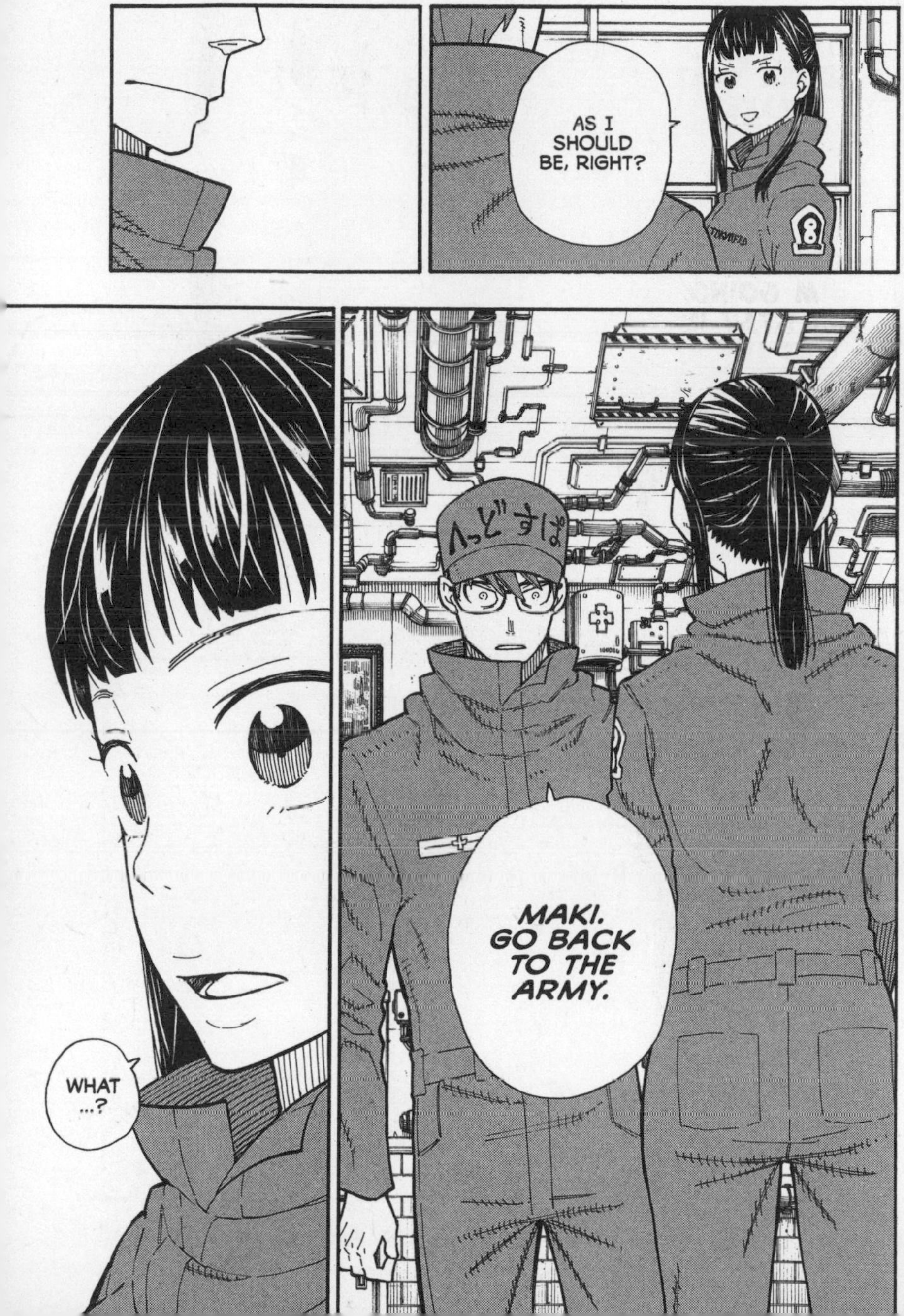
AS I SHOULD BE, RIGHT?
へっどすば
MAKI. GO BACK TO THE ARMY.
WHAT ...?

FIRE FORCE

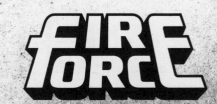

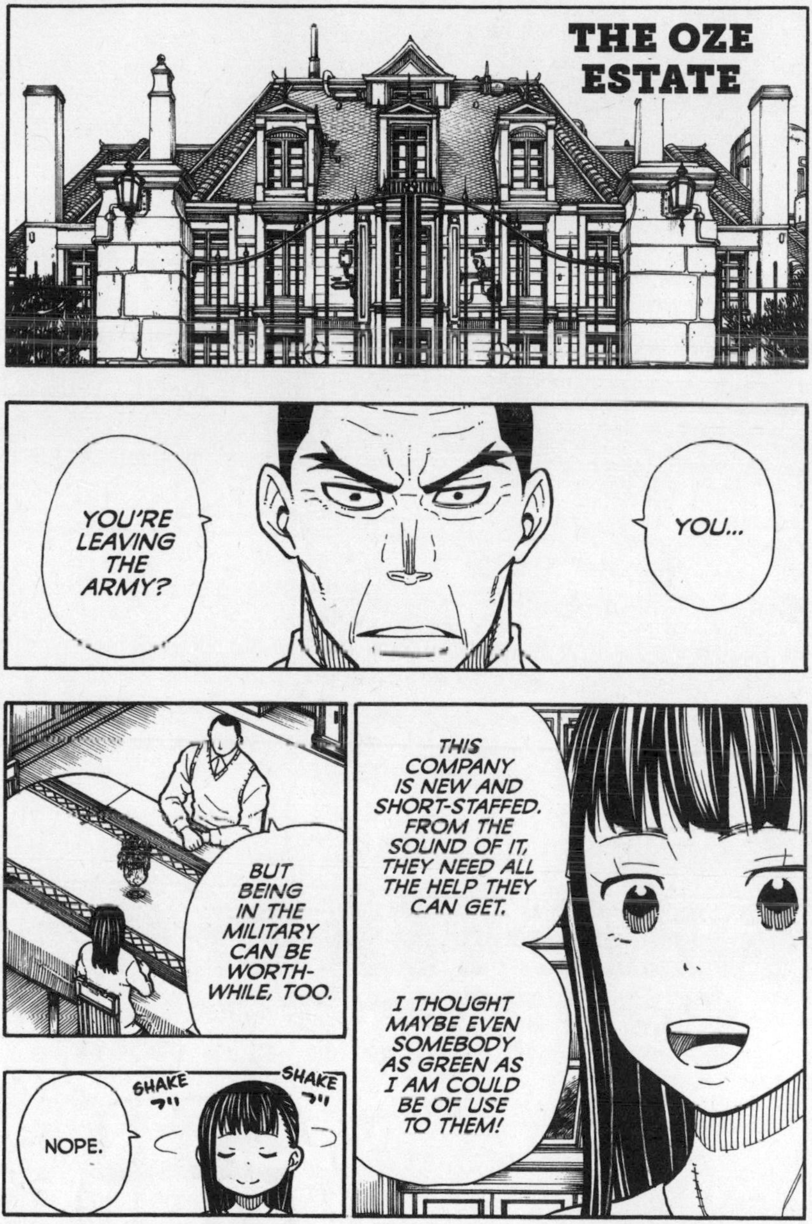
THE OZE ESTATE
YOU...
YOU'RE LEAVING THE ARMY?
THIS COMPANY IS NEW AND SHORT-STAFFED. FROM THE SOUND OF IT, THEY NEED ALL THE HELP THEY CAN GET.
I THOUGHT MAYBE EVEN SOMEBODY AS GREEN AS I AM COULD BE OF USE TO THEM!
BUT BEING IN THE MILITARY CAN BE WORTH-WHILE, TOO.
SHAKE
SHAKE
NOPE.

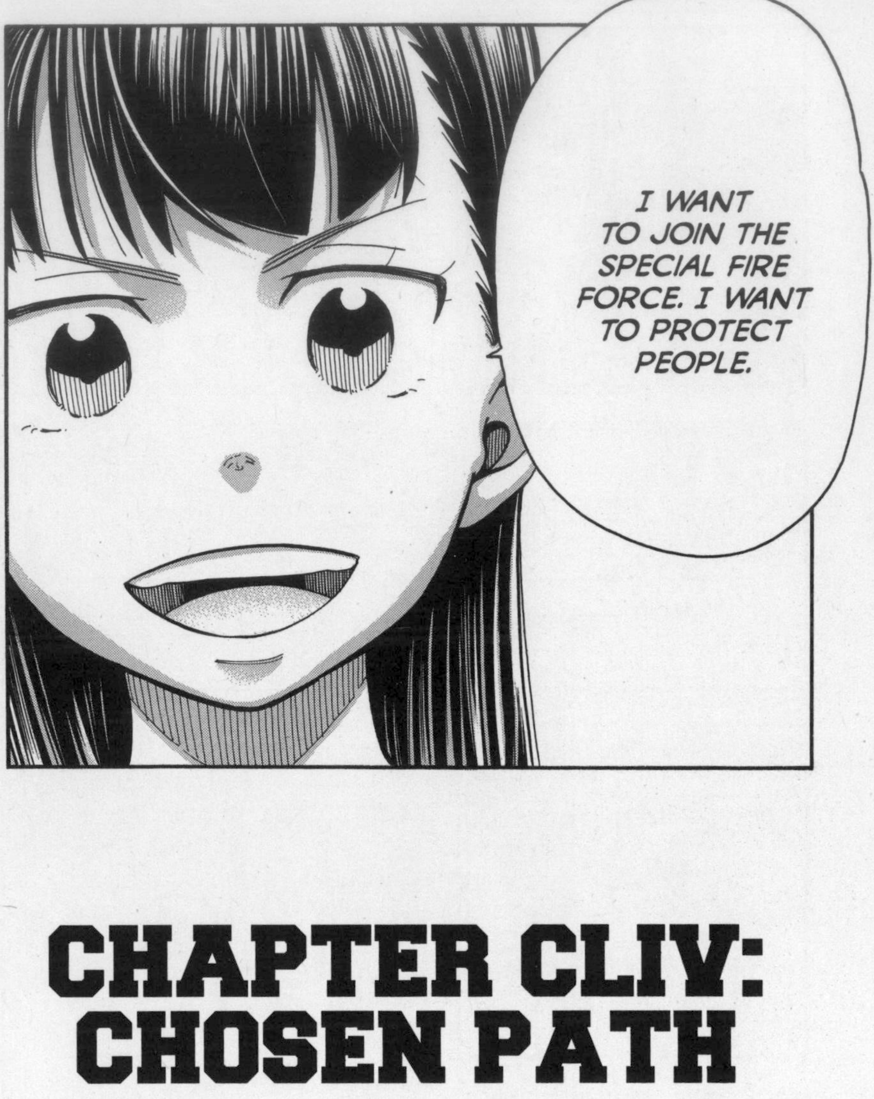
I WANT TO JOIN THE SPECIAL FIRE FORCE. I WANT TO PROTECT PEOPLE.

CHAPTER CLIV: CHOSEN PATH

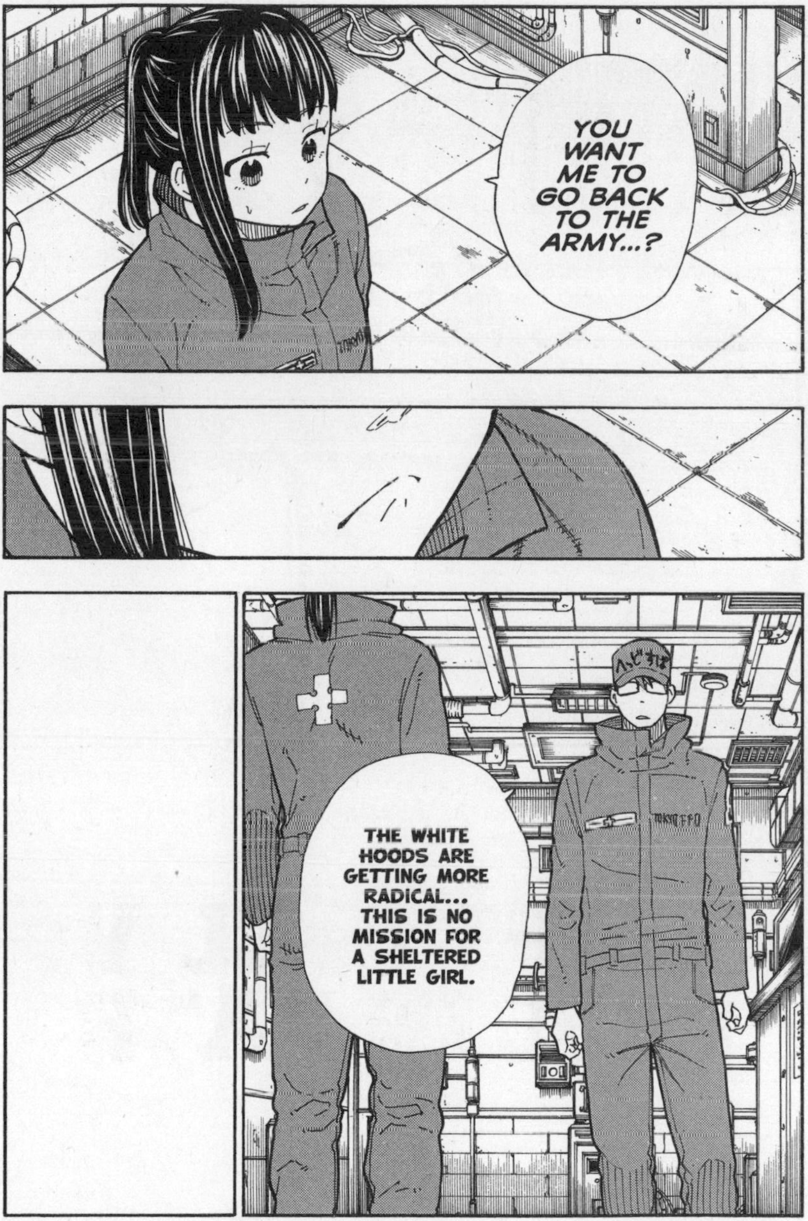
YOU WANT ME TO GO BACK TO THE ARMY...?
THE WHITE HOODS ARE GETTING MORE RADICAL... THIS IS NO MISSION FOR A SHELTERED LITTLE GIRL.

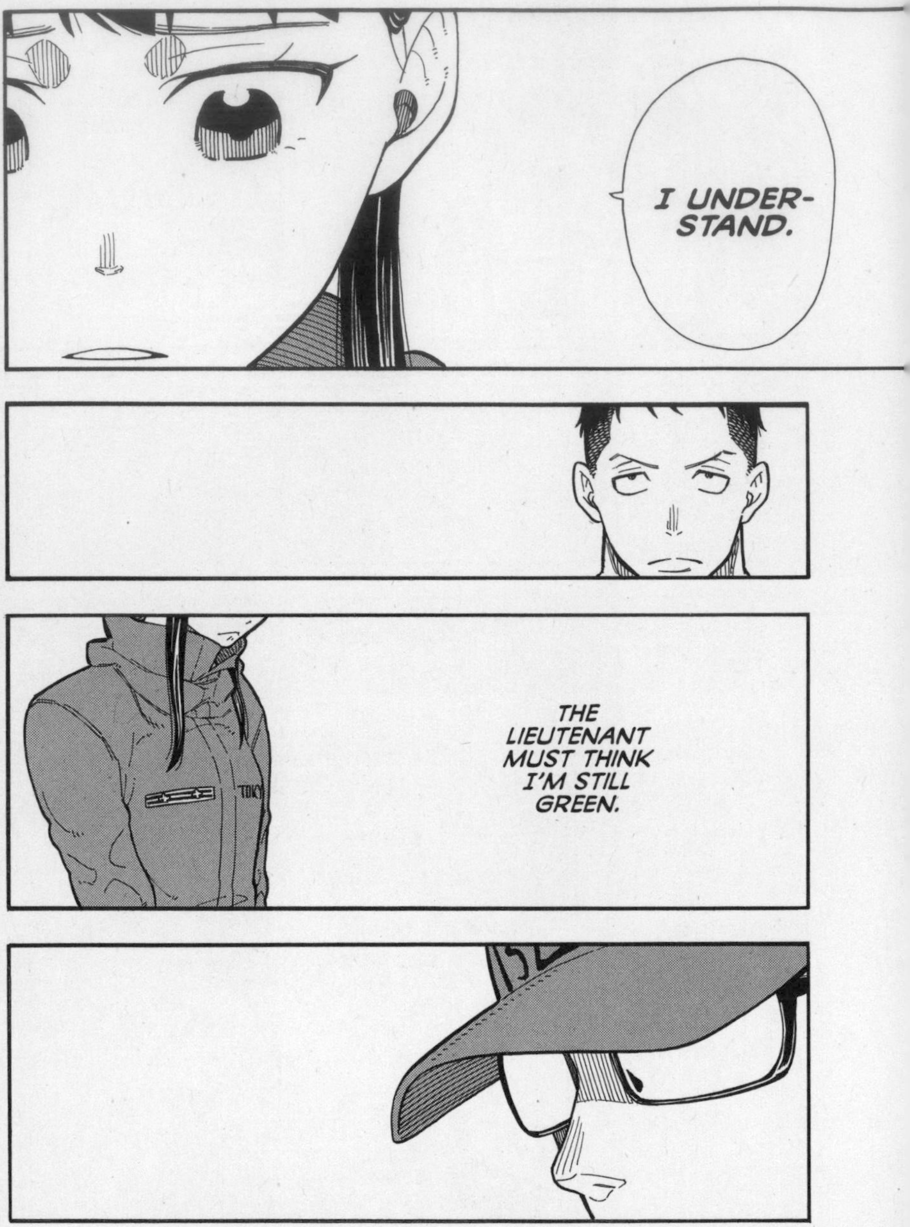
I UNDER-STAND.
THE LIEUTENANT MUST THINK I'M STILL GREEN.

Sign (top to bottom): Hikeshi “Fire Fighting” Fest; Ping-Pong Bungee Tournament Participants

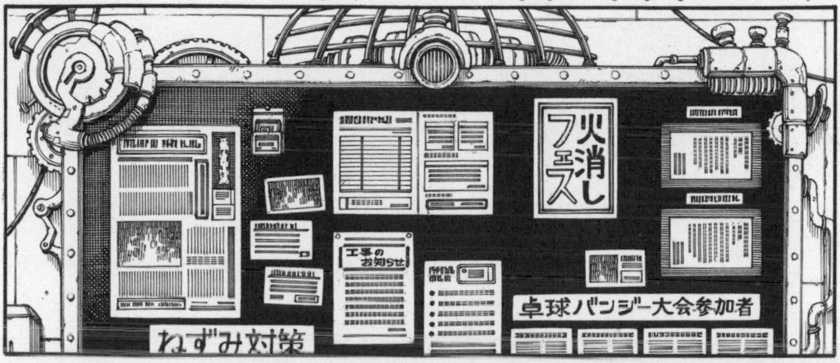
火消しフェス
工事のお知らせ
卓球バンジー大会参加者
ねずみ対策

Sign (R to L): Construction Notice; Keep Rats Away

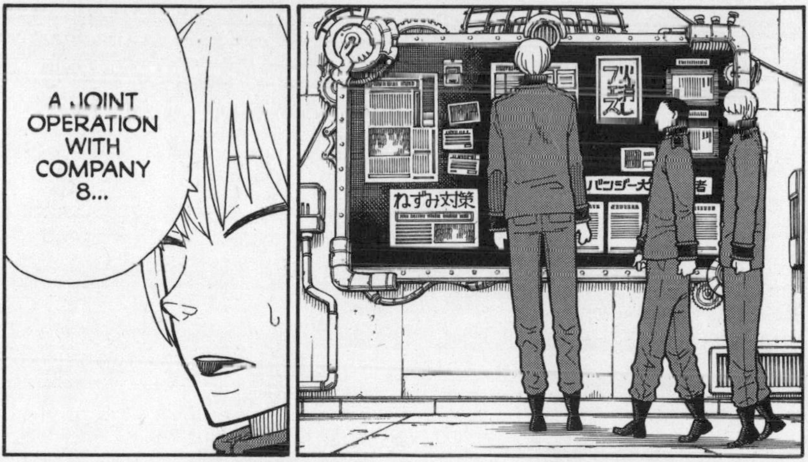
A JOINT OPERATION WITH COMPANY 8...

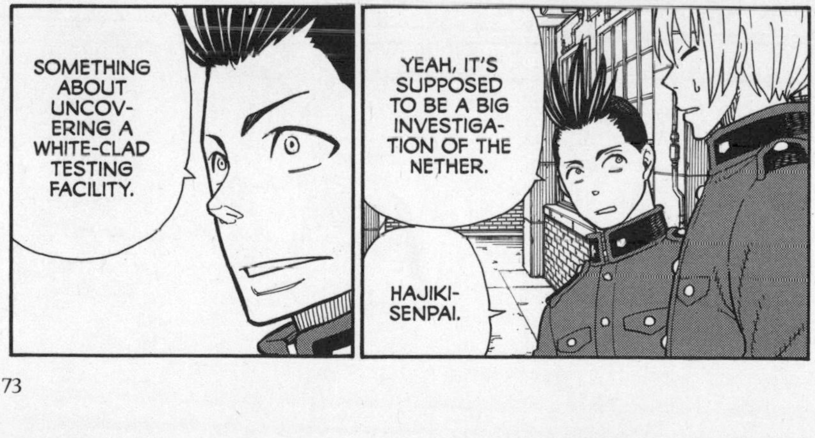
YEAH, IT'S SUPPOSED TO BE A BIG INVESTIGA-TION OF THE NETHER.
HAJIKI-SENPAI.
SOMETHING ABOUT UNCOV-ERING A WHITE-CLAD TESTING FACILITY.

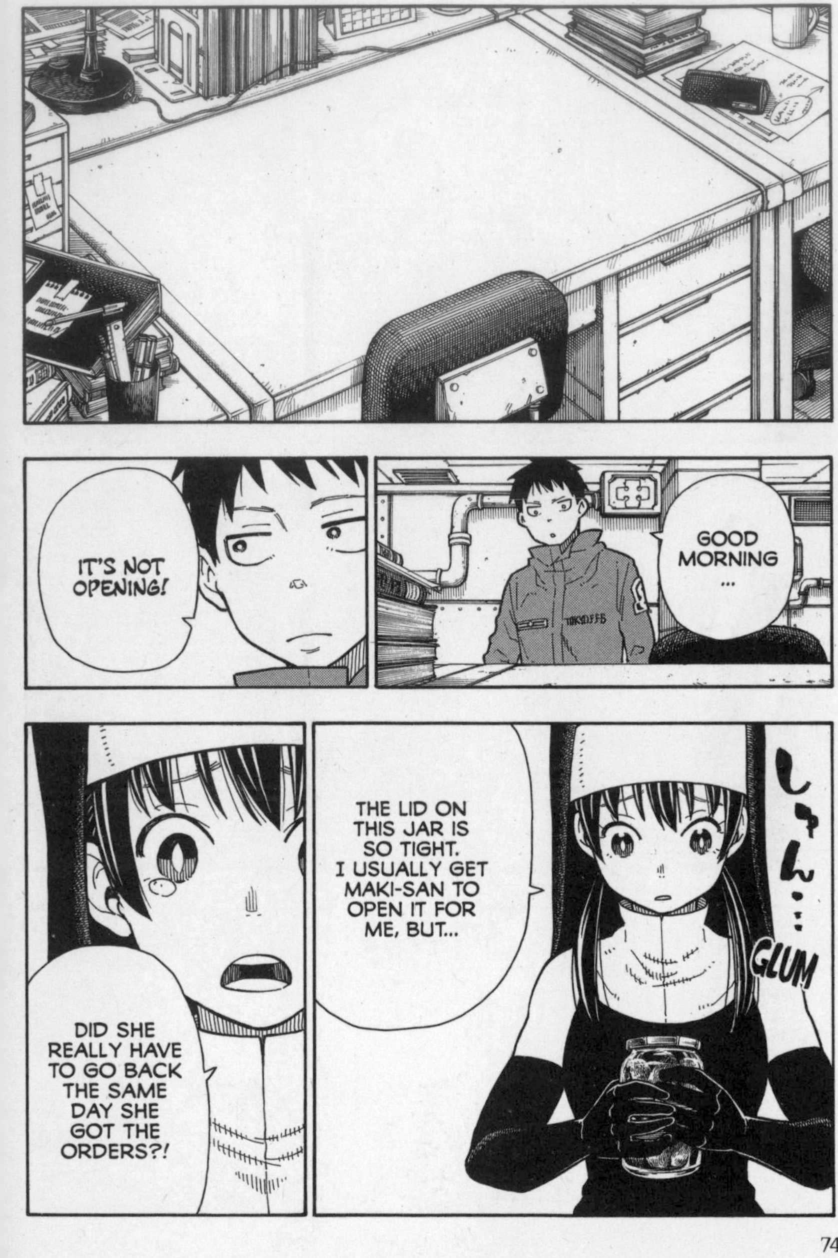
GOOD MORNING ...
IT'S NOT OPENING!
THE LID ON THIS JAR IS SO TIGHT. I USUALLY GET MAKI-SAN TO OPEN IT FOR ME, BUT...
しゅん…
GLUM
DID SHE REALLY HAVE TO GO BACK THE SAME DAY SHE GOT THE ORDERS?!

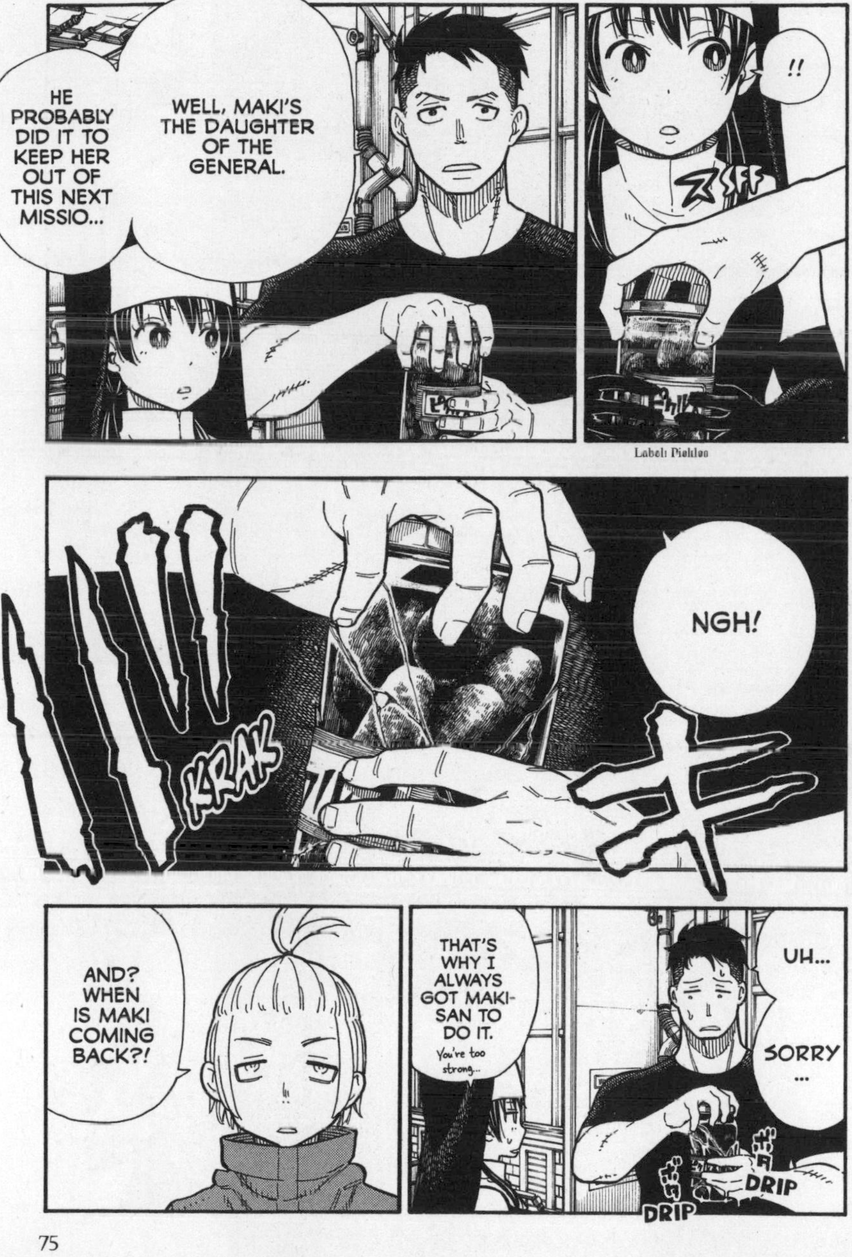
!!
ZSFF
WELL, MAKI'S THE DAUGHTER OF THE GENERAL.
HE PROBABLY DID IT TO KEEP HER OUT OF THIS NEXT MISSIO...
NGH!
KRAK
UH... SORRY...
DRIP
DRIP
THAT'S WHY I ALWAYS GOT MAKI-SAN TO DO IT.
You're too strong...
AND? WHEN IS MAKI COMING BACK?!

Label: Pickles

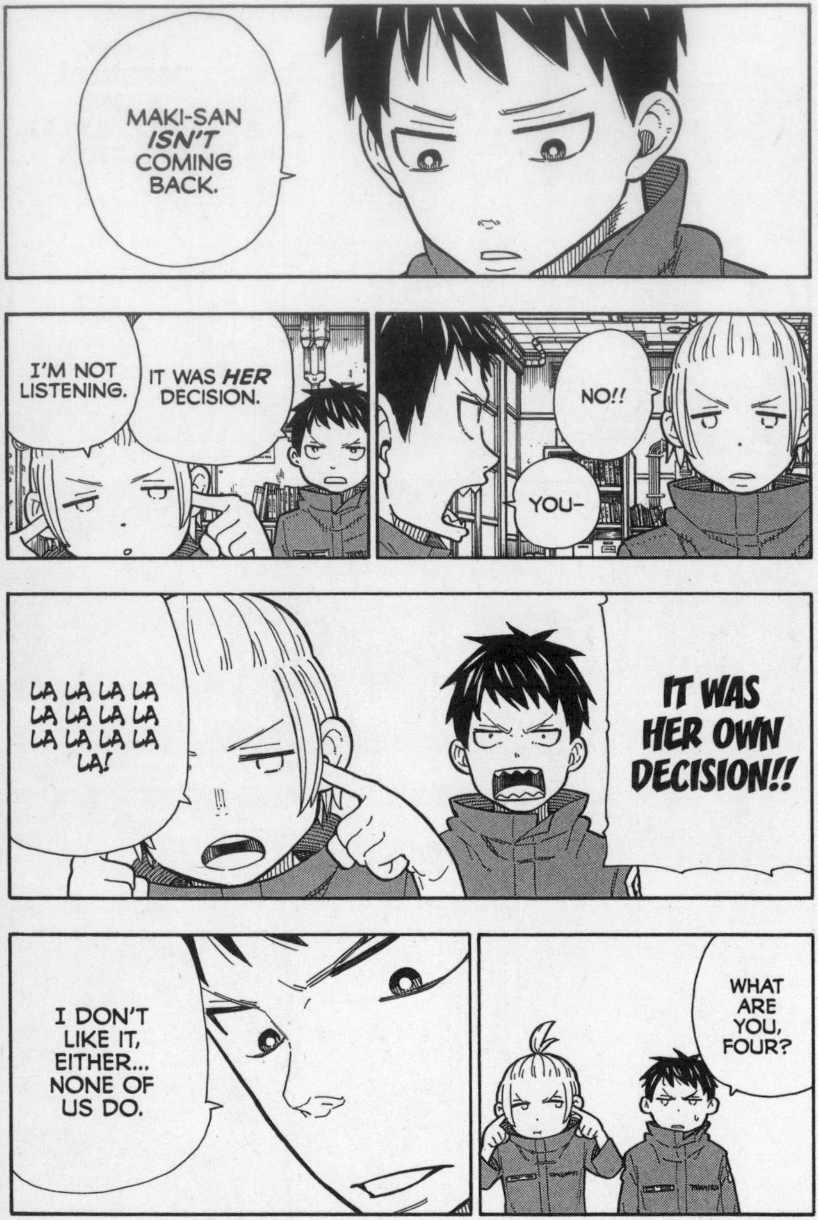
MAKI-SAN *ISN'T* COMING BACK.
NO!!
YOU-
IT WAS *HER* DECISION.
I'M NOT LISTENING.
IT WAS HER OWN DECISION!!
LA LA LA LA LA LA LA LA LA LA LA LA LA!
WHAT ARE YOU, FOUR?
I DON'T LIKE IT, EITHER... NONE OF US DO.

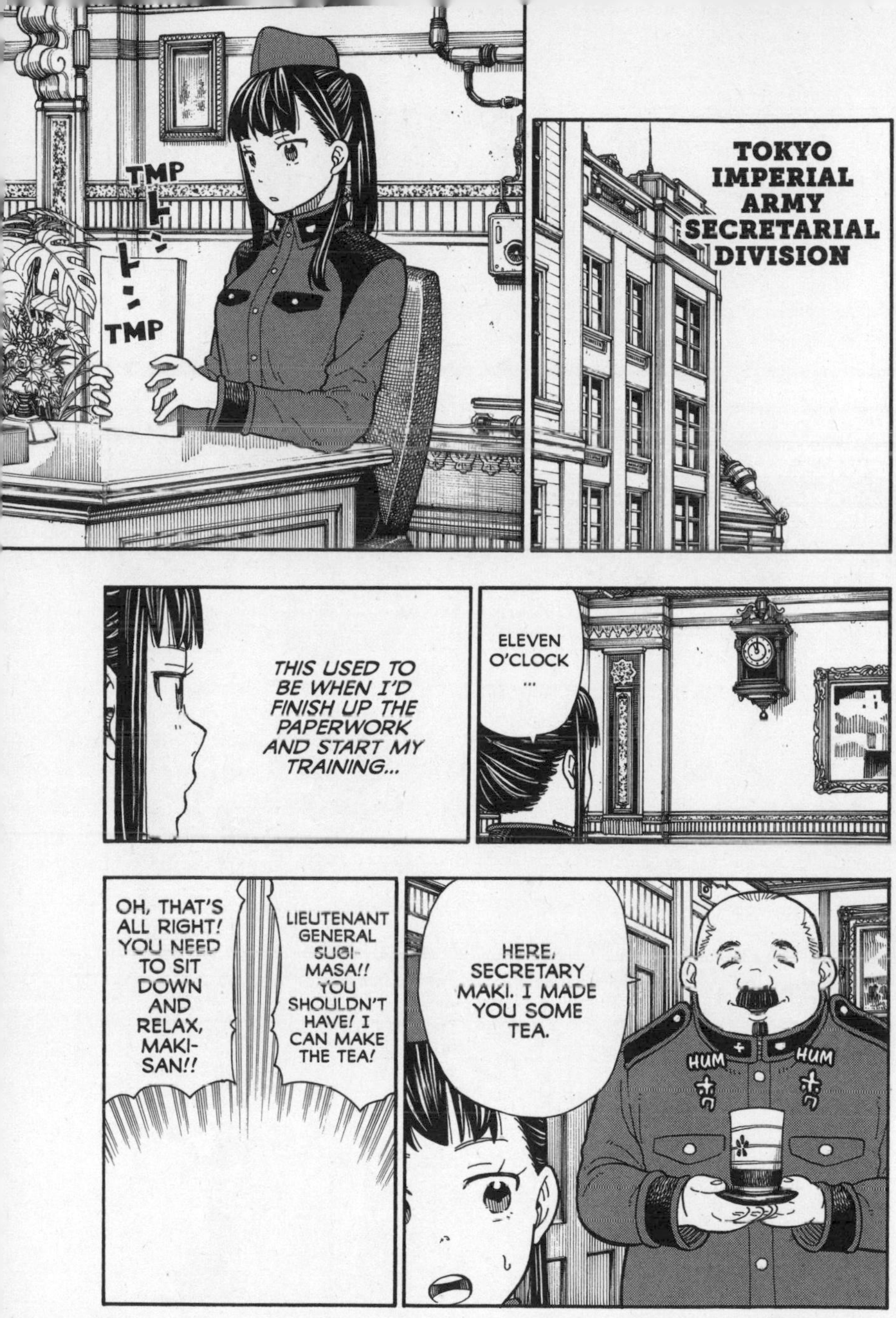
TOKYO IMPERIAL ARMY SECRETARIAL DIVISION
TMP
TMP
ELEVEN O'CLOCK ...
THIS USED TO BE WHEN I'D FINISH UP THE PAPERWORK AND START MY TRAINING...
HERE, SECRETARY MAKI. I MADE YOU SOME TEA.
HUM
HUM
LIEUTENANT GENERAL SUGIMASA!! YOU SHOULDN'T HAVE! I CAN MAKE THE TEA!
OH, THAT'S ALL RIGHT! YOU NEED TO SIT DOWN AND RELAX, MAKI-SAN!!

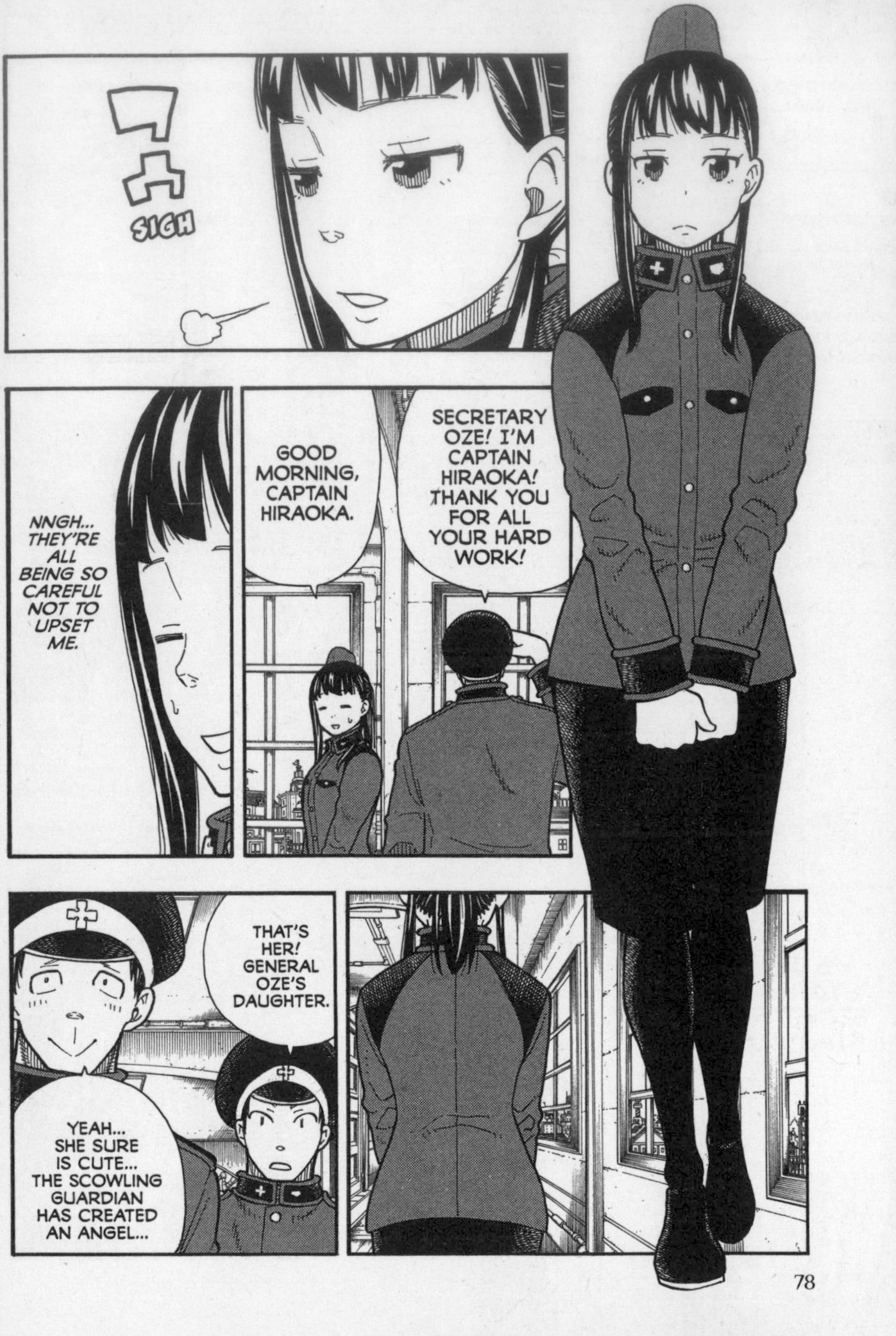
SIGH
SECRETARY OZE! I'M CAPTAIN HIRAOKA! THANK YOU FOR ALL YOUR HARD WORK!
GOOD MORNING, CAPTAIN HIRAOKA.
NNGH... THEY'RE ALL BEING SO CAREFUL NOT TO UPSET ME.
THAT'S HER! GENERAL OZE'S DAUGHTER.
YEAH... SHE SURE IS CUTE... THE SCOWLING GUARDIAN HAS CREATED AN ANGEL...

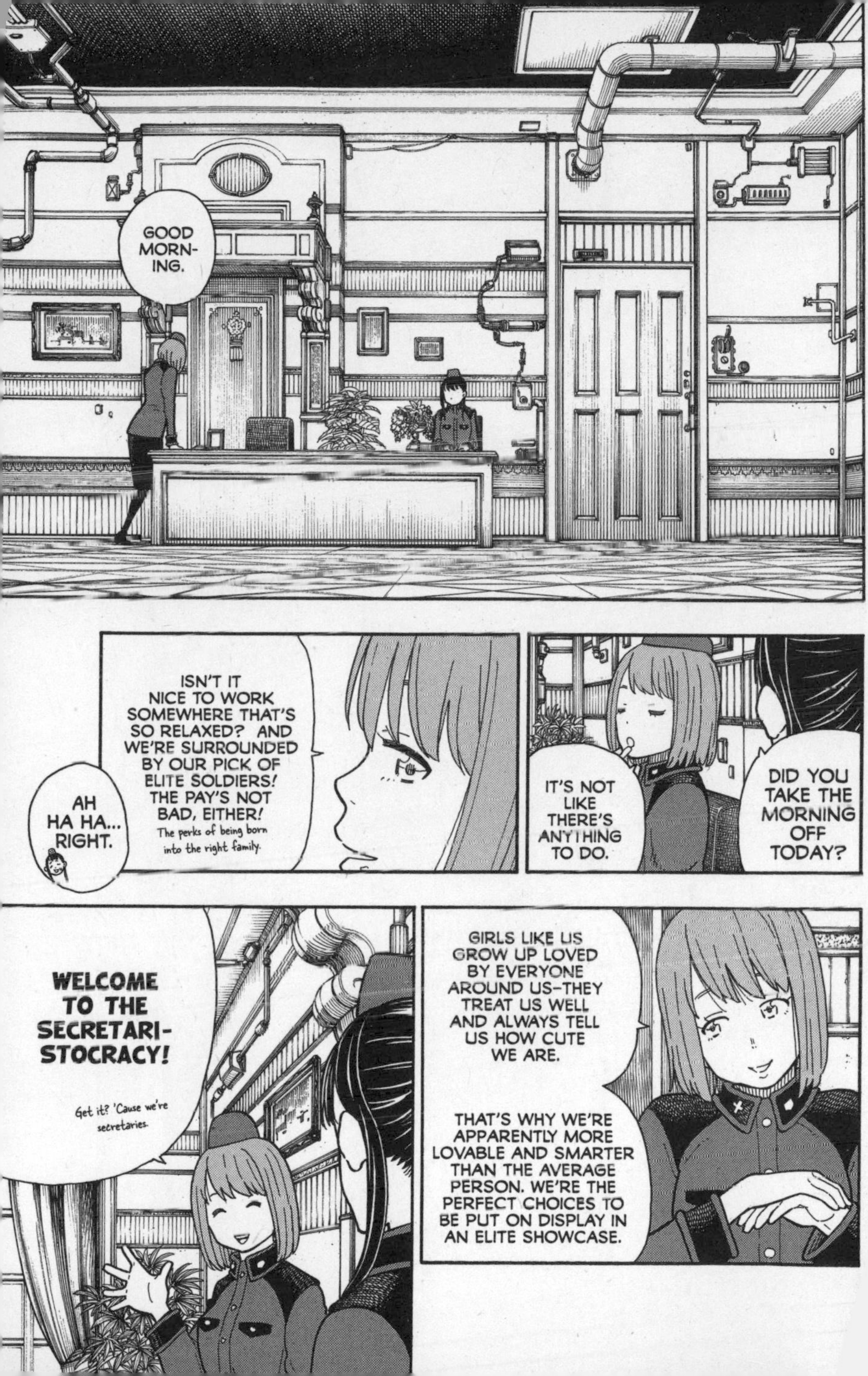
GOOD MORNING-ING.
DID YOU TAKE THE MORNING OFF TODAY?
IT'S NOT LIKE THERE'S ANYTHING TO DO.
ISN'T IT NICE TO WORK SOMEWHERE THAT'S SO RELAXED? AND WE'RE SURROUNDED BY OUR PICK OF ELITE SOLDIERS! THE PAY'S NOT BAD, EITHER!
The perks of being born into the right family.
AH HA HA... RIGHT.
GIRLS LIKE US GROW UP LOVED BY EVERYONE AROUND US—THEY TREAT US WELL AND ALWAYS TELL US HOW CUTE WE ARE.
THAT'S WHY WE'RE APPARENTLY MORE LOVABLE AND SMARTER THAN THE AVERAGE PERSON. WE'RE THE PERFECT CHOICES TO BE PUT ON DISPLAY IN AN ELITE SHOWCASE.
WELCOME TO THE SECRETARI-STOCRACY!
Get it? 'Cause we're secretaries.

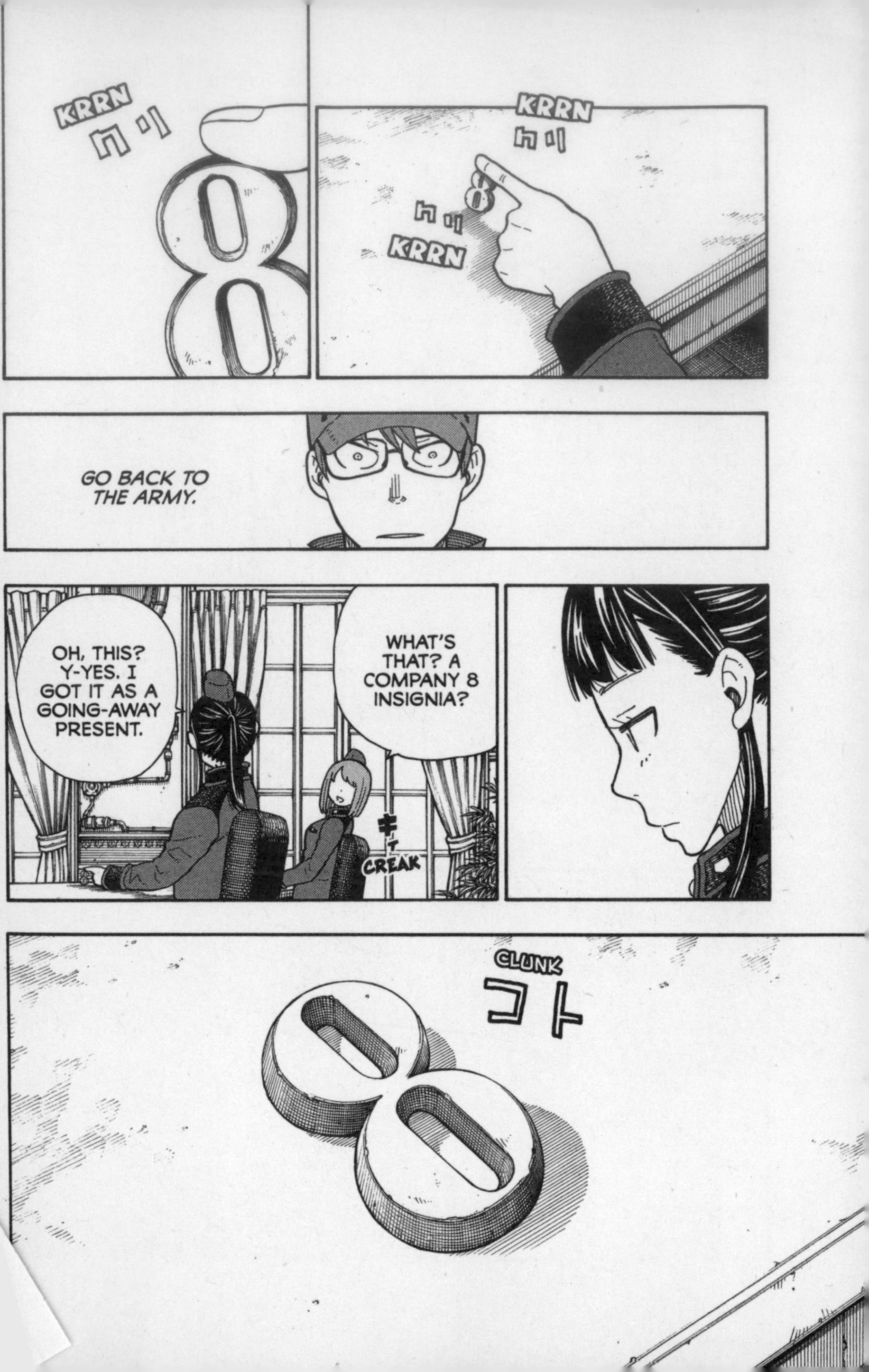
KRRN
カリ
カリ
KRRN
KRRN
カリ
GO BACK TO THE ARMY.
WHAT'S THAT? A COMPANY 8 INSIGNIA?
OH, THIS? Y-YES. I GOT IT AS A GOING-AWAY PRESENT.
キィ
CREAK
CLUNK
コト

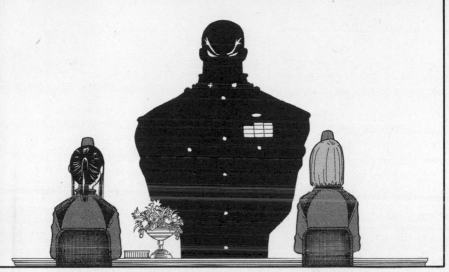

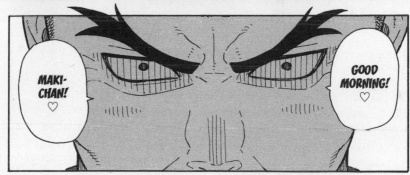

GOOD MORNING! ♡
MAKI-CHAN! ♡
GENERAL OZE ?!!
WHAT?! "MAKI-CHAN" ?!!
I'M SO HAPPY YOU'VE COME BACK TO US, MAKI-CHAN.
THE SCOWLING GUARDIAN OF THE EMPIRE CALLS HIS DAUGHTER MAKI-CHAN?!!
I'LL JUST LEAVE YOU TWO ALONE.
THANK YOU.

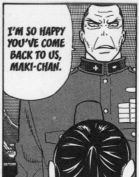

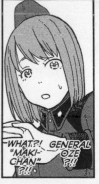

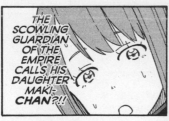

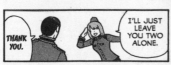

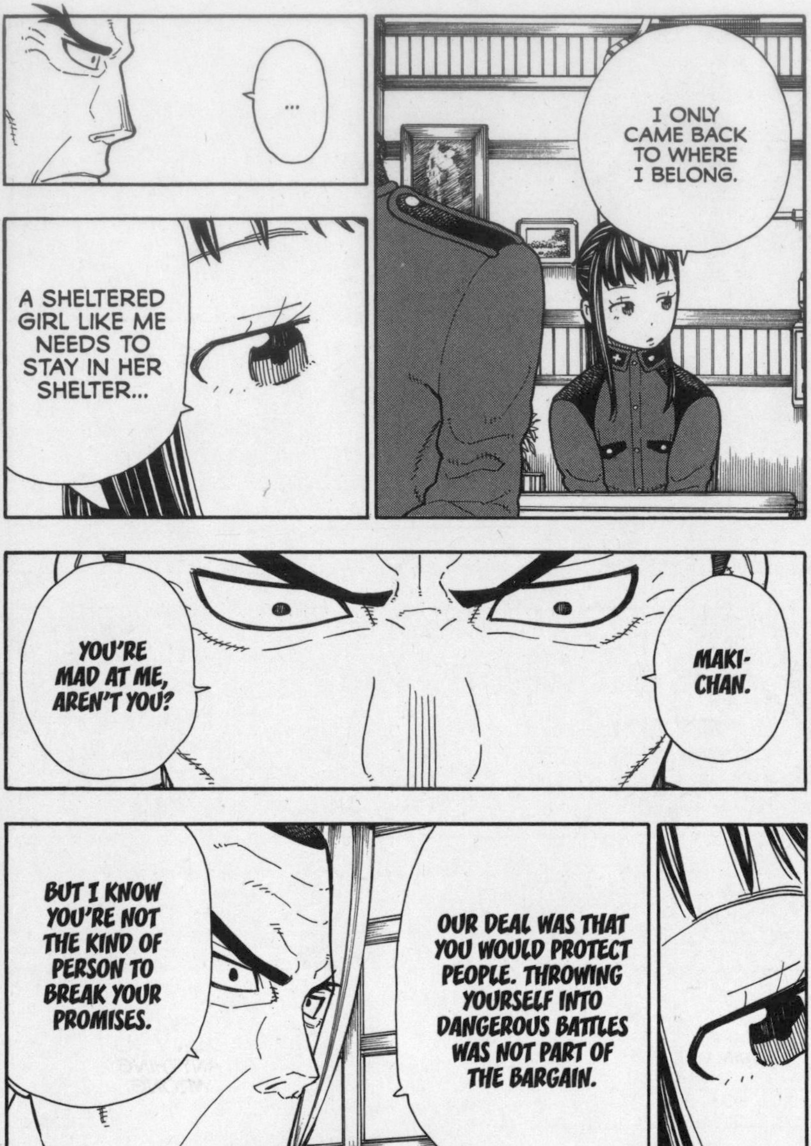
I ONLY CAME BACK TO WHERE I BELONG.
...
A SHELTERED GIRL LIKE ME NEEDS TO STAY IN HER SHELTER...
MAKI-CHAN.
YOU'RE MAD AT ME, AREN'T YOU?
OUR DEAL WAS THAT YOU WOULD PROTECT PEOPLE. THROWING YOURSELF INTO DANGEROUS BATTLES WAS NOT PART OF THE BARGAIN.
BUT I KNOW YOU'RE NOT THE KIND OF PERSON TO BREAK YOUR PROMISES.

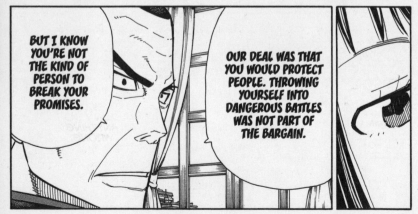

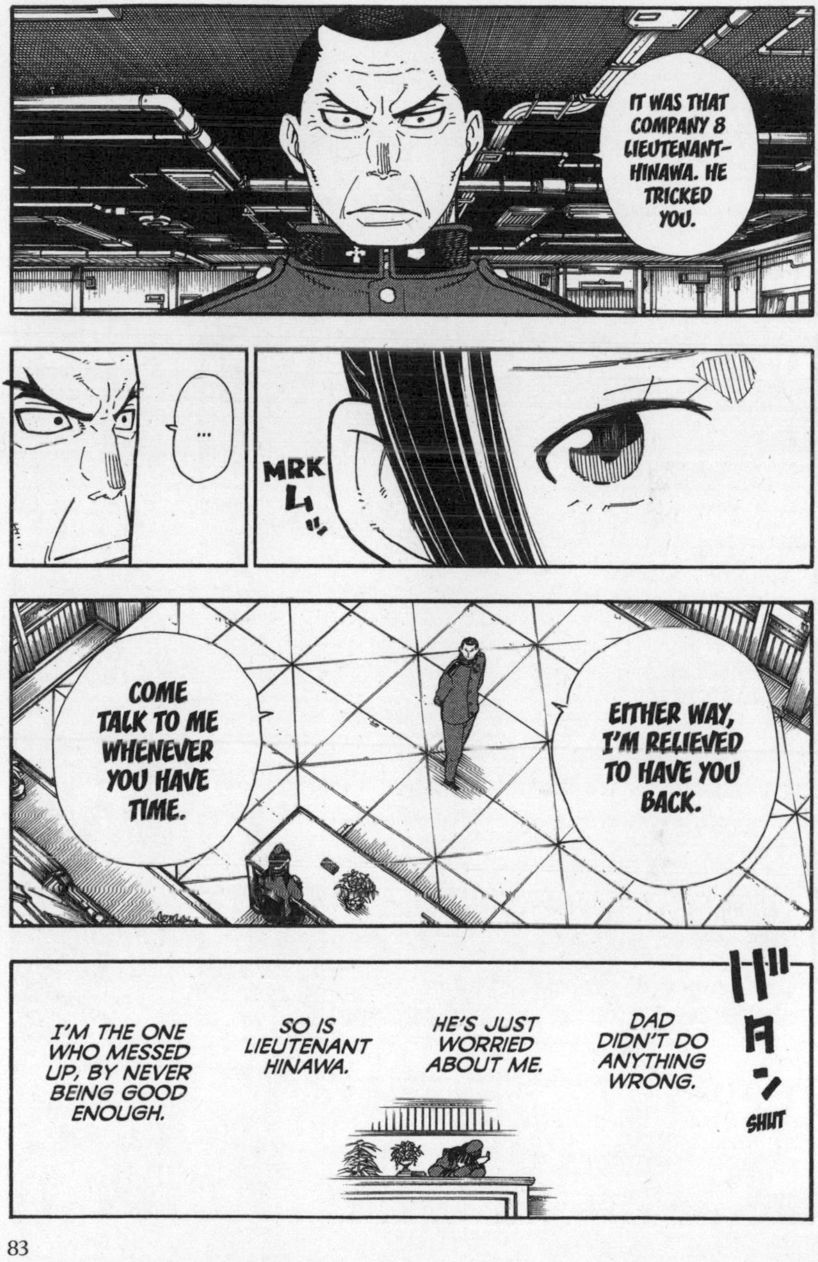
IT WAS THAT COMPANY 8 LIEUTENANT-HINAWA. HE TRICKED YOU.
MRK
...
EITHER WAY, I'M RELIEVED TO HAVE YOU BACK.
COME TALK TO ME WHENEVER YOU HAVE TIME.
SHUT
DAD DIDN'T DO ANYTHING WRONG.
HE'S JUST WORRIED ABOUT ME.
SO IS LIEUTENANT HINAWA.
I'M THE ONE WHO MESSED UP, BY NEVER BEING GOOD ENOUGH.

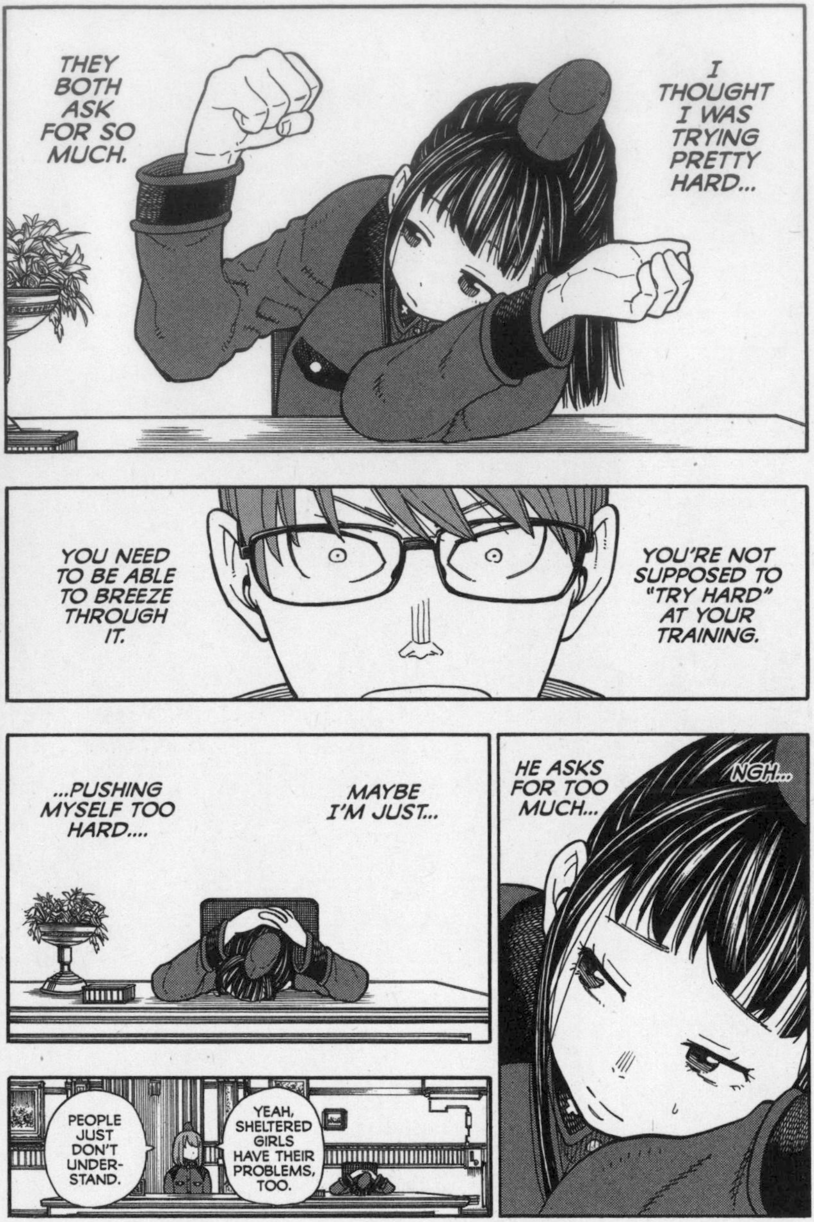
I THOUGHT I WAS TRYING PRETTY HARD...
THEY BOTH ASK FOR SO MUCH.
YOU'RE NOT SUPPOSED TO "TRY HARD" AT YOUR TRAINING.
YOU NEED TO BE ABLE TO BREEZE THROUGH IT.
NGH...
HE ASKS FOR TOO MUCH...
MAYBE I'M JUST...
...PUSHING MYSELF TOO HARD....
YEAH, SHELTERED GIRLS HAVE THEIR PROBLEMS, TOO.
PEOPLE JUST DON'T UNDER-STAND.

SPECIAL FIRE BASE 2

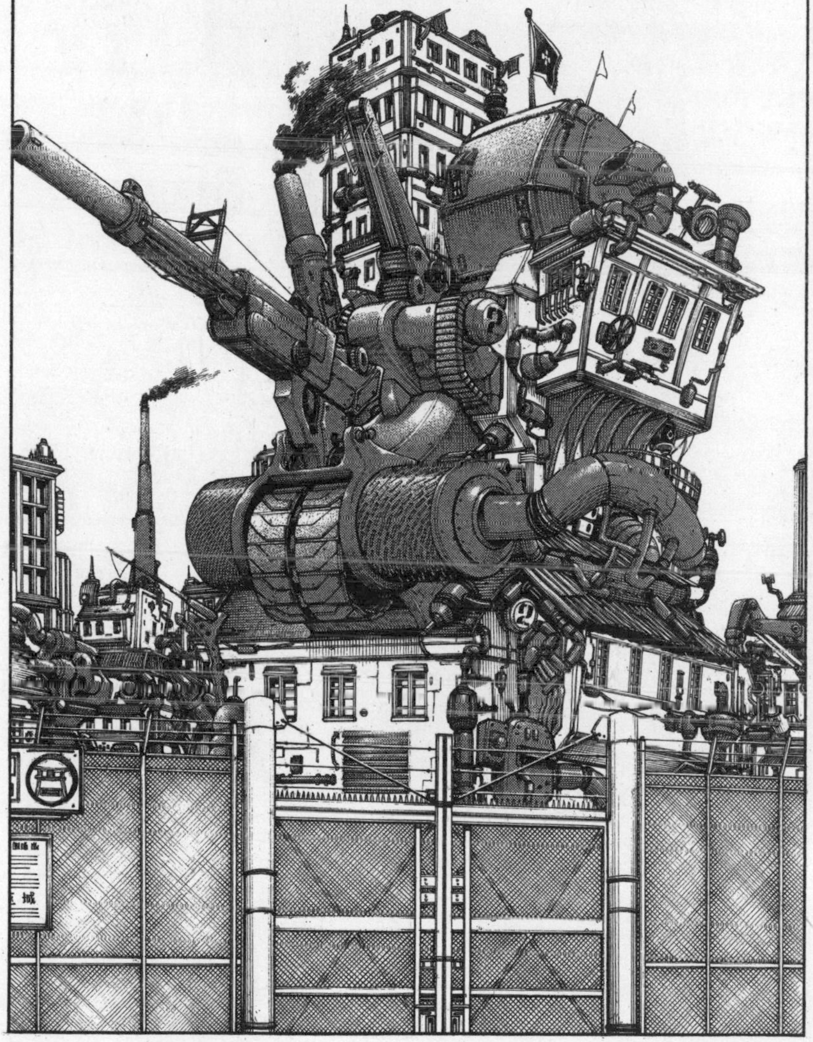

JOINT COMPANY 2/ COMPANY 8 NETHER TESTING FACILITY INVESTIGATION

Hat: 2-Way Mix&Match

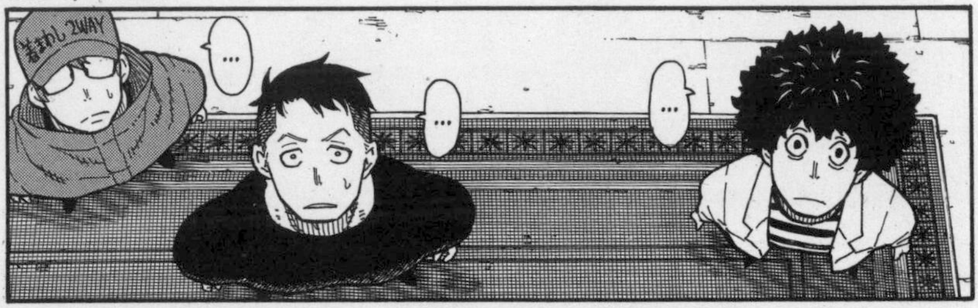
...
...
...

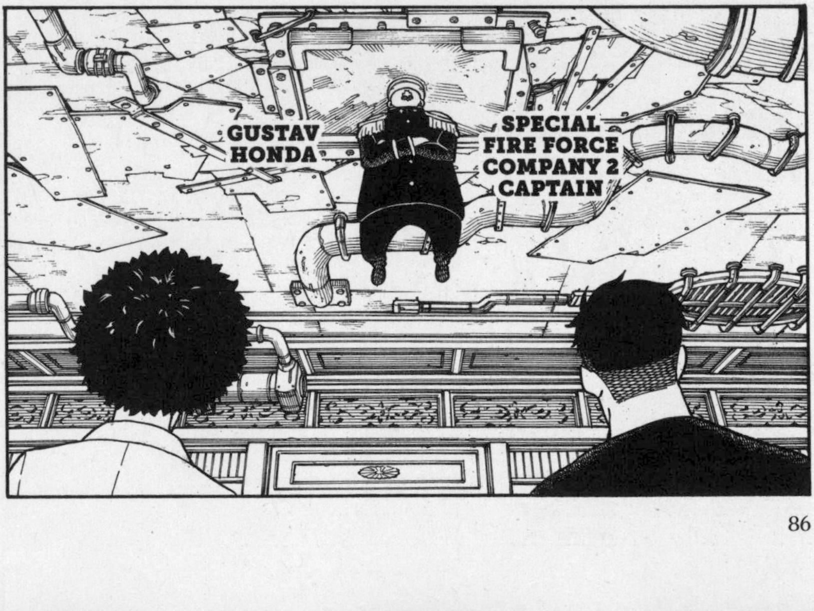
SPECIAL FIRE FORCE COMPANY 2 CAPTAIN
GUSTAV HONDA

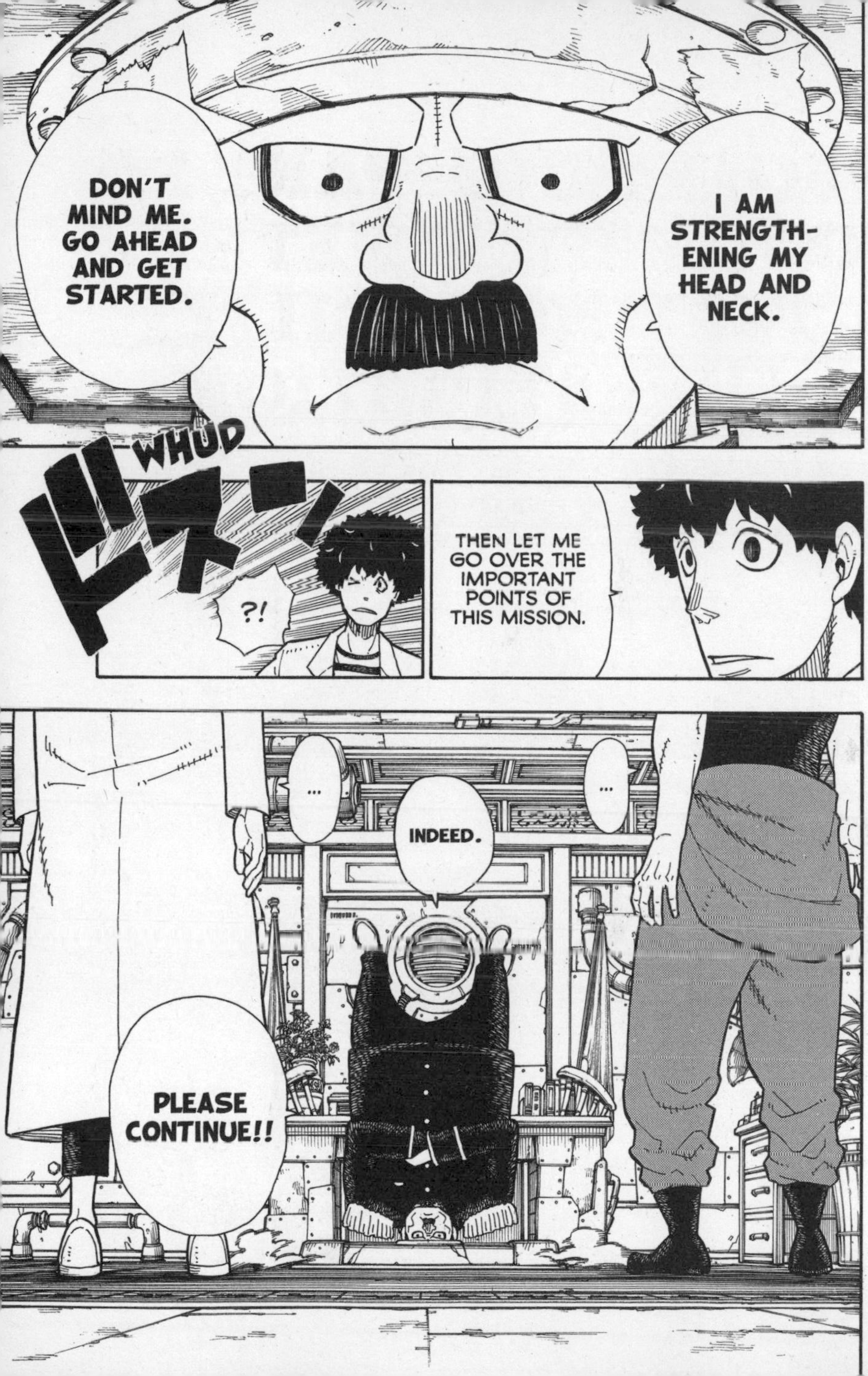
I AM STRENGTH-ENING MY HEAD AND NECK.
DON'T MIND ME. GO AHEAD AND GET STARTED.
THEN LET ME GO OVER THE IMPORTANT POINTS OF THIS MISSION.
WHUD
?!
...
INDEED.
...
PLEASE CONTINUE!!

FIRE FORCE

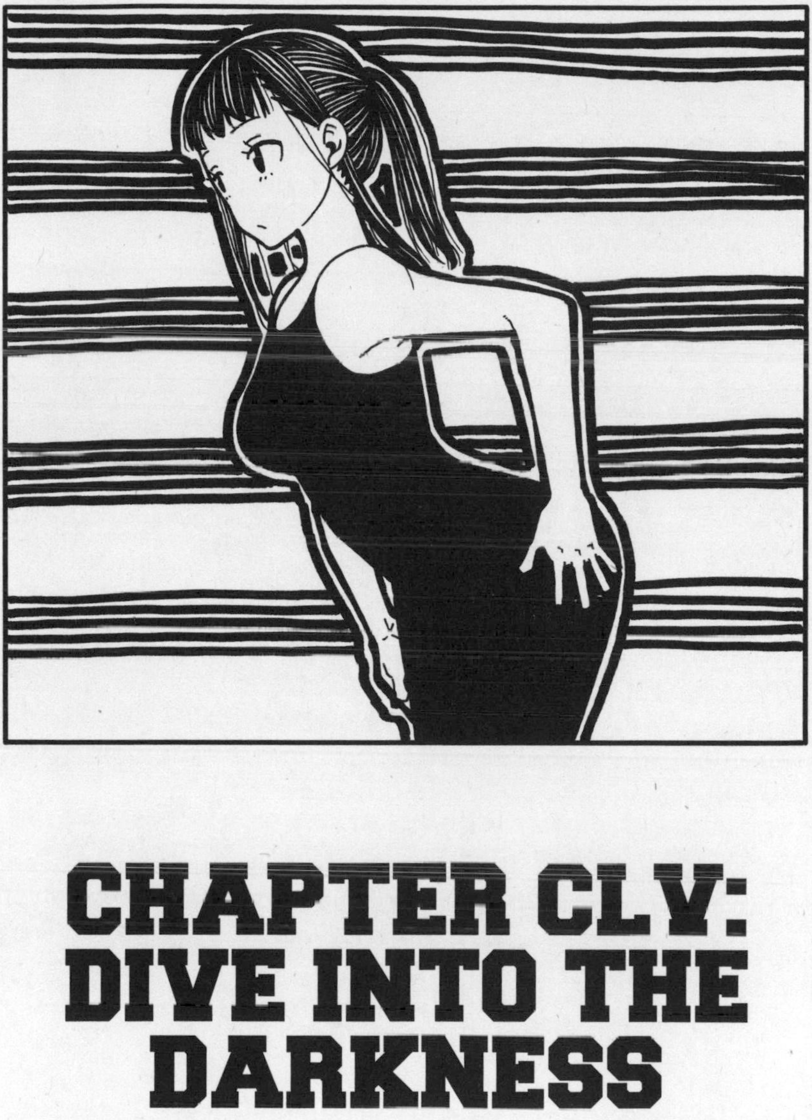

CHAPTER CLV: DIVE INTO THE DARKNESS

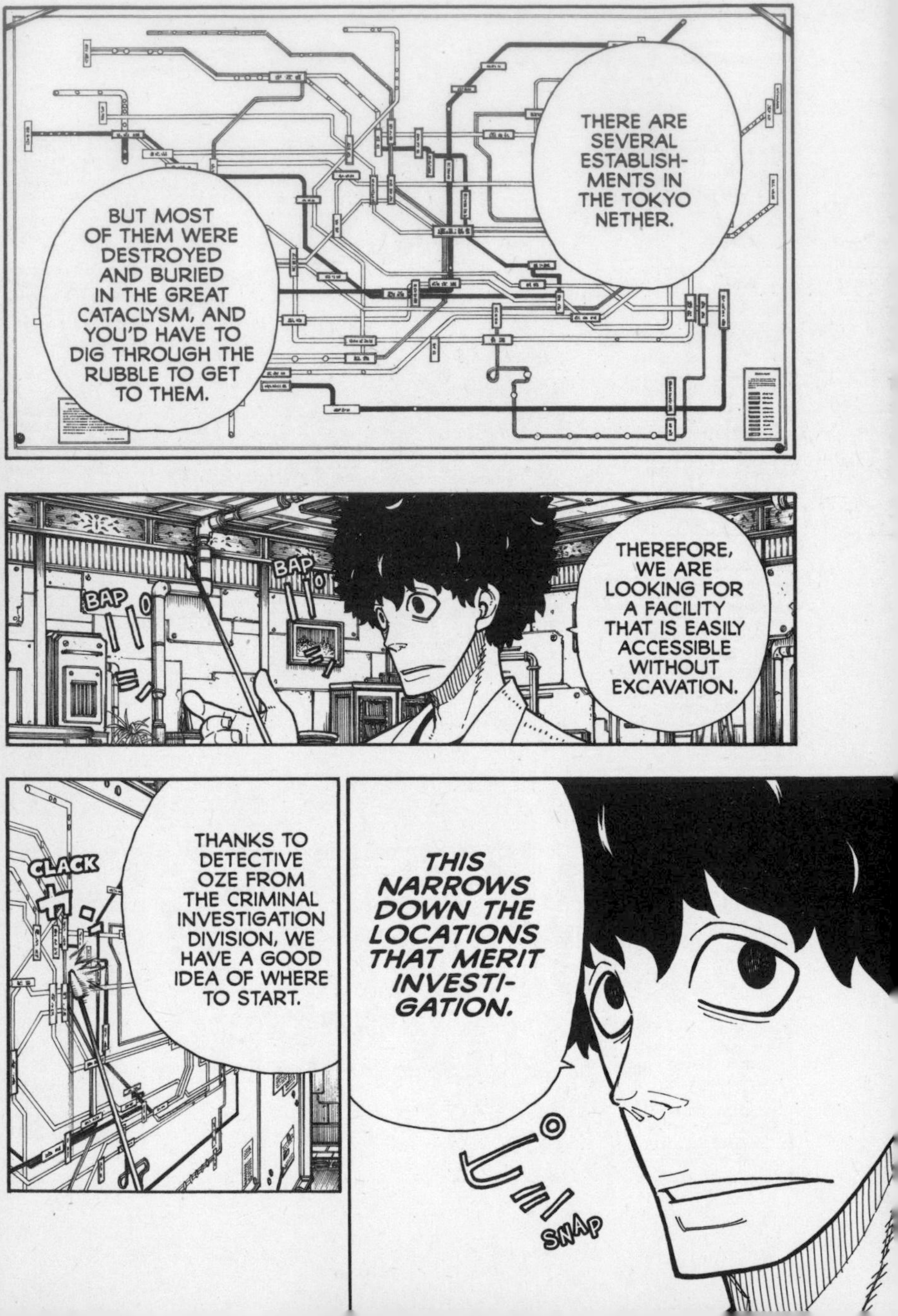
THERE ARE SEVERAL ESTABLISH-MENTS IN THE TOKYO NETHER.
BUT MOST OF THEM WERE DESTROYED AND BURIED IN THE GREAT CATACLYSM, AND YOU'D HAVE TO DIG THROUGH THE RUBBLE TO GET TO THEM.
THEREFORE, WE ARE LOOKING FOR A FACILITY THAT IS EASILY ACCESSIBLE WITHOUT EXCAVATION.
BAP
BAP
THIS NARROWS DOWN THE LOCATIONS THAT MERIT INVESTI-GATION.
SNAP
THANKS TO DETECTIVE OZE FROM THE CRIMINAL INVESTIGATION DIVISION, WE HAVE A GOOD IDEA OF WHERE TO START.
CLACK

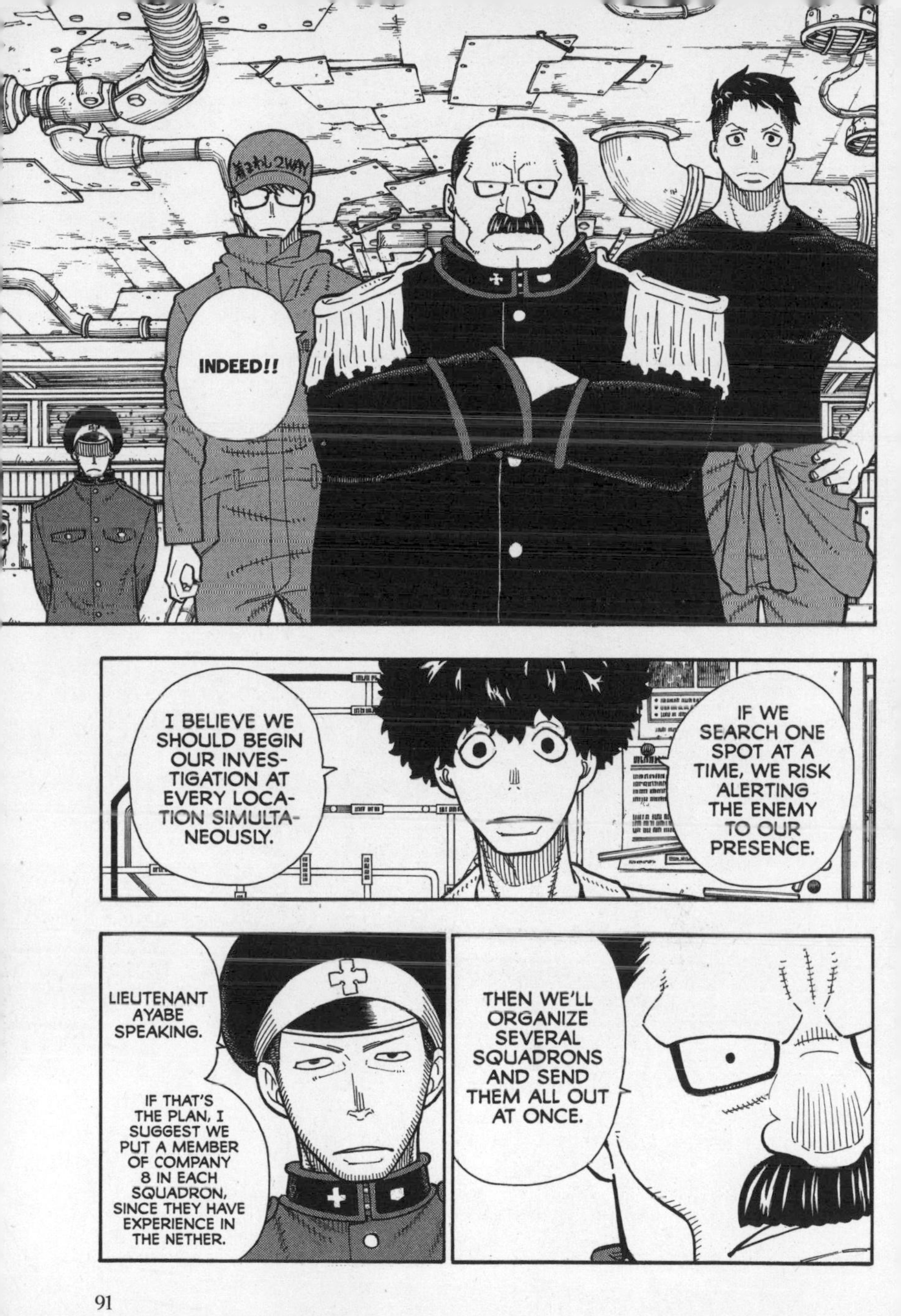
INDEED!!
IF WE SEARCH ONE SPOT AT A TIME, WE RISK ALERTING THE ENEMY TO OUR PRESENCE.
I BELIEVE WE SHOULD BEGIN OUR INVES-TIGATION AT EVERY LOCA-TION SIMULTA-NEOUSLY.
THEN WE'LL ORGANIZE SEVERAL SQUADRONS AND SEND THEM ALL OUT AT ONCE.
LIEUTENANT AYABE SPEAKING.
IF THAT'S THE PLAN, I SUGGEST WE PUT A MEMBER OF COMPANY 8 IN EACH SQUADRON, SINCE THEY HAVE EXPERIENCE IN THE NETHER.

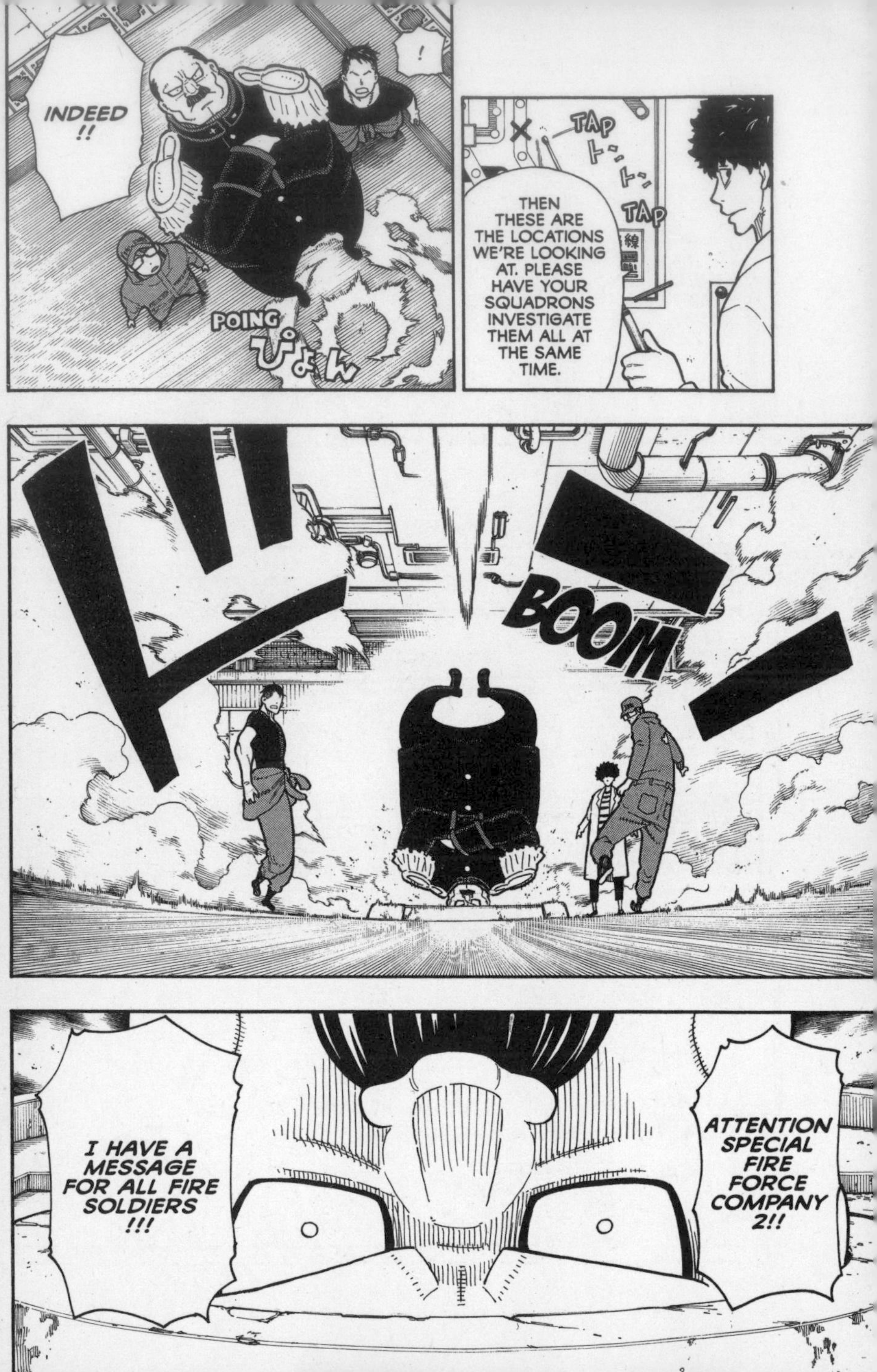
TAP
TAP
THEN THESE ARE THE LOCATIONS WE'RE LOOKING AT. PLEASE HAVE YOUR SQUADRONS INVESTIGATE THEM ALL AT THE SAME TIME.
!
INDEED !!
POING
ぴょん
BOOM
ATTENTION SPECIAL FIRE FORCE COMPANY 2!!
I HAVE A MESSAGE FOR ALL FIRE SOLDIERS !!!

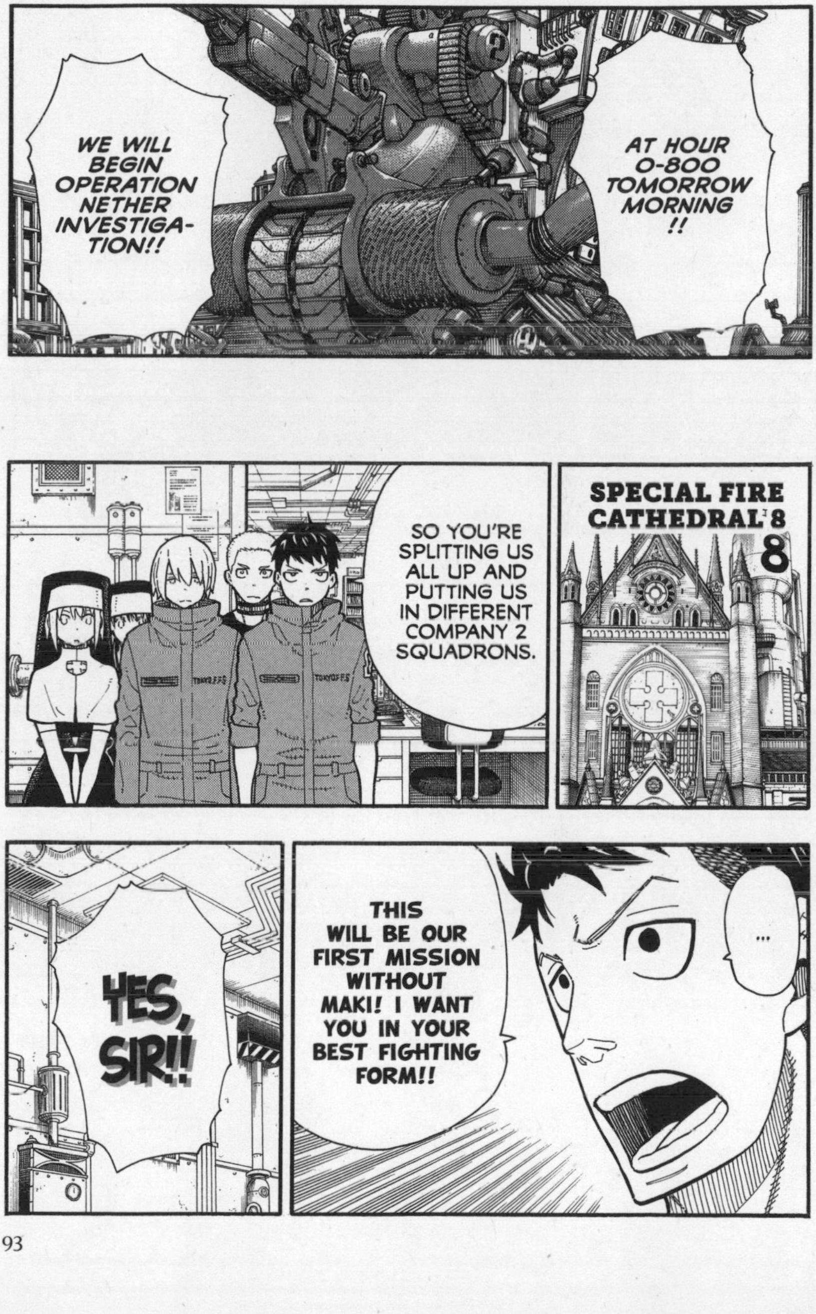
AT HOUR 0-800 TOMORROW MORNING!!
WE WILL BEGIN OPERATION NETHER INVESTIGATION!!
SPECIAL FIRE CATHEDRAL 8
8
SO YOU'RE SPLITTING US ALL UP AND PUTTING US IN DIFFERENT COMPANY 2 SQUADRONS.
...
THIS WILL BE OUR FIRST MISSION WITHOUT MAKI! I WANT YOU IN YOUR BEST FIGHTING FORM!!
YES, SIR!!

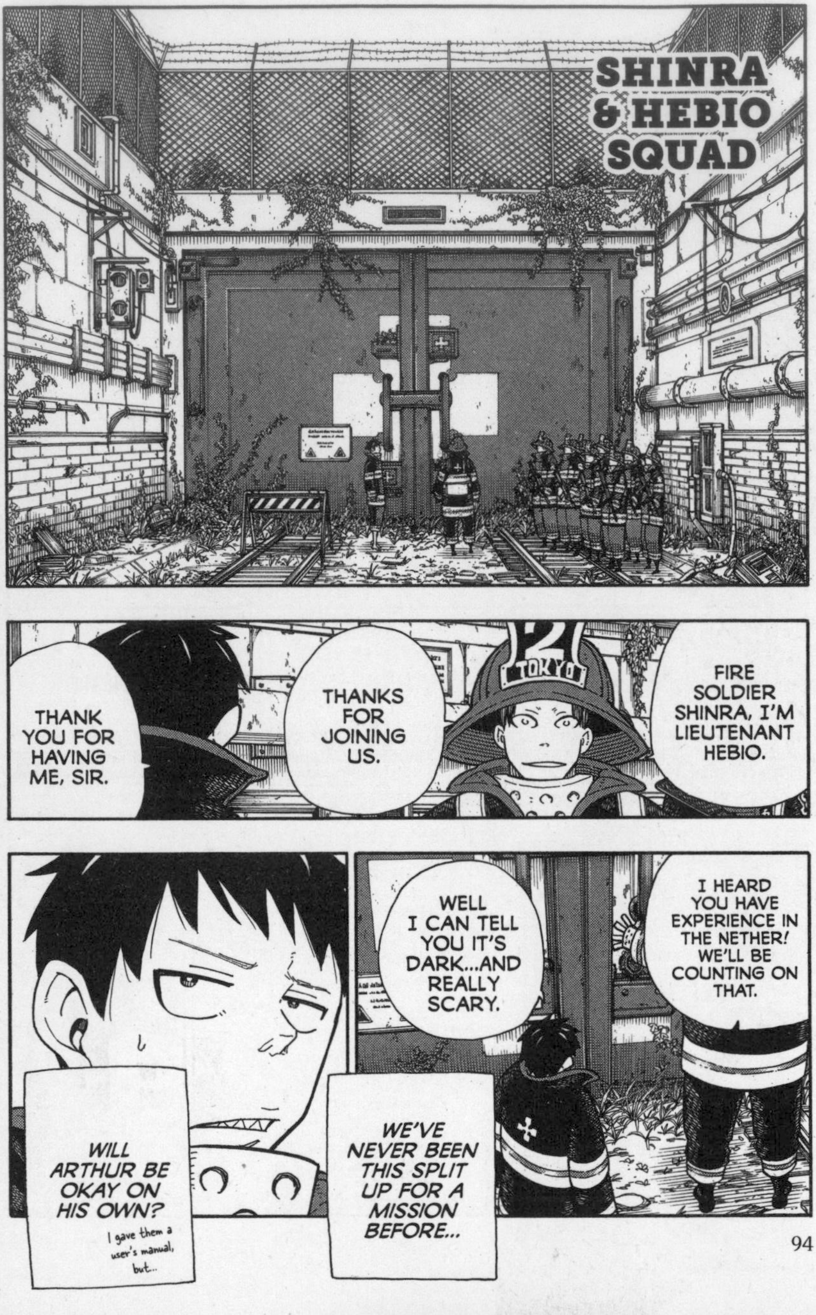
SHINRA & HEBIO SQUAD
FIRE SOLDIER SHINRA, I'M LIEUTENANT HEBIO.
THANKS FOR JOINING US.
THANK YOU FOR HAVING ME, SIR.
I HEARD YOU HAVE EXPERIENCE IN THE NETHER! WE'LL BE COUNTING ON THAT.
WELL I CAN TELL YOU IT'S DARK...AND REALLY SCARY.
WE'VE NEVER BEEN THIS SPLIT UP FOR A MISSION BEFORE...
WILL ARTHUR BE OKAY ON HIS OWN?
I gave them a user's manual, but...

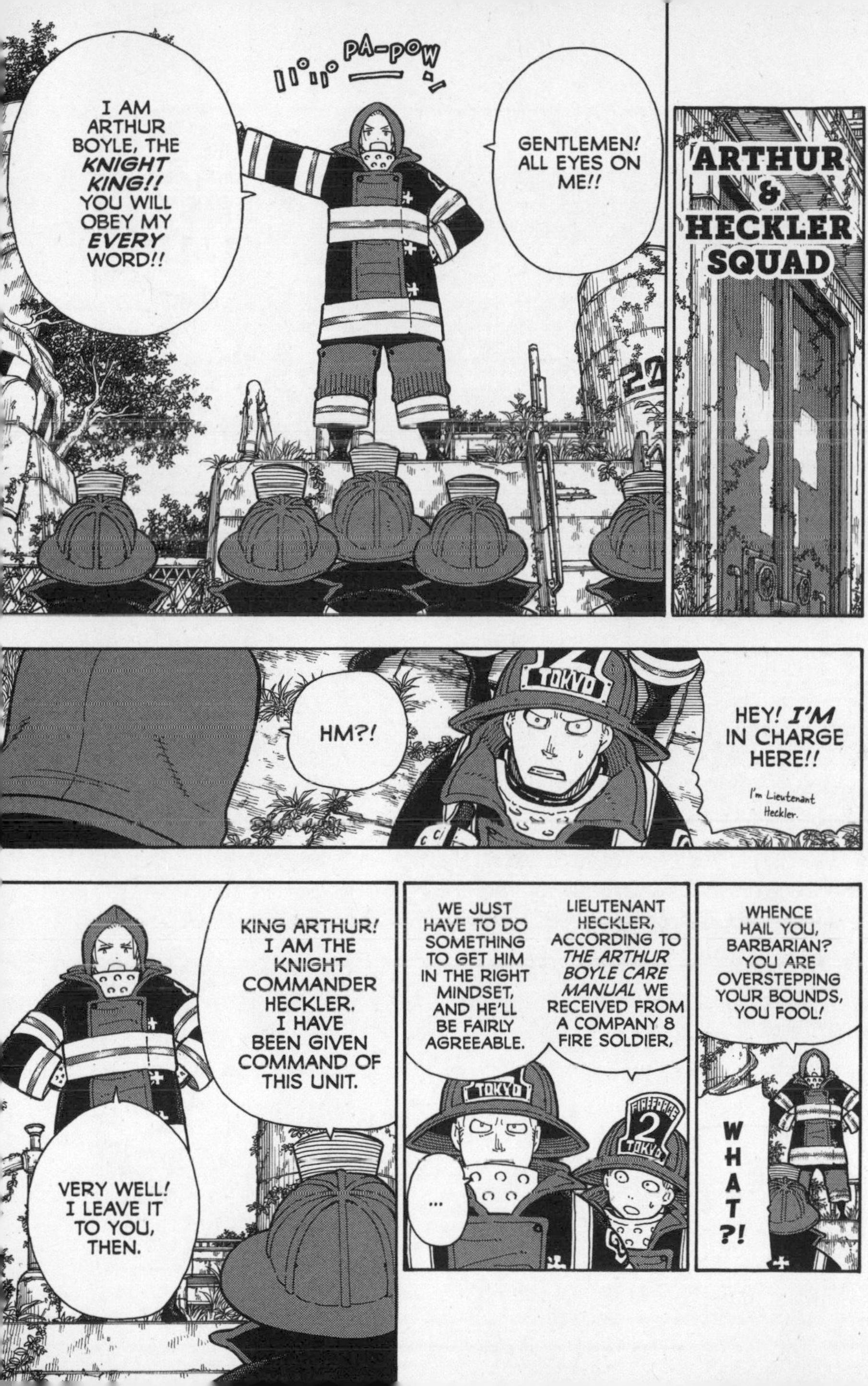
ARTHUR & HECKLER SQUAD
GENTLEMEN! ALL EYES ON ME!!
PA-POW
I AM ARTHUR BOYLE, THE KNIGHT KING!! YOU WILL OBEY MY EVERY WORD!!
HEY! I'M IN CHARGE HERE!!
I'm Lieutenant Heckler.
HM?!
WHENCE HAIL YOU, BARBARIAN? YOU ARE OVERSTEPPING YOUR BOUNDS, YOU FOOL!
WHAT?!
LIEUTENANT HECKLER, ACCORDING TO THE ARTHUR BOYLE CARE MANUAL WE RECEIVED FROM A COMPANY 8 FIRE SOLDIER,
WE JUST HAVE TO DO SOMETHING TO GET HIM IN THE RIGHT MINDSET, AND HE'LL BE FAIRLY AGREEABLE.
...
KING ARTHUR! I AM THE KNIGHT COMMANDER HECKLER. I HAVE BEEN GIVEN COMMAND OF THIS UNIT.
VERY WELL! I LEAVE IT TO YOU, THEN.

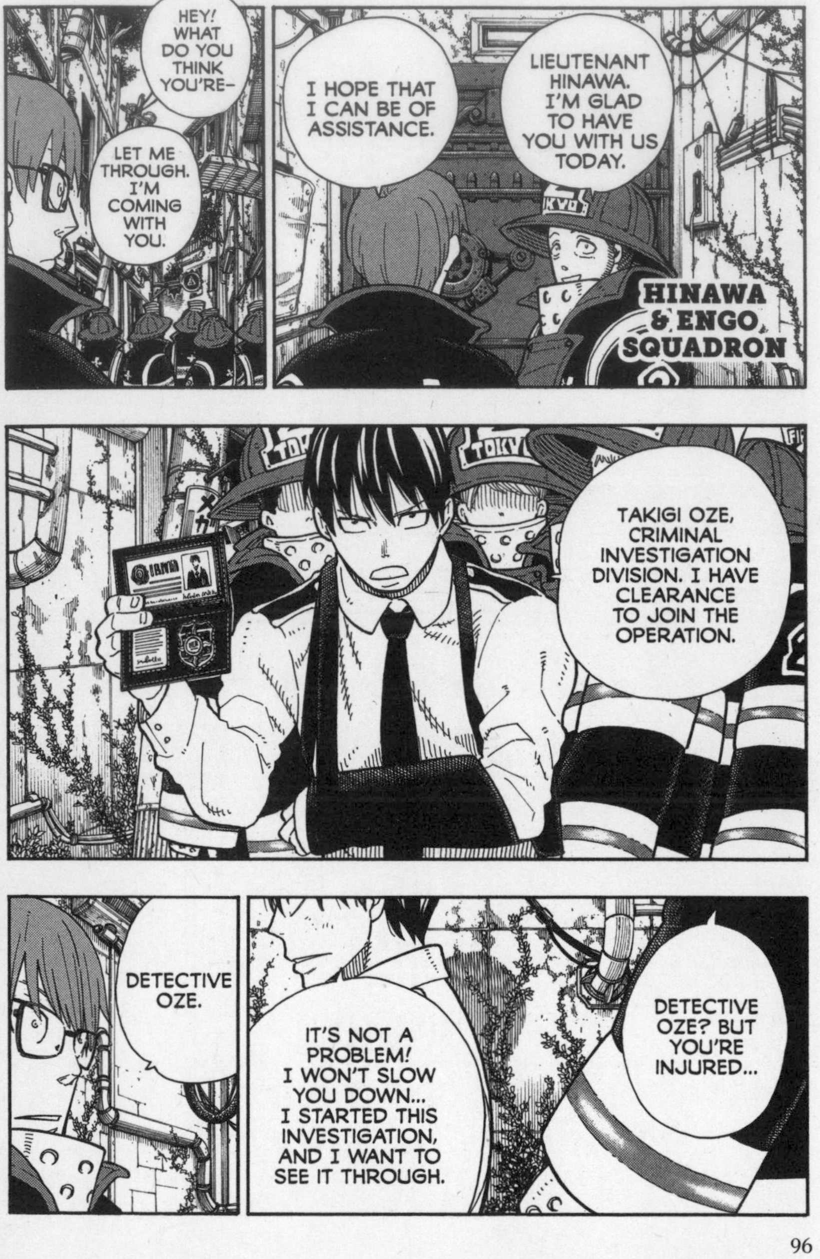
LIEUTENANT HINAWA. I'M GLAD TO HAVE YOU WITH US TODAY.
I HOPE THAT I CAN BE OF ASSISTANCE.
HINAWA & ENGO SQUADRON
HEY! WHAT DO YOU THINK YOU'RE–
LET ME THROUGH. I'M COMING WITH YOU.
TAKIGI OZE, CRIMINAL INVESTIGATION DIVISION. I HAVE CLEARANCE TO JOIN THE OPERATION.
DETECTIVE OZE? BUT YOU'RE INJURED...
IT'S NOT A PROBLEM! I WON'T SLOW YOU DOWN... I STARTED THIS INVESTIGATION, AND I WANT TO SEE IT THROUGH.
DETECTIVE OZE.

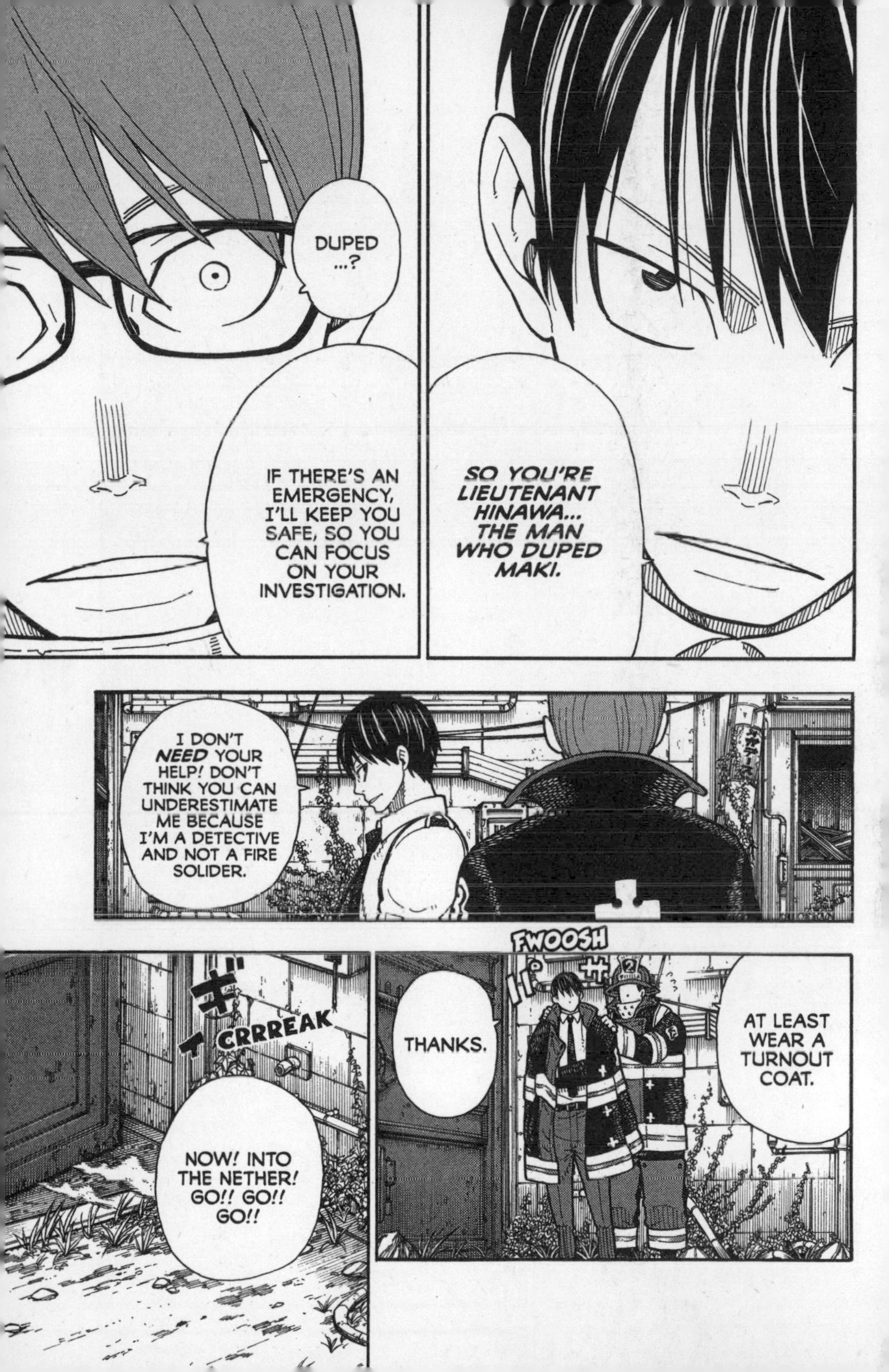
SO YOU'RE LIEUTENANT HINAWA... THE MAN WHO DUPED MAKI.
DUPED ...?
IF THERE'S AN EMERGENCY, I'LL KEEP YOU SAFE, SO YOU CAN FOCUS ON YOUR INVESTIGATION.
I DON'T NEED YOUR HELP! DON'T THINK YOU CAN UNDERESTIMATE ME BECAUSE I'M A DETECTIVE AND NOT A FIRE SOLIDER.
FWOOSH
AT LEAST WEAR A TURNOUT COAT.
THANKS.
CRRREAK
NOW! INTO THE NETHER! GO!! GO!! GO!!

Signs (L to R): Ladies' Apparel, Kusaya Books, Ladies' Apparel, Sale

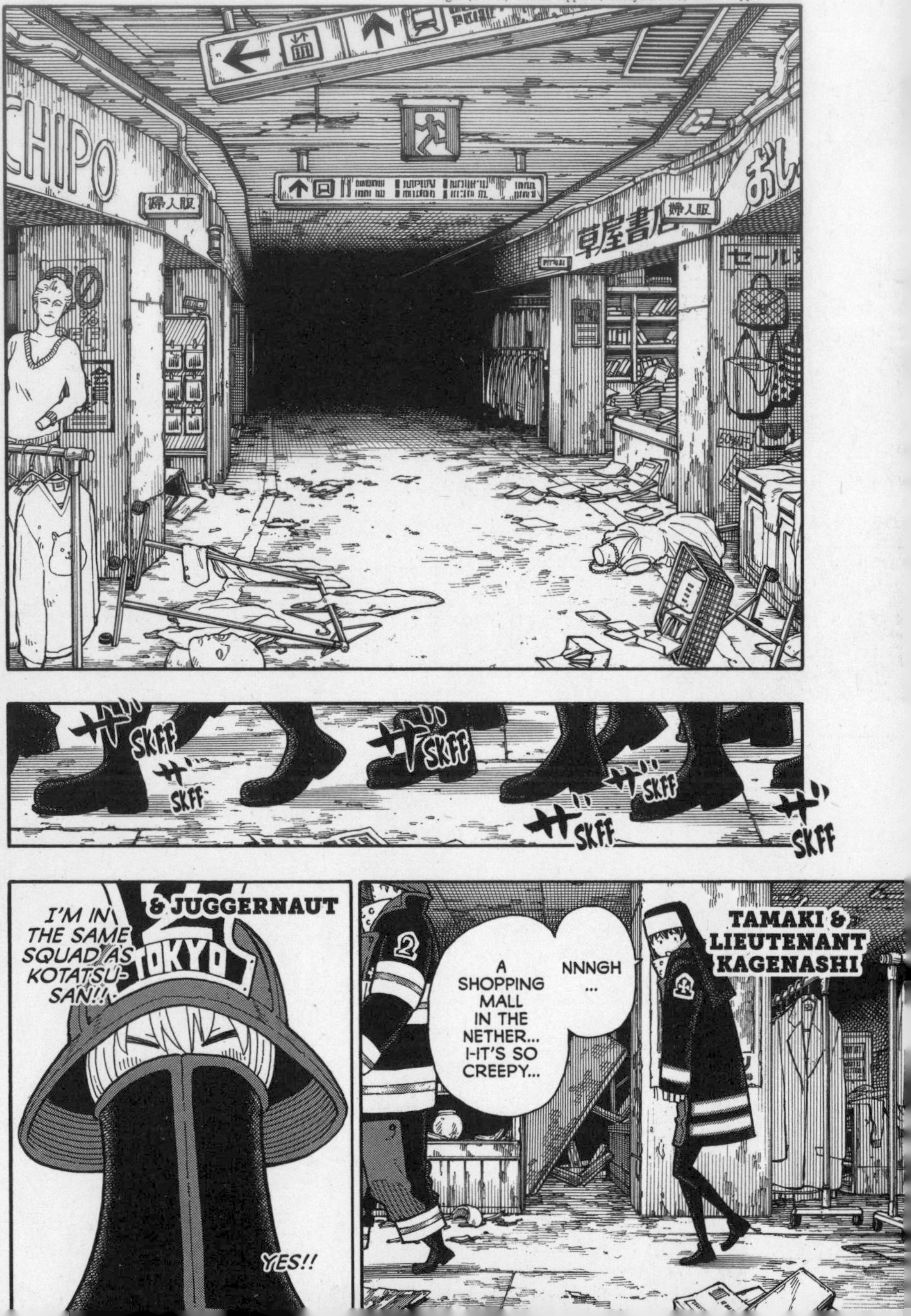
CHIPO
婦人服
草屋書店
婦人服
セール
SKFF
SKFF
SKFF
SKFF
SKFF
SKFF
TAMAKI & LIEUTENANT KAGENASHI
NNNGH ...
A SHOPPING MALL IN THE NETHER... I-IT'S SO CREEPY...
& JUGGERNAUT
TOKYO
I'M IN THE SAME SQUAD AS KOTATSU-SAN!!
YES!!

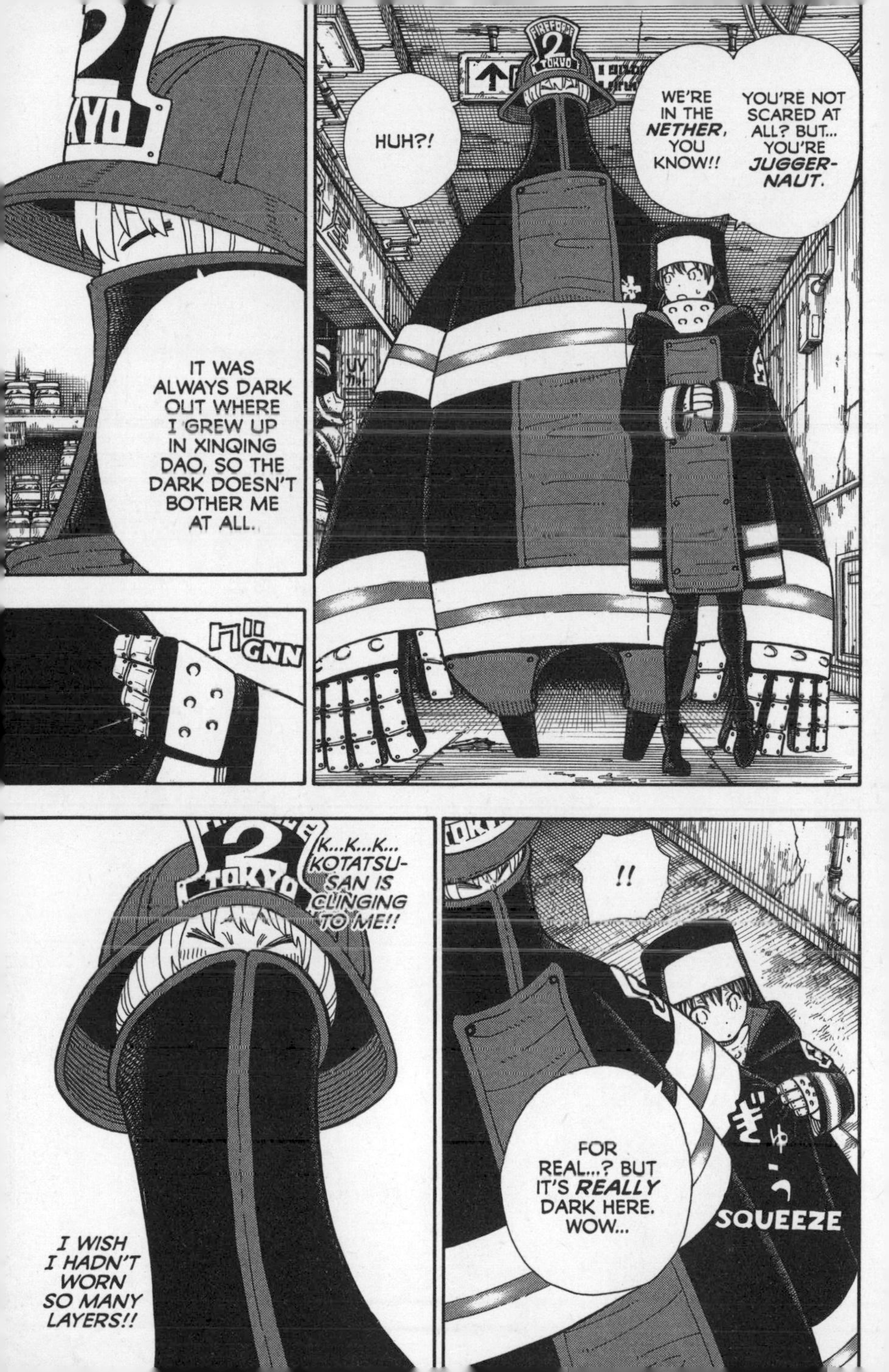

YOU'RE NOT SCARED AT ALL? BUT... YOU'RE *JUGGERNAUT*.
WE'RE IN THE *NETHER*, YOU KNOW!!
HUH?!
UV
IT WAS ALWAYS DARK OUT WHERE I GREW UP IN XINQING DAO, SO THE DARK DOESN'T BOTHER ME AT ALL.
GNN
!!
SQUEEZE
FOR REAL...? BUT IT'S *REALLY* DARK HERE. WOW...
K...K...K... KOTATSU-SAN IS CLINGING TO ME!!
I WISH I HADN'T WORN SO MANY LAYERS!!

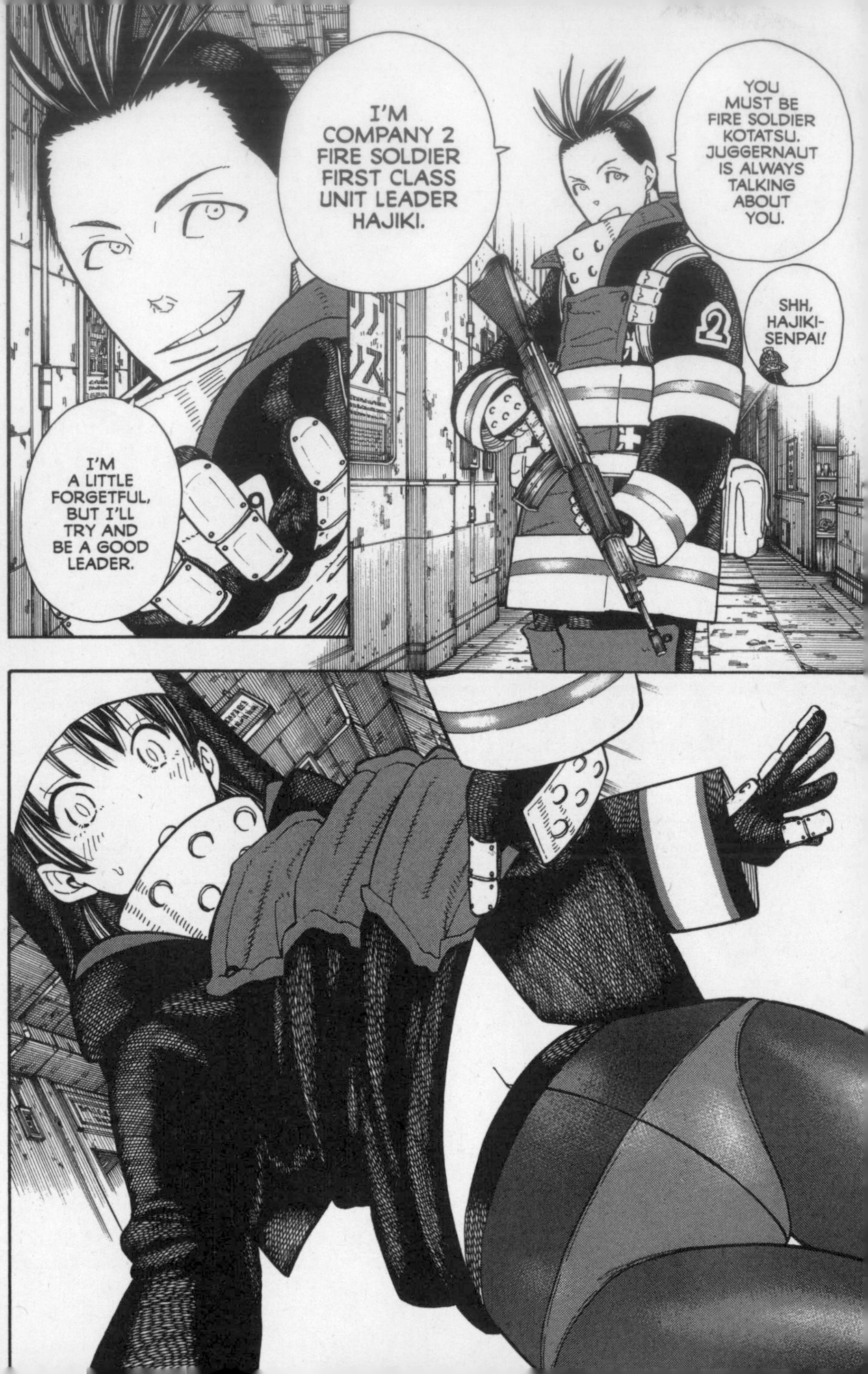
YOU MUST BE FIRE SOLDIER KOTATSU. JUGGERNAUT IS ALWAYS TALKING ABOUT YOU.
SHH, HAJIKI-SENPAI!
I'M COMPANY 2 FIRE SOLDIER FIRST CLASS UNIT LEADER HAJIKI.
I'M A LITTLE FORGETFUL, BUT I'LL TRY AND BE A GOOD LEADER.

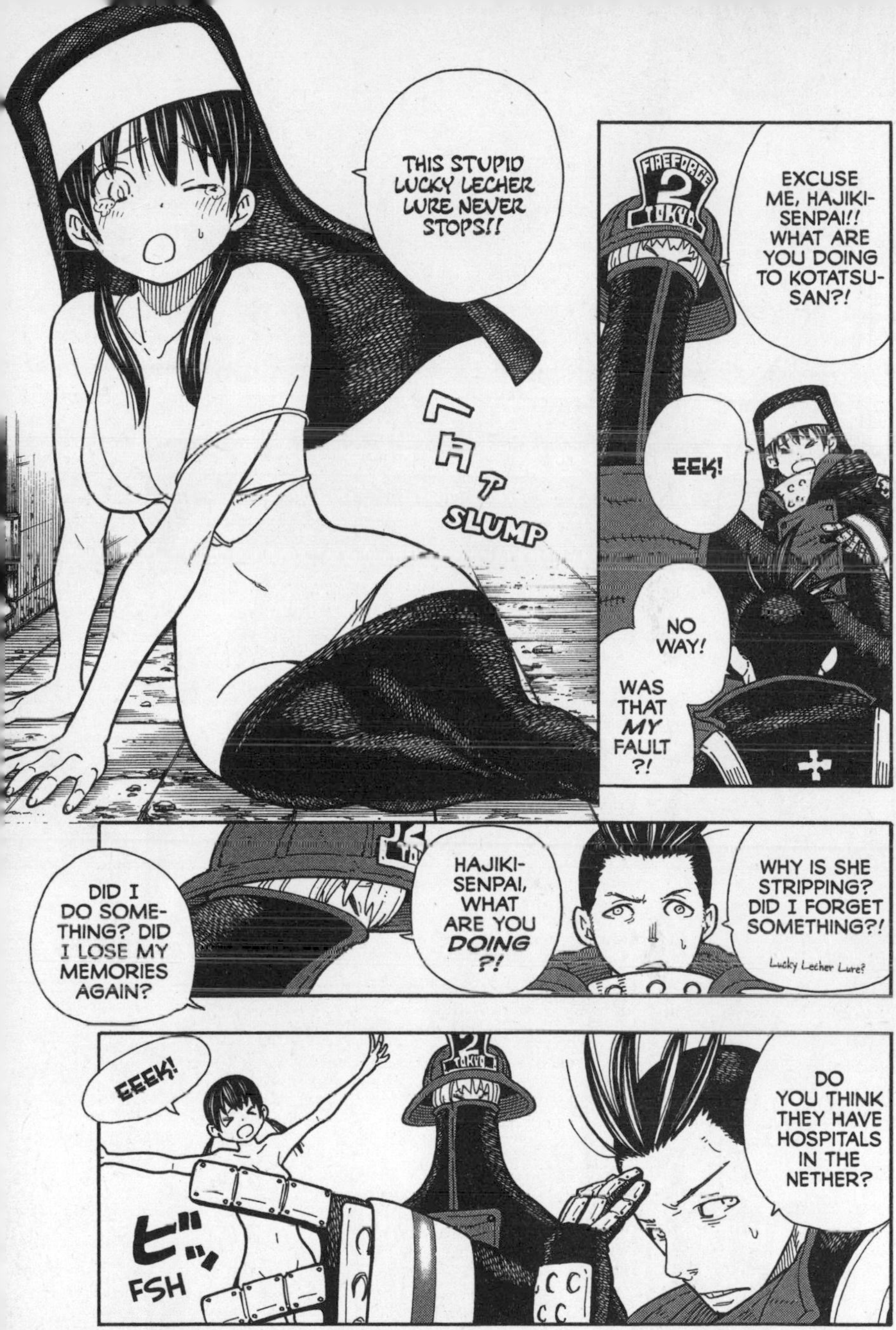
EXCUSE ME, HAJIKI-SENPAI!! WHAT ARE YOU DOING TO KOTATSU-SAN?!
EEK!
NO WAY!
WAS THAT MY FAULT?!
THIS STUPID LUCKY LECHER LURE NEVER STOPS!!
SLUMP
WHY IS SHE STRIPPING? DID I FORGET SOMETHING?!
Lucky Lecher Lure?
HAJIKI-SENPAI, WHAT ARE YOU DOING?!
DID I DO SOME-THING? DID I LOSE MY MEMORIES AGAIN?
DO YOU THINK THEY HAVE HOSPITALS IN THE NETHER?
EEEK!
FSH

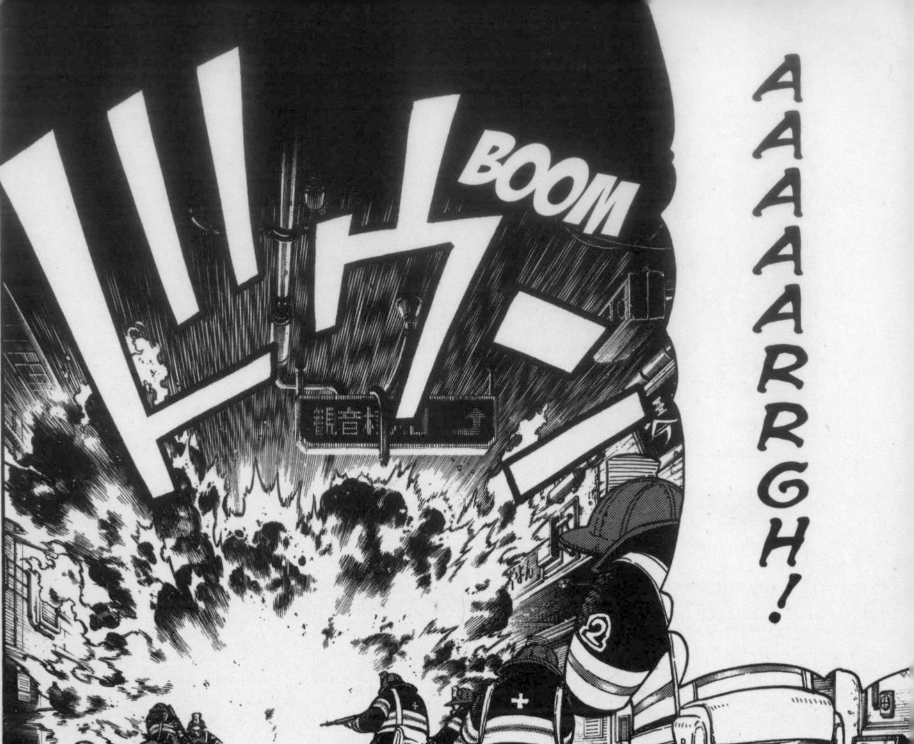
AAAARRGH!
BOOM

Sign: Kannon

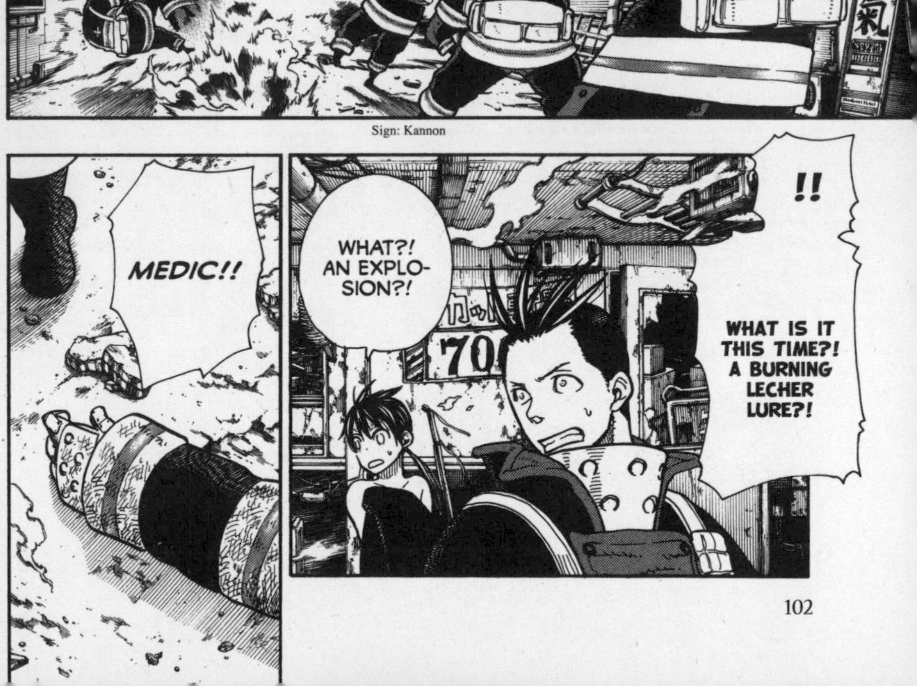
!!
WHAT IS IT THIS TIME?! A BURNING LECHER LURE?!
WHAT?! AN EXPLOSION?!
70
MEDIC!!

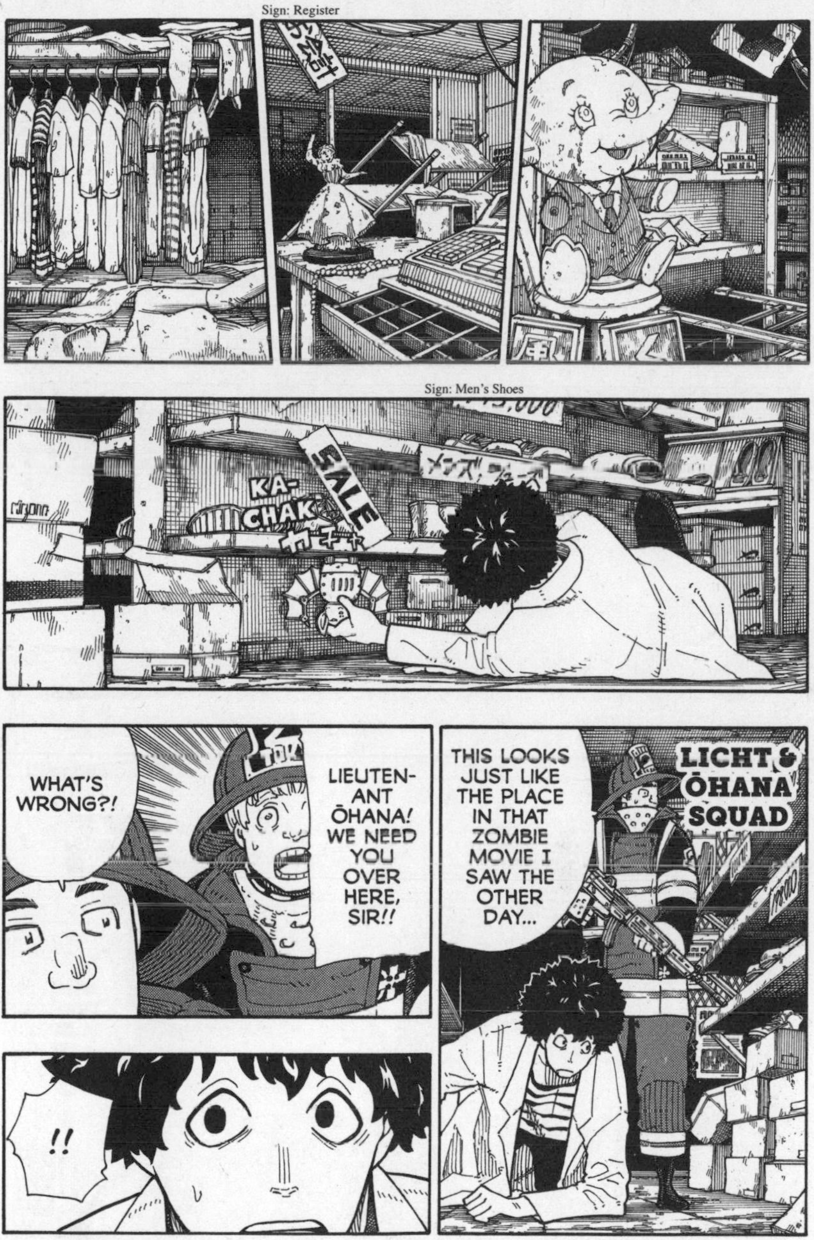
Sign: Register
Sign: Men's Shoes
KA-CHAK
SALE
LICHT & ŌHANA SQUAD
THIS LOOKS JUST LIKE THE PLACE IN THAT ZOMBIE MOVIE I SAW THE OTHER DAY...
LIEUTEN-ANT ŌHANA! WE NEED YOU OVER HERE, SIR!!
WHAT'S WRONG?!
!!

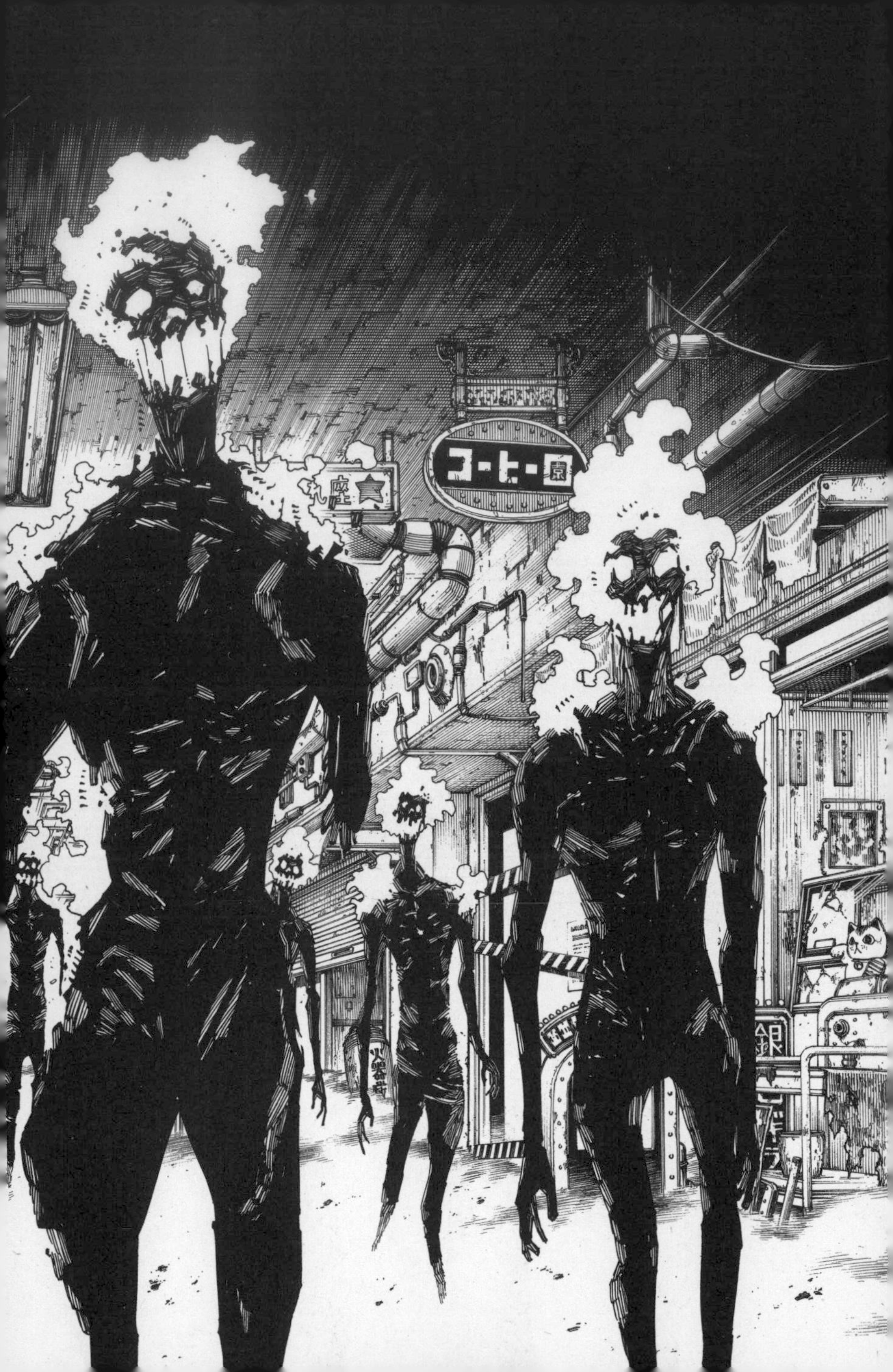

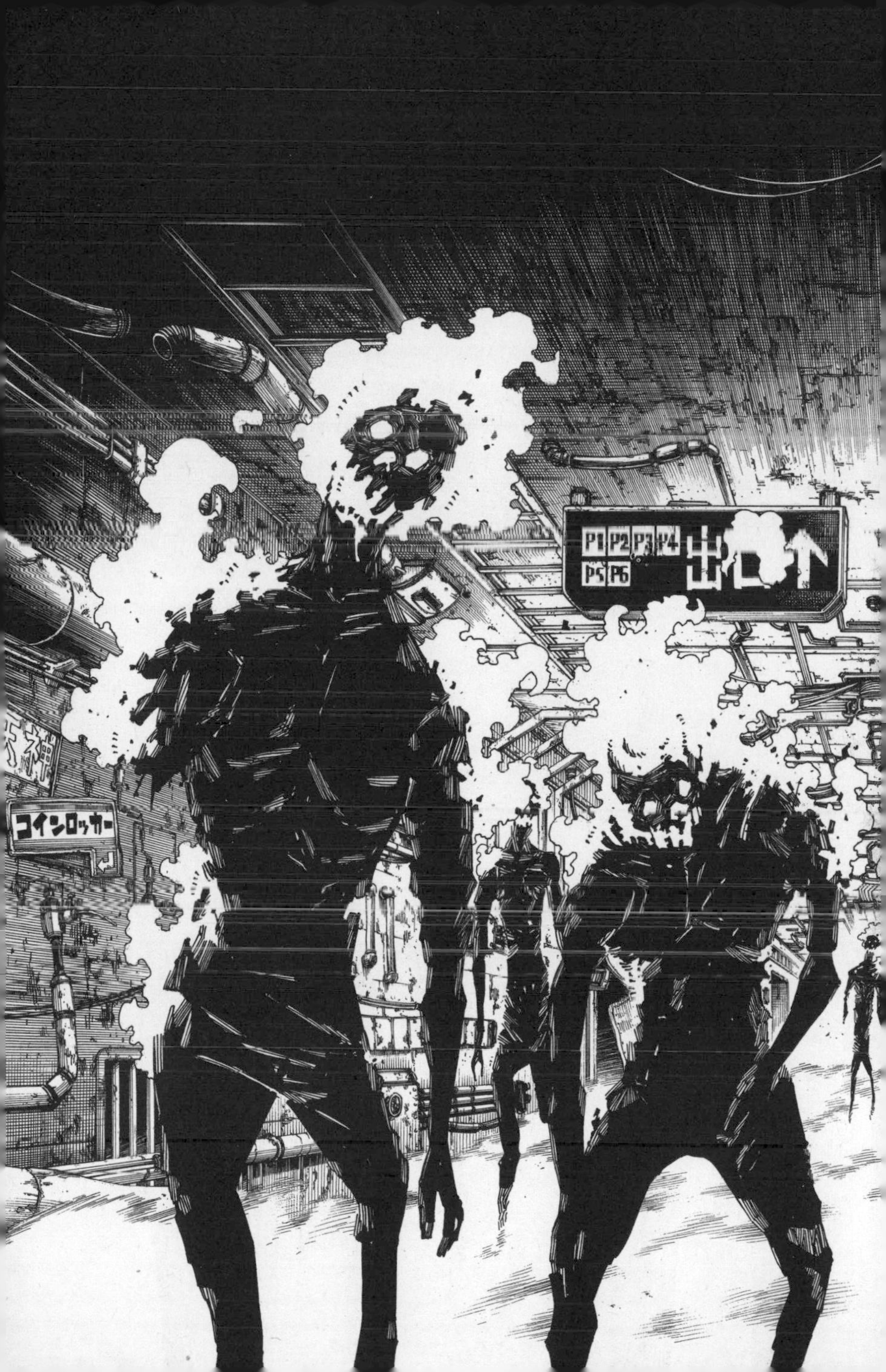
P1 P2 P3 P4
P5 P6
コインロッカー

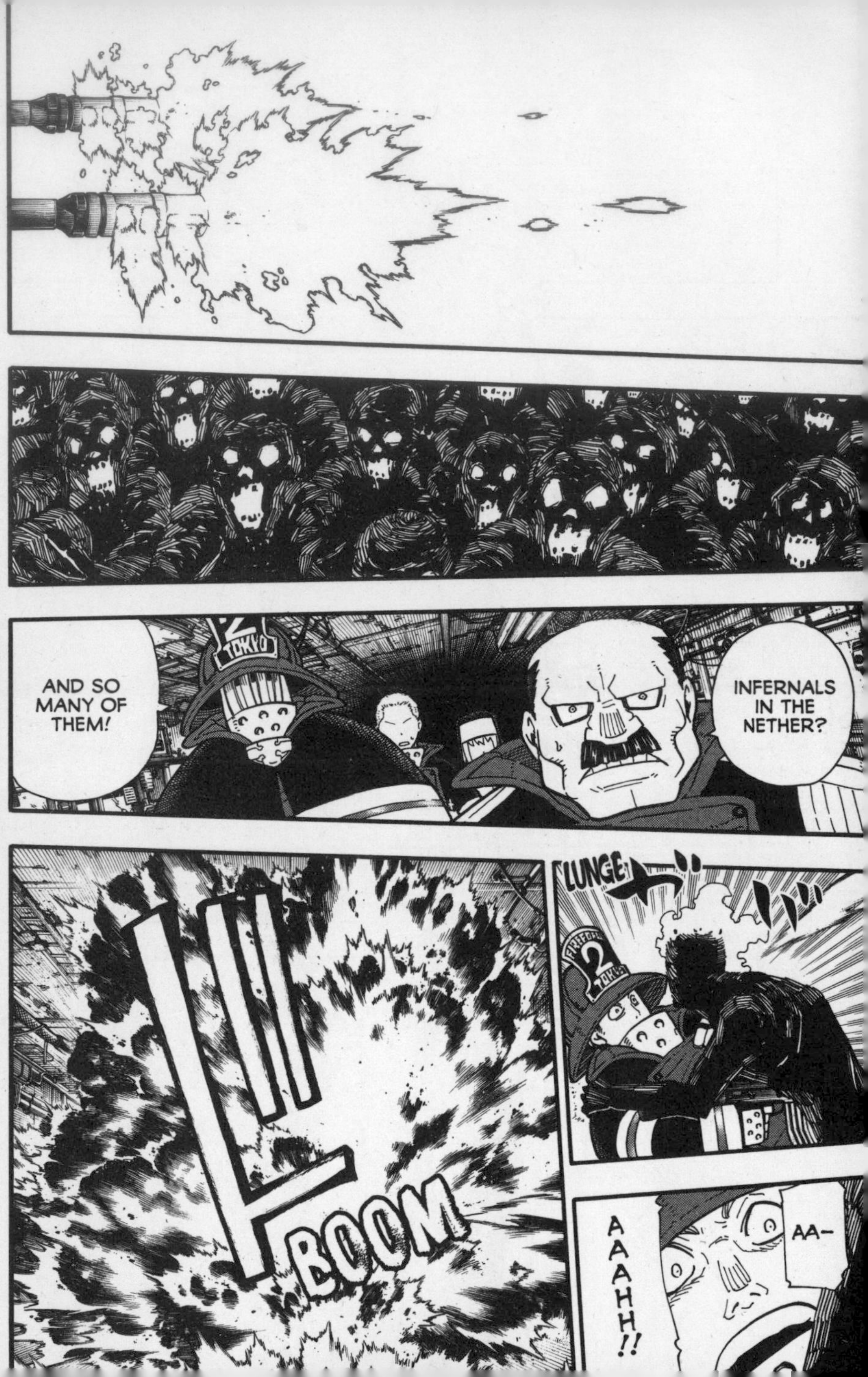
INFERNALS IN THE NETHER?
AND SO MANY OF THEM!
LUNGE
AA-
AAAHH!!
BOOM

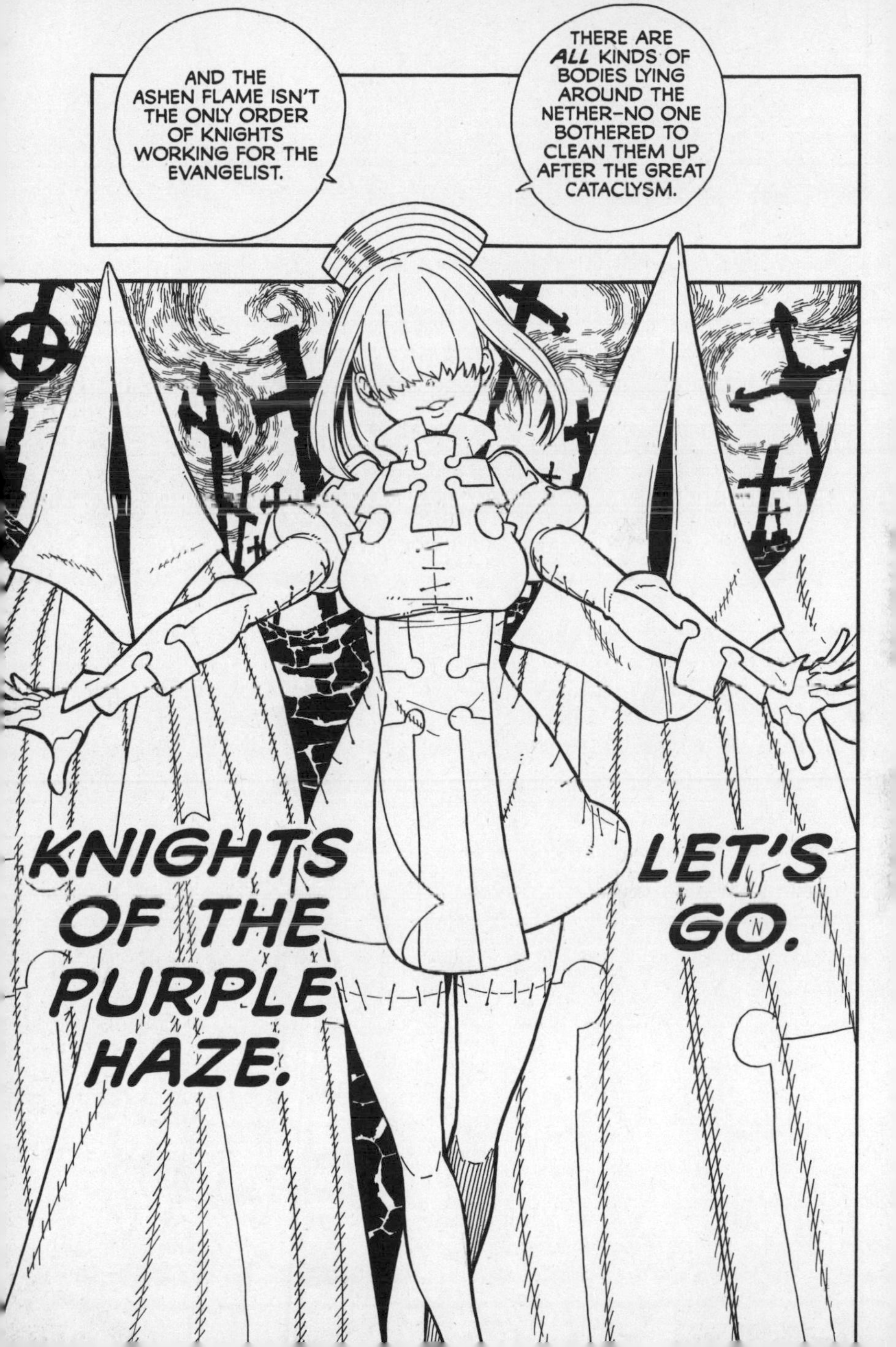
THERE ARE ALL KINDS OF BODIES LYING AROUND THE NETHER–NO ONE BOTHERED TO CLEAN THEM UP AFTER THE GREAT CATACLYSM.
AND THE ASHEN FLAME ISN'T THE ONLY ORDER OF KNIGHTS WORKING FOR THE EVANGELIST.
LET'S GO.
KNIGHTS OF THE PURPLE HAZE.

FIRE FORCE

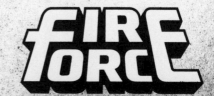

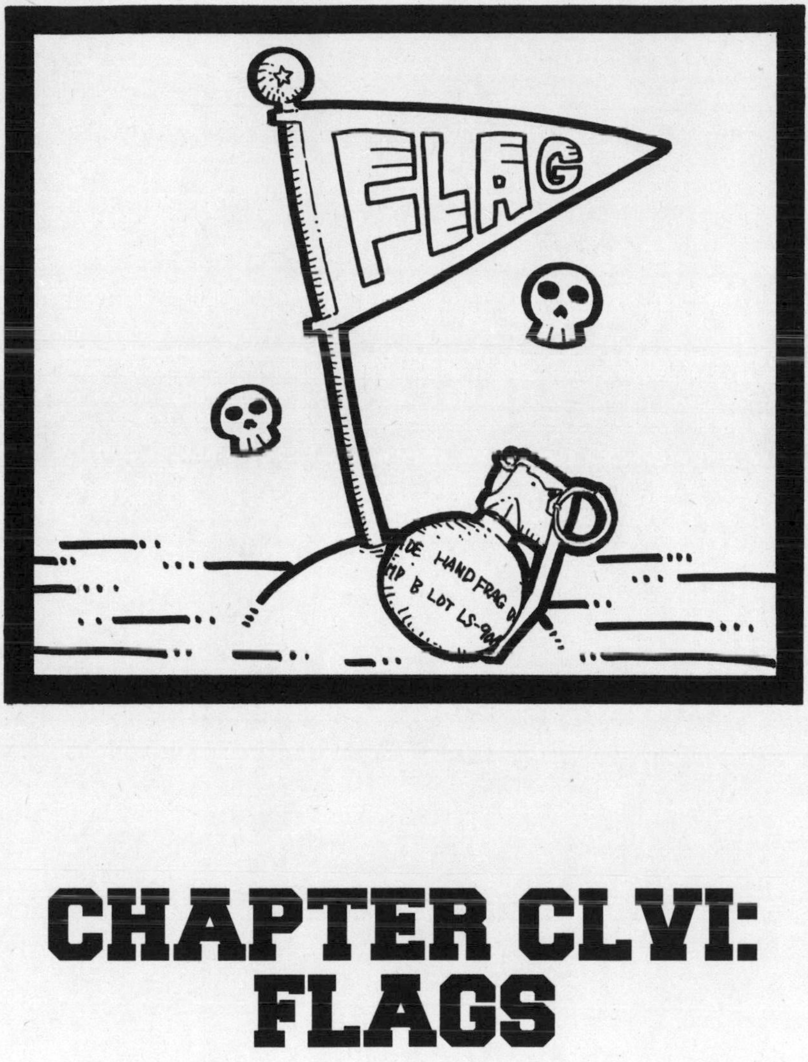
FLAG

CHAPTER CLVI: FLAGS

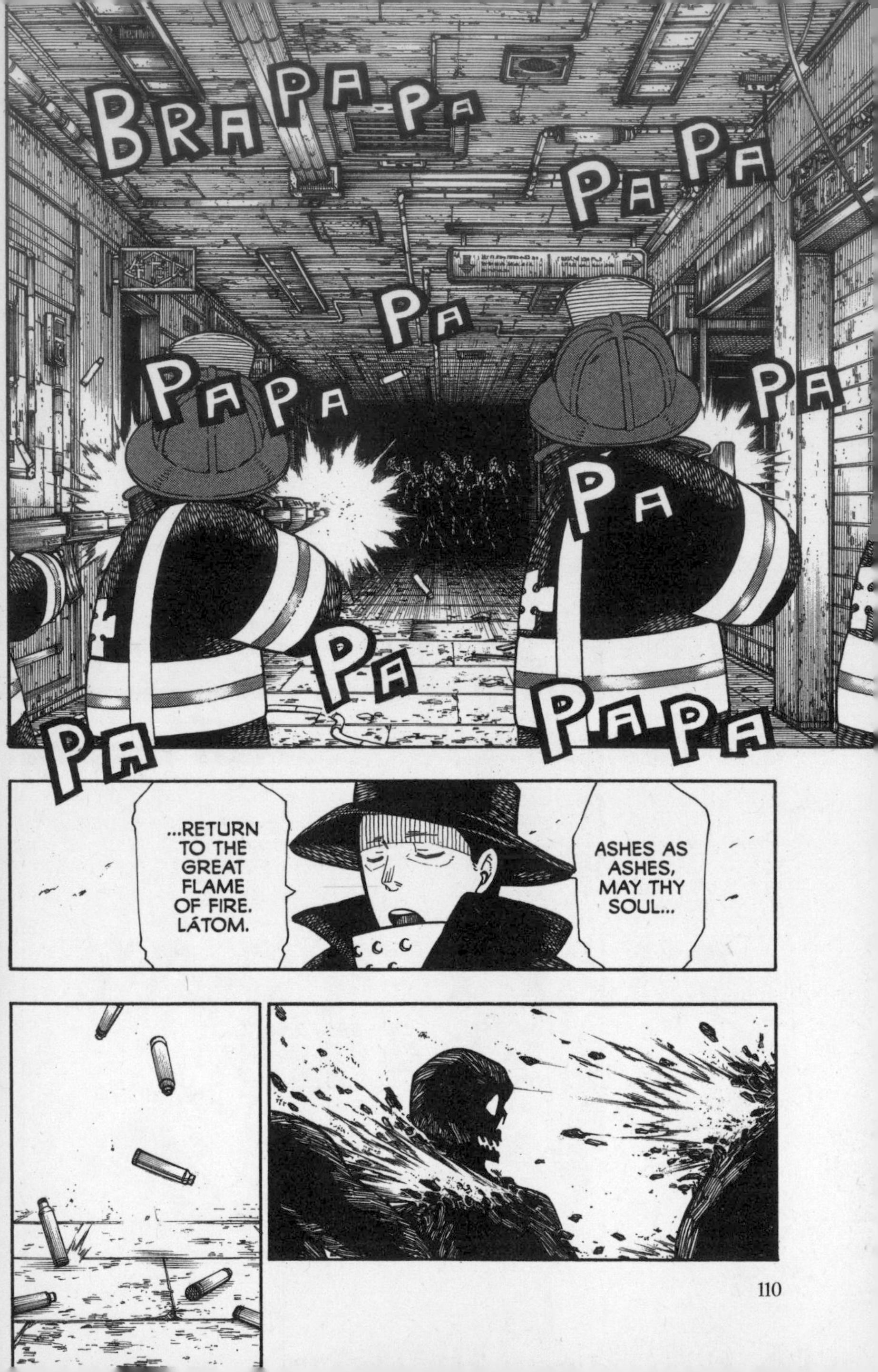
BRAPA-PA
PA PA
PA PA
PAPA-PA
PA PA
PA PA
PAPAPA
PA
ASHES AS ASHES, MAY THY SOUL...
...RETURN TO THE GREAT FLAME OF FIRE. LÁTOM.

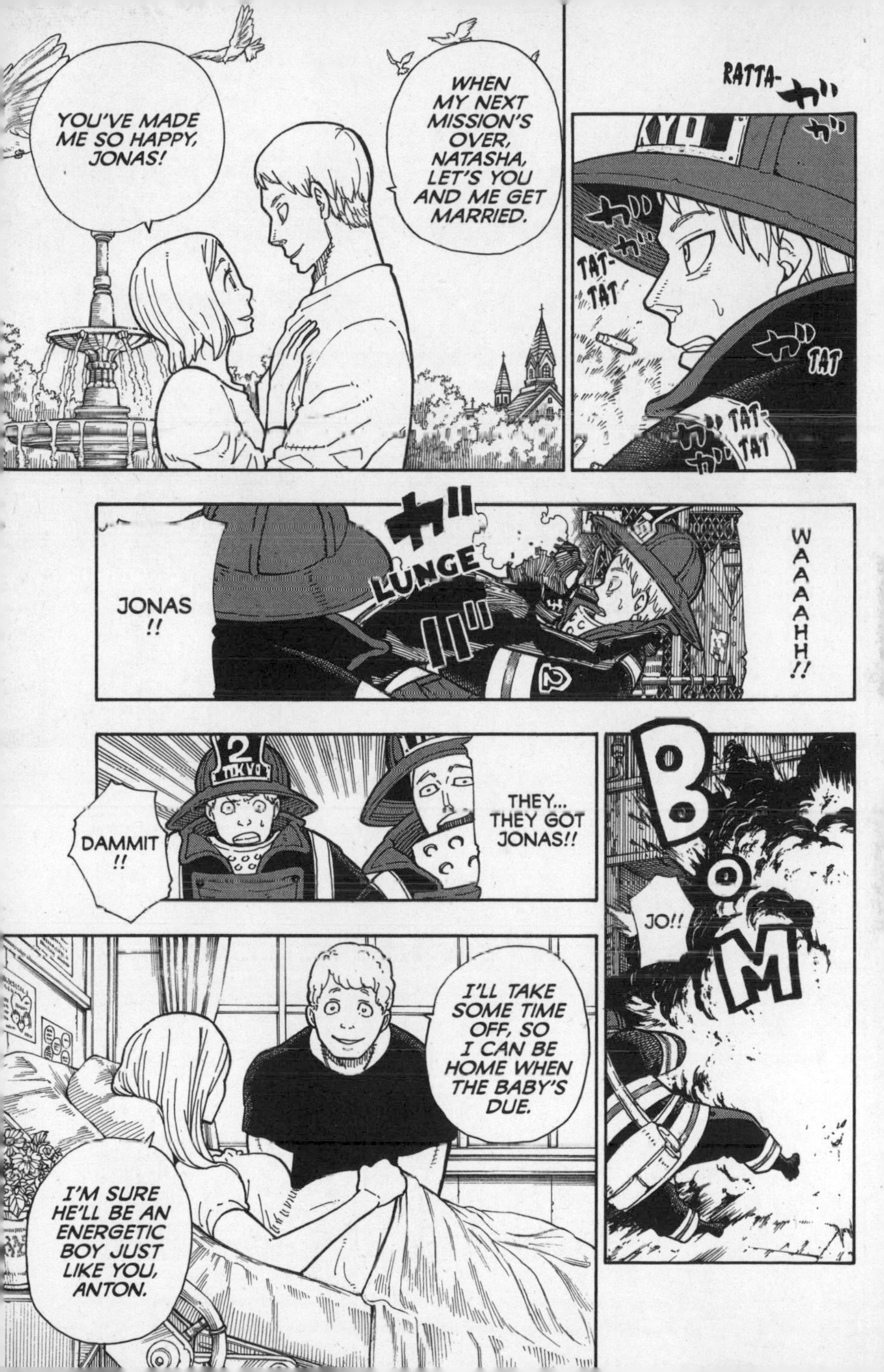
RATTA-
TAT-TAT
TAT
TAT-TAT
WHEN MY NEXT MISSION'S OVER, NATASHA, LET'S YOU AND ME GET MARRIED.
YOU'VE MADE ME SO HAPPY, JONAS!
WAAAAAHH!!
LUNGE
JONAS!!
BOOM
JO!!
THEY... THEY GOT JONAS!!
DAMMIT!!
I'LL TAKE SOME TIME OFF, SO I CAN BE HOME WHEN THE BABY'S DUE.
I'M SURE HE'LL BE AN ENERGETIC BOY JUST LIKE YOU, ANTON.

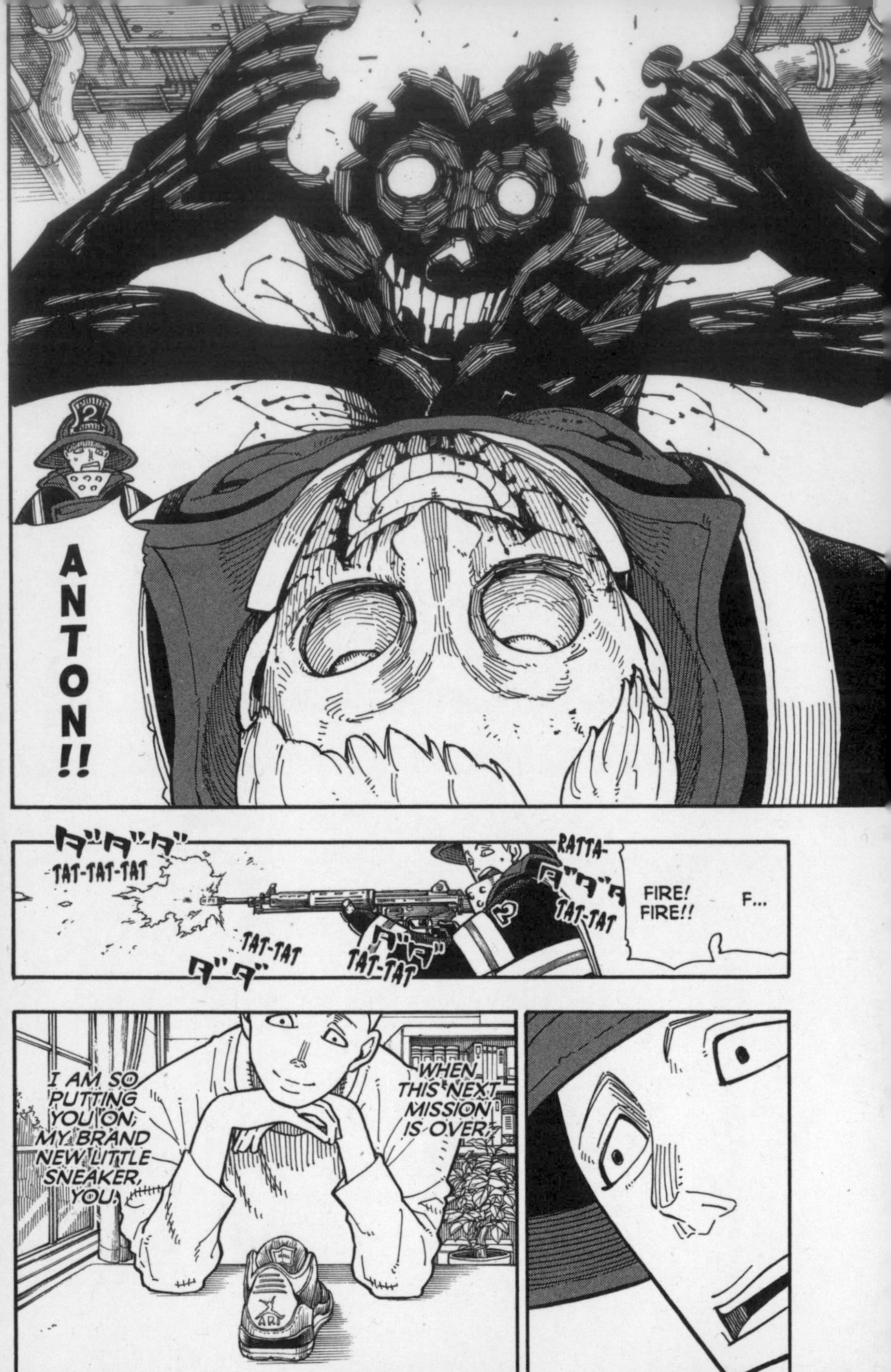
ANTON!!
F...
FIRE! FIRE!!
RATTA-TAT-TAT
TAT-TAT
TAT-TAT
TAT-TAT-TAT
WHEN THIS NEXT MISSION IS OVER,
I AM SO PUTTING YOU ON, MY BRAND NEW LITTLE SNEAKER, YOU.

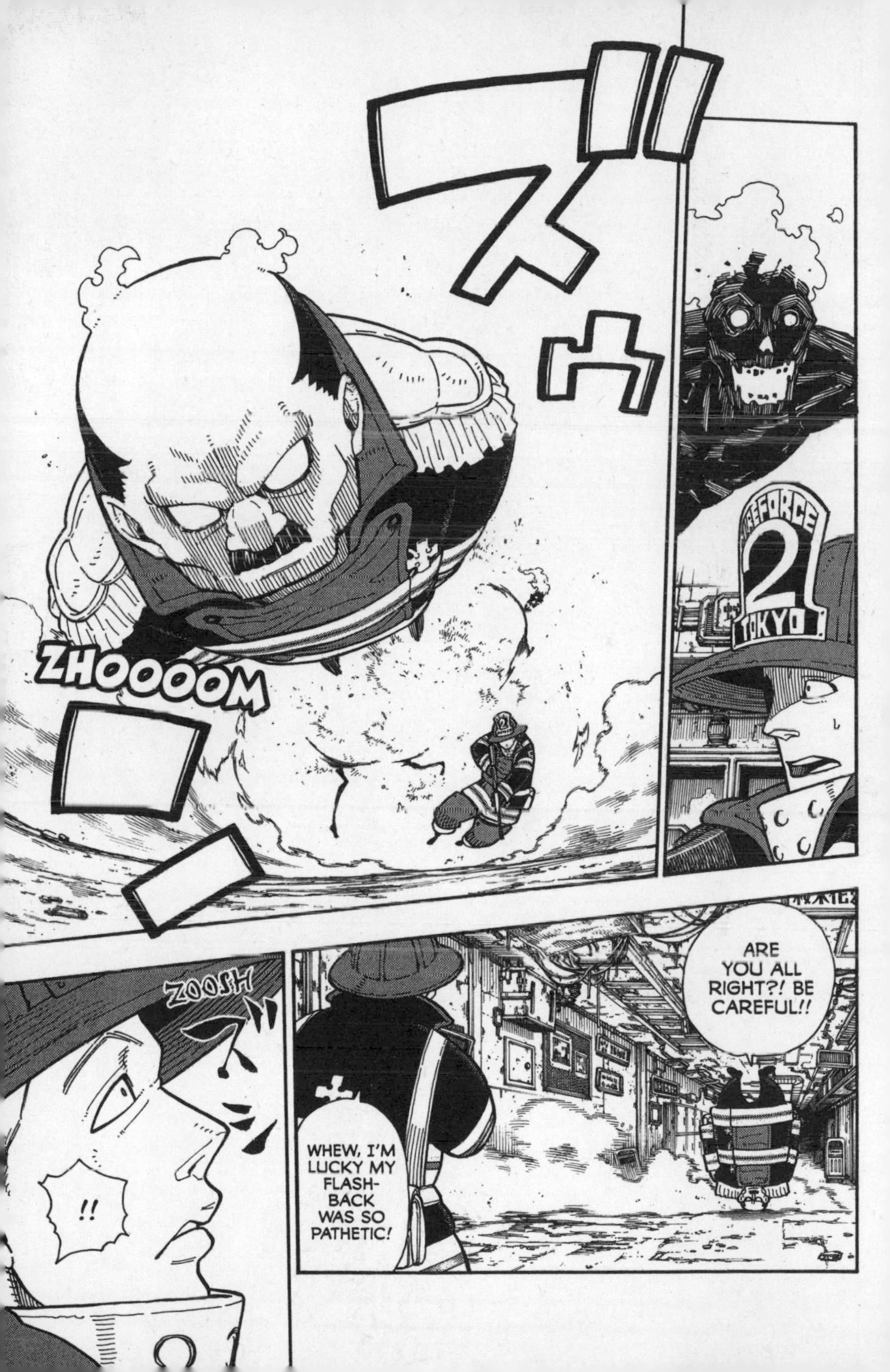
TOKYO
ZHOOOOM
ARE YOU ALL RIGHT?! BE CAREFUL!!
WHEW, I'M LUCKY MY FLASH-BACK WAS SO PATHETIC!
ZOOSH
!!

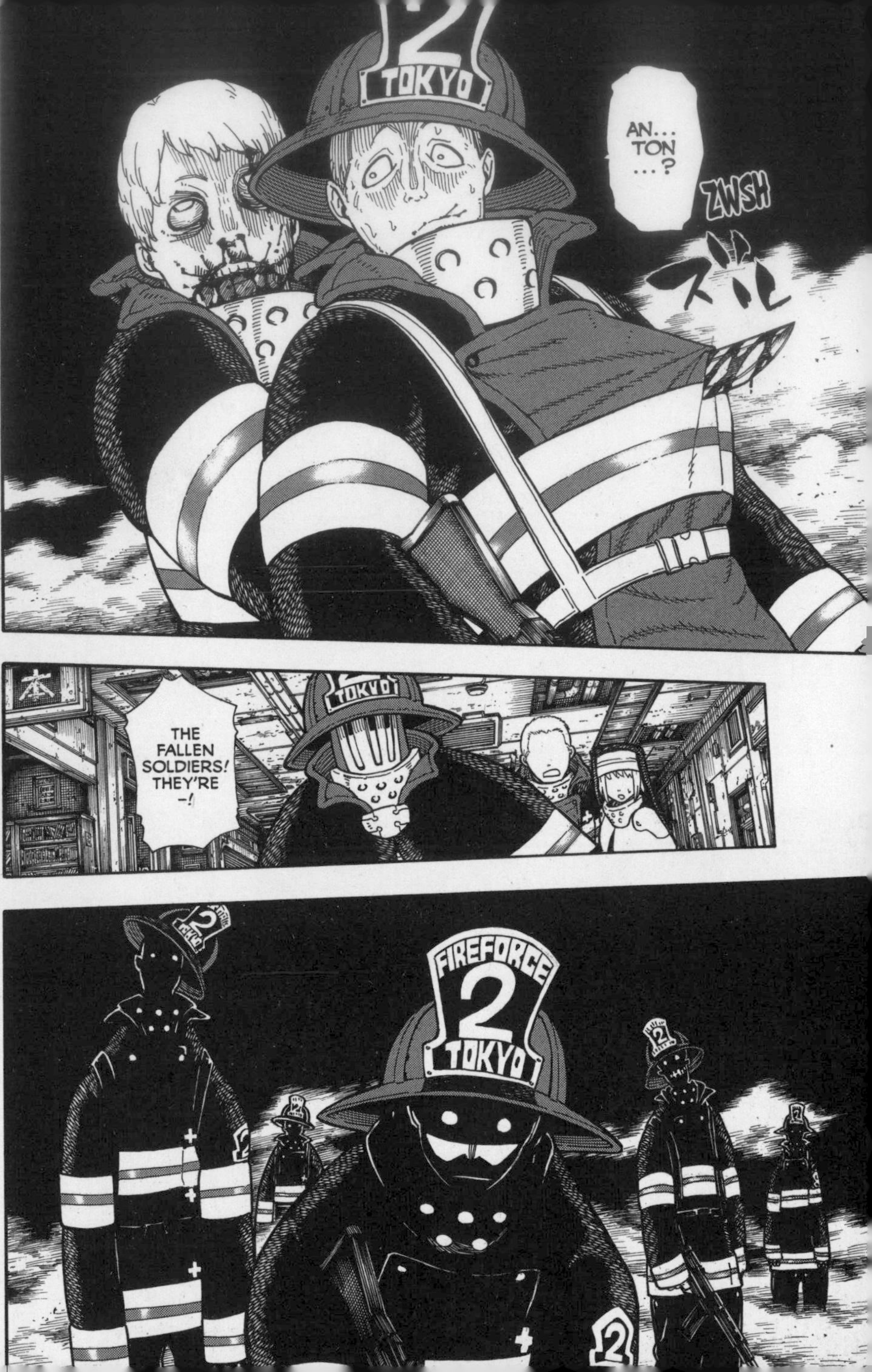
AN... TON ...?
ZWSH
THE FALLEN SOLDIERS! THEY'RE —!

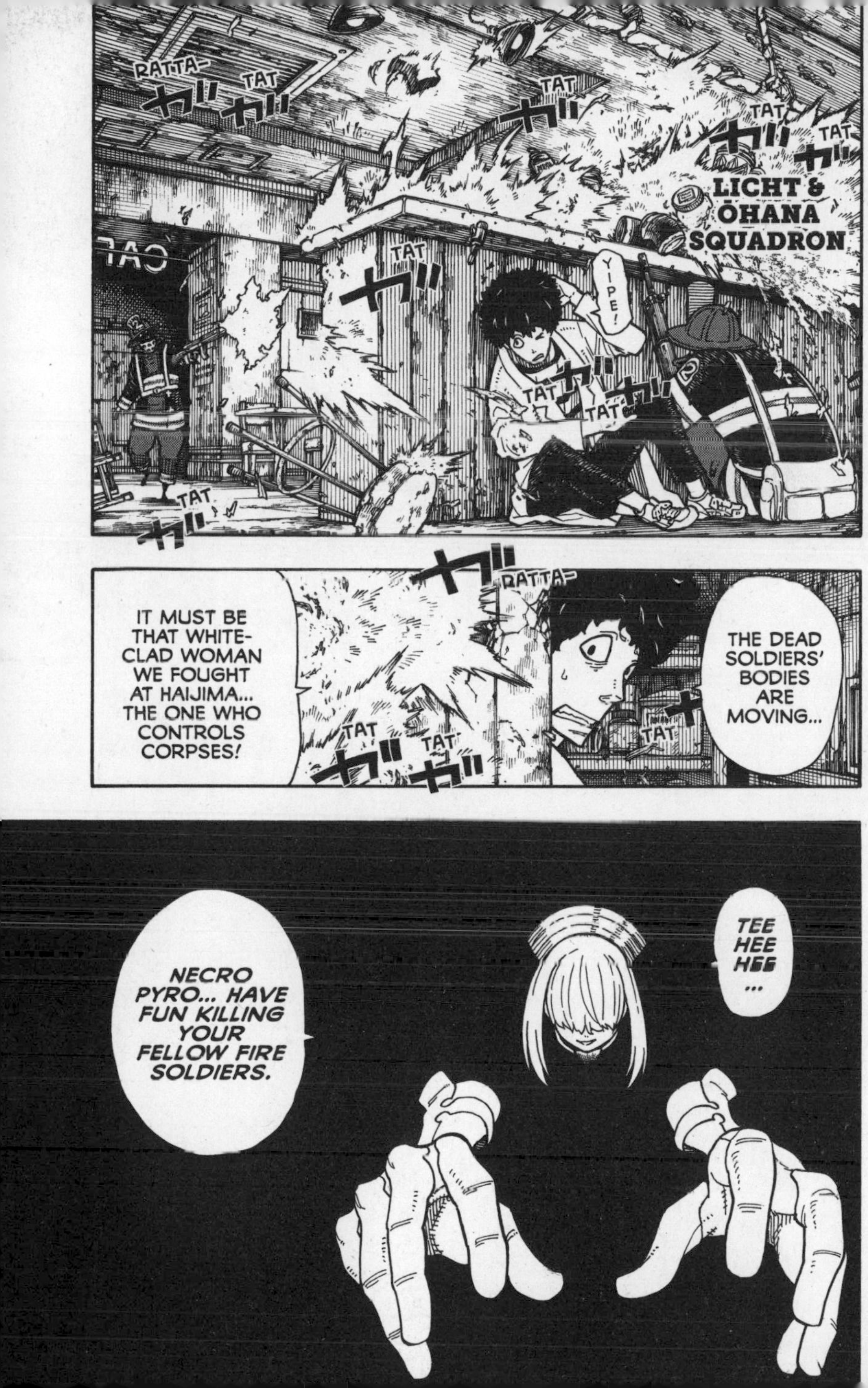
RATTA-
TAT
TAT
TAT
TAT
LICHT & ŌHANA SQUADRON
YIPE!
TAT
TAT
TAT
TAT
RATTA-
THE DEAD SOLDIERS' BODIES ARE MOVING...
IT MUST BE THAT WHITE-CLAD WOMAN WE FOUGHT AT HAIJIMA... THE ONE WHO CONTROLS CORPSES!
TAT
TAT
TAT
TEE HEE HEE ...
NECRO PYRO... HAVE FUN KILLING YOUR FELLOW FIRE SOLDIERS.

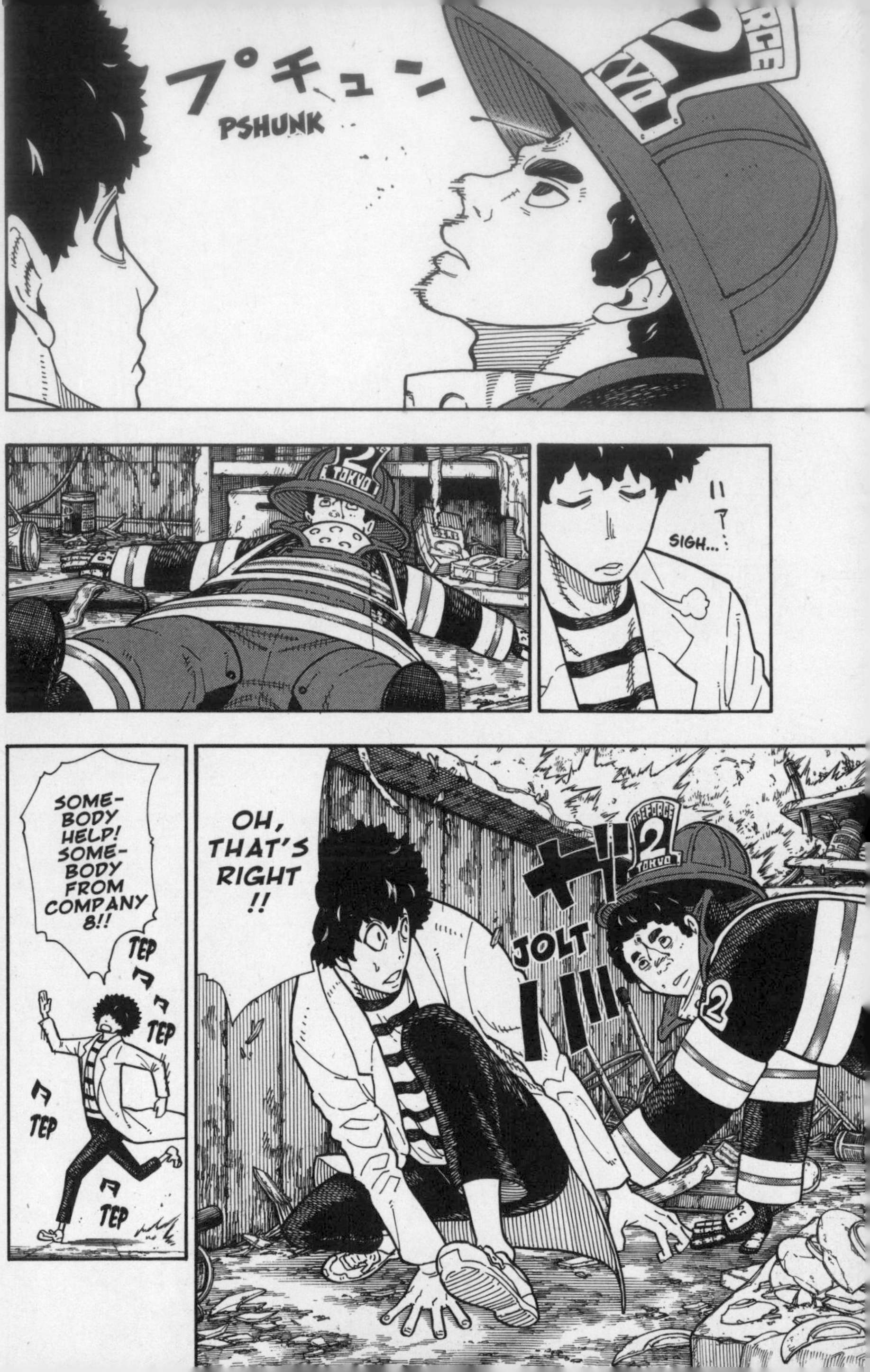
プチューン
PSHUNK
ハァ
SIGH...
OH, THAT'S RIGHT!!
JOLT
SOME-BODY HELP! SOME-BODY FROM COMPANY 8!!
TEP
TEP
TEP
TEP

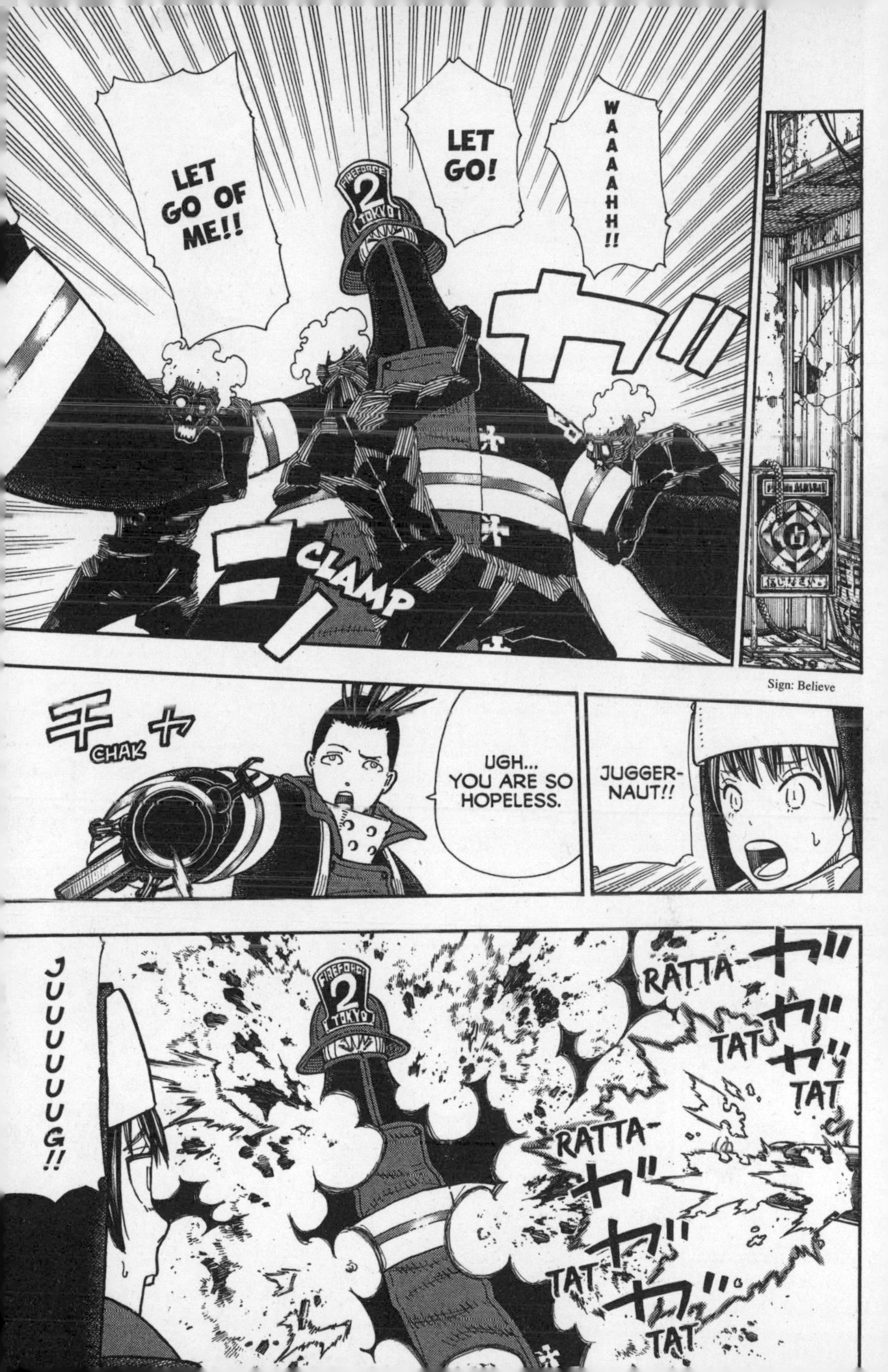
WAAAAHH!!
LET GO!
LET GO OF ME!!
CLAMP
JUGGER-NAUT!!
UGH... YOU ARE SO HOPELESS.
CHAK
RATTA-TAT
TAT
RATTA-TAT
TAT
TAT
JUUUUUUUG!!
Sign: Believe

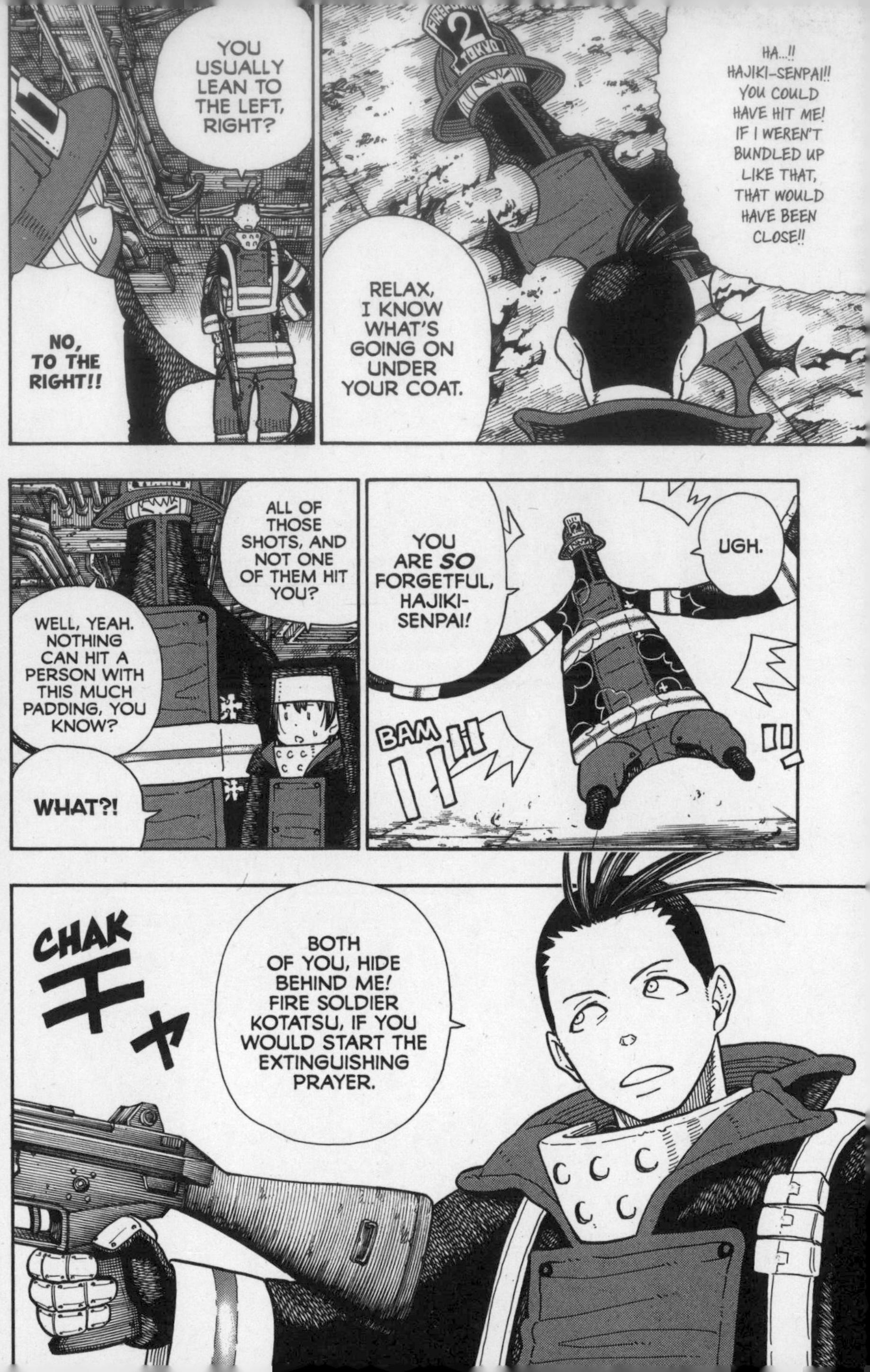
HA...!! HAJIKI-SENPAI!! YOU COULD HAVE HIT ME! IF I WEREN'T BUNDLED UP LIKE THAT, THAT WOULD HAVE BEEN CLOSE!!
RELAX, I KNOW WHAT'S GOING ON UNDER YOUR COAT.
YOU USUALLY LEAN TO THE LEFT, RIGHT?
NO, TO THE RIGHT!!
UGH.
YOU ARE SO FORGETFUL, HAJIKI-SENPAI!
BAM
ALL OF THOSE SHOTS, AND NOT ONE OF THEM HIT YOU?
WELL, YEAH. NOTHING CAN HIT A PERSON WITH THIS MUCH PADDING, YOU KNOW?
WHAT?!
BOTH OF YOU, HIDE BEHIND ME! FIRE SOLDIER KOTATSU, IF YOU WOULD START THE EXTINGUISHING PRAYER.
CHAK
チャ

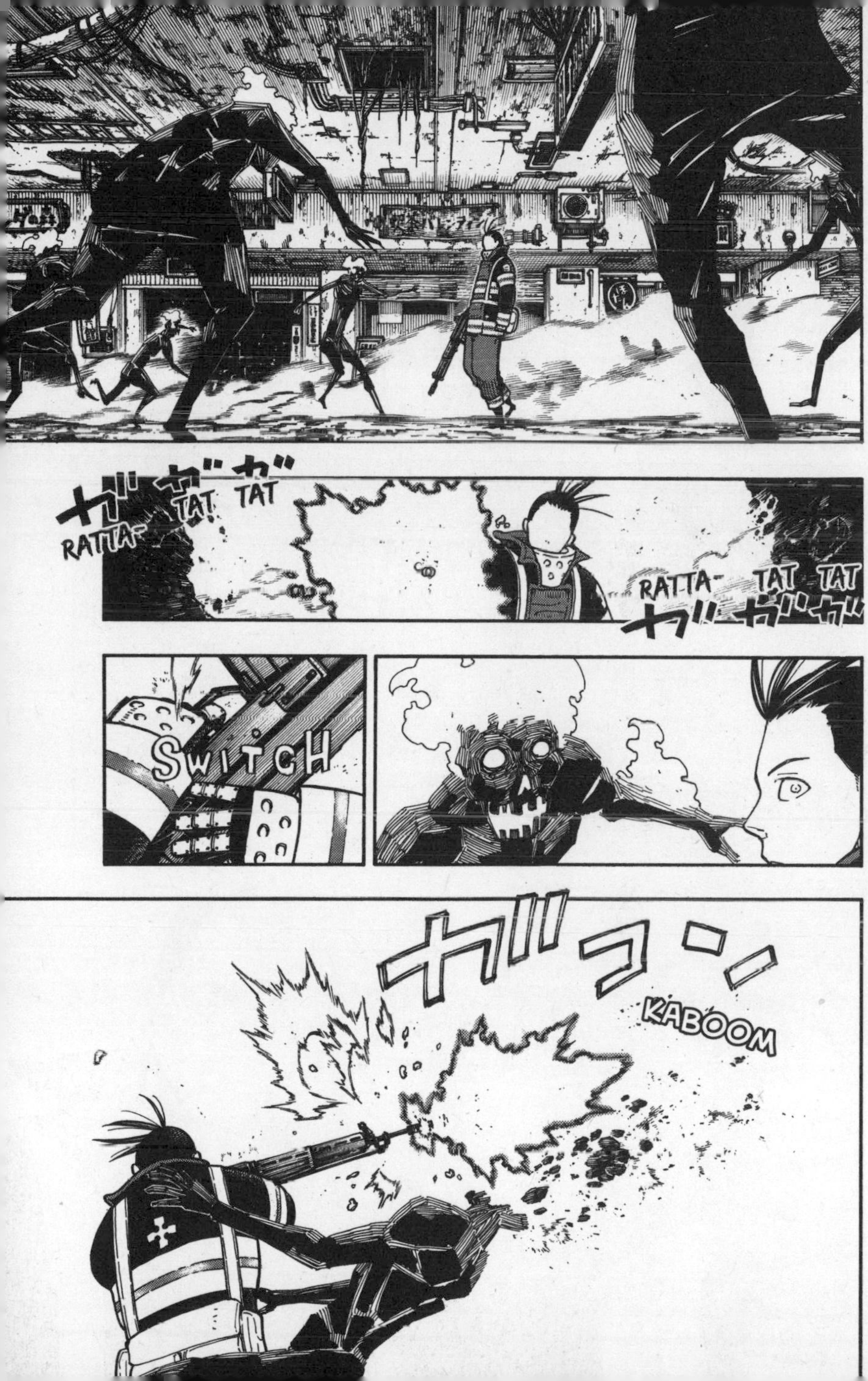
RATTA- TAT TAT
RATTA- TAT! TAT
SWITCH
KABOOM

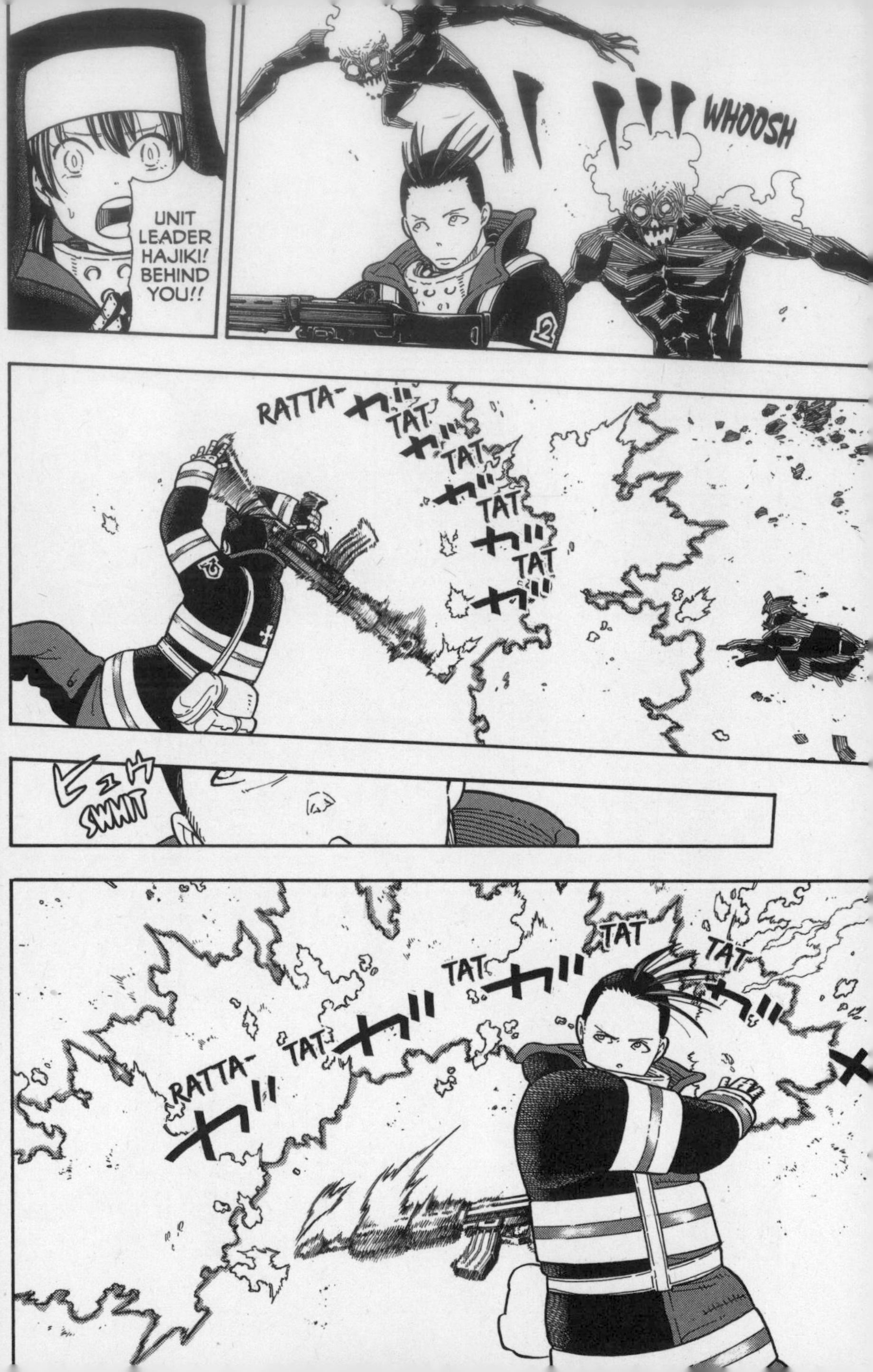
WHOOSH
UNIT LEADER HAJIKI! BEHIND YOU!!
RATTA-TAT TAT TAT TAT
SWMIT
RATTA-TAT TAT TAT TAT

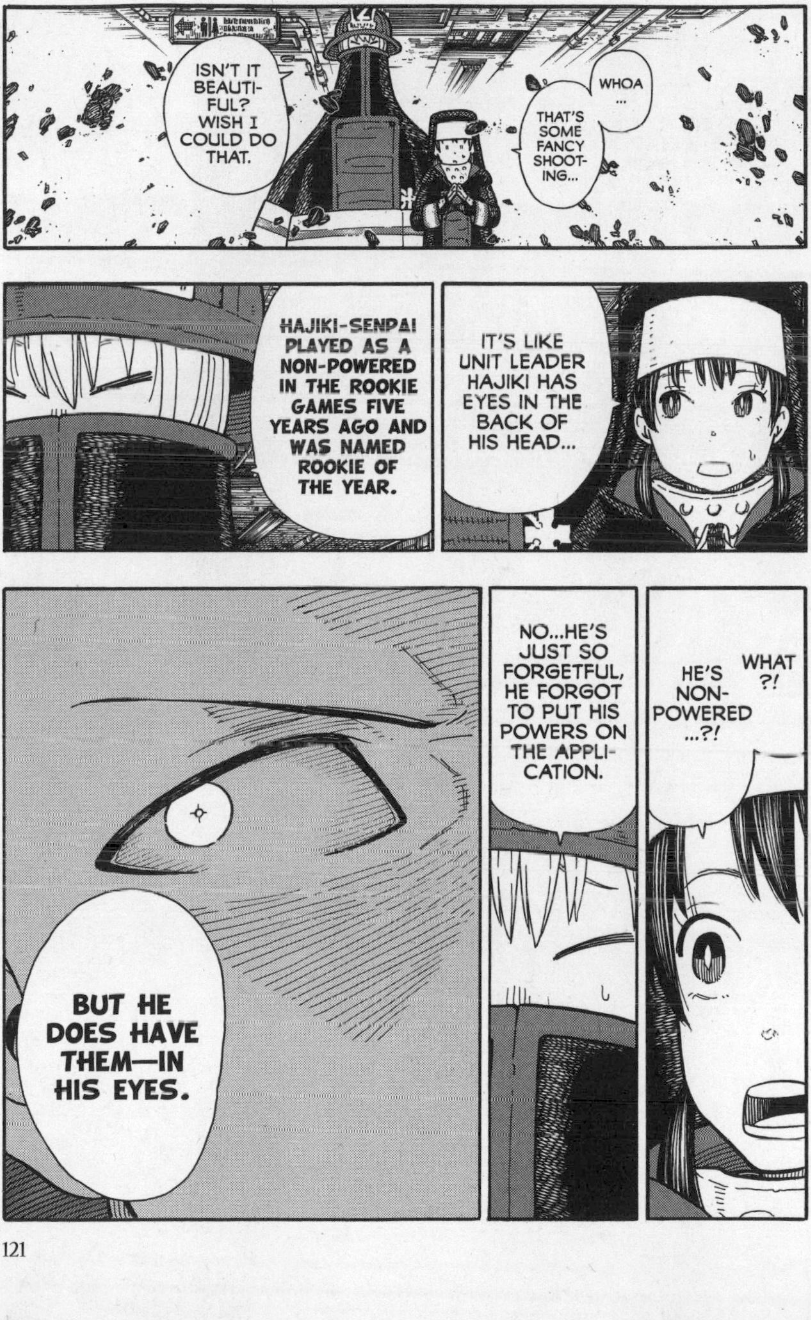
WHOA ...
THAT'S SOME FANCY SHOOTING...
ISN'T IT BEAUTIFUL? WISH I COULD DO THAT.
IT'S LIKE UNIT LEADER HAJIKI HAS EYES IN THE BACK OF HIS HEAD...
HAJIKI-SENPAI PLAYED AS A NON-POWERED IN THE ROOKIE GAMES FIVE YEARS AGO AND WAS NAMED ROOKIE OF THE YEAR.
WHAT ?!
HE'S NON-POWERED ...?!
NO...HE'S JUST SO FORGETFUL, HE FORGOT TO PUT HIS POWERS ON THE APPLICATION.
BUT HE DOES HAVE THEM—IN HIS EYES.

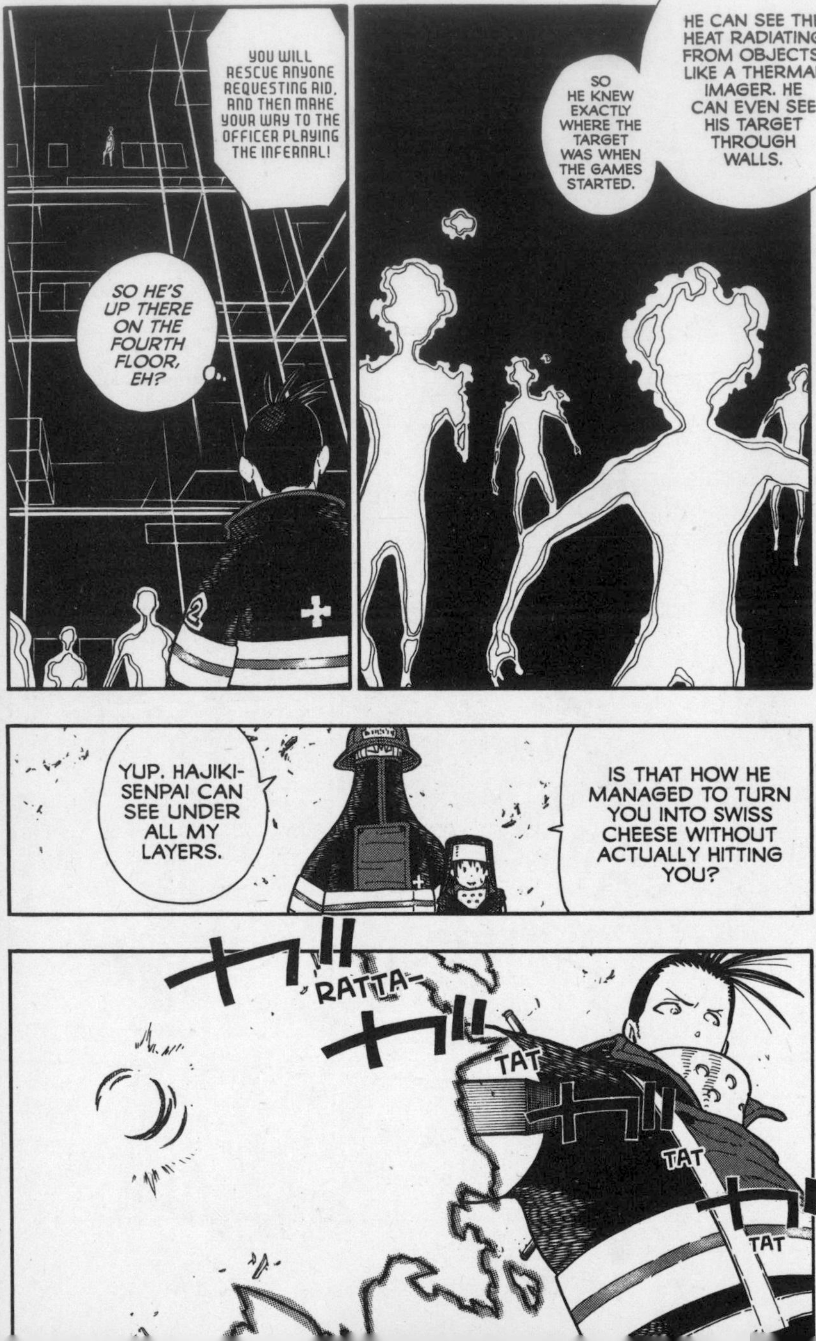
HE CAN SEE THE HEAT RADIATING FROM OBJECTS, LIKE A THERMAL IMAGER. HE CAN EVEN SEE HIS TARGET THROUGH WALLS.
SO HE KNEW EXACTLY WHERE THE TARGET WAS WHEN THE GAMES STARTED.
YOU WILL RESCUE ANYONE REQUESTING AID, AND THEN MAKE YOUR WAY TO THE OFFICER PLAYING THE INFERNAL!
SO HE'S UP THERE ON THE FOURTH FLOOR, EH?
IS THAT HOW HE MANAGED TO TURN YOU INTO SWISS CHEESE WITHOUT ACTUALLY HITTING YOU?
YUP. HAJIKI-SENPAI CAN SEE UNDER ALL MY LAYERS.
RATTA-
TAT
TAT
TAT

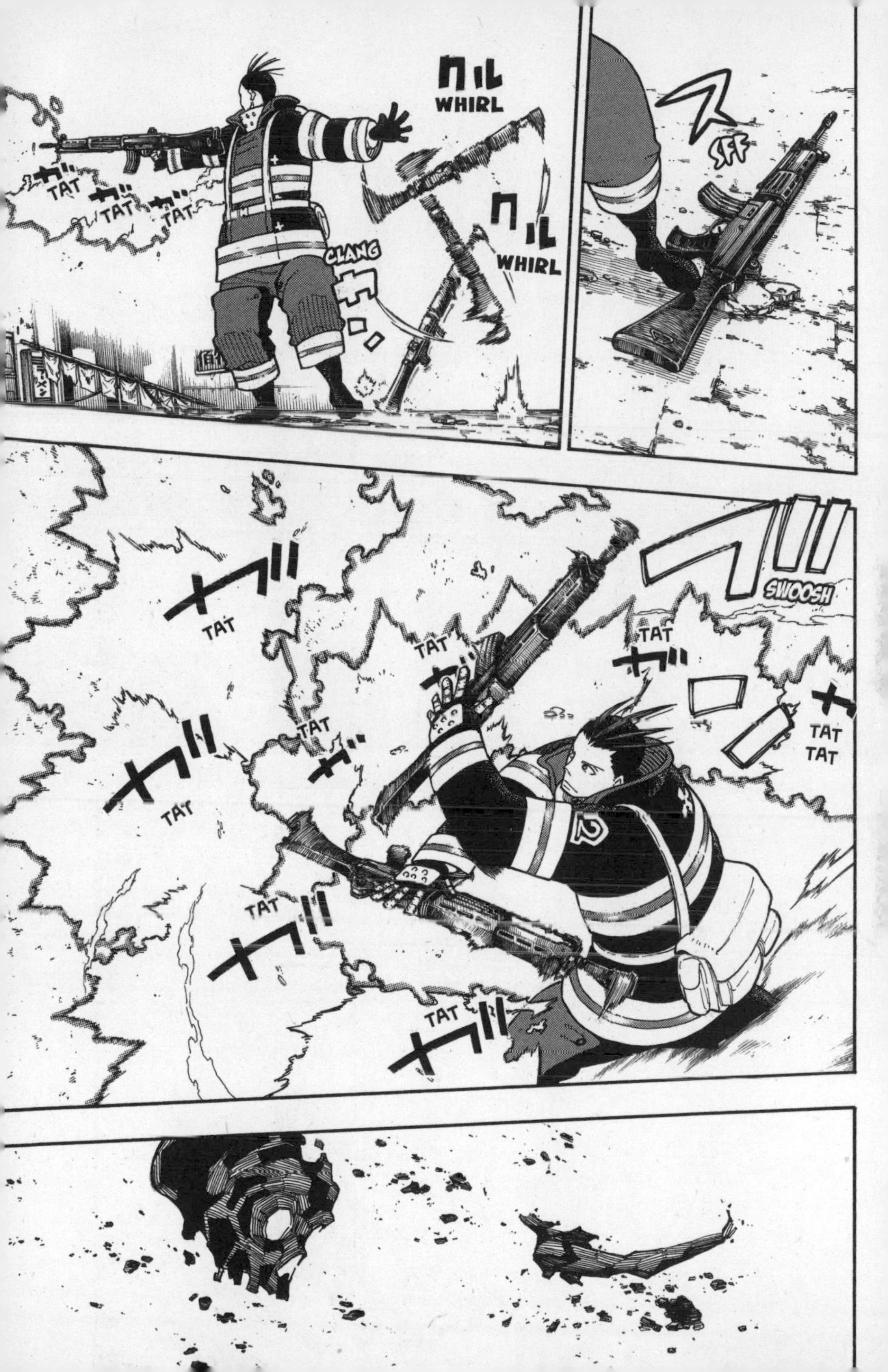
SFF
WHIRL
WHIRL
CLANG
TAT
TAT
TAT
SWOOSH
TAT
TAT
TAT
TAT
TAT
TAT
TAT
TAT
TAT

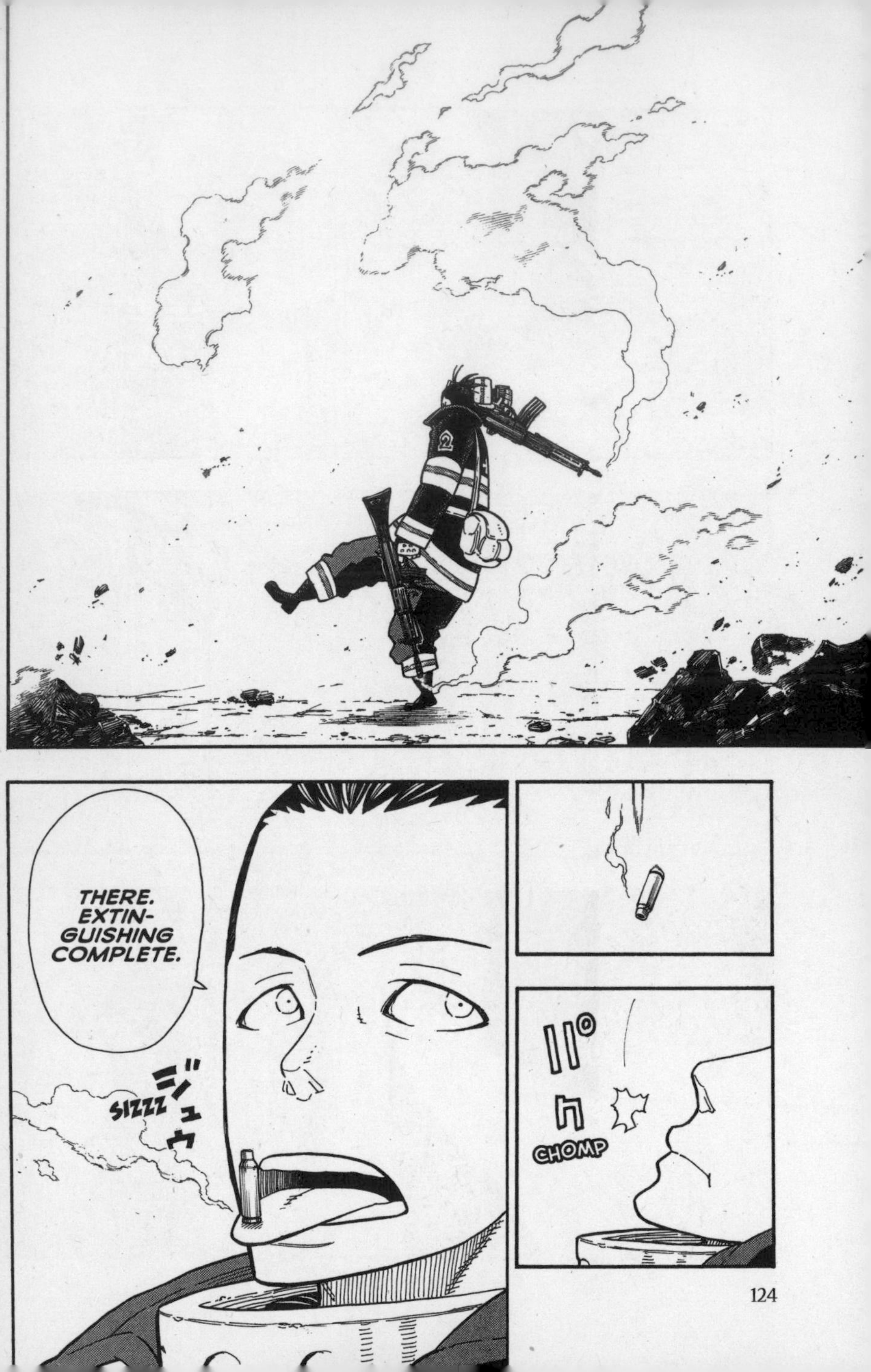
パク
CHOMP
THERE. EXTIN-GUISHING COMPLETE.
ジュウ
SIZZZ

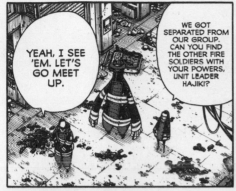

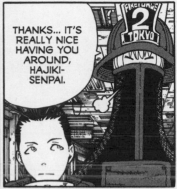

THANKS... IT'S REALLY NICE HAVING YOU AROUND, HAJIKI-SENPAI.
WE GOT SEPARATED FROM OUR GROUP. CAN YOU FIND THE OTHER FIRE SOLDIERS WITH YOUR POWERS, UNIT LEADER HAJIKI?
YEAH, I SEE 'EM. LET'S GO MEET UP.
WAIT. THAT'S–
SFF
FWOOSH

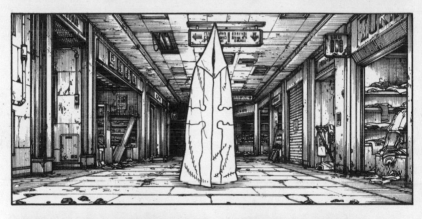

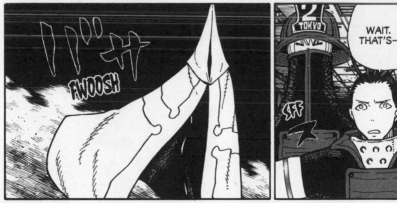

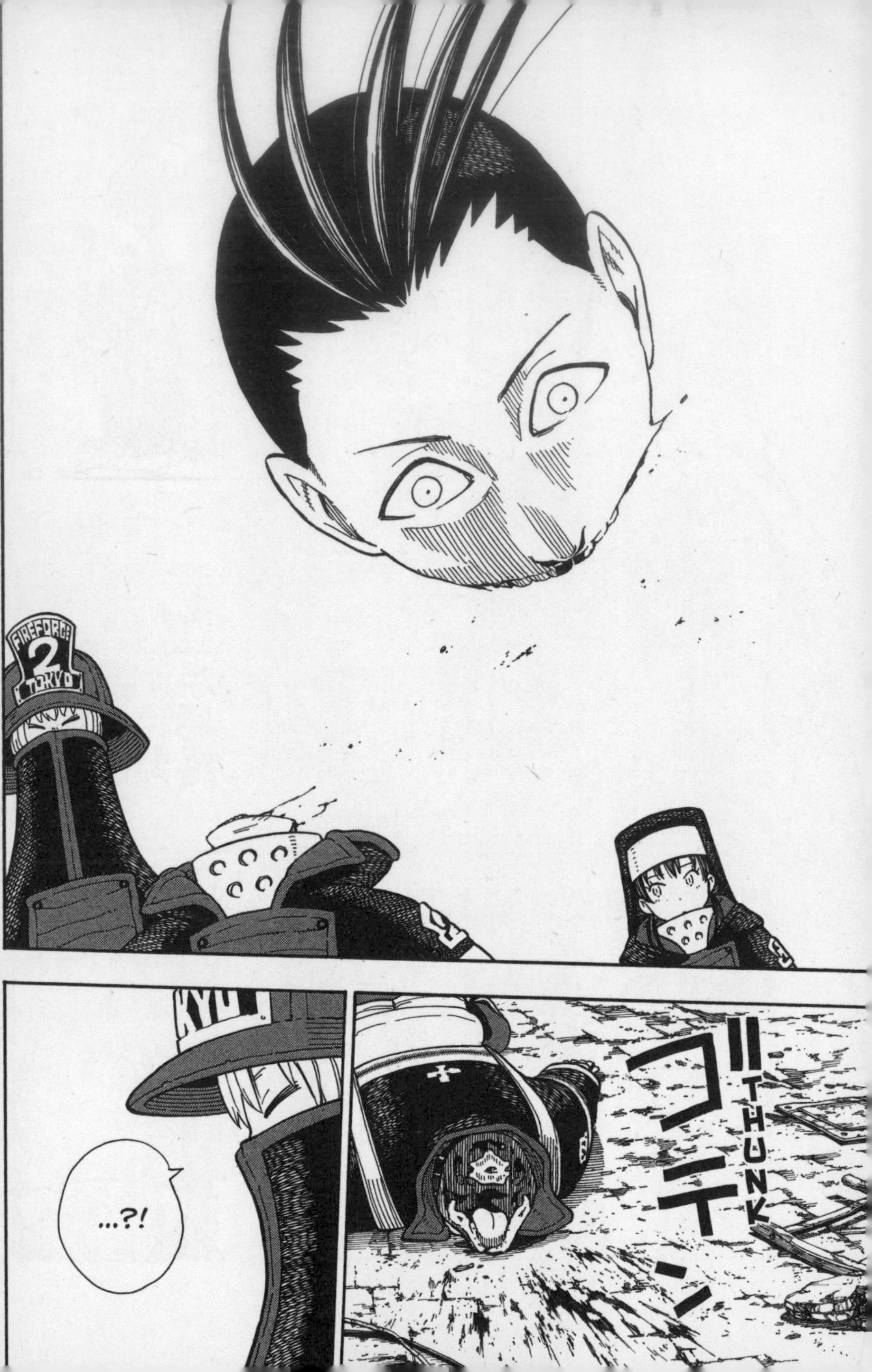
FIREFORCE
2
TOKYO
THUNK
...?!

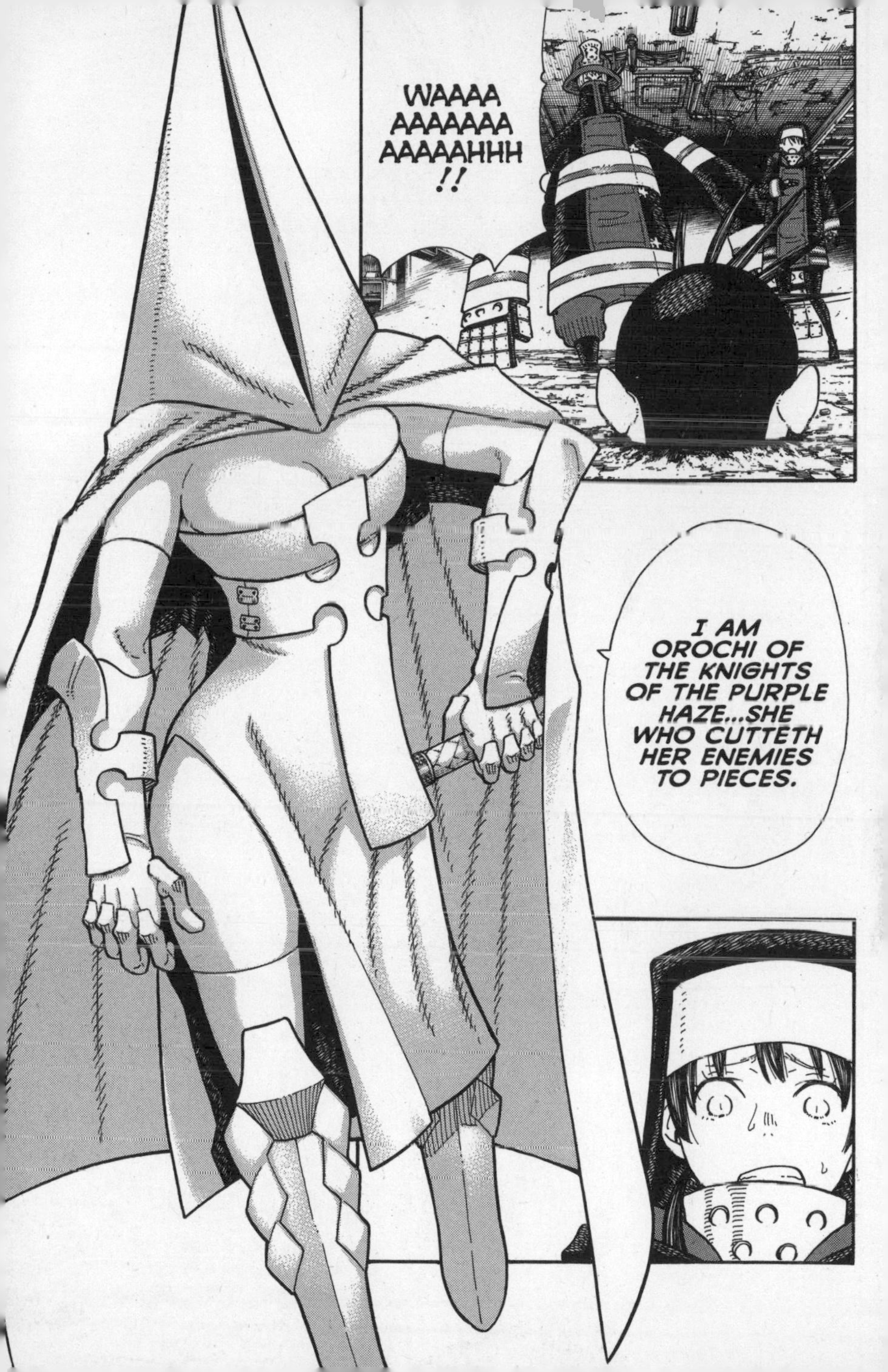
WAAAA AAAAAAA AAAAAHHH !!
I AM OROCHI OF THE KNIGHTS OF THE PURPLE HAZE...SHE WHO CUTTETH HER ENEMIES TO PIECES.

FIRE FORCE

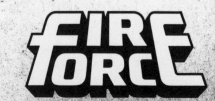

CHAPTER CLVII: BATTLE OF RESOLVE

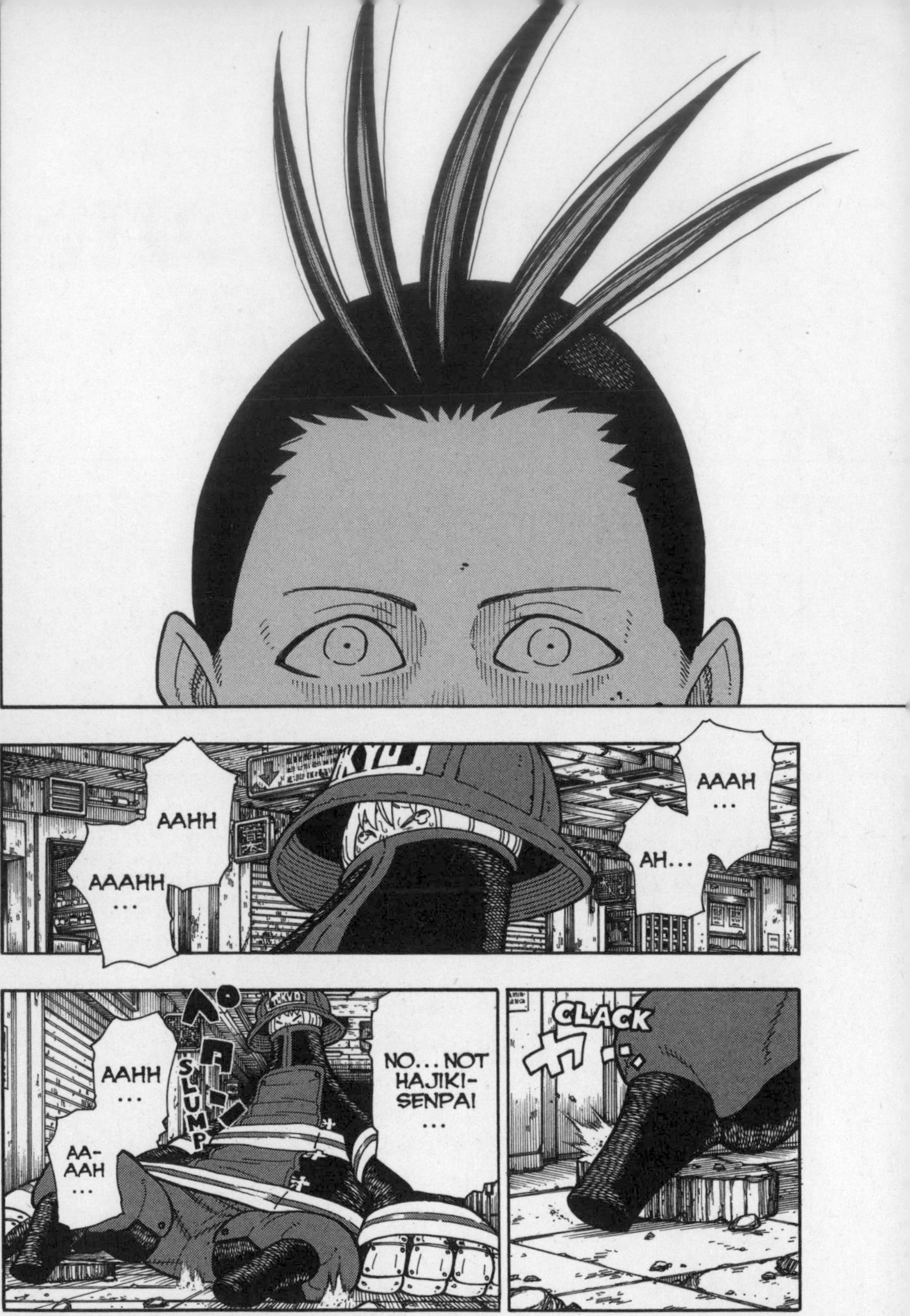
AAAH . . .
AH . . .
AAHH
AAAAHH . . .
CLACK
NO . . . NOT HAJIKI-SENPAI . . .
SLUMP
AAHH . . .
AA-AAH . . .

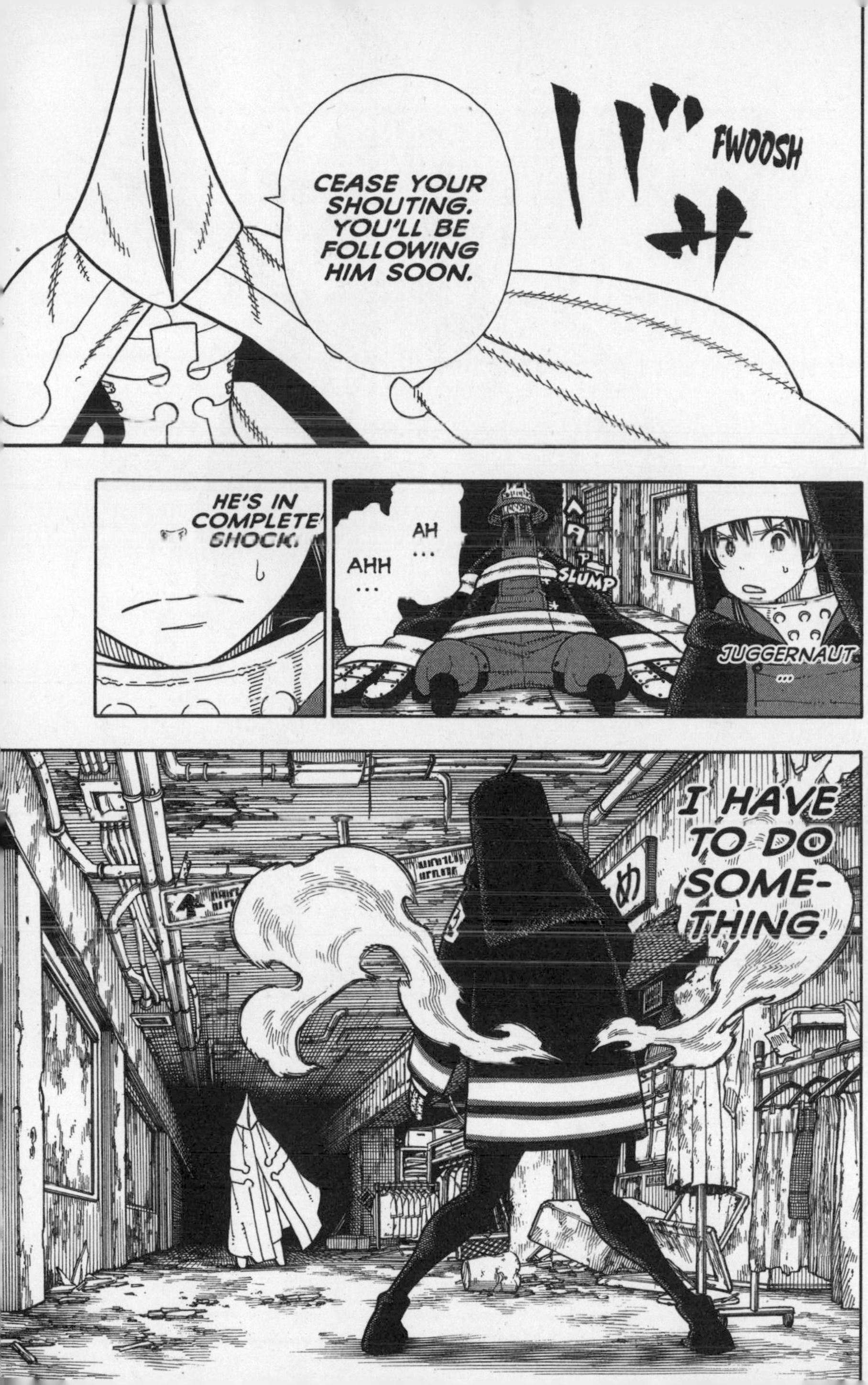
FWOOSH
CEASE YOUR SHOUTING. YOU'LL BE FOLLOWING HIM SOON.
JUGGERNAUT ...
AH ...
AHH ...
SLUMP
HE'S IN COMPLETE SHOCK.
I HAVE TO DO SOME-THING.

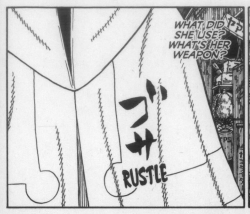

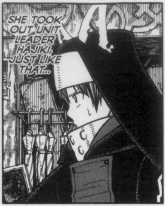

SHE TOOK OUT UNIT LEADER HAJIKI, JUST LIKE THAT...
WHAT DID SHE USE? WHAT'S HER WEAPON?
RUSTLE
IF UNIT LEADER HAJIKI COULDN'T DODGE HER ATTACK, EVEN WITH HIS INFRARED EYES...
THEN THERE'S NO WAY I CAN DODGE IT.
BUT IF THE ATTACK IS MADE OF FLAME,
THEN I HAVE HIGH FIRE RESISTANCE. I MIGHT BE ABLE TO SURVIVE IT.

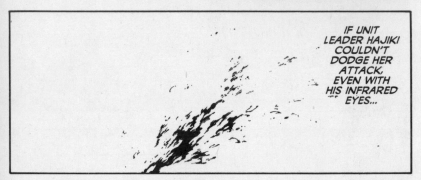

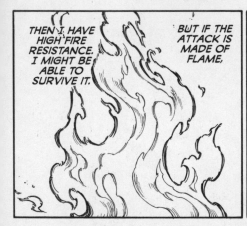

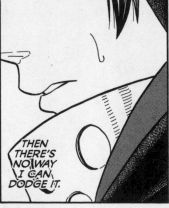

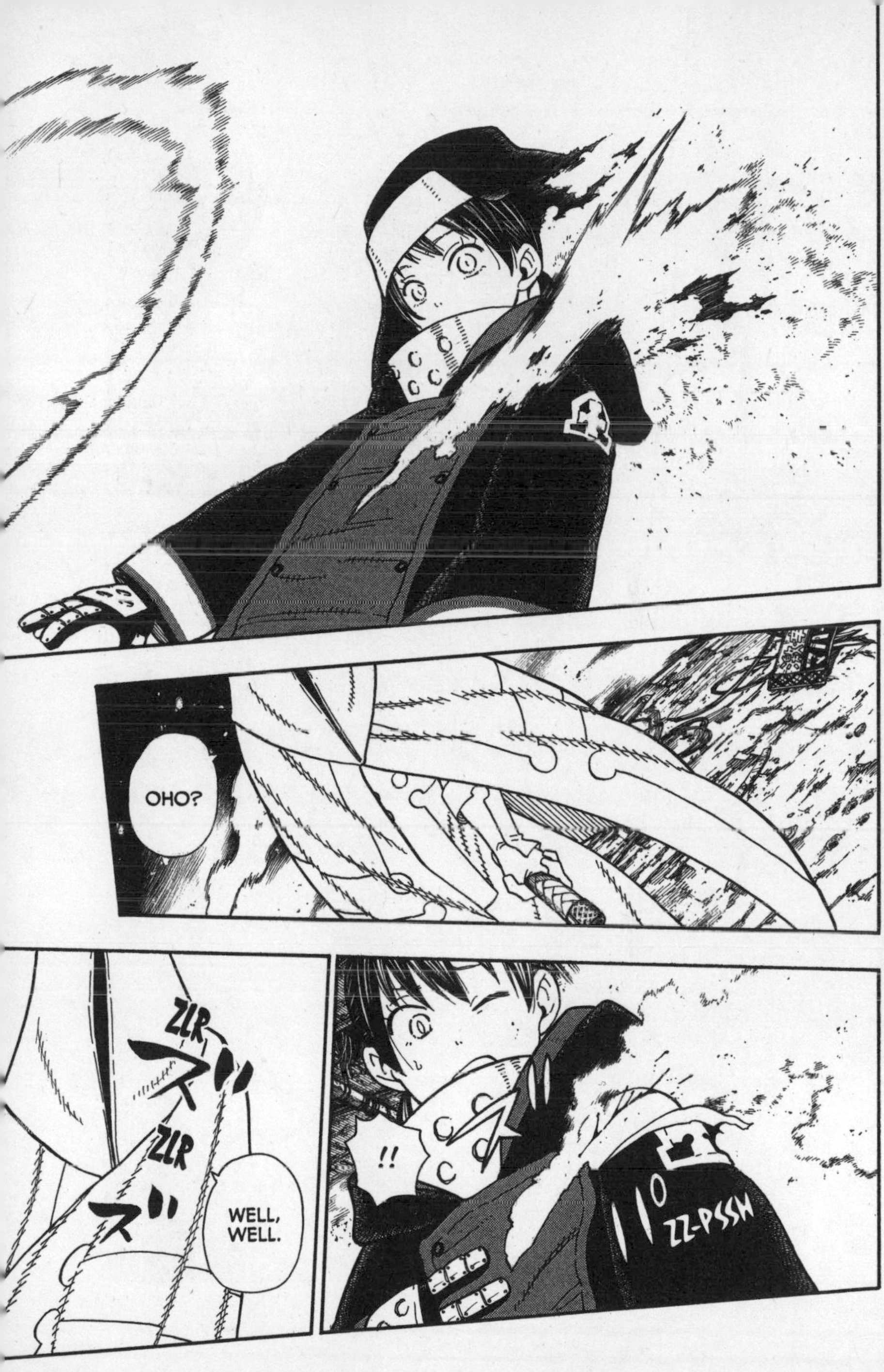
OHO?
!!
ZZ-PSSH
ZZR
ZZR
WELL, WELL.

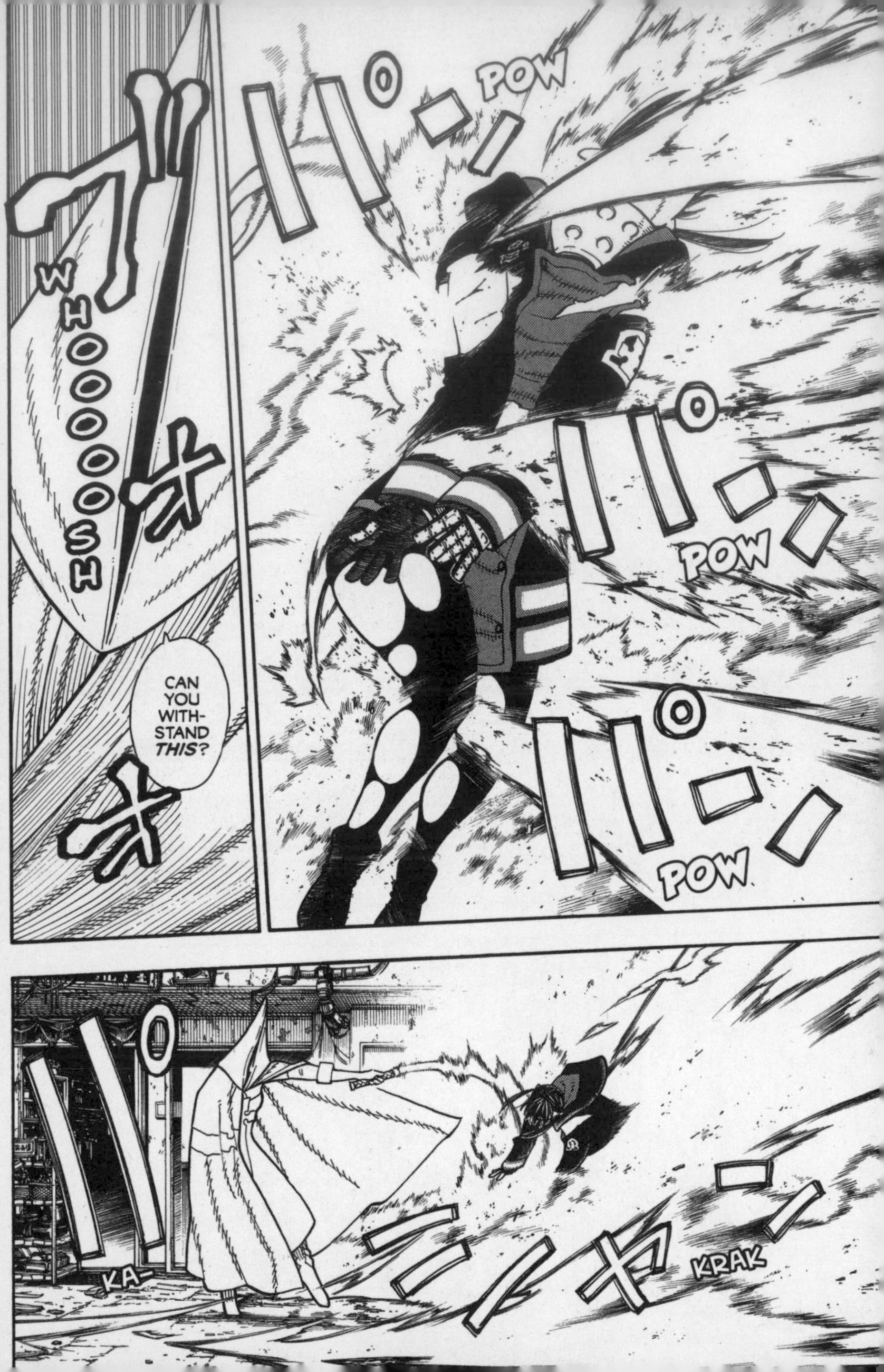
POW
POW
POW
WHOOOOOOSH
CAN YOU WITHSTAND *THIS*?
KRAK
KA-

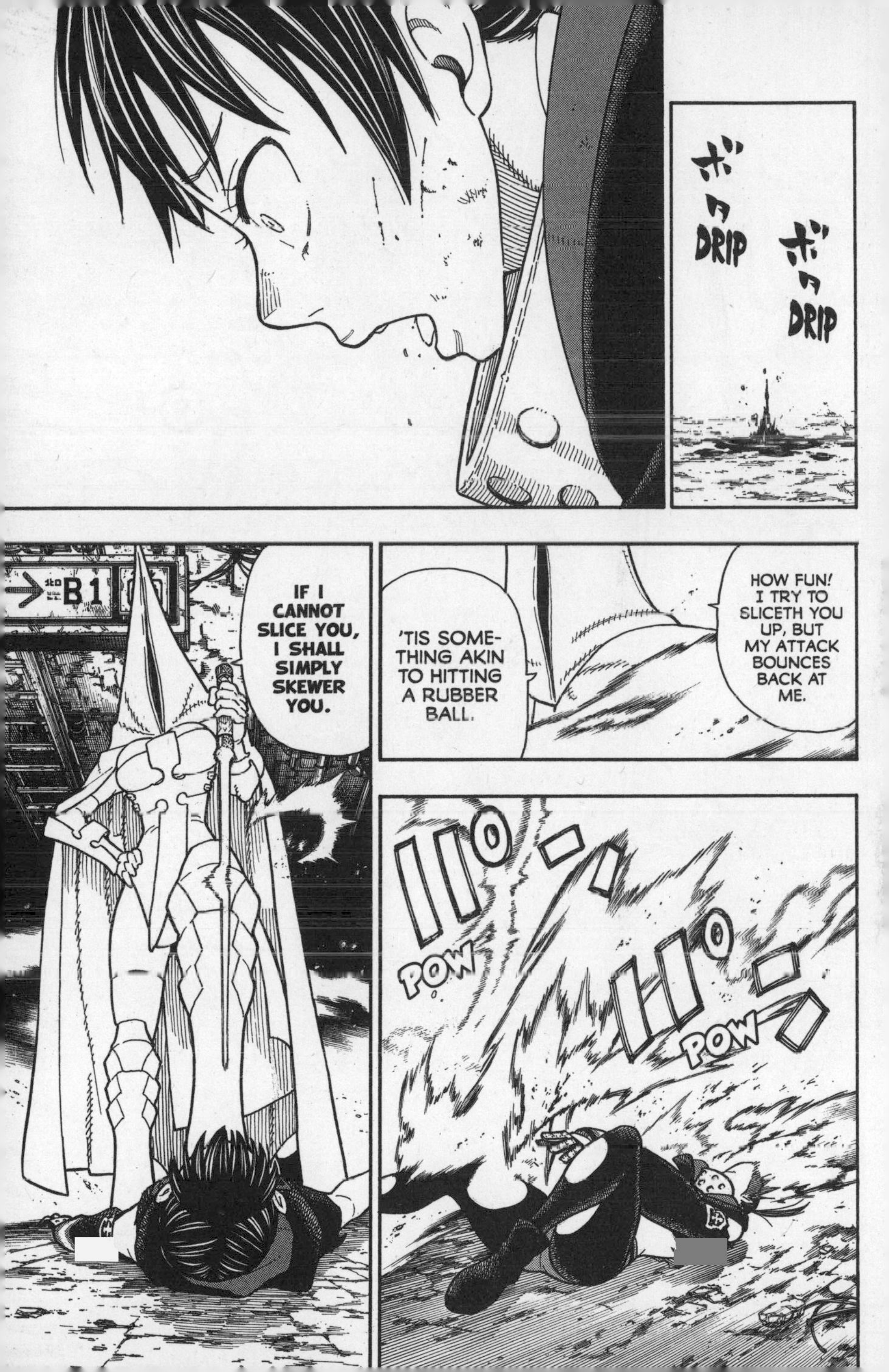

ボワ
DRIP
ボワ
DRIP
HOW FUN! I TRY TO SLICETH YOU UP, BUT MY ATTACK BOUNCES BACK AT ME.
'TIS SOMETHING AKIN TO HITTING A RUBBER BALL.
POW
POW
B1
IF I CANNOT SLICE YOU, I SHALL SIMPLY SKEWER YOU.

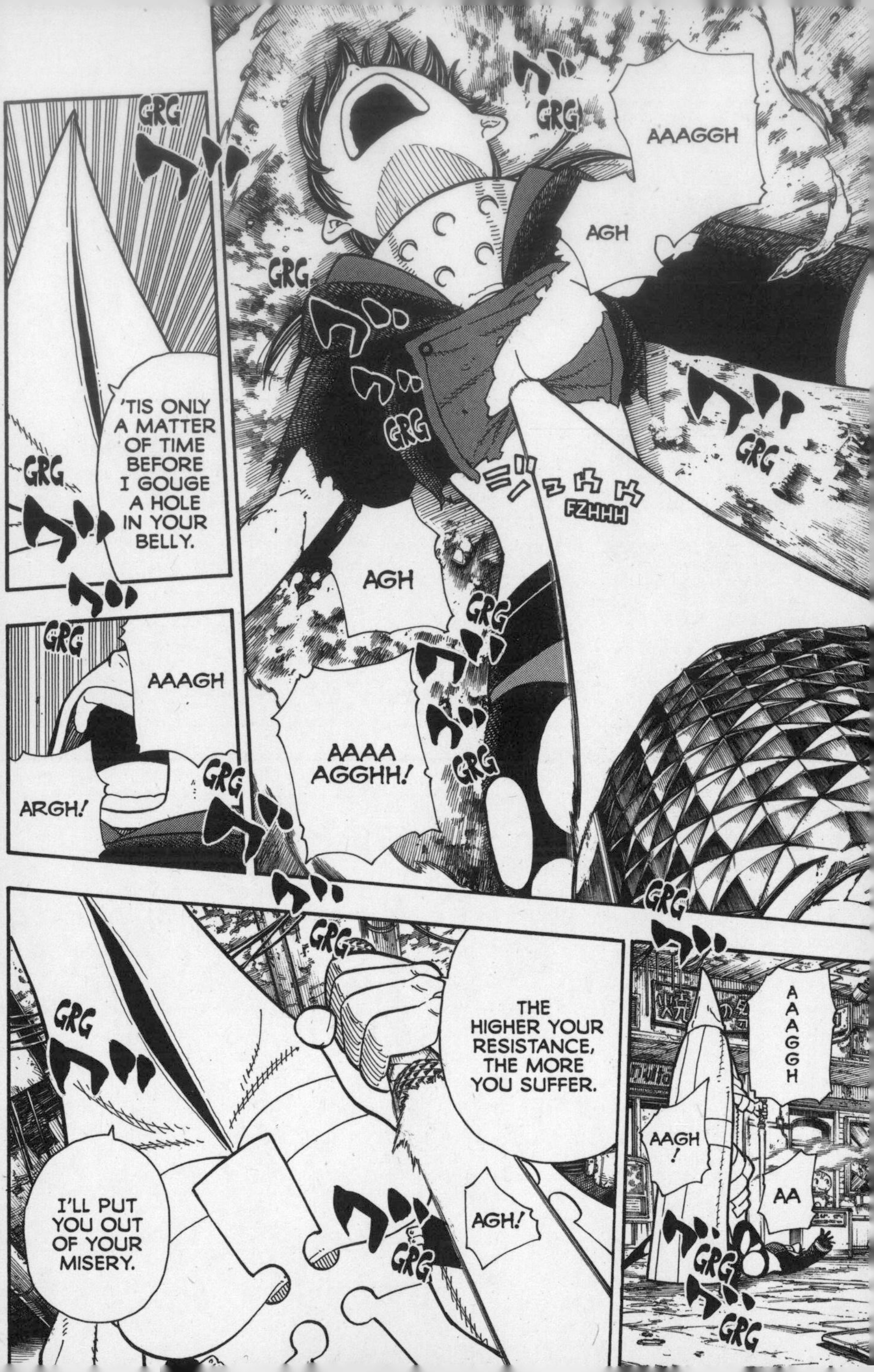
GRG
AAAGGH
AGH
GRG
FZHHH
GRG
GRG
AGH
GRG
GRG
AAAA AGGHH!
GRG
'TIS ONLY A MATTER OF TIME BEFORE I GOUGE A HOLE IN YOUR BELLY.
GRG
GRG
AAAGH
GRG
ARGH!
GRG
AAAGGH
AAGH!
AA
GRG
GRG
GRG
THE HIGHER YOUR RESISTANCE, THE MORE YOU SUFFER.
AGH!
GRG
GRG
I'LL PUT YOU OUT OF YOUR MISERY.

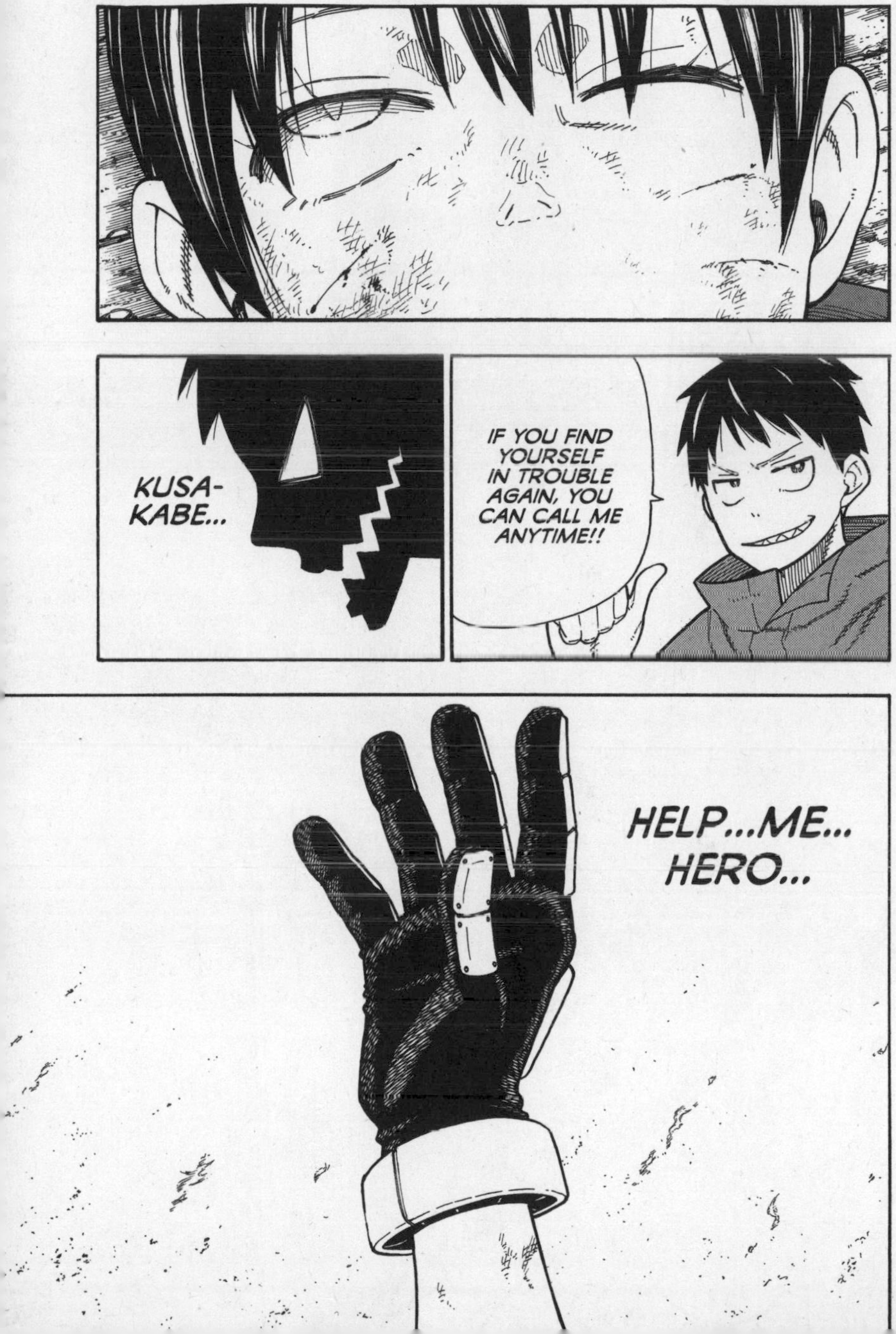
IF YOU FIND YOURSELF IN TROUBLE AGAIN, YOU CAN CALL ME ANYTIME!!
KUSA-KABE...
HELP...ME... HERO...

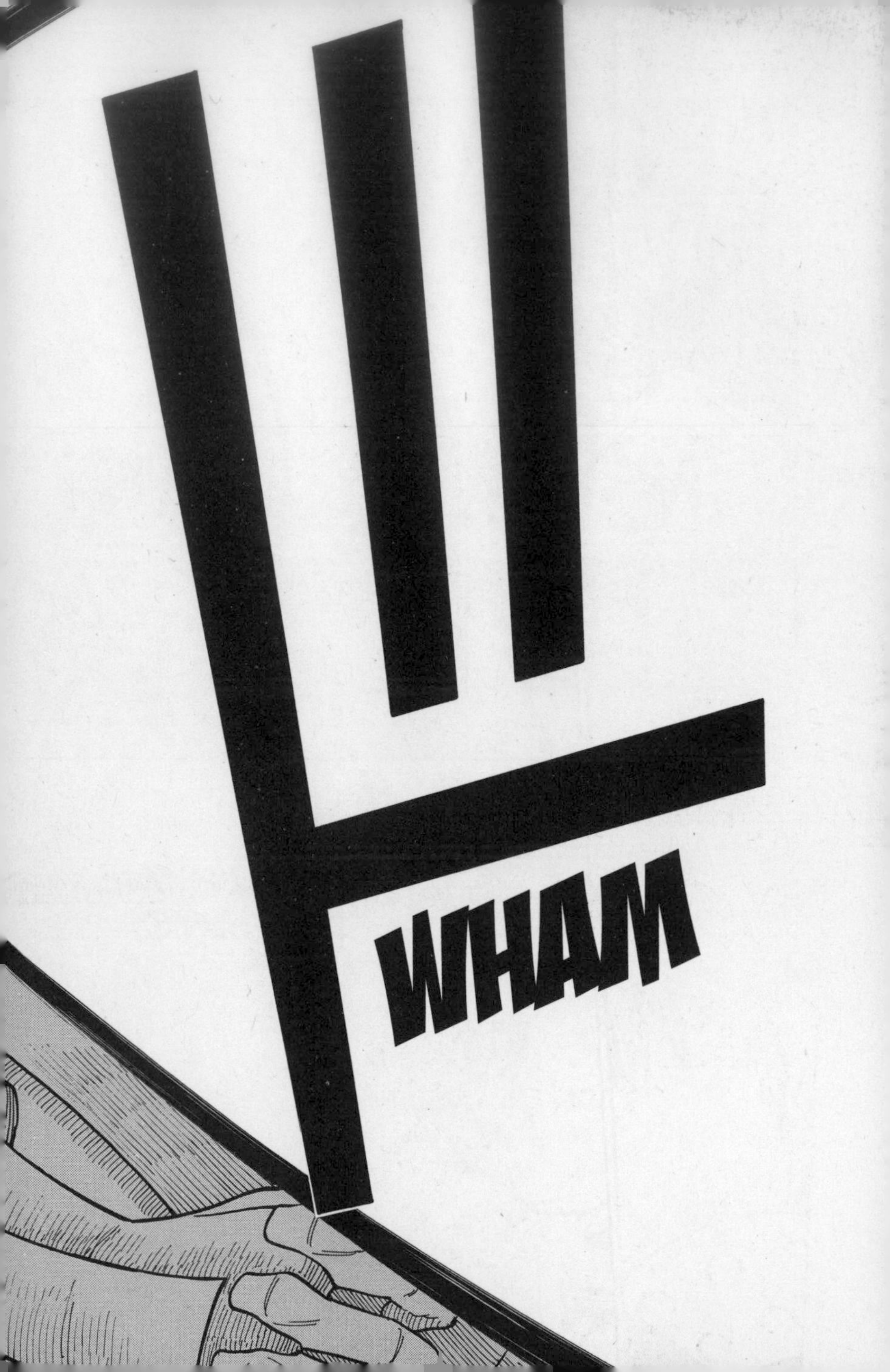
WHAM

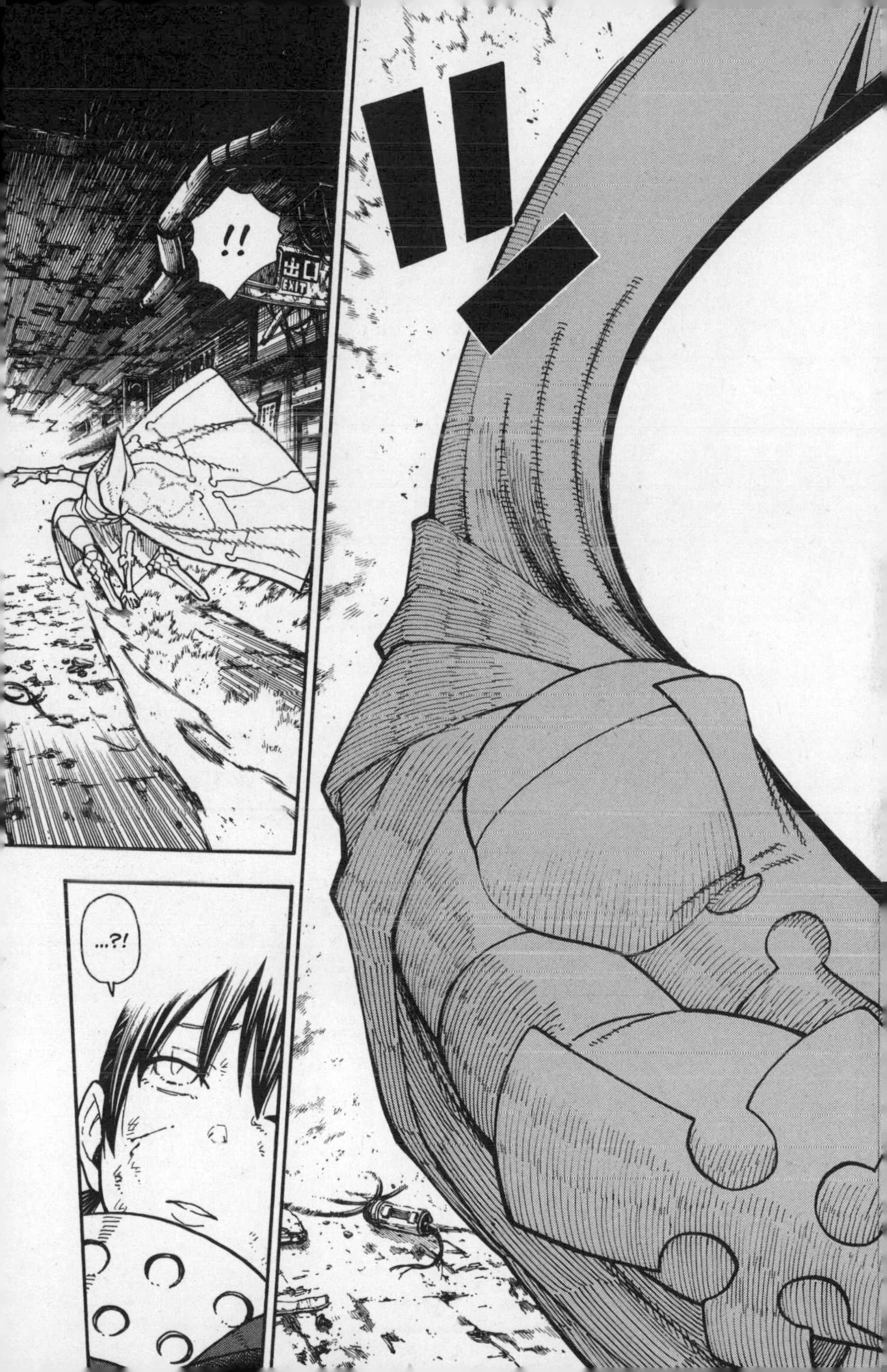
!!
出口
EXIT
...?!

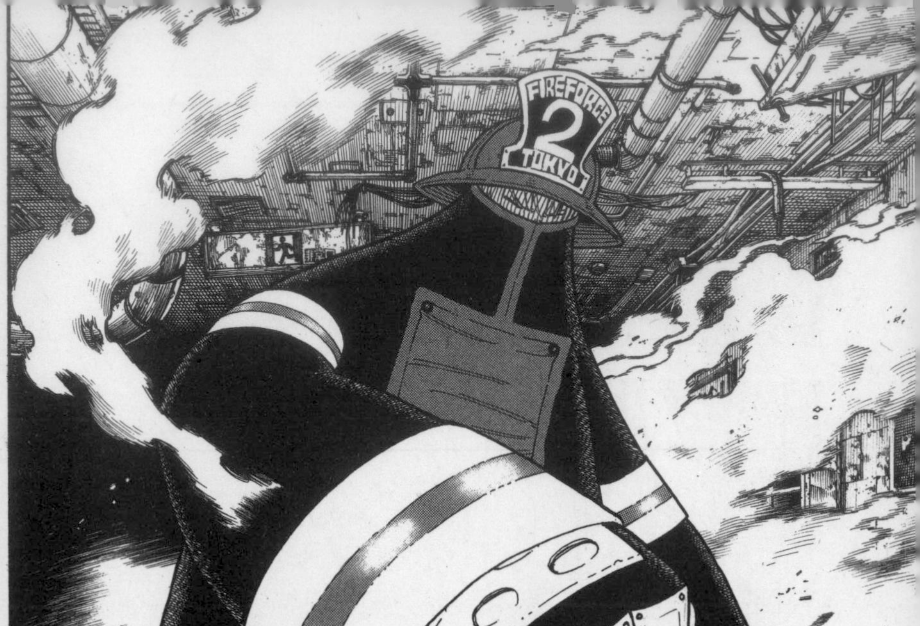
FIREFORCE
2
TOKYO
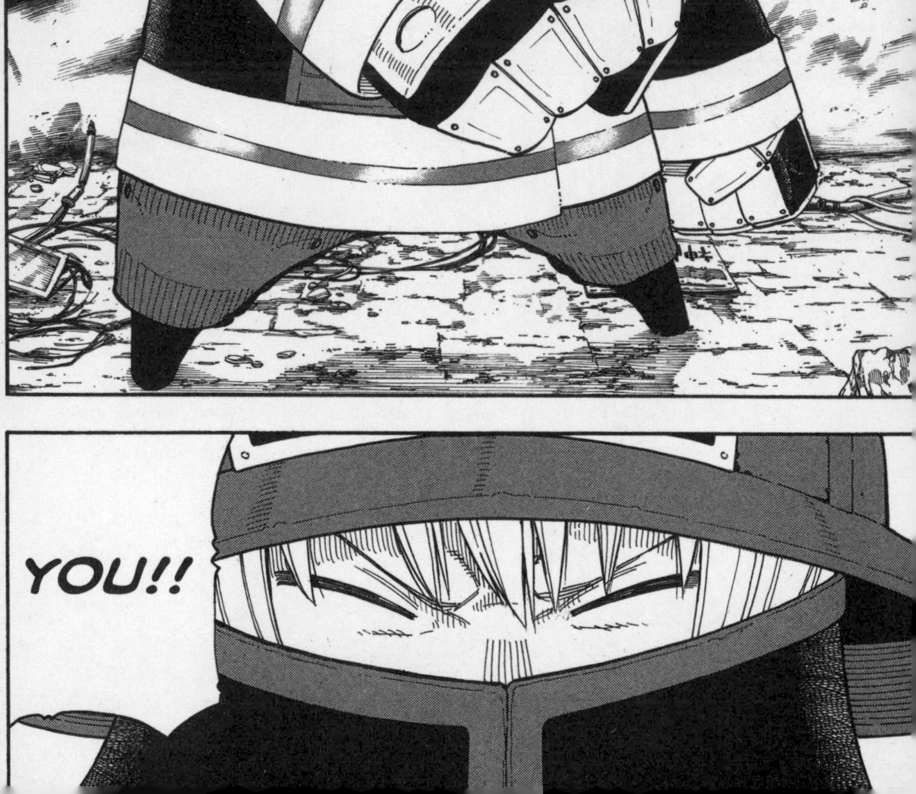
YOU!!

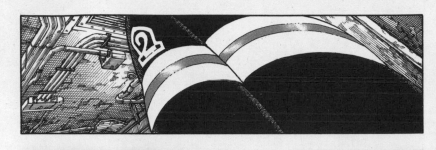

TUG...

THAT'S A 2....

FWOOSH

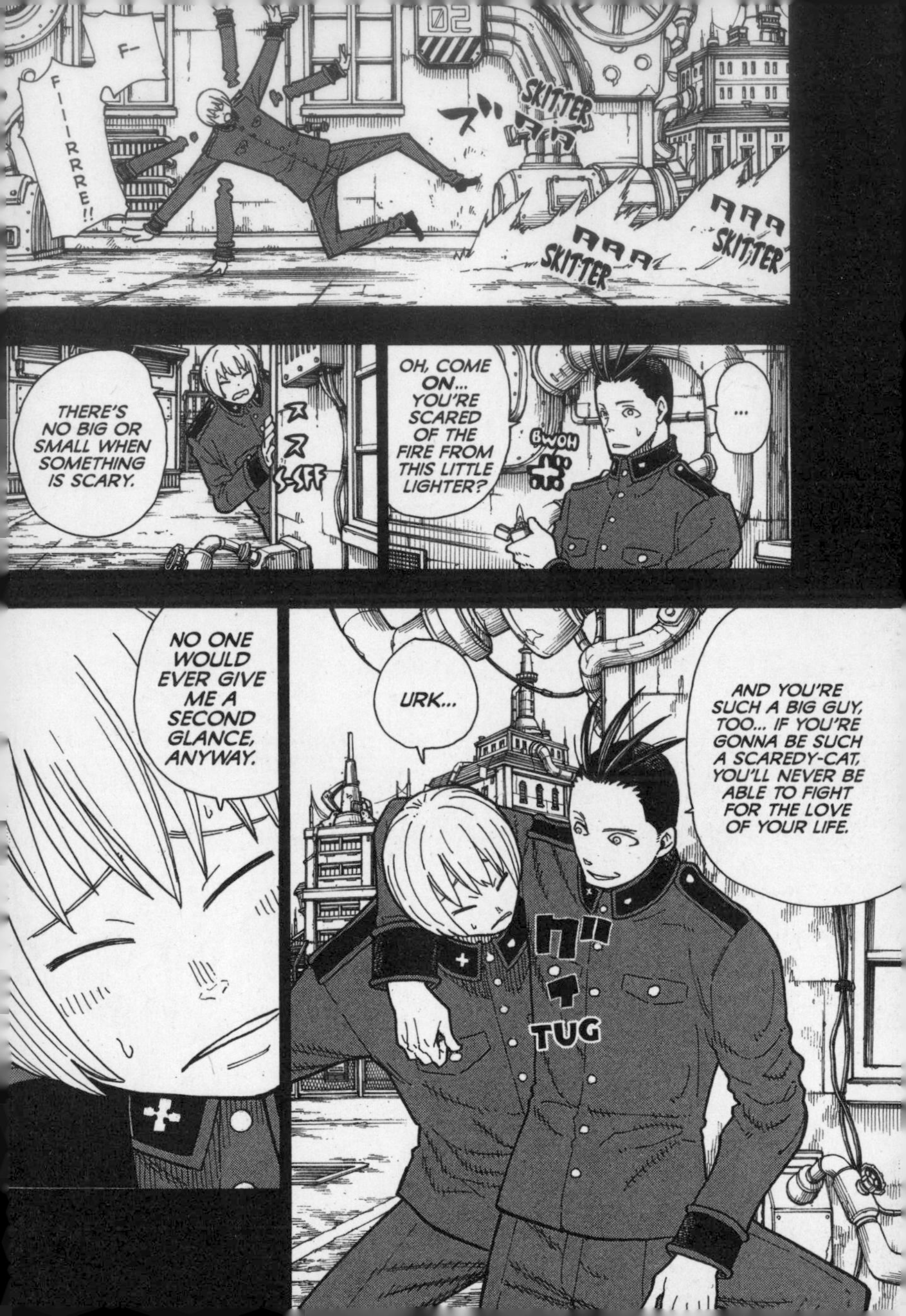
SKITTER
SKITTER
SKITTER
F-
FIIIRRRE!!
...
OH, COME ON... YOU'RE SCARED OF THE FIRE FROM THIS LITTLE LIGHTER?
BWOH
S-SFF
THERE'S NO BIG OR SMALL WHEN SOMETHING IS SCARY.
AND YOU'RE SUCH A BIG GUY, TOO... IF YOU'RE GONNA BE SUCH A SCAREDY-CAT, YOU'LL NEVER BE ABLE TO FIGHT FOR THE LOVE OF YOUR LIFE.
URK...
TUG
NO ONE WOULD EVER GIVE ME A SECOND GLANCE, ANYWAY.

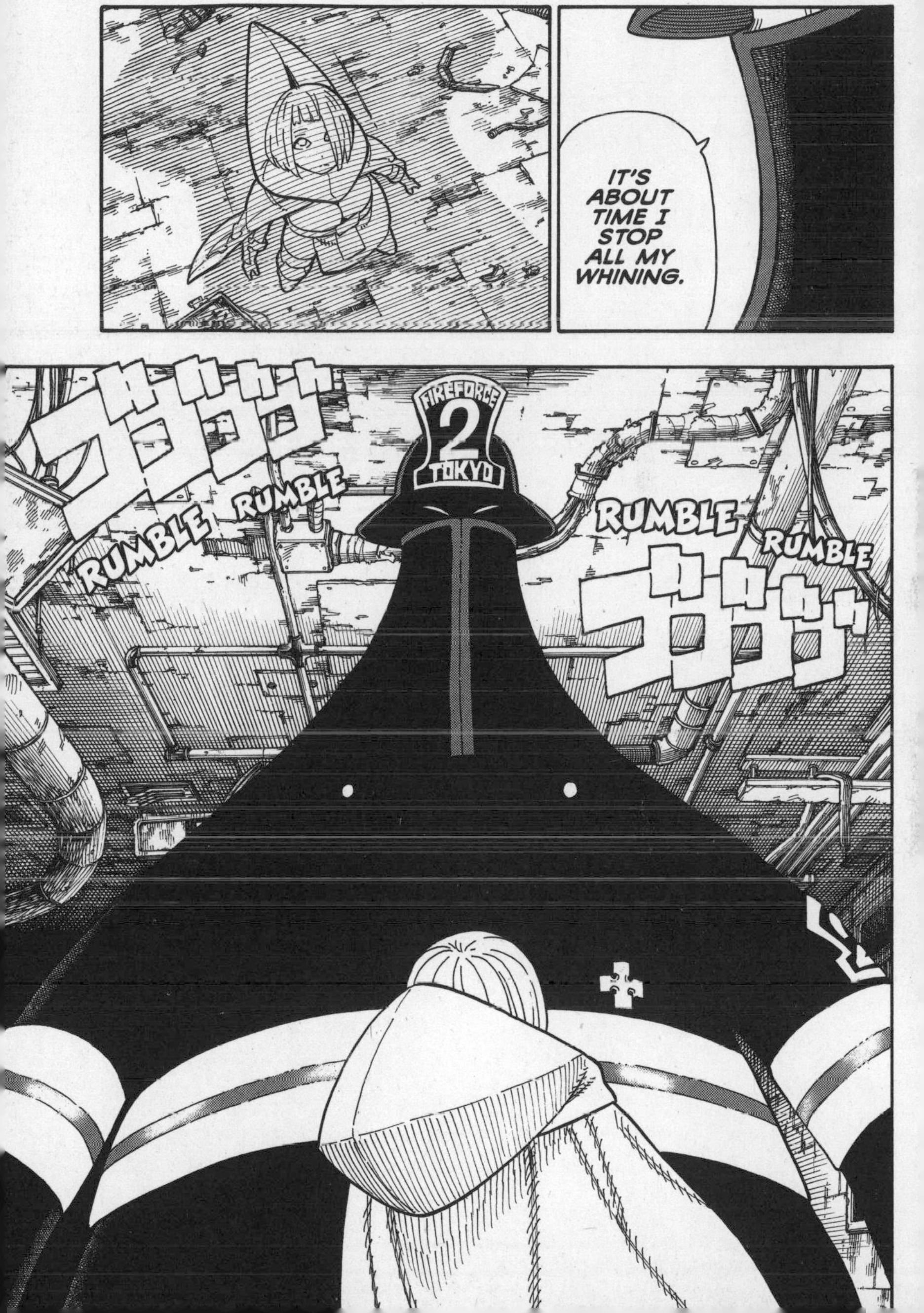
IT'S ABOUT TIME I STOP ALL MY WHINING.
FIREFORCE
2
TOKYO
RUMBLE RUMBLE
RUMBLE RUMBLE

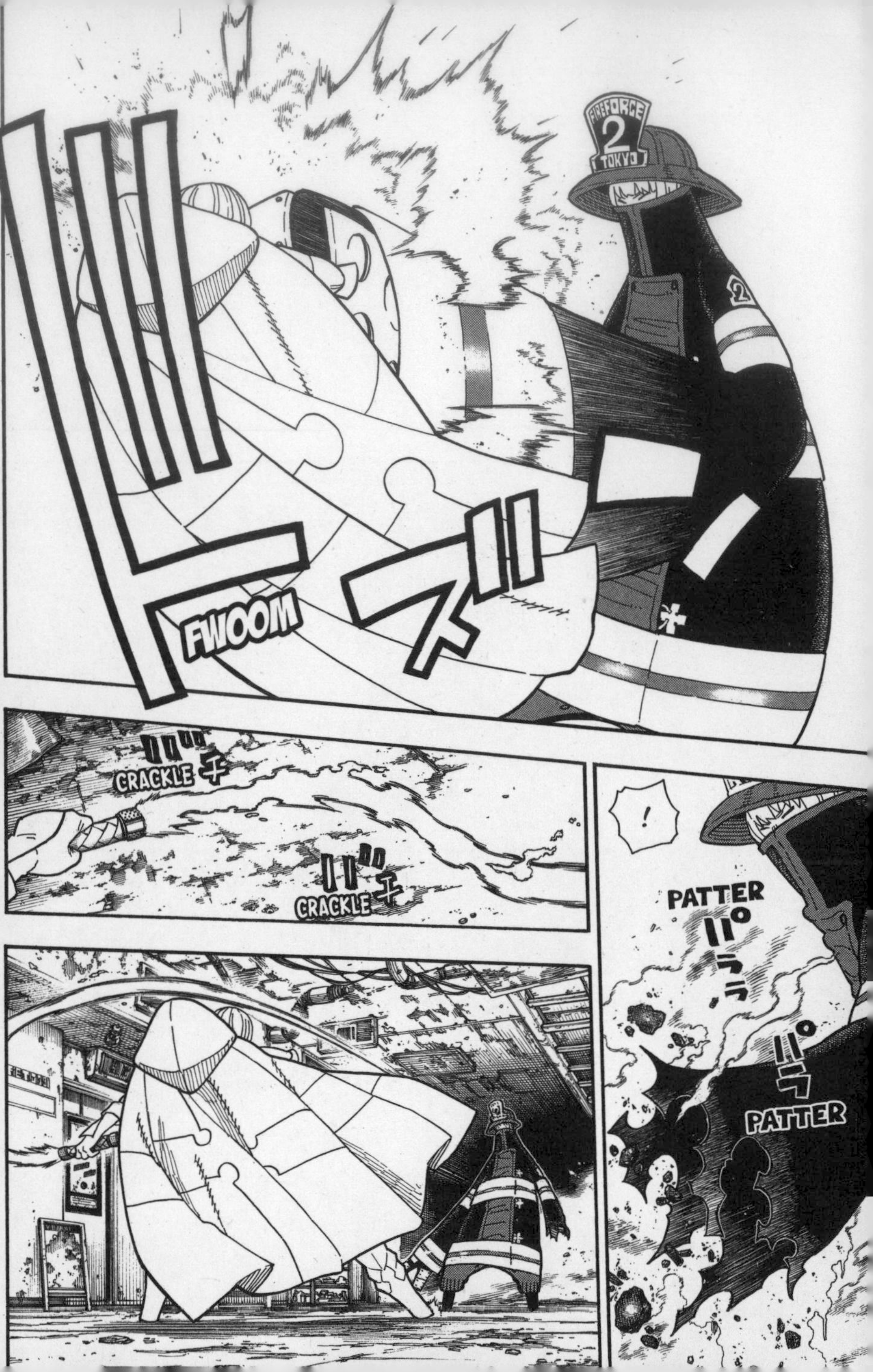
FWOOM
!
PATTER
PATTER
CRACKLE
CRACKLE

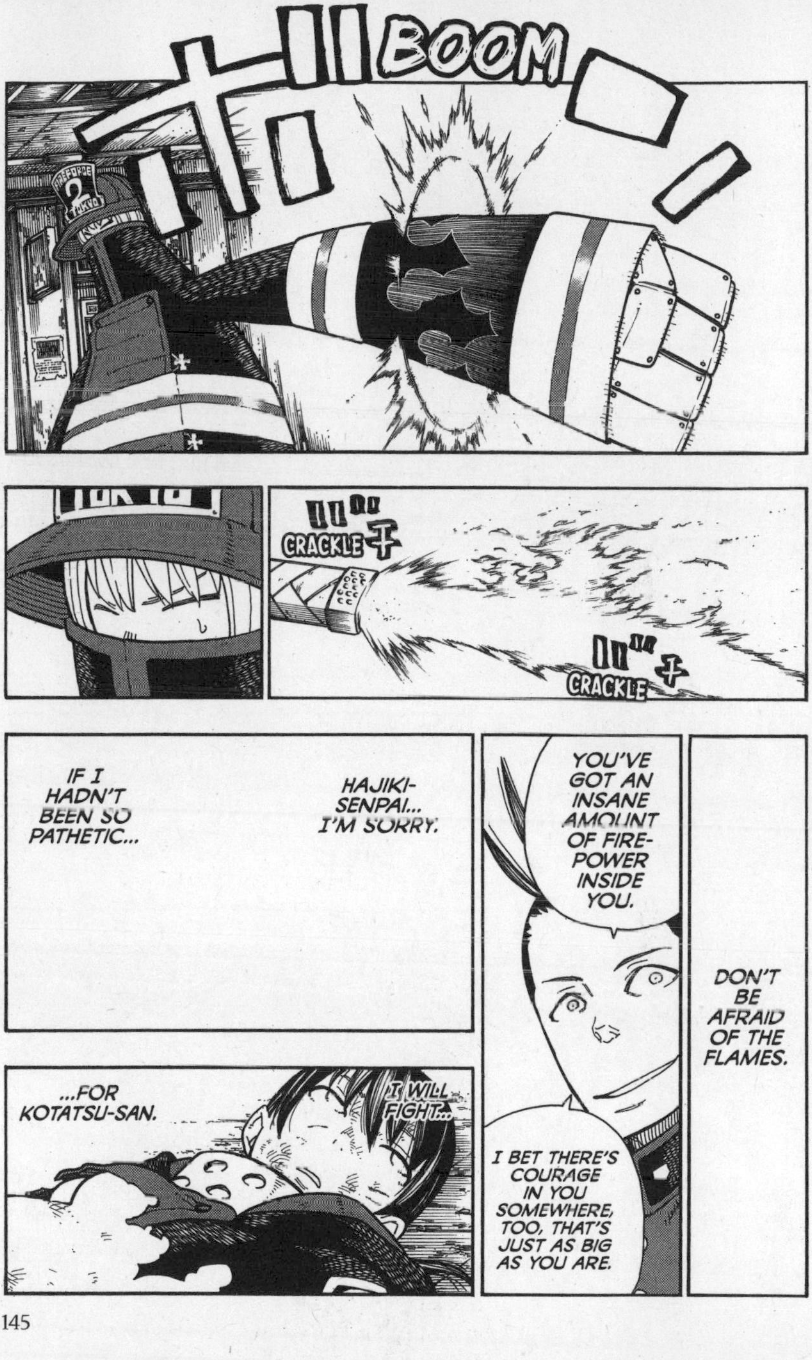
BOOM
CRACKLE
CRACKLE
DON'T BE AFRAID OF THE FLAMES.
YOU'VE GOT AN INSANE AMOUNT OF FIRE-POWER INSIDE YOU.
I BET THERE'S COURAGE IN YOU SOMEWHERE, TOO, THAT'S JUST AS BIG AS YOU ARE.
HAJIKI-SENPAI... I'M SORRY.
IF I HADN'T BEEN SO PATHETIC...
I WILL FIGHT...
...FOR KOTATSU-SAN.

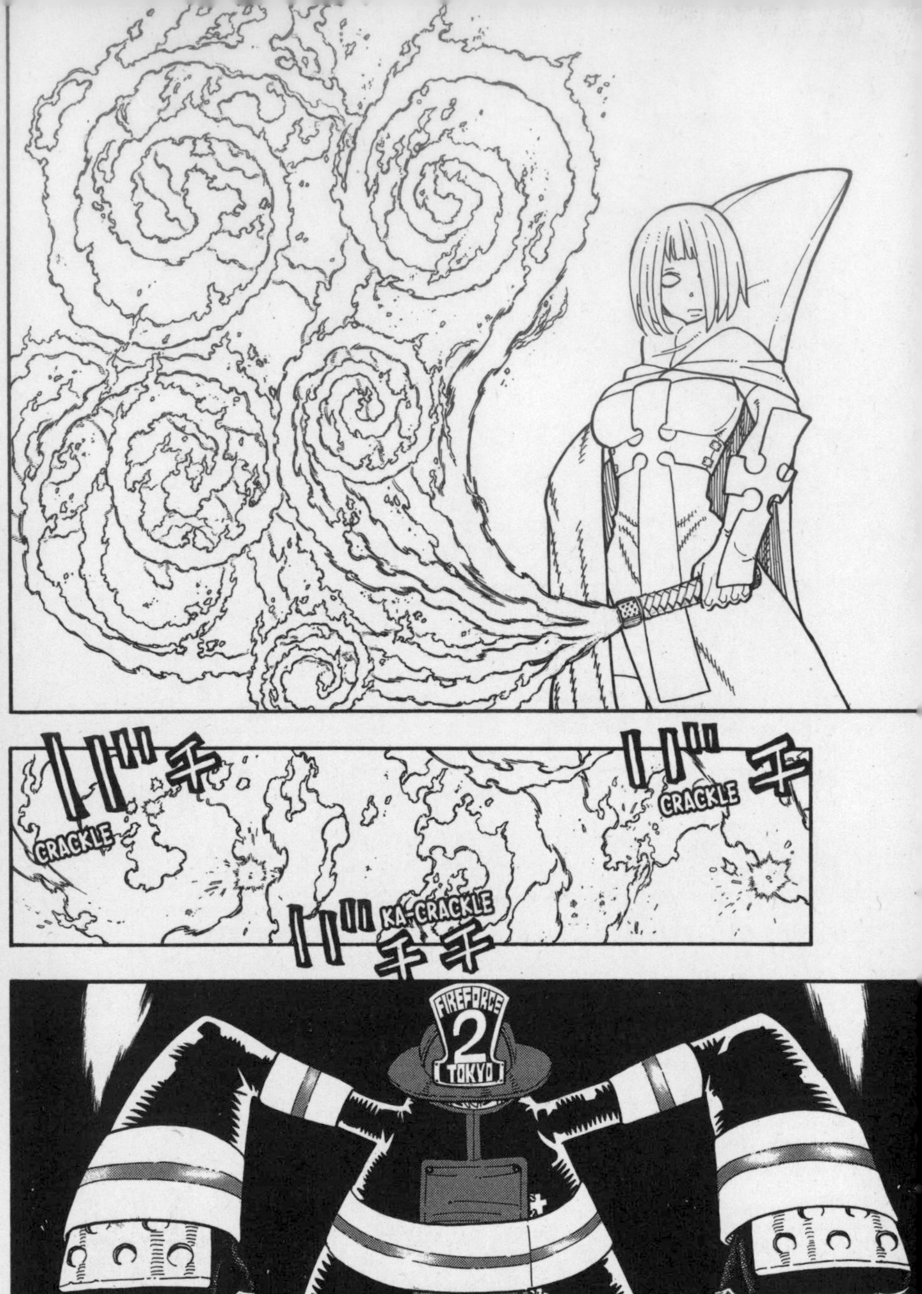
CRACKLE
CRACKLE
KA-CRACKLE
FIREFORCE
2
TOKYO

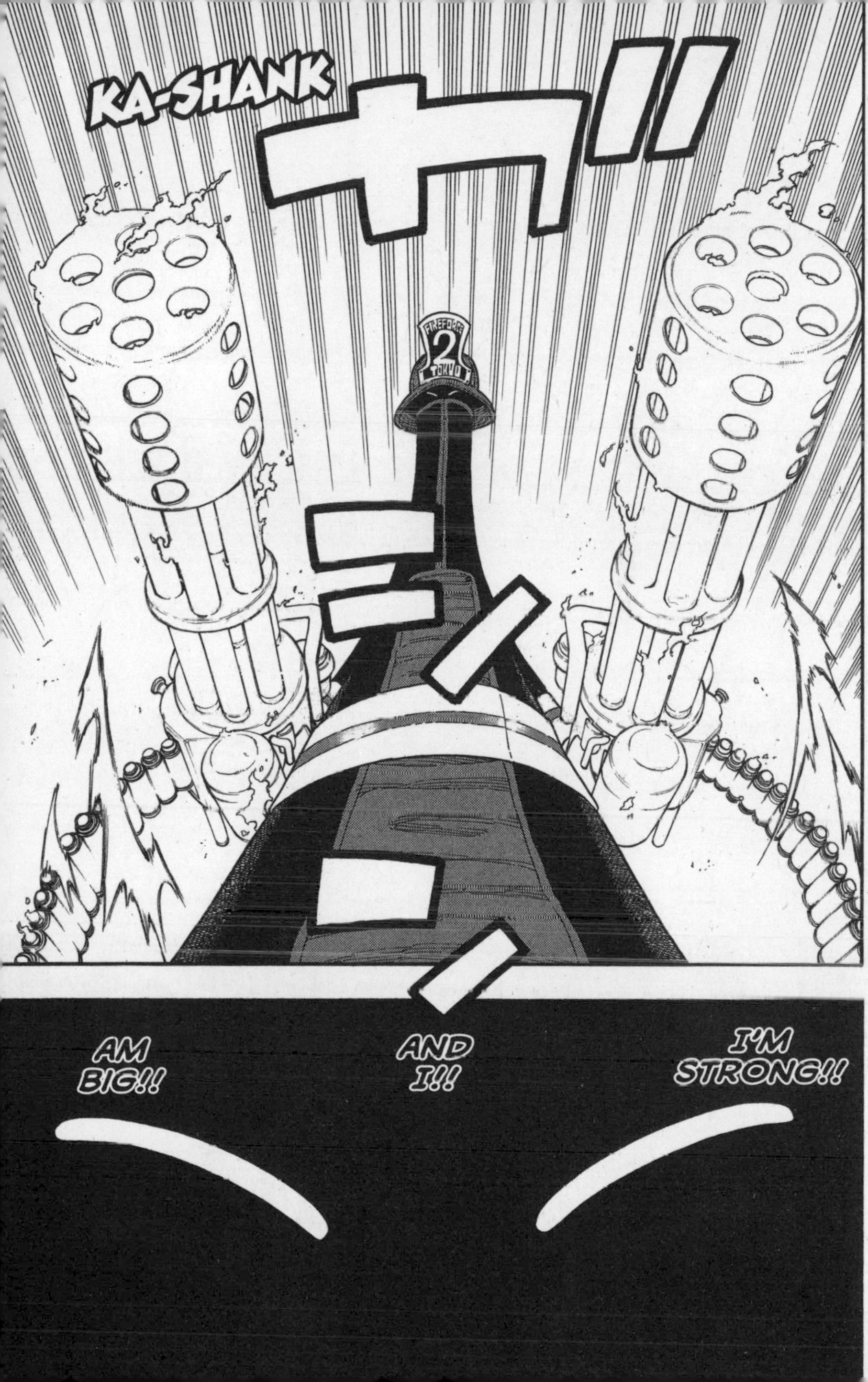
KA-SHANK
I'M STRONG!!
AND I!!
AM BIG!!

FIRE FORCE

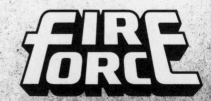

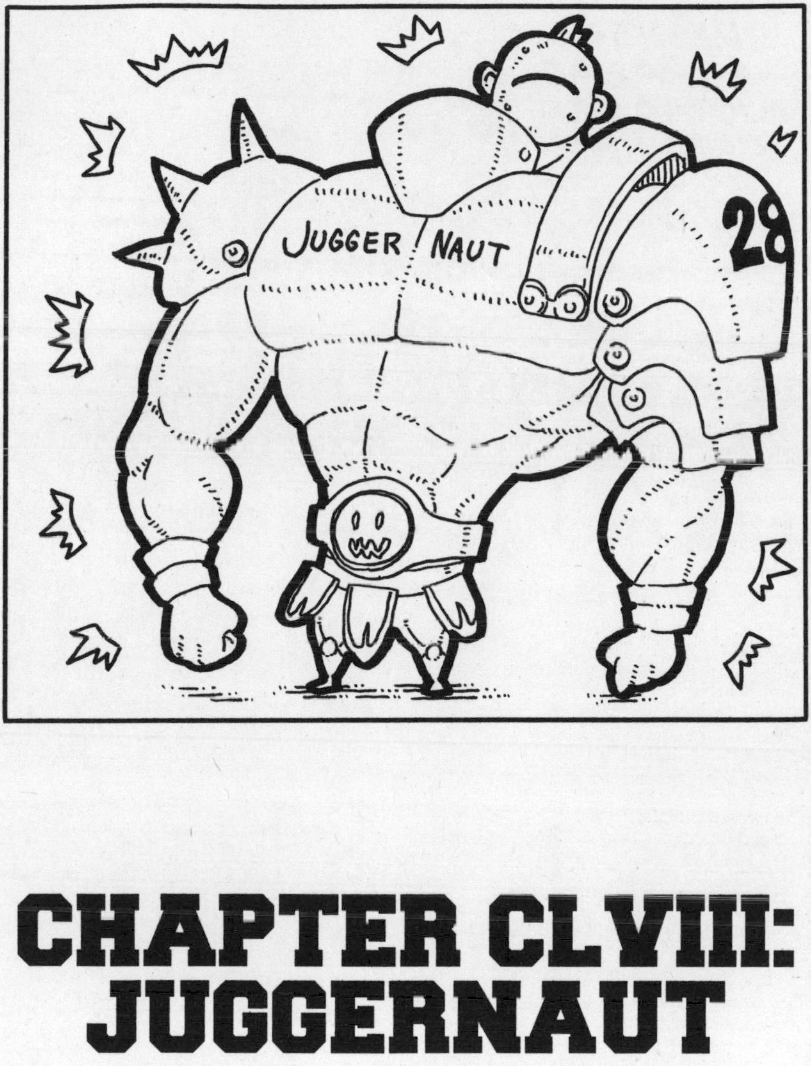
JUGGER NAUT
28

CHAPTER CLVIII: JUGGERNAUT

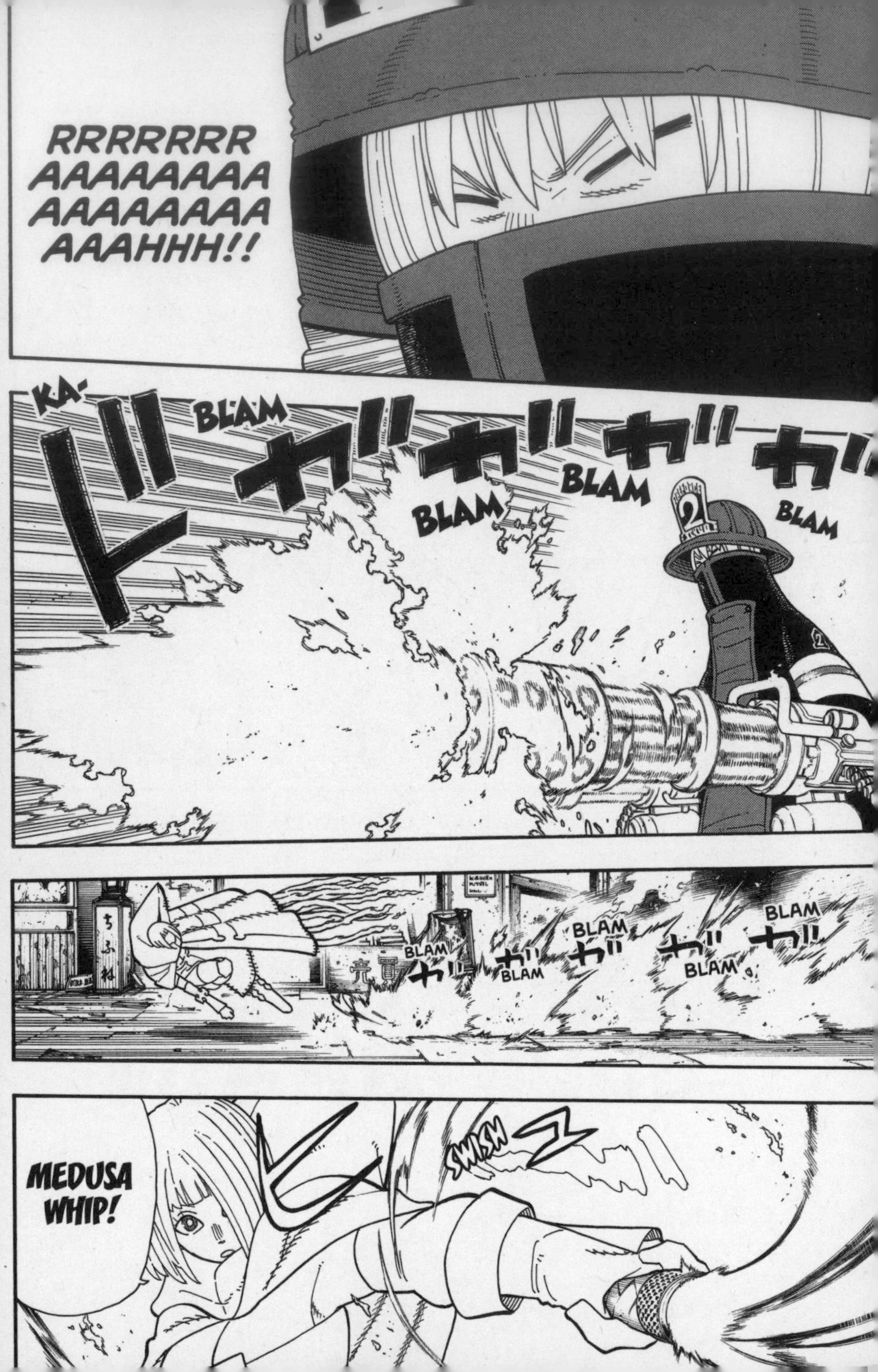
RRRRRRR
AAAAAAAA
AAAAAAAA
AAAHHH!!
BLAM
BLAM
BLAM
BLAM
KA-
BLAM
BLAM
BLAM
BLAM
BLAM
SWISH
MEDUSA WHIP!

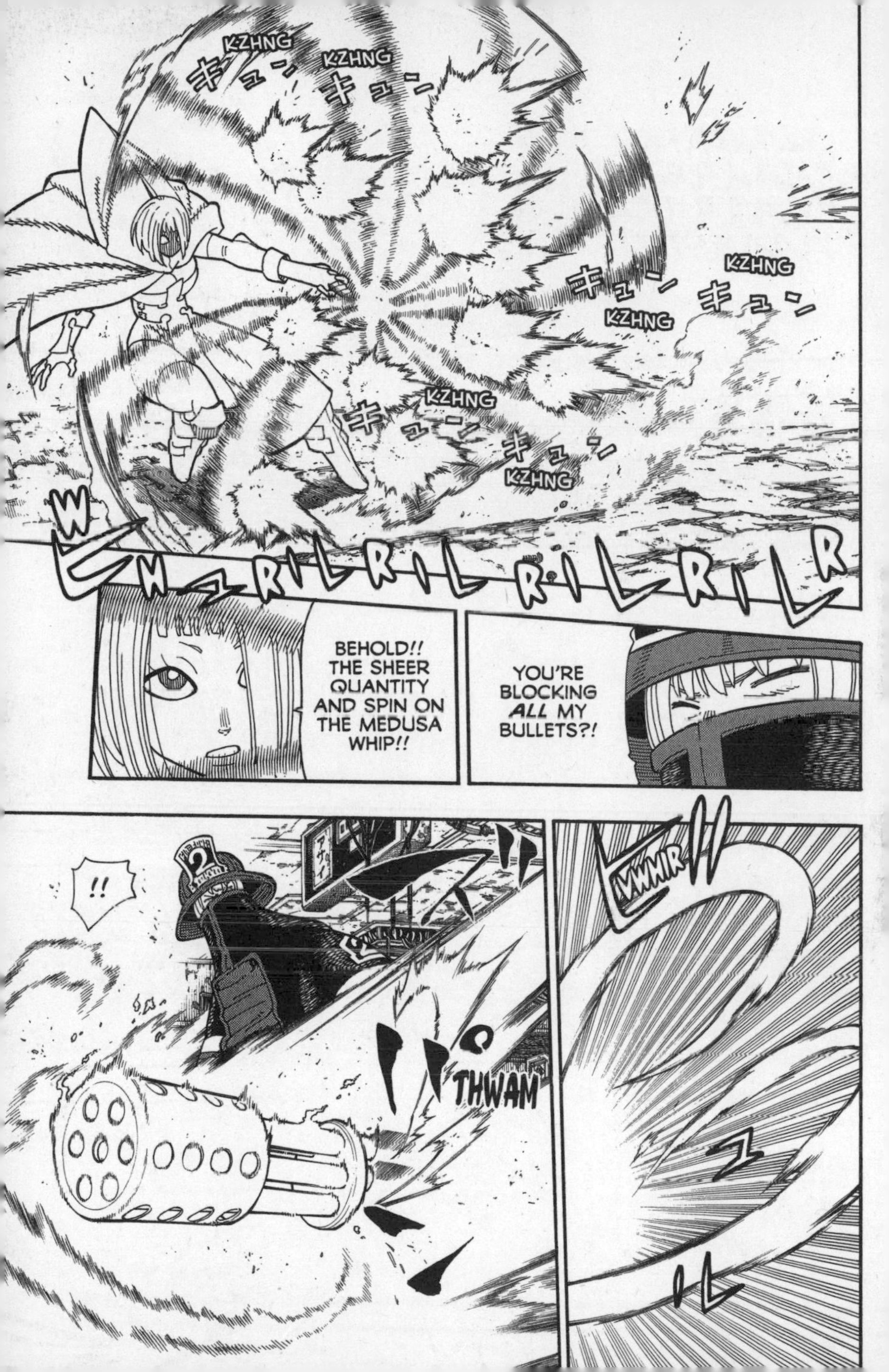
KZHNG
KZHNG
KZHNG
KZHNG
KZHNG
KZHNG
YOU'RE BLOCKING *ALL* MY BULLETS?!
BEHOLD!! THE SHEER QUANTITY AND SPIN ON THE MEDUSA WHIP!!
VWHIR
!!
THWAM

I IRON-WALL MYSELF BY TURNING MY WHIP TO DEFENSE,

AND AT THE SAME TIME, THE QUANTITY RAGETH VIOLENTLY AS I ATTACK.

BE-HOLD.

THE MEDUSA WHIP.

SHOONK

OKAY, THEN!!

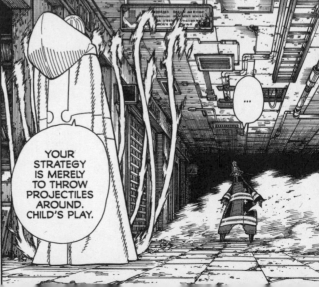

YOUR STRATEGY IS MERELY TO THROW PROJECTILES AROUND. CHILD'S PLAY.

...

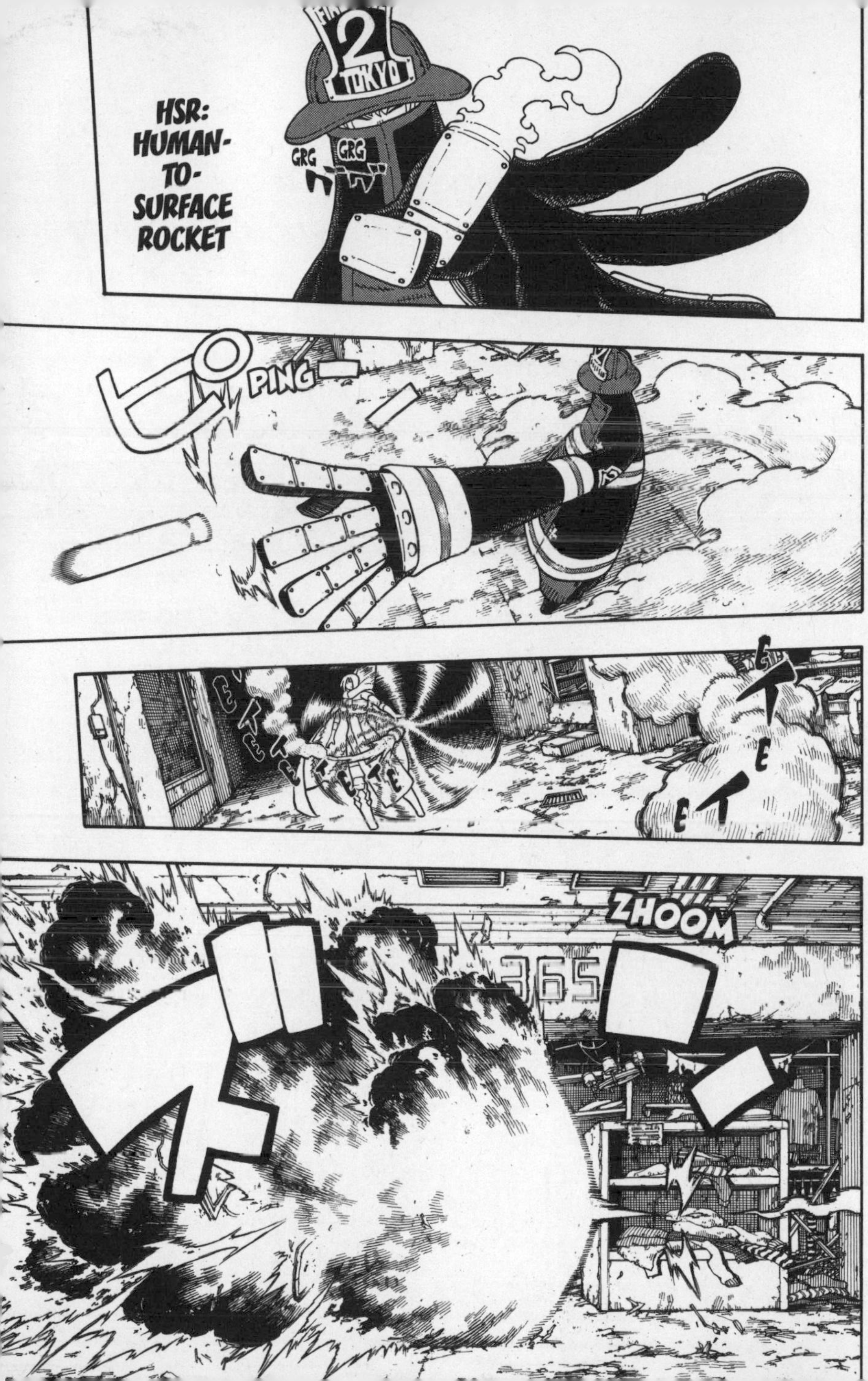
HSR: HUMAN-TO-SURFACE ROCKET
GRG
GRG
PING
ZHOOM

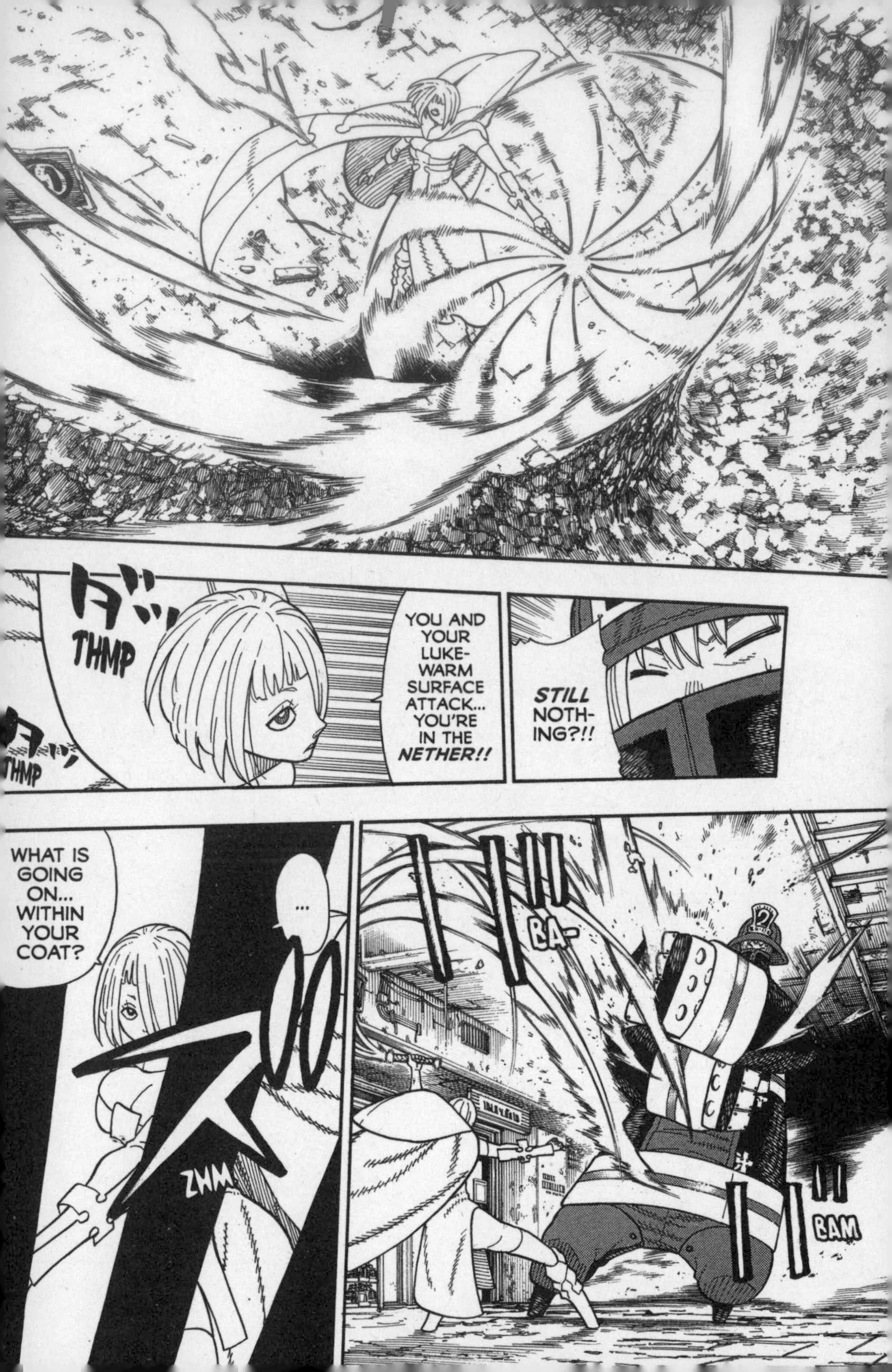

STILL NOTHING?!!
THMP
THMP
YOU AND YOUR LUKEWARM SURFACE ATTACK... YOU'RE IN THE NETHER!!
BA-
BAM
...
WHAT IS GOING ON... WITHIN YOUR COAT?
ZHM

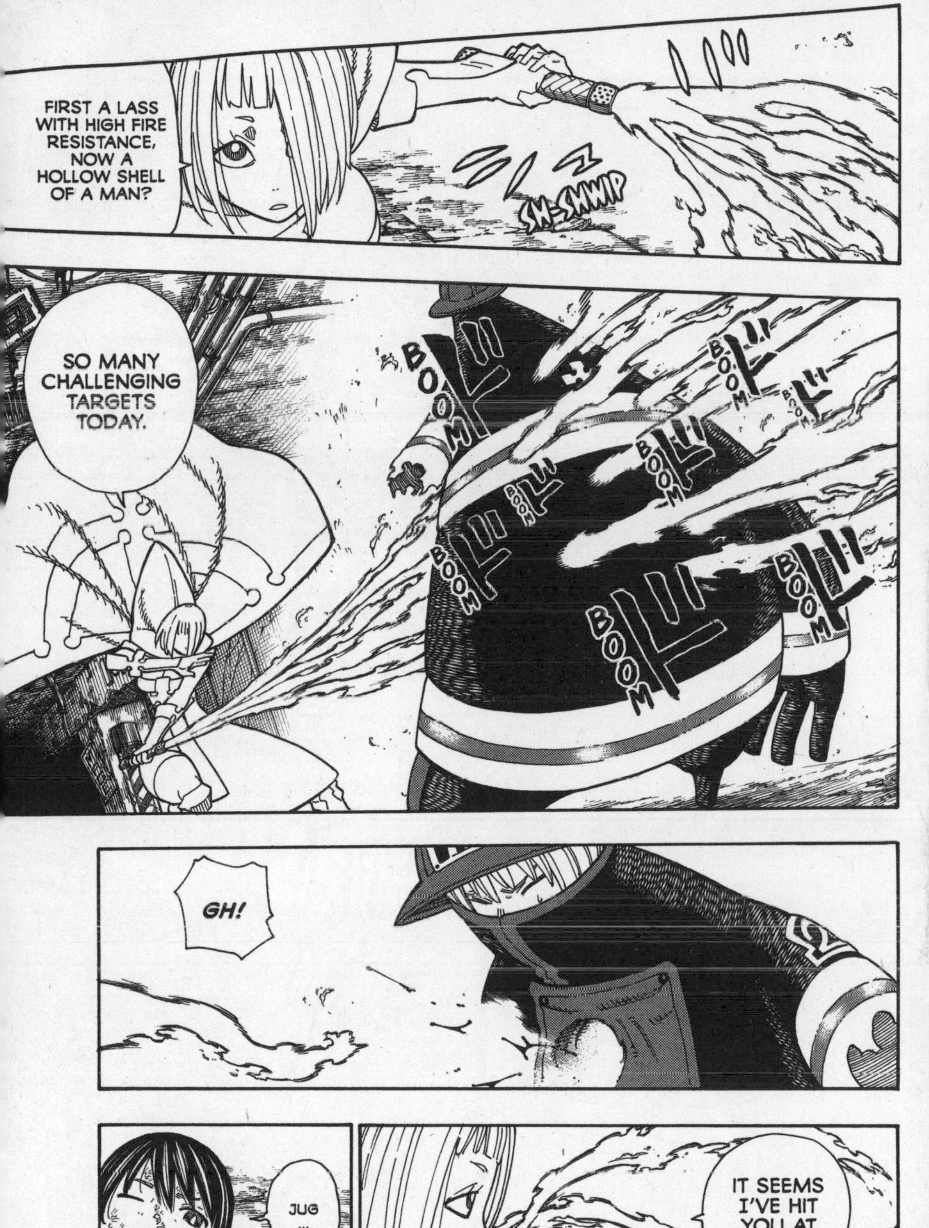
FIRST A LASS WITH HIGH FIRE RESISTANCE, NOW A HOLLOW SHELL OF A MAN?
SH-SHWIP
SO MANY CHALLENGING TARGETS TODAY.
BOOM
BOOM
BOOM
BOOM
BOOM
BOOM
BOOM
BOOM
GH!
IT SEEMS I'VE HIT YOU AT LAST.
JUG ...

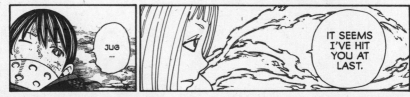

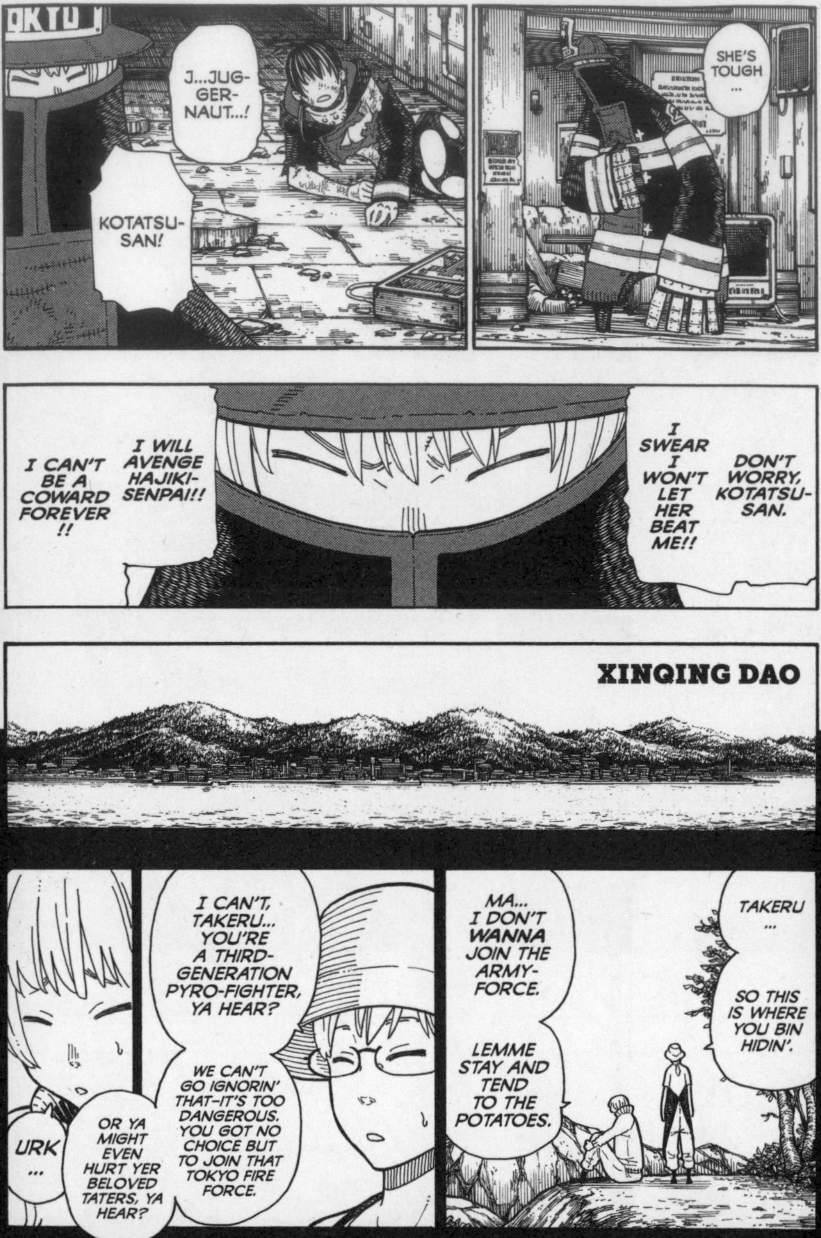
SHE'S TOUGH ...
J...JUGGERNAUT...!
KOTATSU-SAN!
DON'T WORRY, KOTATSU-SAN.
I SWEAR I WON'T LET HER BEAT ME!!
I WILL AVENGE HAJIKI-SENPAI!!
I CAN'T BE A COWARD FOREVER !!
XINQING DAO
TAKERU ...
SO THIS IS WHERE YOU BIN HIDIN'.
MA... I DON'T WANNA JOIN THE ARMY-FORCE.
LEMME STAY AND TEND TO THE POTATOES.
I CAN'T, TAKERU... YOU'RE A THIRD-GENERATION PYRO-FIGHTER, YA HEAR?
WE CAN'T GO IGNORIN' THAT—IT'S TOO DANGEROUS. YOU GOT NO CHOICE BUT TO JOIN THAT TOKYO FIRE FORCE.
OR YA MIGHT EVEN HURT YER BELOVED TATERS, YA HEAR?
URK ...

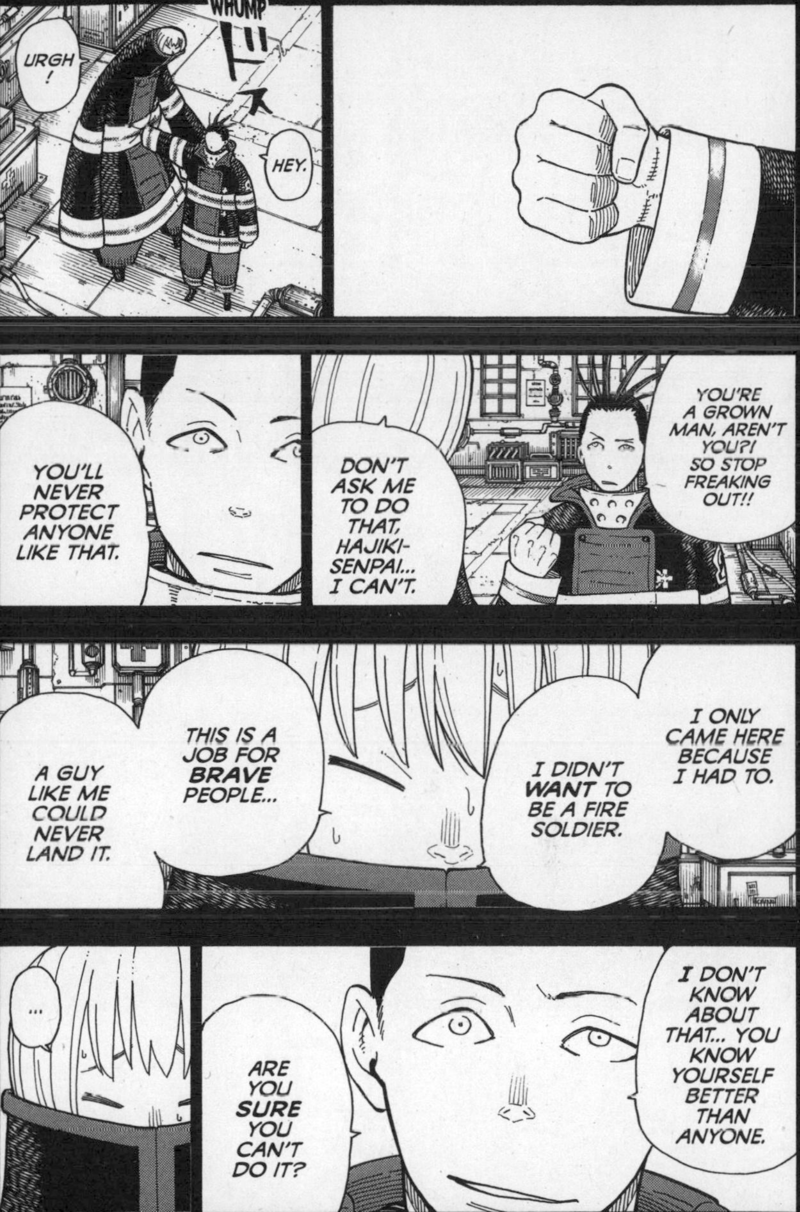
WHUMP
ドッ
URGH!
HEY.
YOU'RE A GROWN MAN, AREN'T YOU?! SO STOP FREAKING OUT!!
DON'T ASK ME TO DO THAT, HAJIKI-SENPAI... I CAN'T.
YOU'LL NEVER PROTECT ANYONE LIKE THAT.
I ONLY CAME HERE BECAUSE I HAD TO.
I DIDN'T WANT TO BE A FIRE SOLDIER.
THIS IS A JOB FOR BRAVE PEOPLE...
A GUY LIKE ME COULD NEVER LAND IT.
I DON'T KNOW ABOUT THAT... YOU KNOW YOURSELF BETTER THAN ANYONE.
ARE YOU SURE YOU CAN'T DO IT?
...

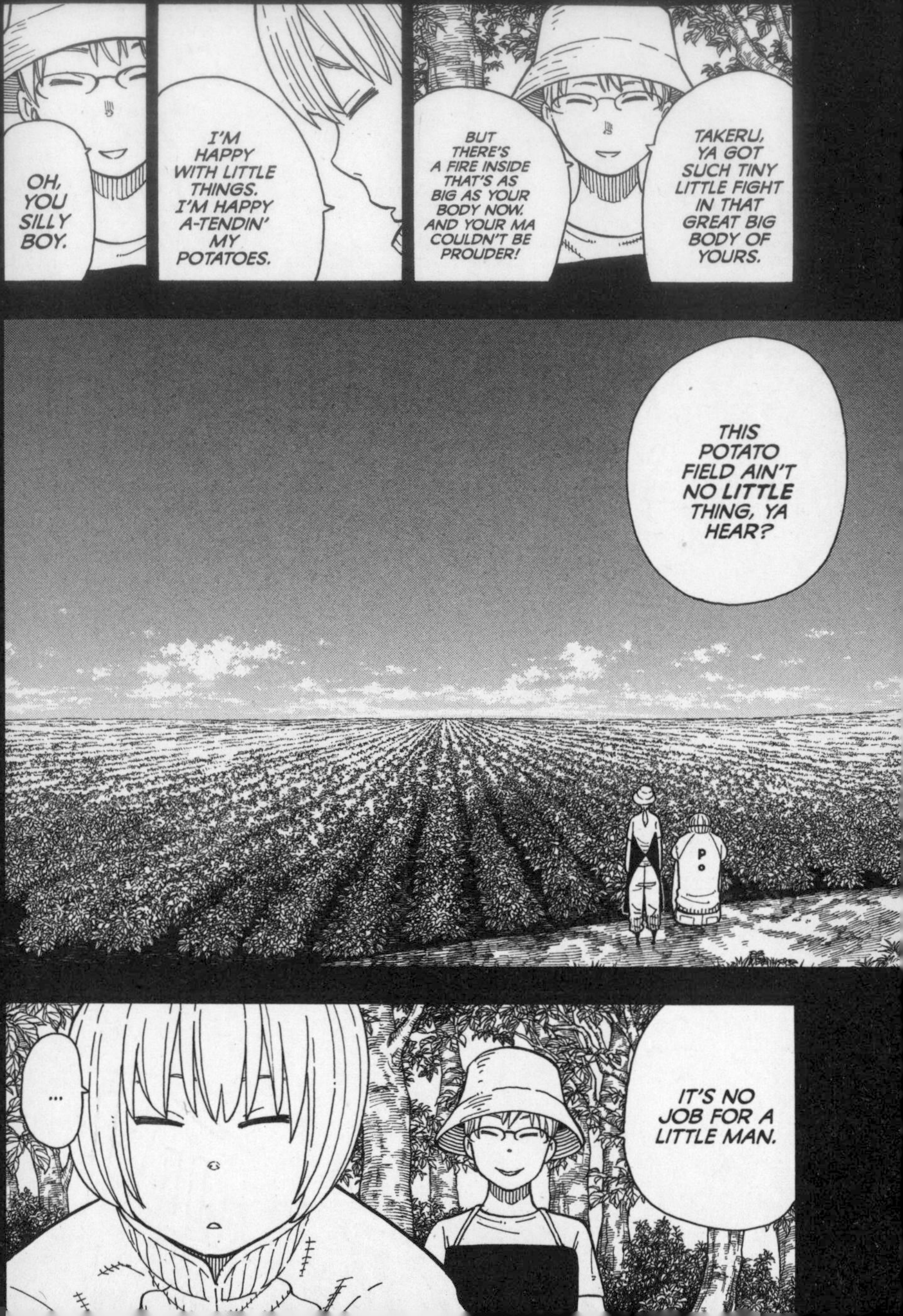
TAKERU, YA GOT SUCH TINY LITTLE FIGHT IN THAT GREAT BIG BODY OF YOURS.
BUT THERE'S A FIRE INSIDE THAT'S AS BIG AS YOUR BODY NOW. AND YOUR MA COULDN'T BE PROUDER!
I'M HAPPY WITH LITTLE THINGS. I'M HAPPY A-TENDIN' MY POTATOES.
OH, YOU SILLY BOY.
THIS POTATO FIELD AIN'T NO LITTLE THING, YA HEAR?
IT'S NO JOB FOR A LITTLE MAN.
...

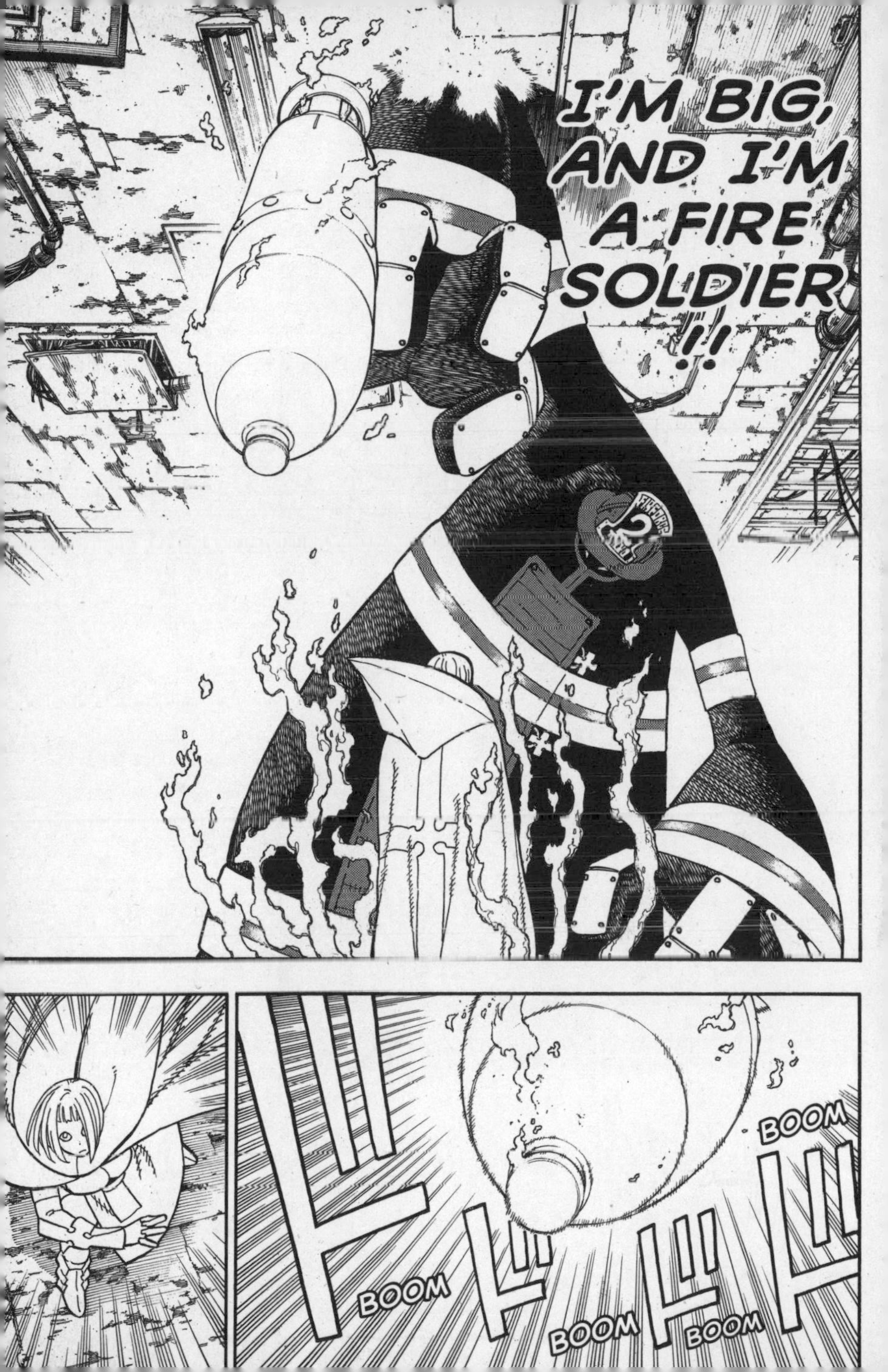
I'M BIG, AND I'M A FIRE SOLDIER!!
BOOM
BOOM
BOOM
BOOM

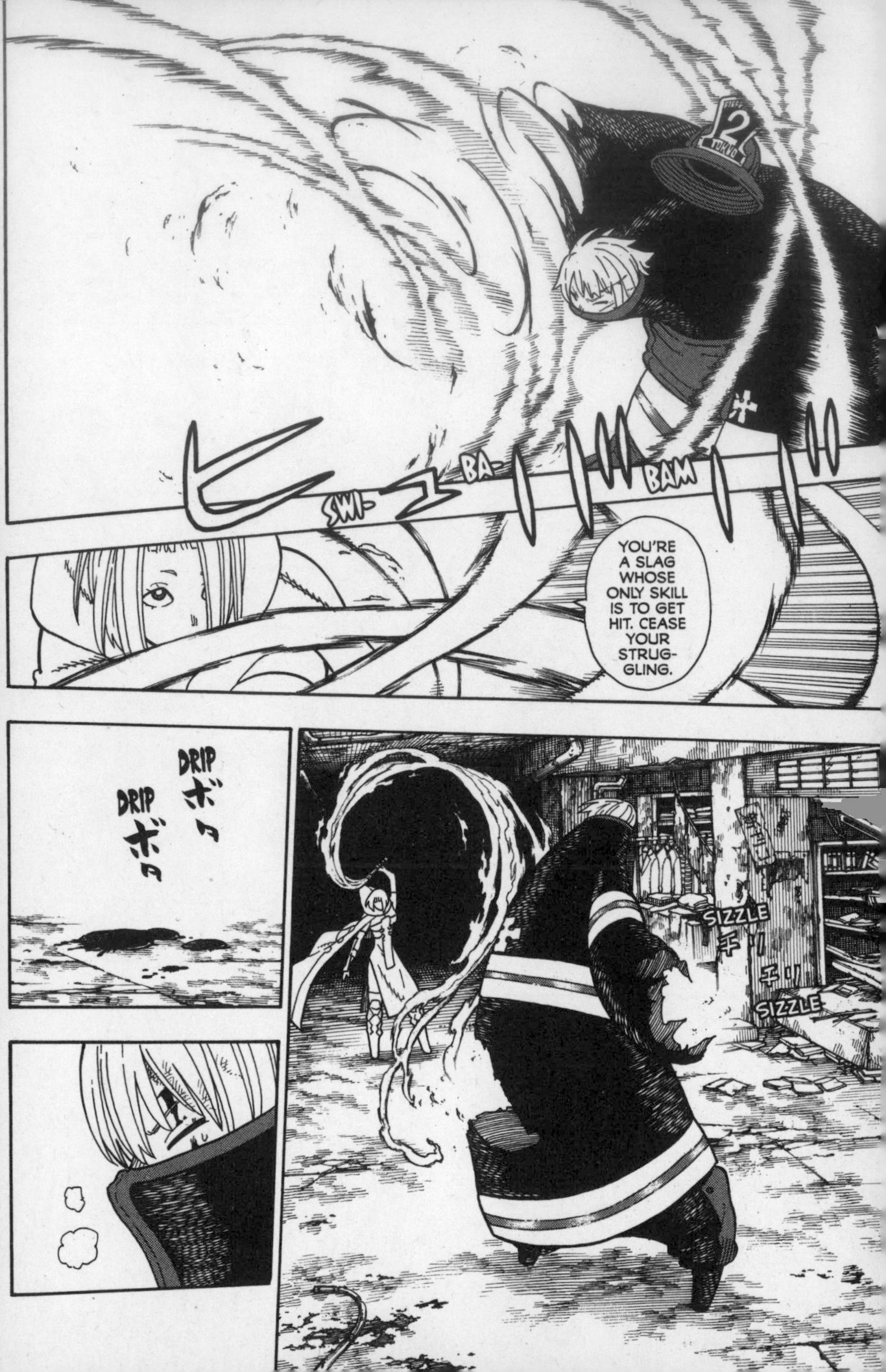
SWI-
BA-
BAM
YOU'RE A SLAG WHOSE ONLY SKILL IS TO GET HIT. CEASE YOUR STRUG-GLING.
SIZZLE チリ
チリ SIZZLE
DRIP ボタ
DRIP ボタ

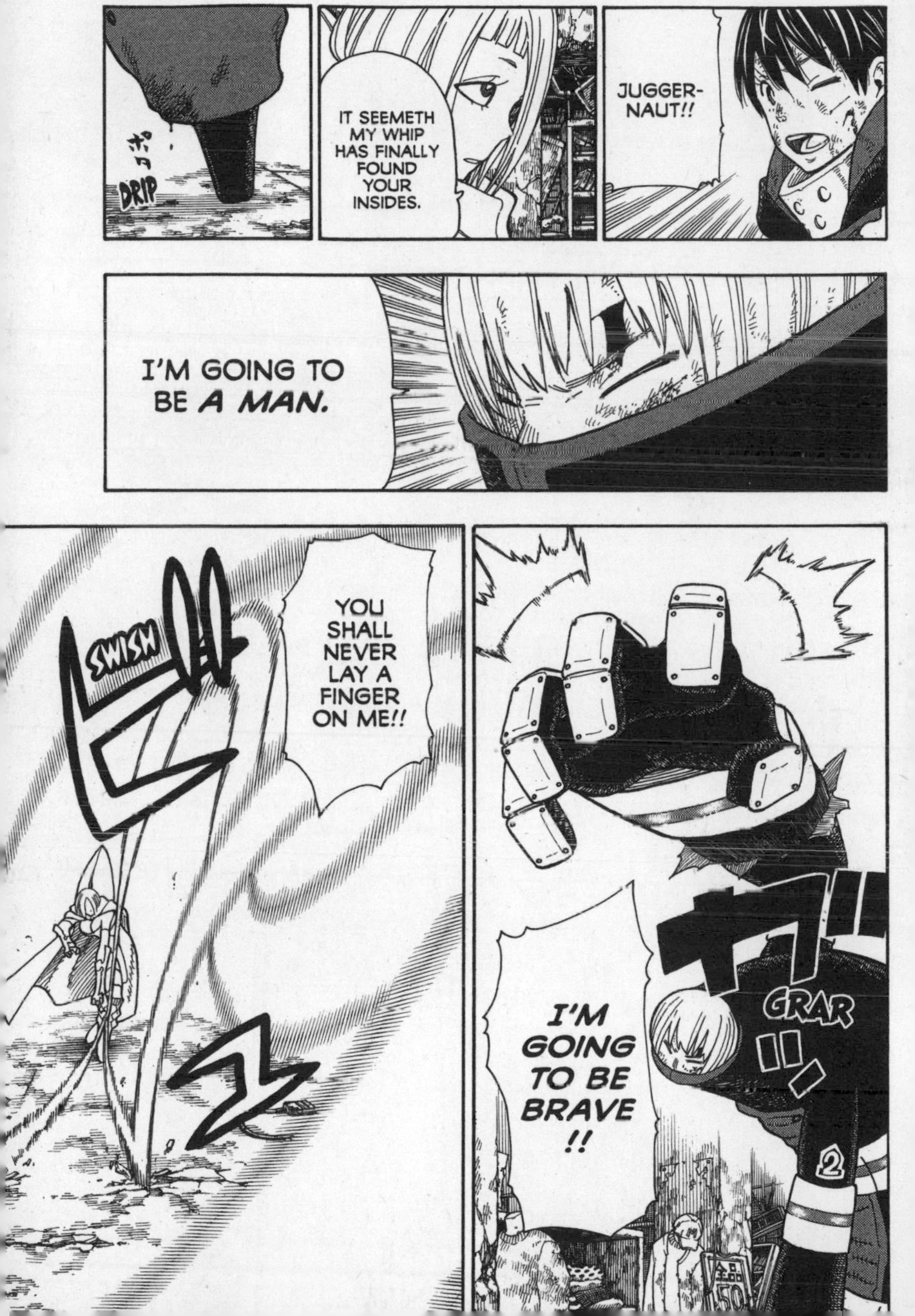
JUGGER-
NAUT!!
IT SEEMETH MY WHIP HAS FINALLY FOUND YOUR INSIDES.
DRIP
I'M GOING TO BE *A MAN.*
I'M GOING TO BE BRAVE!!
GRAR
YOU SHALL NEVER LAY A FINGER ON ME!!
SWISH

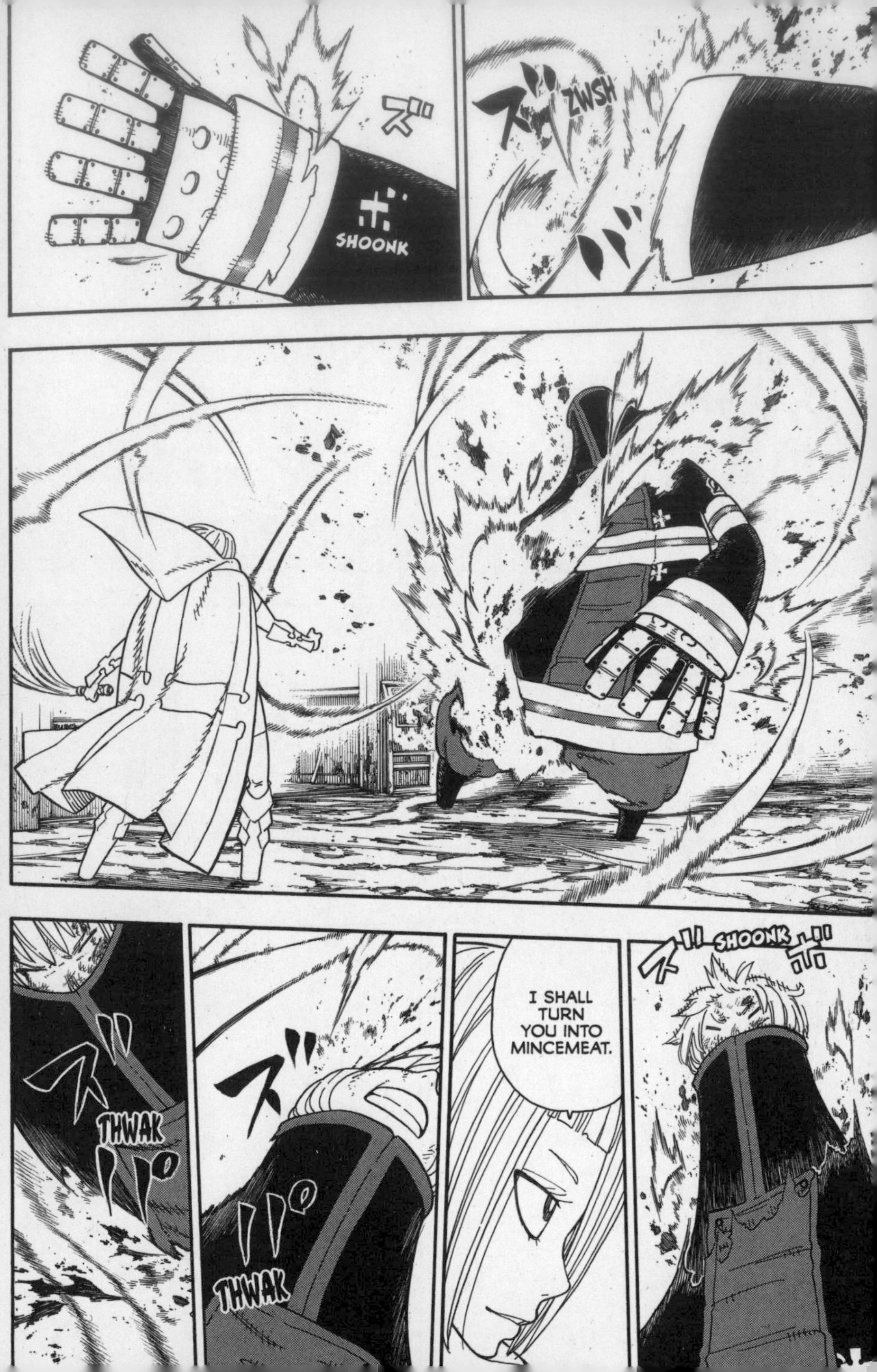
ZWSH
SHOONK
SHOONK
I SHALL TURN YOU INTO MINCEMEAT.
THWAK
THWAK

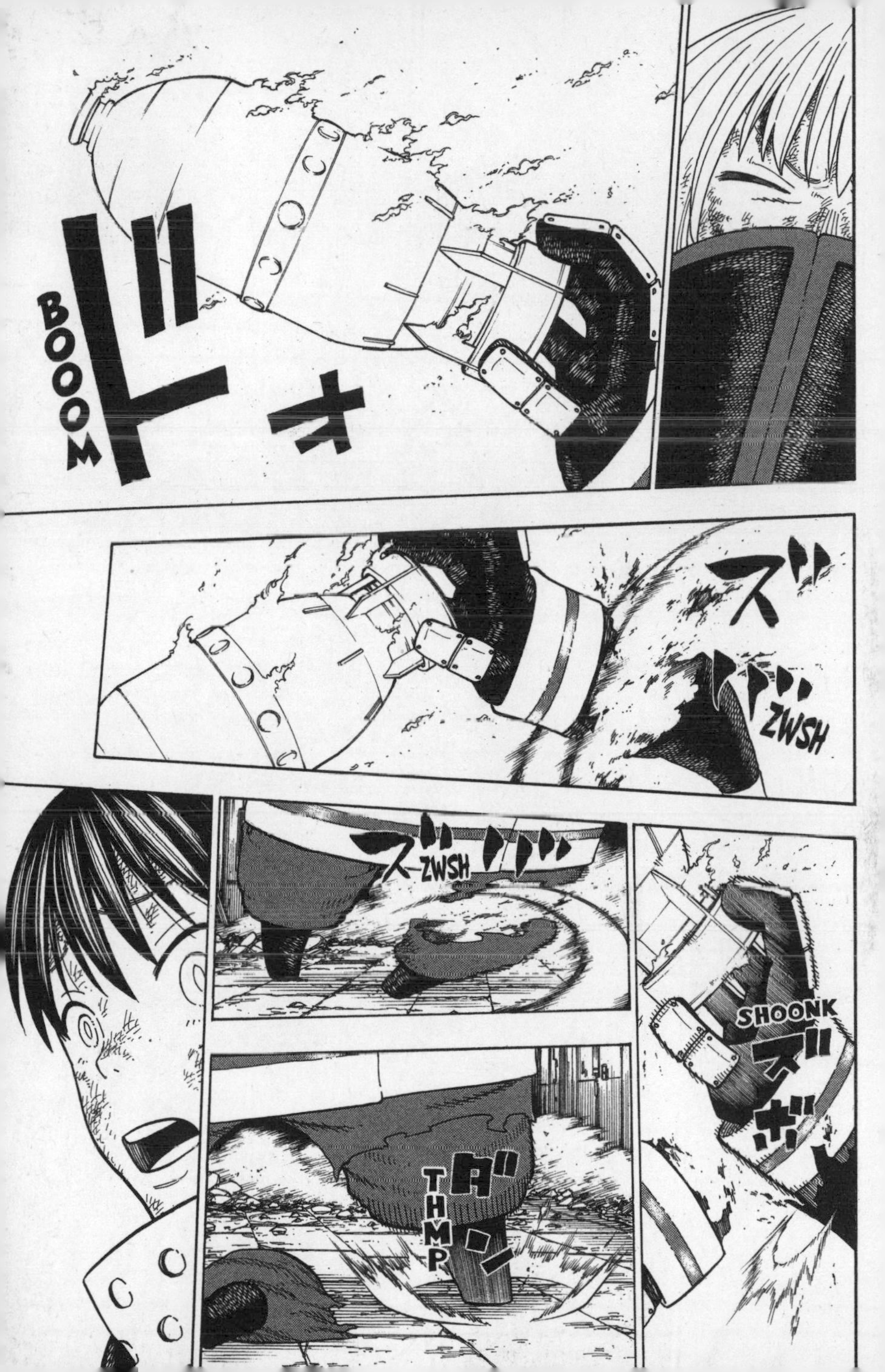
BOOOM
ZWSH
SHOONK
ZWSH
THMP

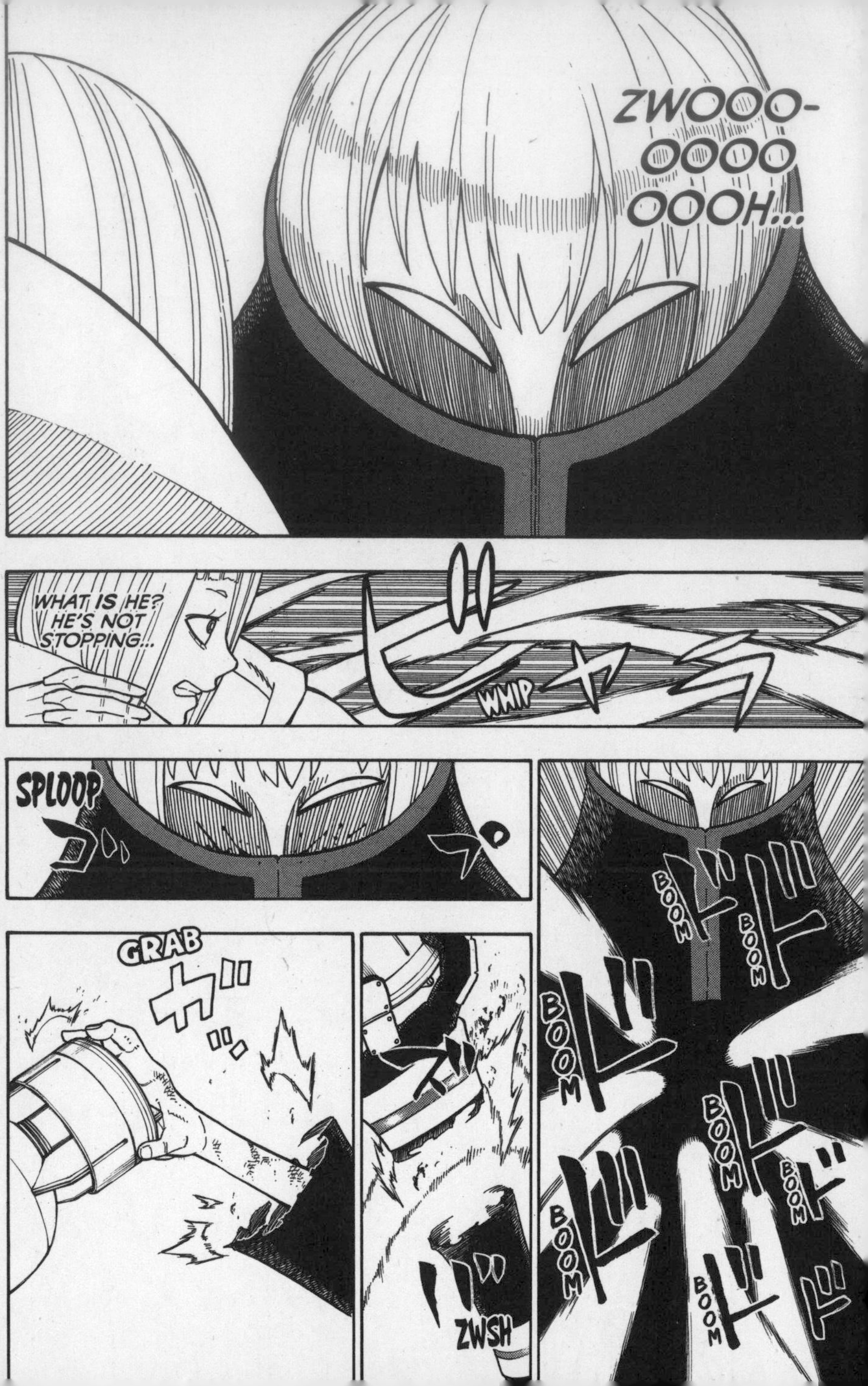
ZWOOO-OOOO OOOH...
WHIP
WHAT IS HE? HE'S NOT STOPPING...
SPLOOP
BOOM BOOM BOOM BOOM BOOM BOOM BOOM
ZWSH
GRAB

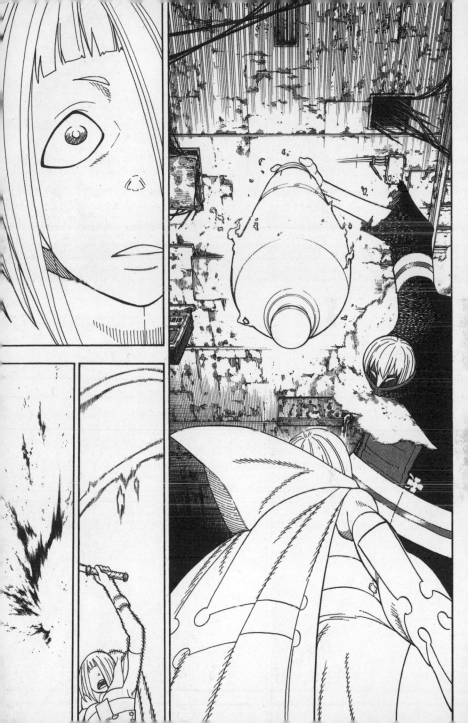

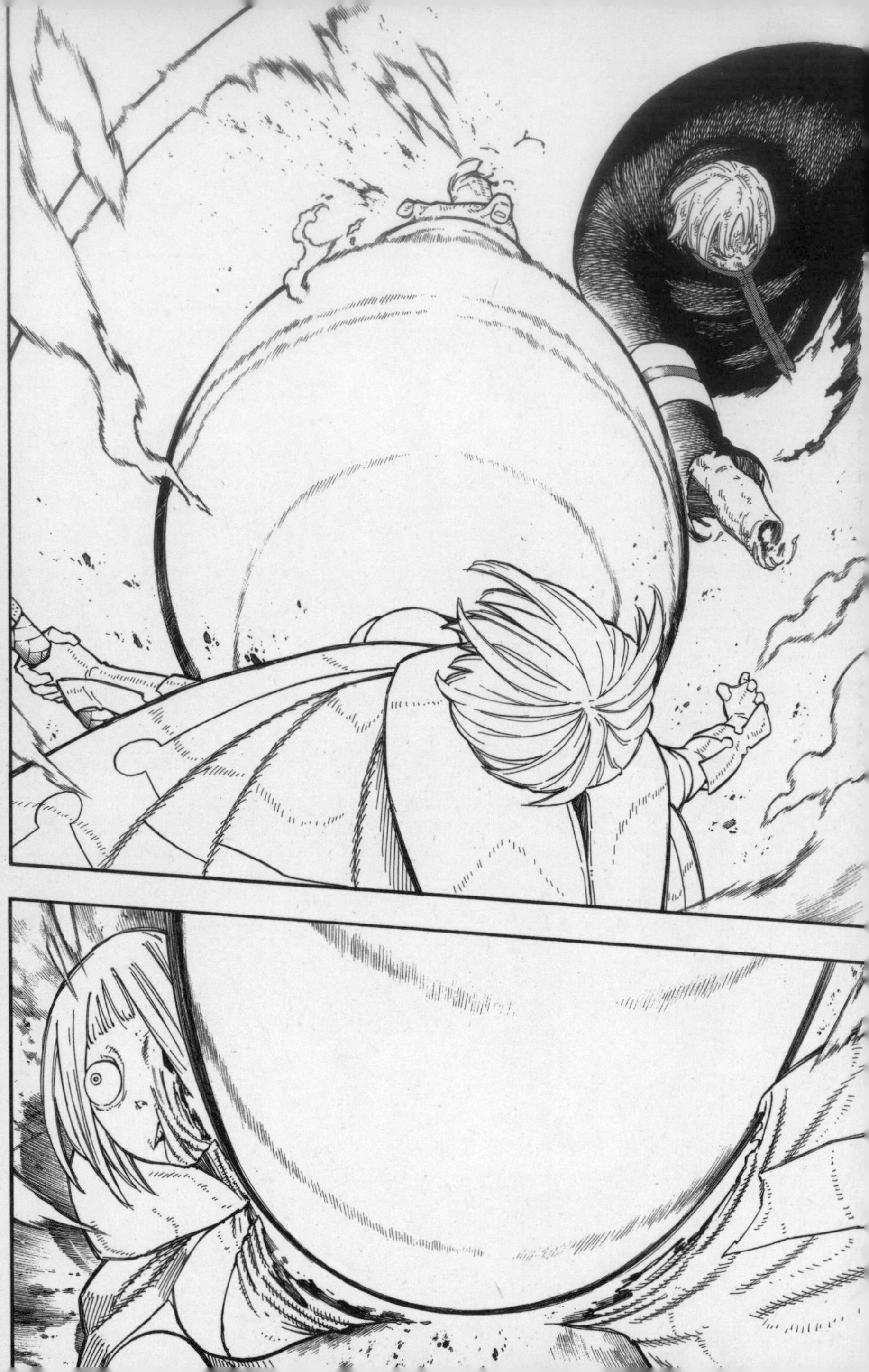

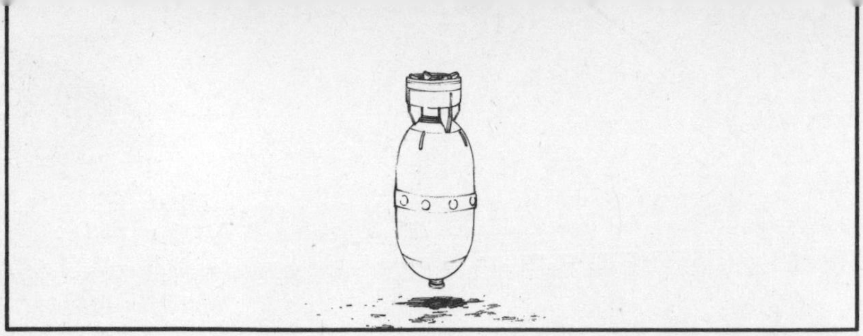

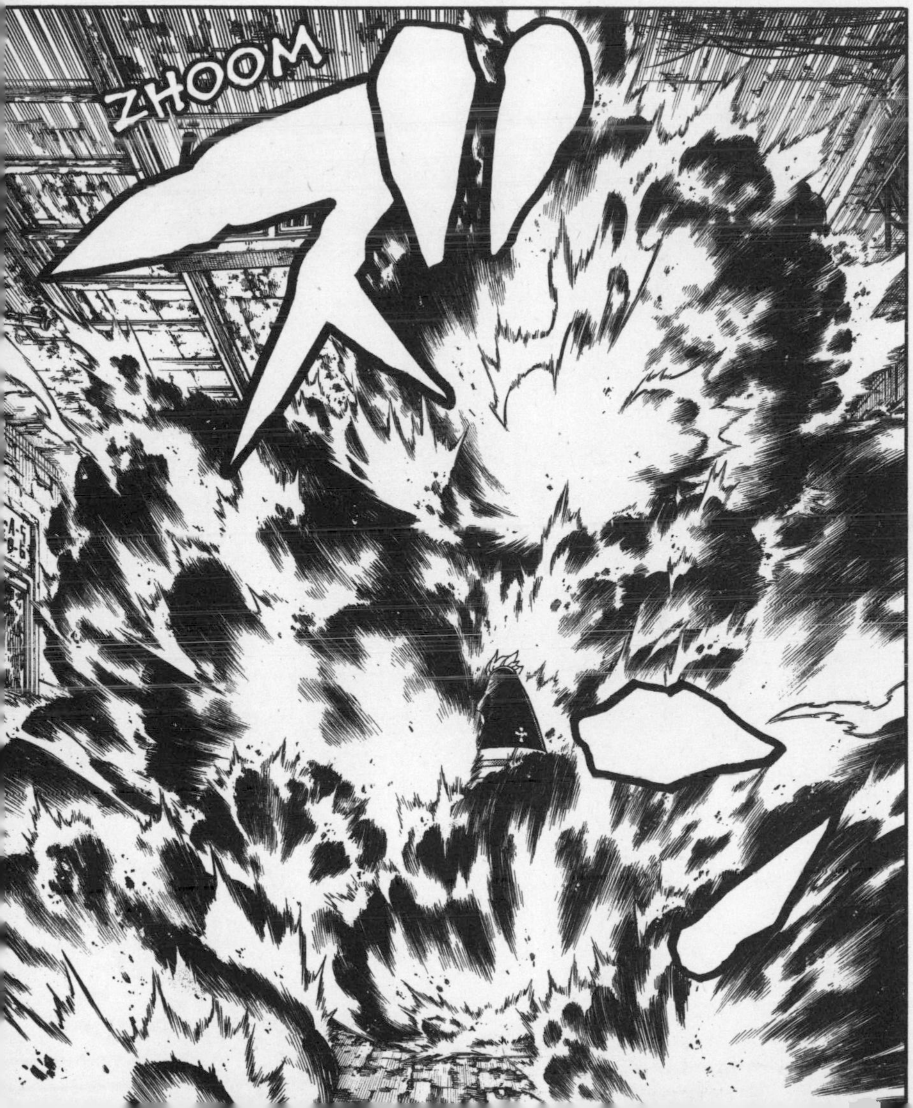
ZHOOM

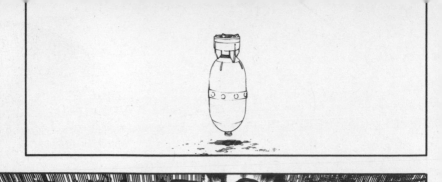

FIRE FORCE

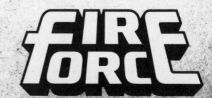

CHAPTER CLIX: ENEMY CONTACT

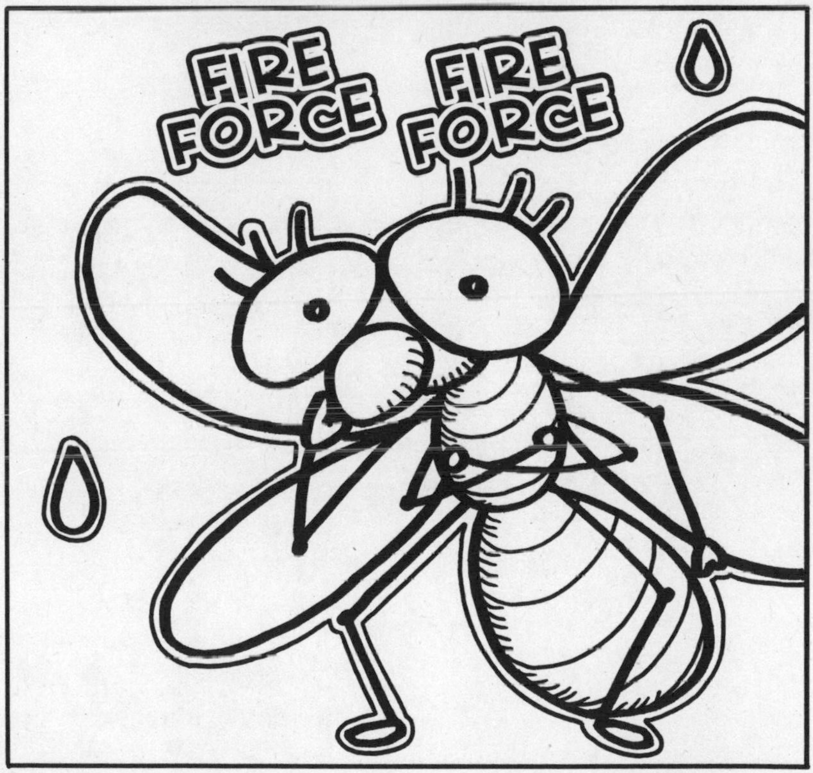
FIRE FORCE
FIRE FORCE

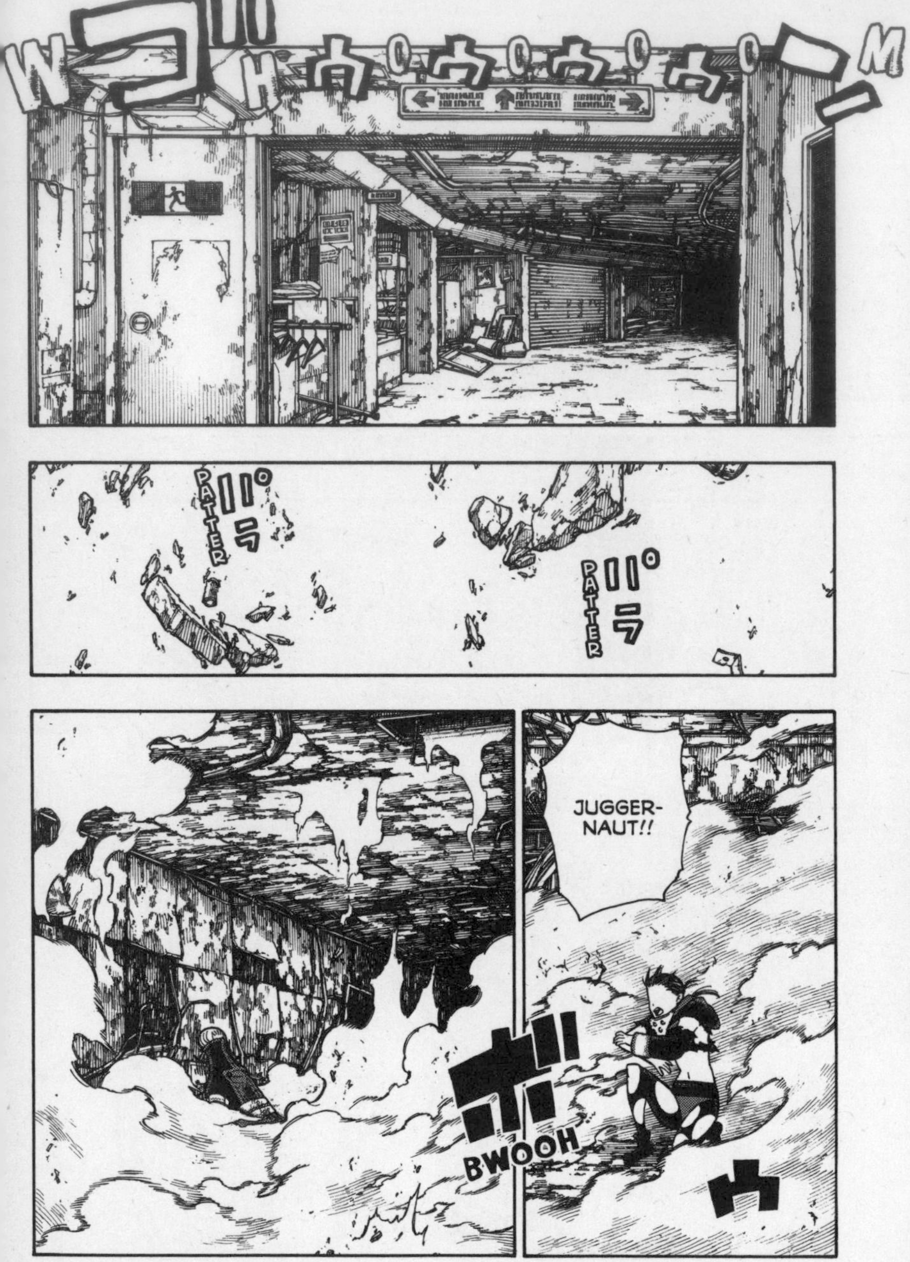
WHOOOOM
PATTER
PATTER
JUGGER-
NAUT!!
BWOOH

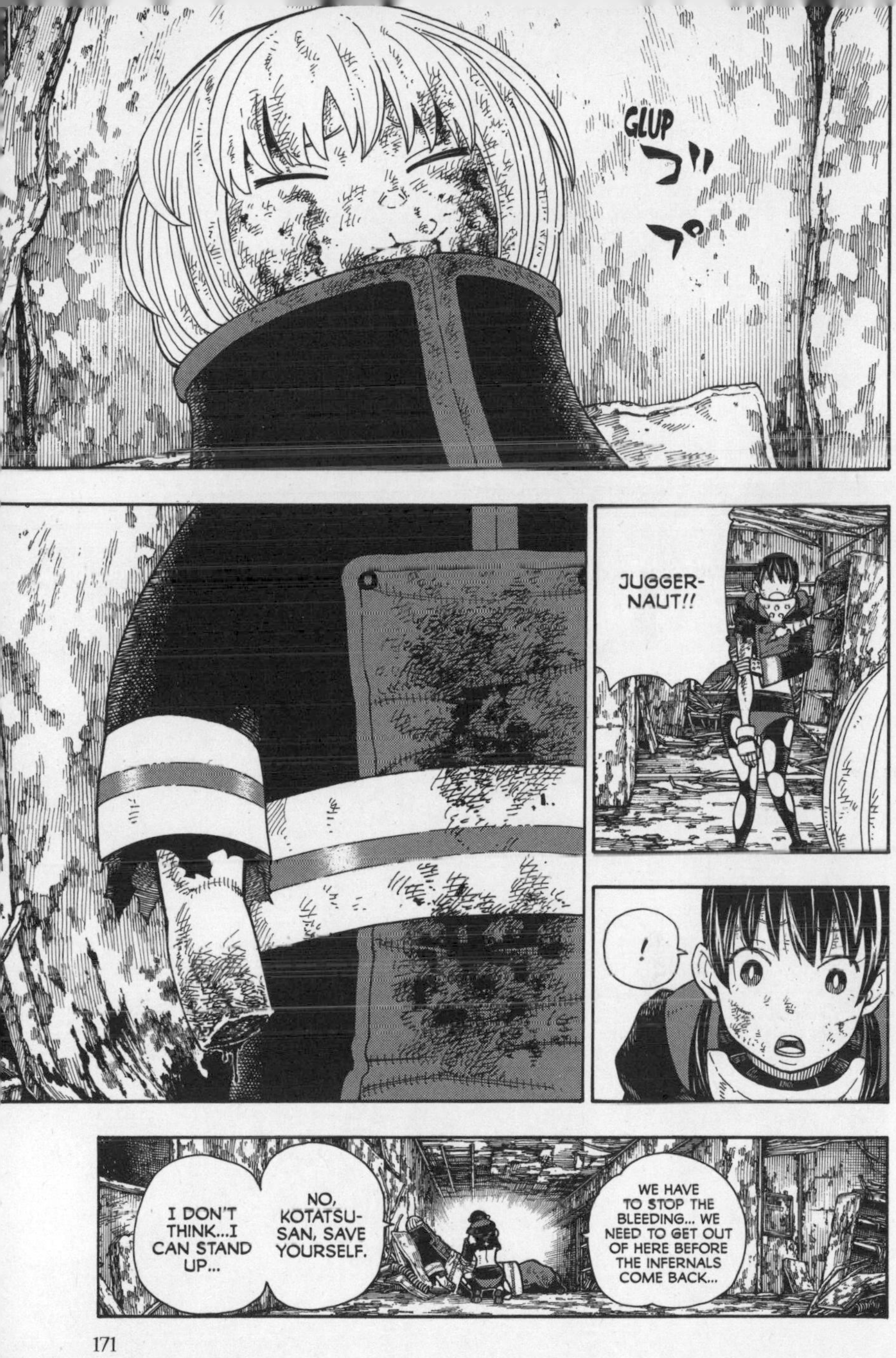
GLUP
ゴップ
JUGGER-NAUT!!
!
WE HAVE TO STOP THE BLEEDING... WE NEED TO GET OUT OF HERE BEFORE THE INFERNALS COME BACK...
NO, KOTATSU-SAN, SAVE YOURSELF.
I DON'T THINK...I CAN STAND UP...

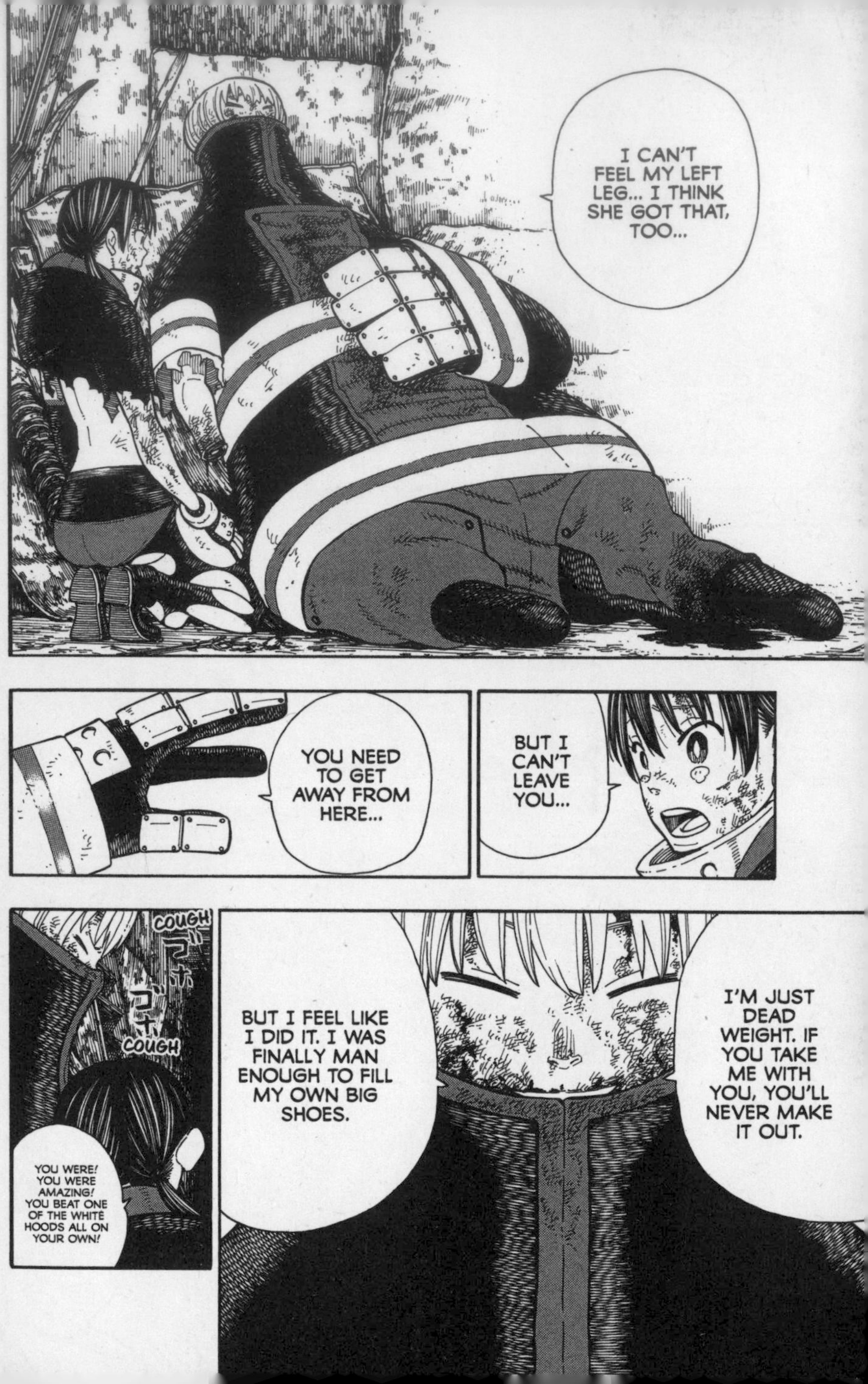
I CAN'T FEEL MY LEFT LEG... I THINK SHE GOT THAT, TOO...
BUT I CAN'T LEAVE YOU...
YOU NEED TO GET AWAY FROM HERE...
I'M JUST DEAD WEIGHT. IF YOU TAKE ME WITH YOU, YOU'LL NEVER MAKE IT OUT.
BUT I FEEL LIKE I DID IT. I WAS FINALLY MAN ENOUGH TO FILL MY OWN BIG SHOES.
COUGH
ゴホ
ゴホ
COUGH
YOU WERE! YOU WERE AMAZING! YOU BEAT ONE OF THE WHITE HOODS ALL ON YOUR OWN!

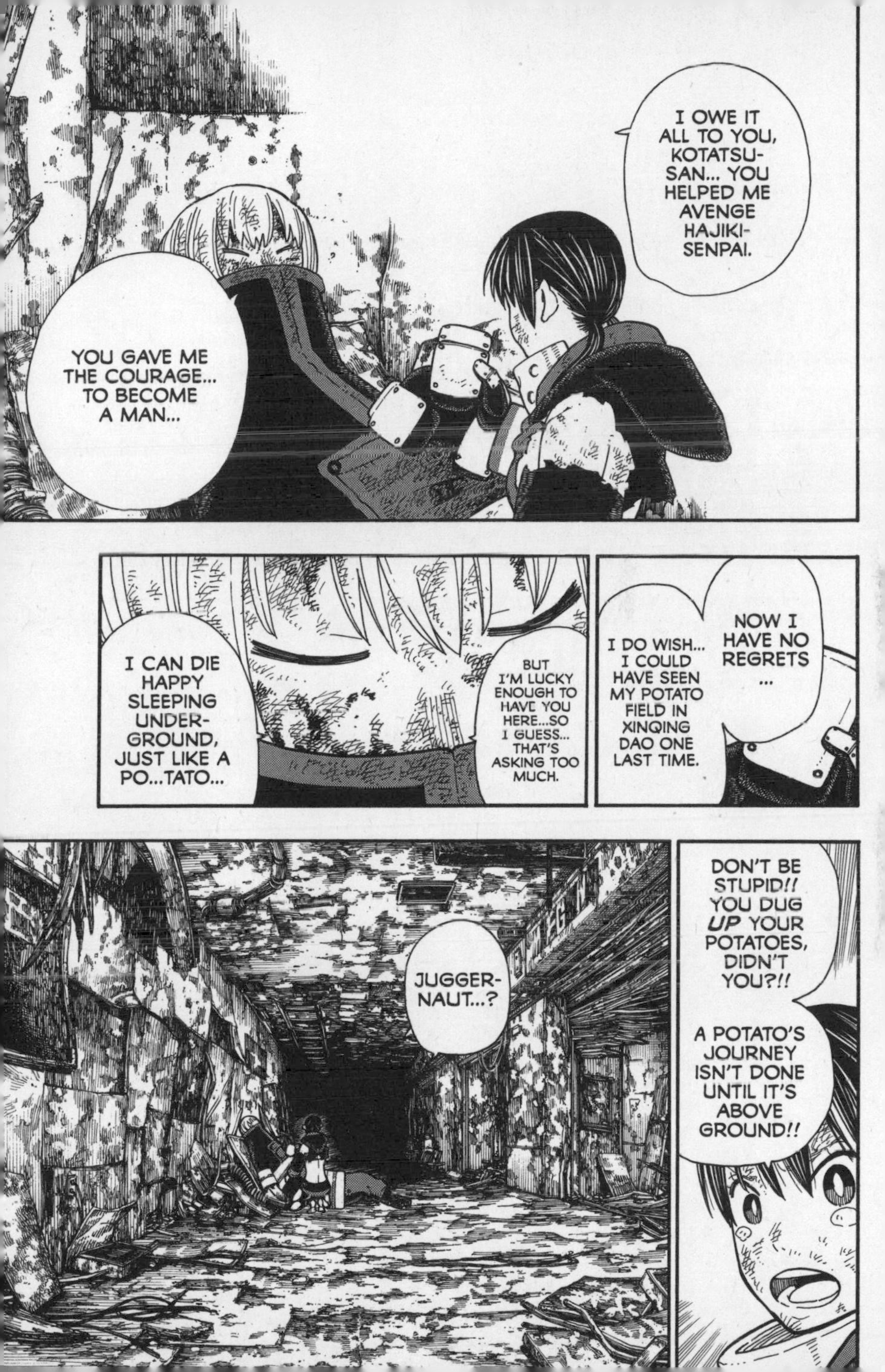
I OWE IT ALL TO YOU, KOTATSU-SAN... YOU HELPED ME AVENGE HAJIKI-SENPAI.
YOU GAVE ME THE COURAGE... TO BECOME A MAN...
NOW I HAVE NO REGRETS ...
I DO WISH... I COULD HAVE SEEN MY POTATO FIELD IN XINQING DAO ONE LAST TIME.
BUT I'M LUCKY ENOUGH TO HAVE YOU HERE...SO I GUESS... THAT'S ASKING TOO MUCH.
I CAN DIE HAPPY SLEEPING UNDER-GROUND, JUST LIKE A PO...TATO...
DON'T BE STUPID!! YOU DUG *UP* YOUR POTATOES, DIDN'T YOU?!!
A POTATO'S JOURNEY ISN'T DONE UNTIL IT'S ABOVE GROUND!!
JUGGER-NAUT...?

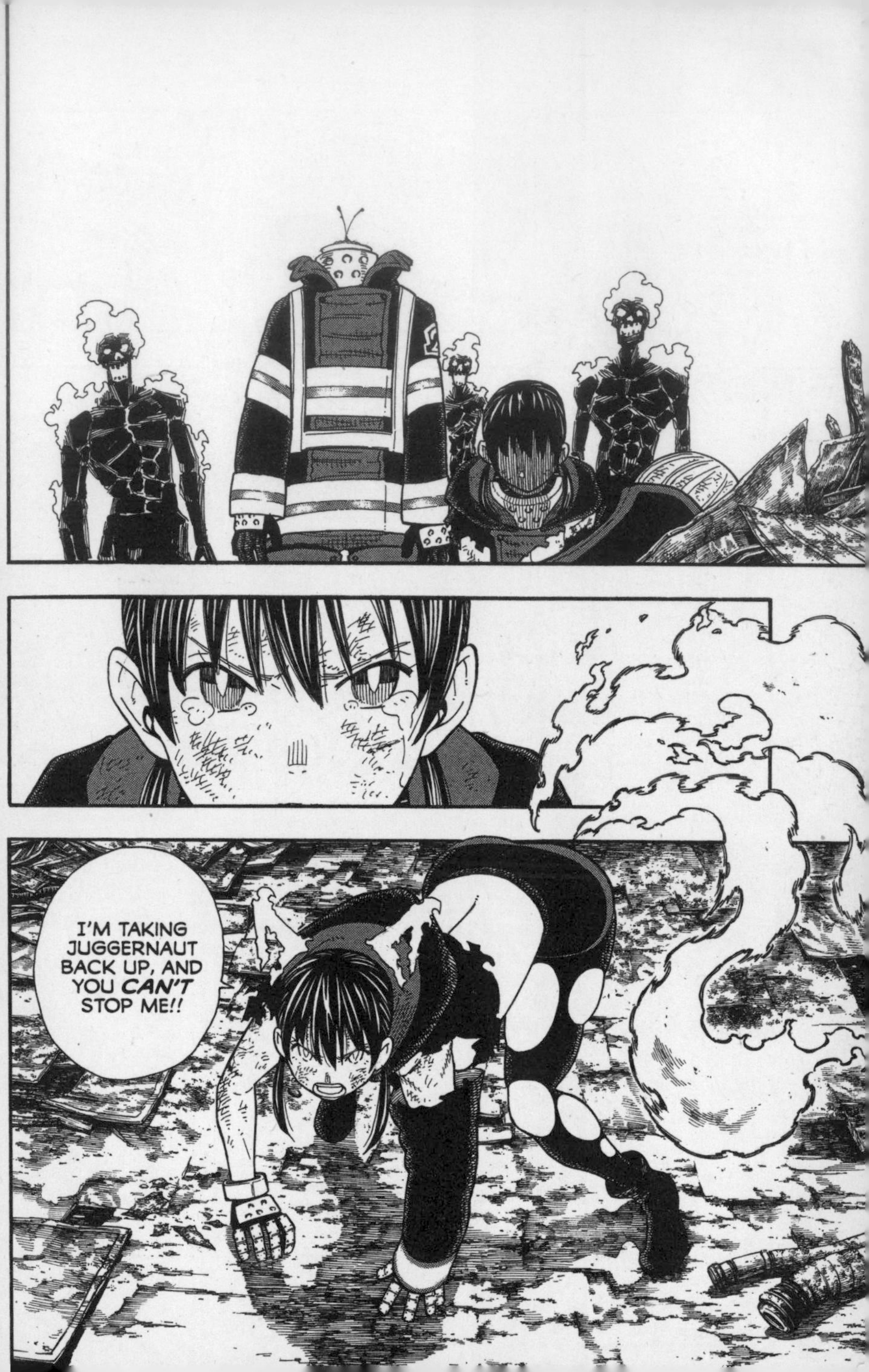
I'M TAKING JUGGERNAUT BACK UP, AND YOU CAN'T STOP ME!!

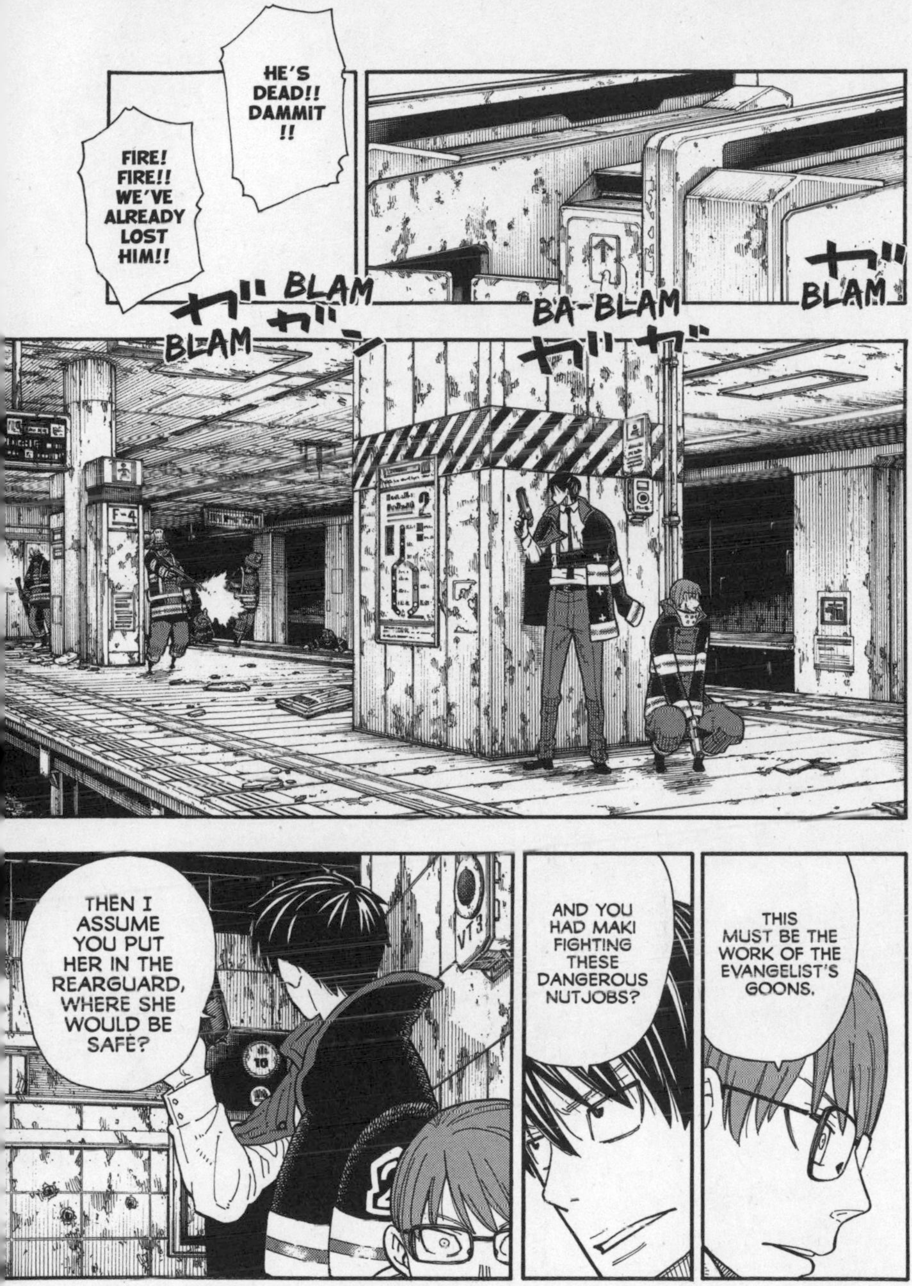
BLAM
HE'S DEAD!! DAMMIT !!
FIRE! FIRE!! WE'VE ALREADY LOST HIM!!
BA-BLAM
BLAM
BLAM
THIS MUST BE THE WORK OF THE EVANGELIST'S GOONS.
AND YOU HAD MAKI FIGHTING THESE DANGEROUS NUTJOBS?
THEN I ASSUME YOU PUT HER IN THE REARGUARD, WHERE SHE WOULD BE SAFE?

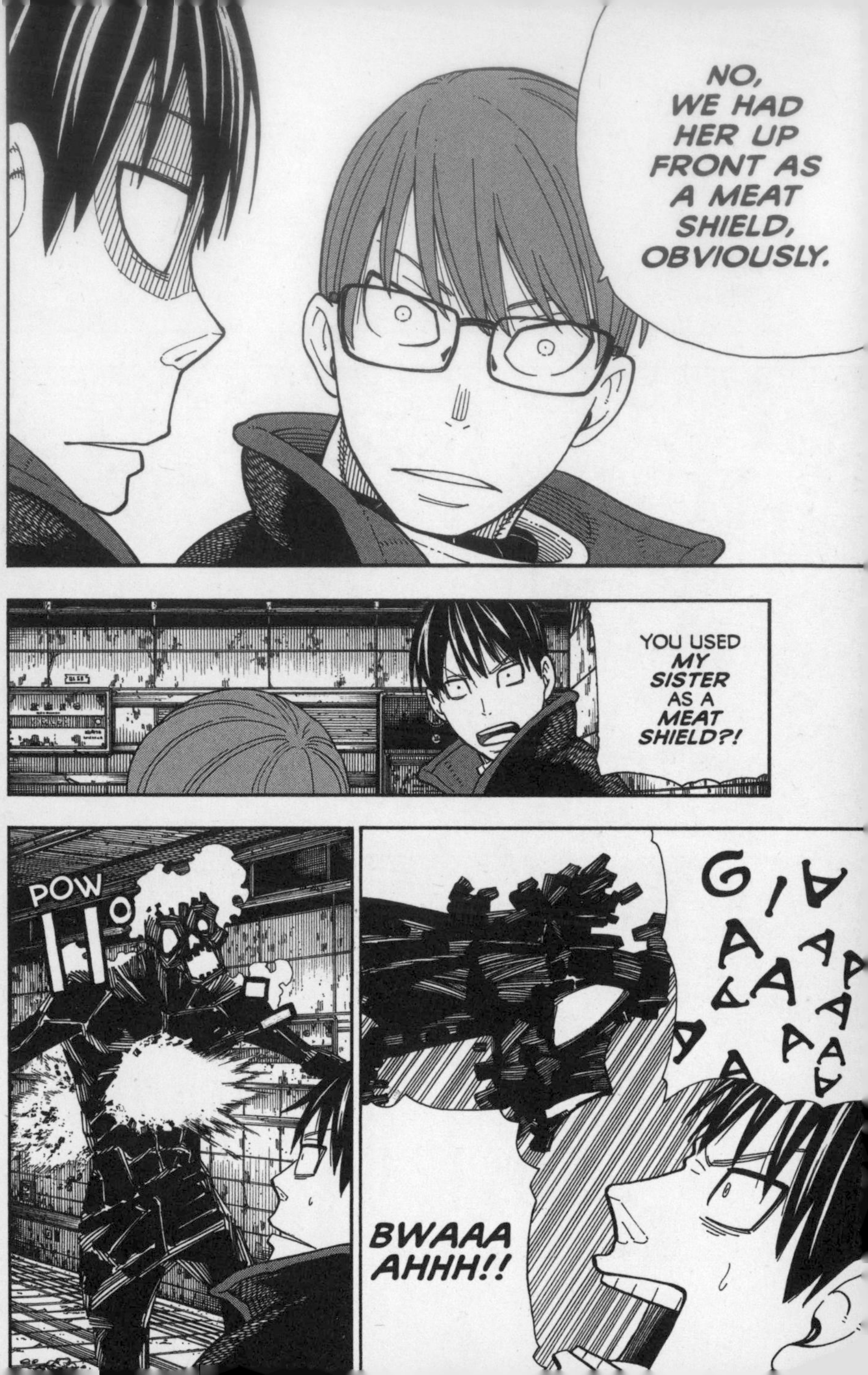
NO, WE HAD HER UP FRONT AS A MEAT SHIELD, OBVIOUSLY.
YOU USED *MY SISTER* AS A *MEAT SHIELD?!*
GIAAAAAAAAAAAAA
BWAAA AHHH!!
POW

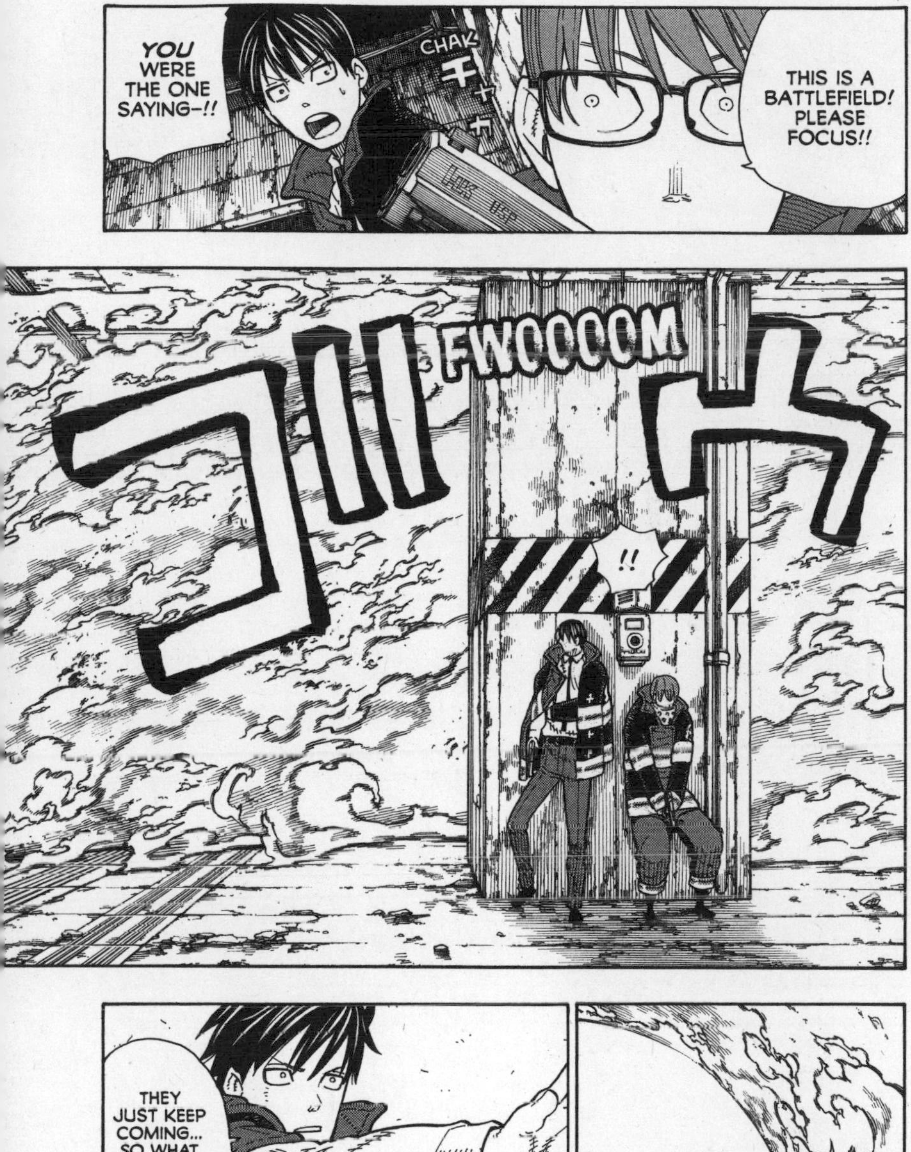
THIS IS A BATTLEFIELD! PLEASE FOCUS!!
CHAK
YOU WERE THE ONE SAYING–!!
FWOOOOM
!!
THEY JUST KEEP COMING... SO WHAT IS IT THIS TIME?!

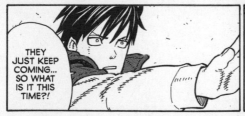

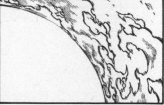

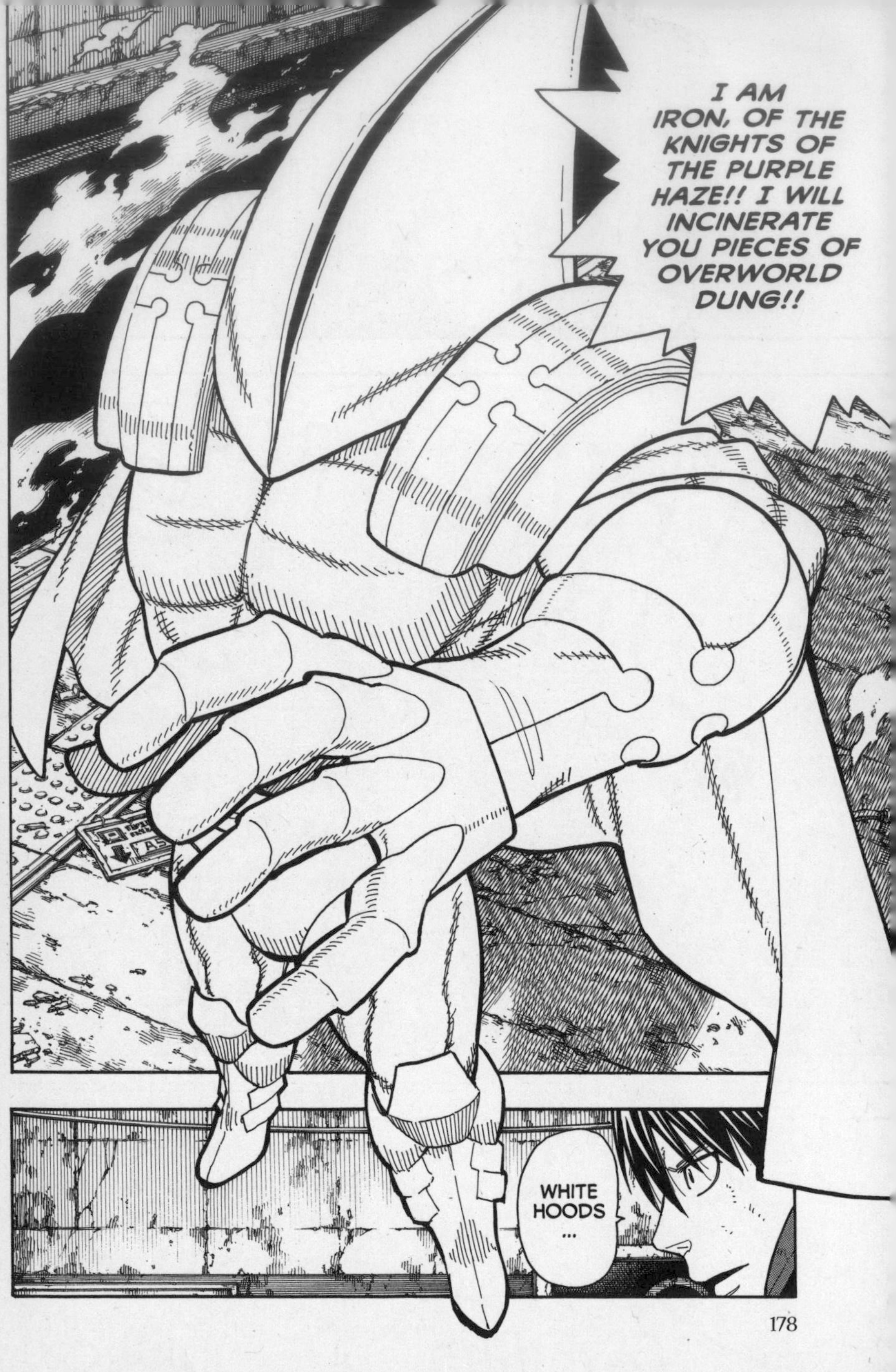
I AM IRON, OF THE KNIGHTS OF THE PURPLE HAZE!! I WILL INCINERATE YOU PIECES OF OVERWORLD DUNG!!
WHITE HOODS ...

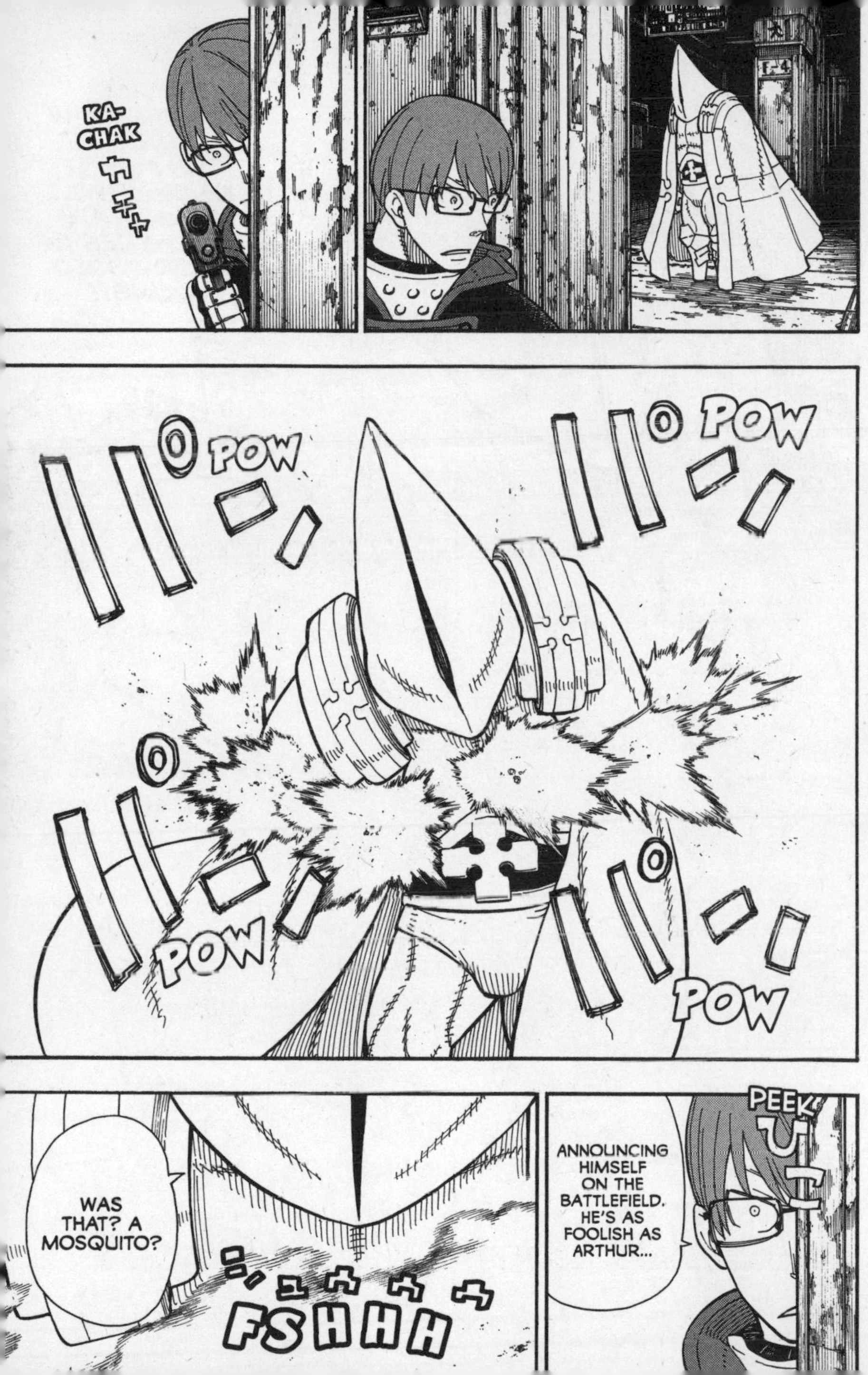
KA-CHAK
POW
POW
POW
POW
PEEK
ANNOUNCING HIMSELF ON THE BATTLEFIELD. HE'S AS FOOLISH AS ARTHUR...
WAS THAT? A MOSQUITO?
FSHHH

MY GUN DOESN'T WORK ON HIM?! BUT HOW...?

...

I STILL HAVE THINGS TO ASK YOU ABOUT MAKI!

GET BEHIND ME!!

HA!! YOUR LUKEWARM ATTACKS COULD NEVER EVEN SCRATCH MY FLESH OF STEEL!!

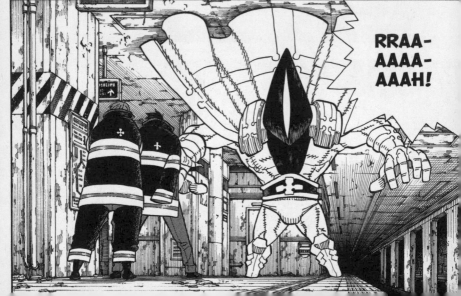

RRAA-AAAA-AAAH!

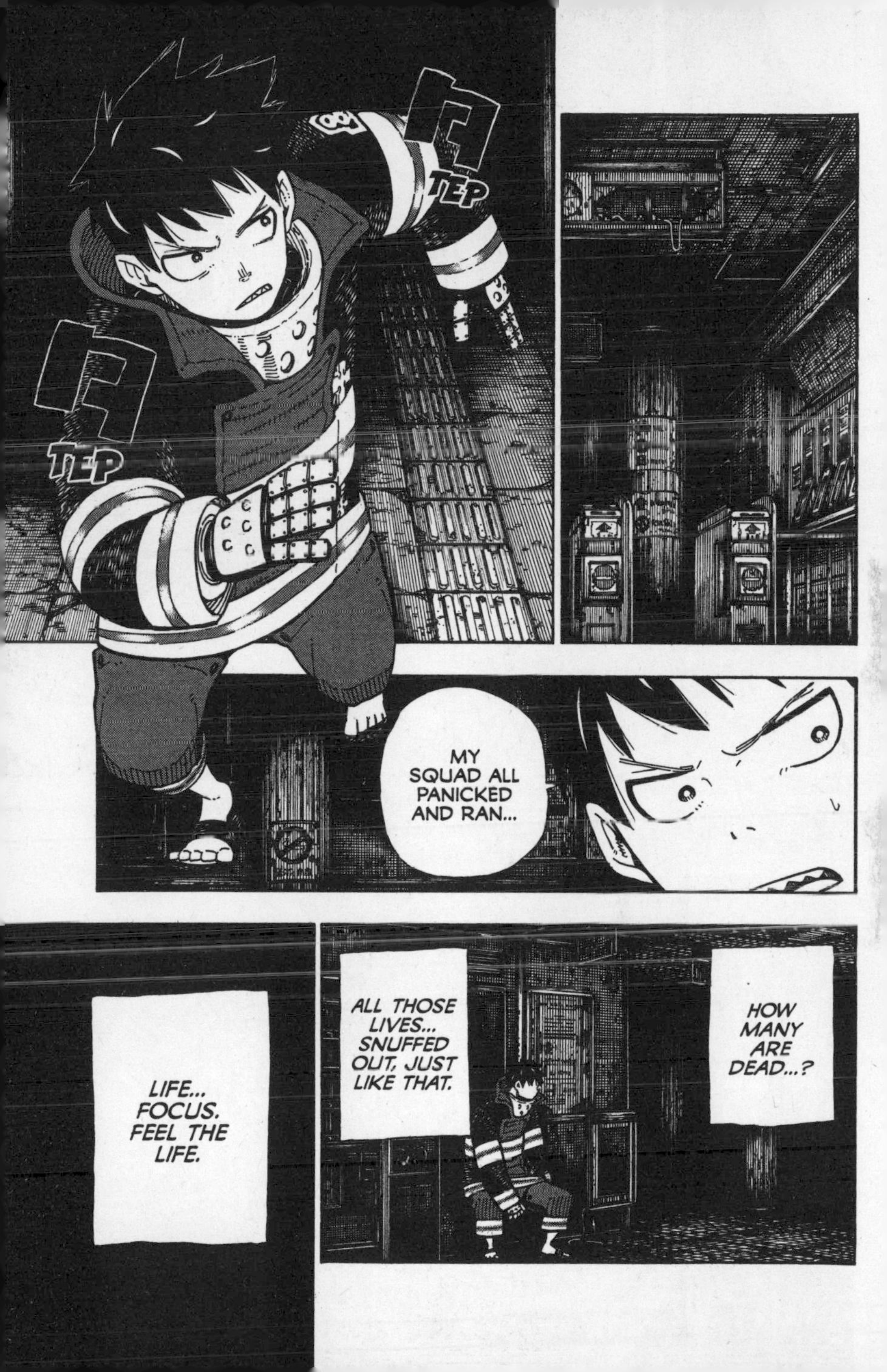
TEP
TEP
MY SQUAD ALL PANICKED AND RAN...
HOW MANY ARE DEAD...?
ALL THOSE LIVES... SNUFFED OUT, JUST LIKE THAT.
LIFE... FOCUS. FEEL THE LIFE.

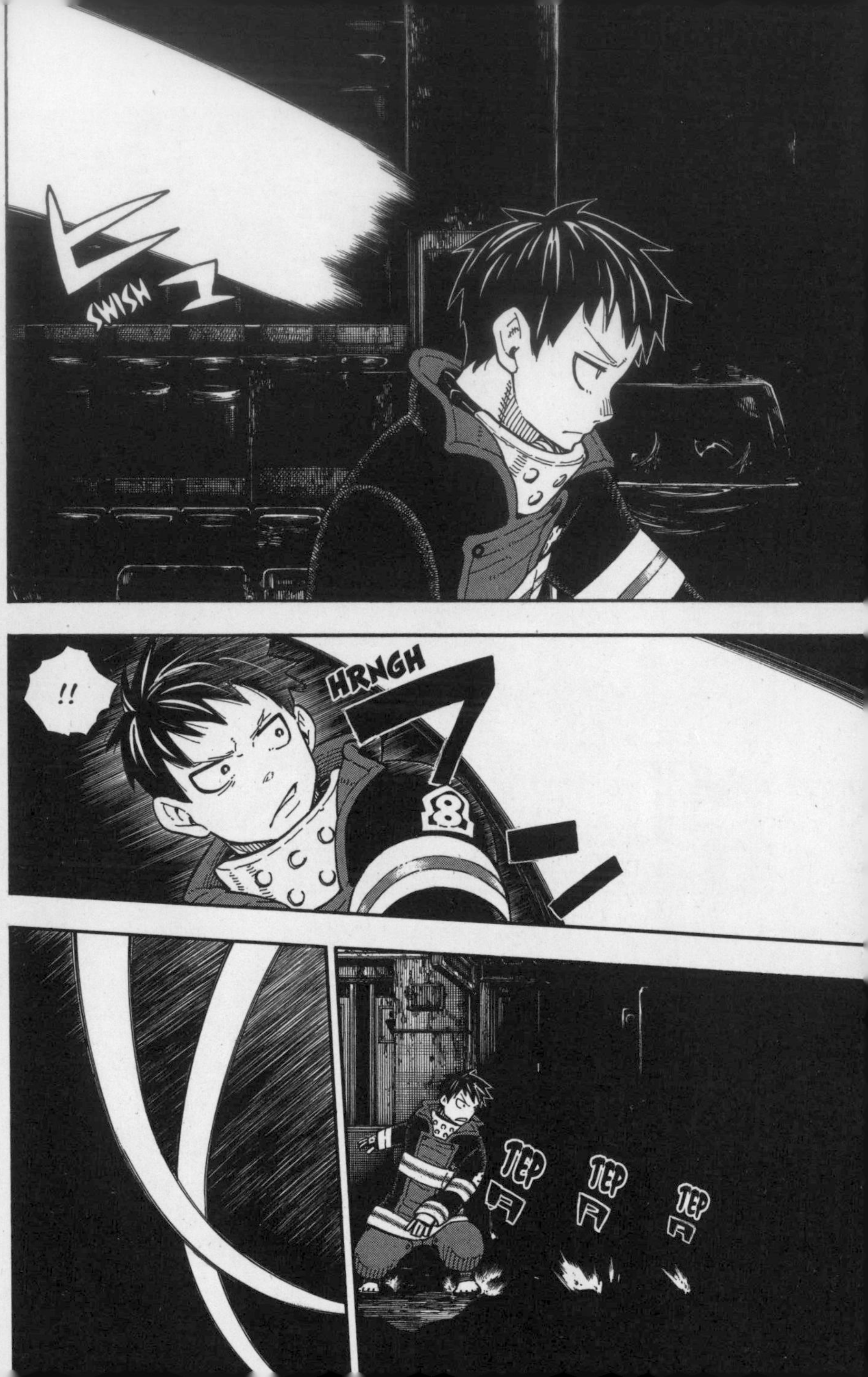
SWISH
HRNGH
!!
TEP
TEP
TEP

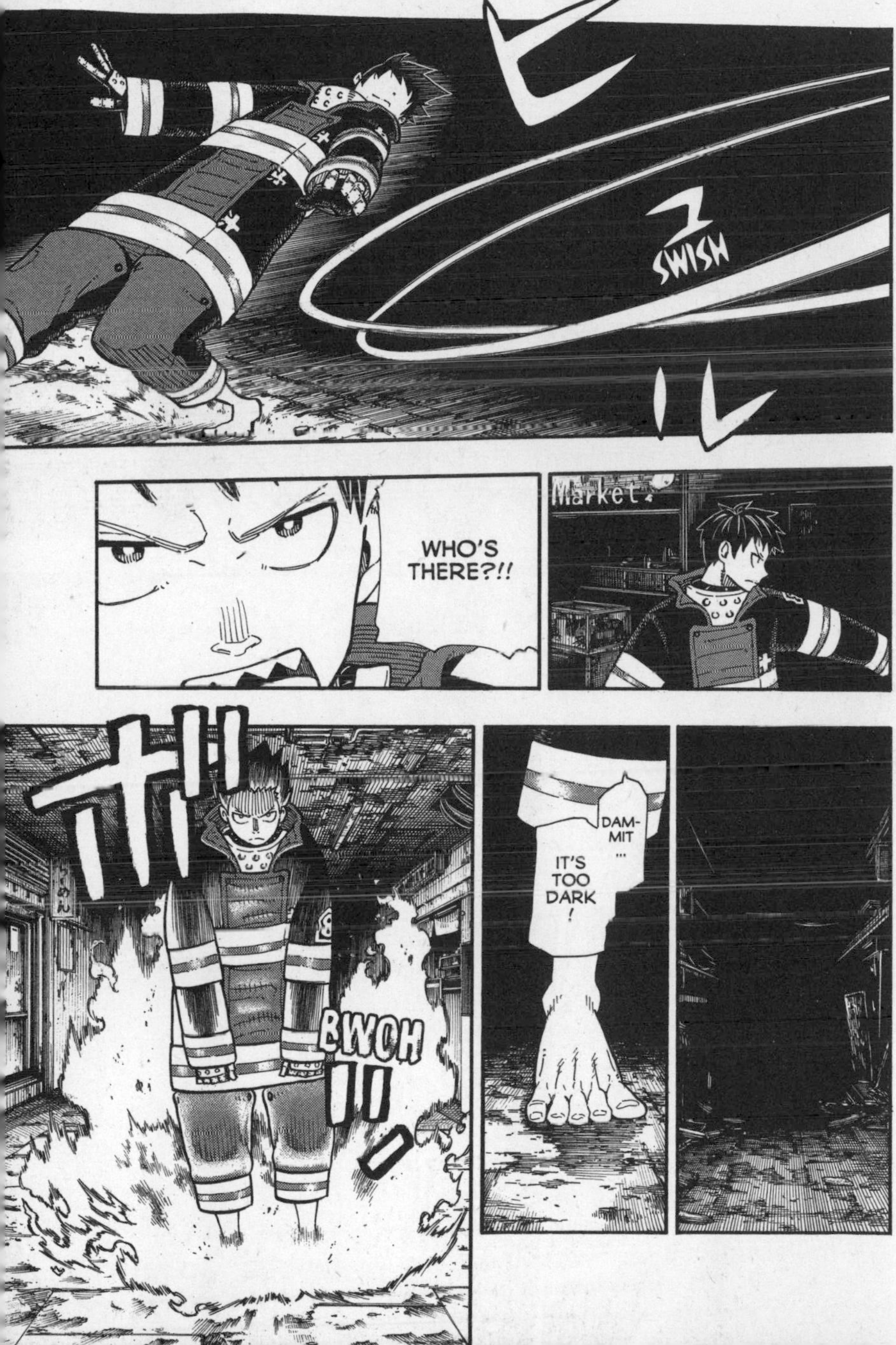
SWISH
Market
WHO'S THERE?!!
DAM-MIT ...
IT'S TOO DARK!
BWOH

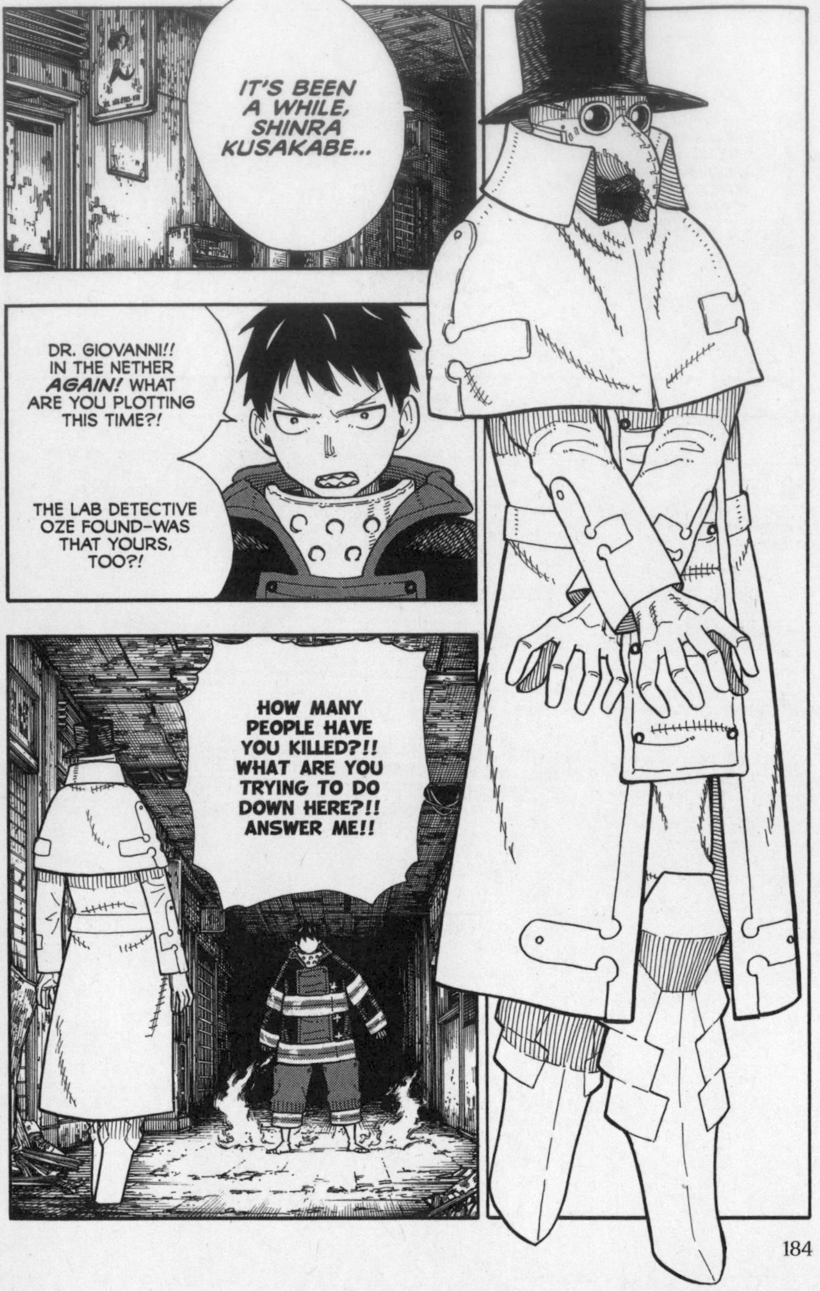
IT'S BEEN A WHILE, SHINRA KUSAKABE...
DR. GIOVANNI!! IN THE NETHER AGAIN! WHAT ARE YOU PLOTTING THIS TIME?!
THE LAB DETECTIVE OZE FOUND—WAS THAT YOURS, TOO?!
HOW MANY PEOPLE HAVE YOU KILLED?!! WHAT ARE YOU TRYING TO DO DOWN HERE?!! ANSWER ME!!

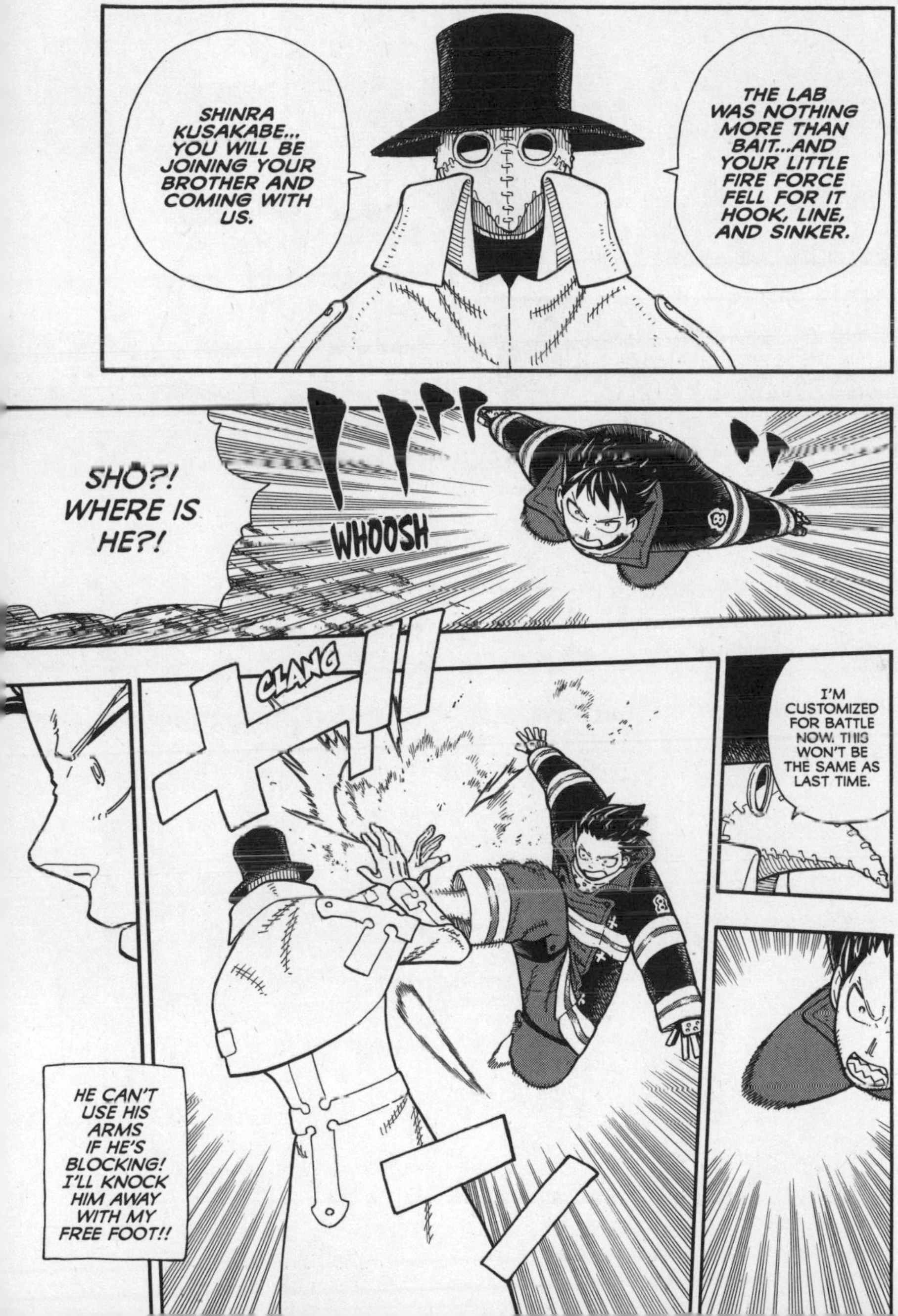
THE LAB WAS NOTHING MORE THAN BAIT...AND YOUR LITTLE FIRE FORCE FELL FOR IT HOOK, LINE, AND SINKER.
SHINRA KUSAKABE... YOU WILL BE JOINING YOUR BROTHER AND COMING WITH US.
WHOOSH
SHO?! WHERE IS HE?!
I'M CUSTOMIZED FOR BATTLE NOW. THIS WON'T BE THE SAME AS LAST TIME.
CLANG
HE CAN'T USE HIS ARMS IF HE'S BLOCKING! I'LL KNOCK HIM AWAY WITH MY FREE FOOT!!

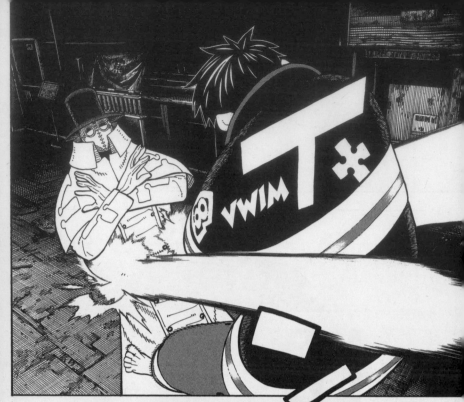

DID
SOMETHING
GRAZE ME?

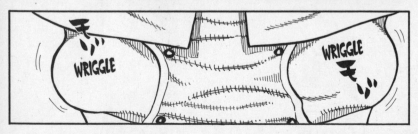

WRIGGLE

WRIGGLE

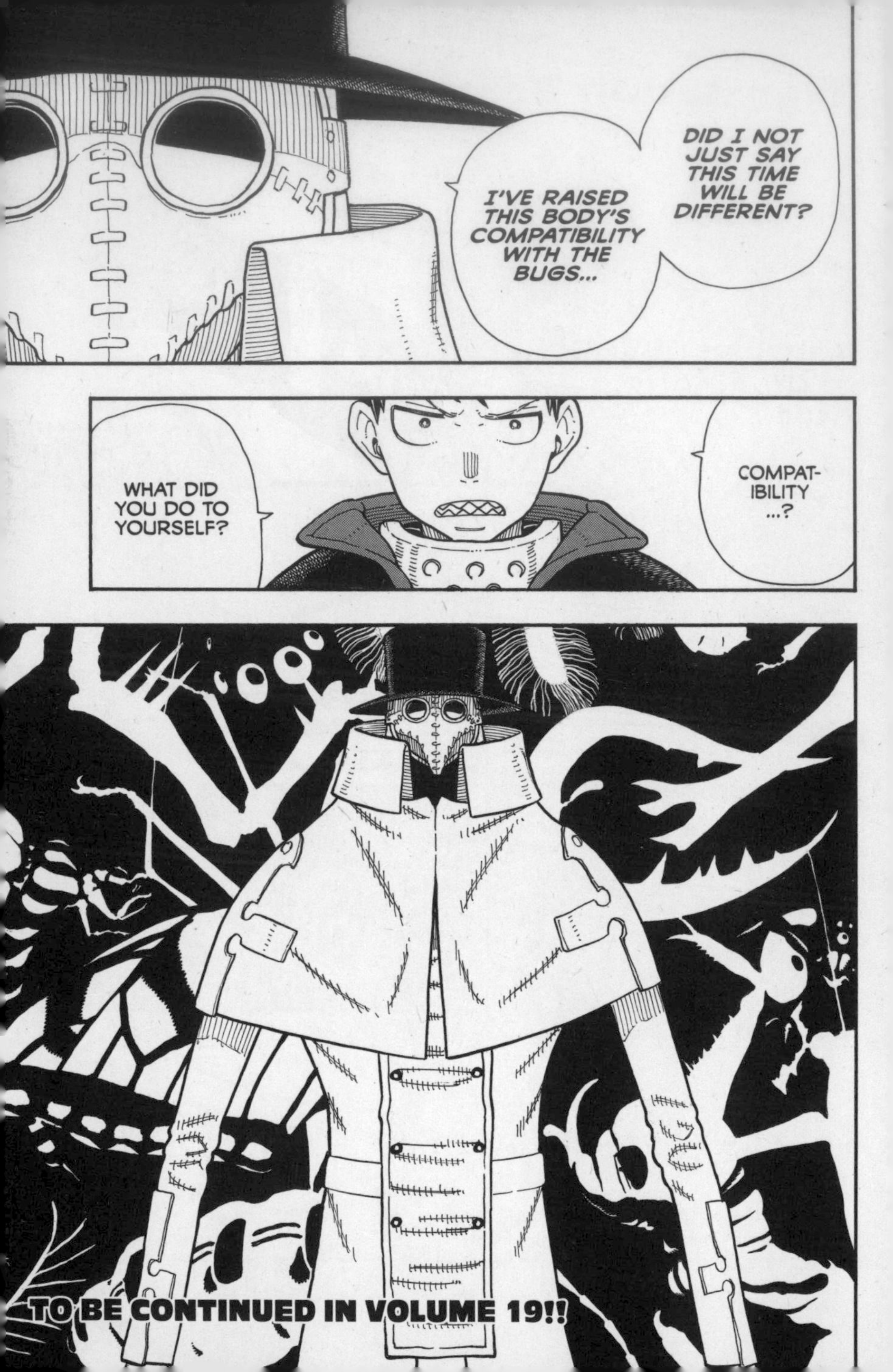
DID I NOT JUST SAY THIS TIME WILL BE DIFFERENT?
I'VE RAISED THIS BODY'S COMPATIBILITY WITH THE BUGS...
COMPAT-IBILITY ...?
WHAT DID YOU DO TO YOURSELF?
TO BE CONTINUED IN VOLUME 19!!

Translation Notes:

Juggernaut, page 2

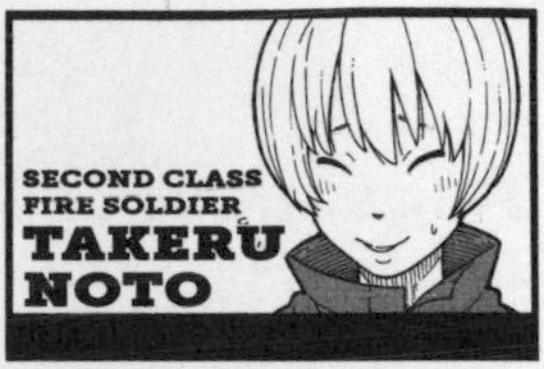
SECOND CLASS FIRE SOLDIER
TAKERU NOTO

In Japanese, "Jaga" means "potato." Hence the nickname Jaga-Noto, or Juggernaut.

Scowling Guardian of the Empire, page 37

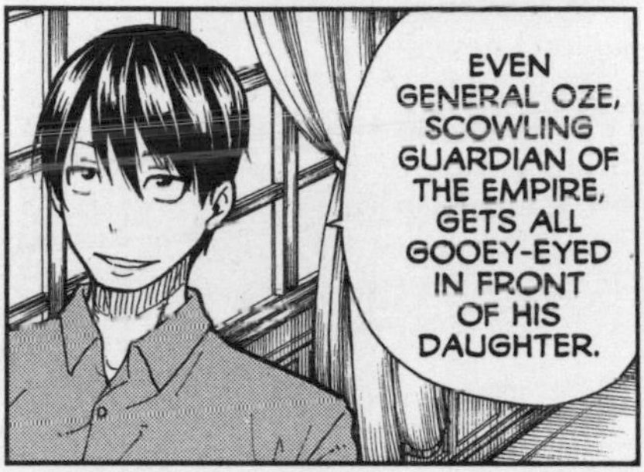
EVEN GENERAL OZE, SCOWLING GUARDIAN OF THE EMPIRE, GETS ALL GOOEY-EYED IN FRONT OF HIS DAUGHTER.

More specifically, General Oze's original nickname is Niō of the Empire. *Niō* refers to the guardian deities of Buddhist temples, often depicted in statue form. They are big, intimidating, and wear perpetual scowls.

The black goat always eats his letters, page 61

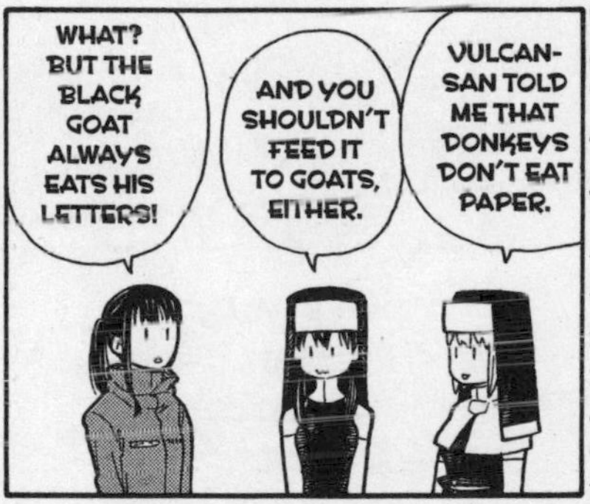
VULCAN-SAN TOLD ME THAT DONKEYS DON'T EAT PAPER.
AND YOU SHOULDN'T FEED IT TO GOATS, EITHER.
WHAT? BUT THE BLACK GOAT ALWAYS EATS HIS LETTERS!

This is a reference to a famous Japanese children's song *Yagi-san no Yūbin* (meaning roughly "Goat Mail"), which sings the tale of White Goat writing a letter to Black Goat, who eats it without reading it. The only solution is to write a letter to White Goat, asking what was in the letter, but White Goat in turn eats Black Goat's letter without reading it, and on and on in endless repeat.

Lucky Lecher Lure, page 101

In anime and manga, romantic comedies sometimes use a trope of the "lucky *sukebe*" or the "lucky lecher." The trope occurs when some miraculous incident results in one "lucky" young man accidentally finding his hand on a woman's breast, or catching sight of her undergarments.

Flags, page 109

In the world of Japanese entertainment, the world "flag" is used to describe an action or event that acts as foreshadowing. Most commonly, flags signal either future romantic developments between characters, or a character's untimely demise. "Flag" and "frag" are pronounced the same way in Japanese.

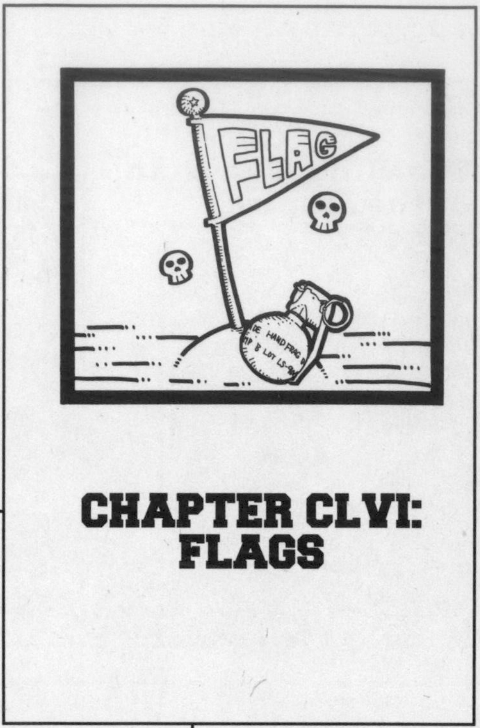
FLAG
CHAPTER CLVI:
FLAGS

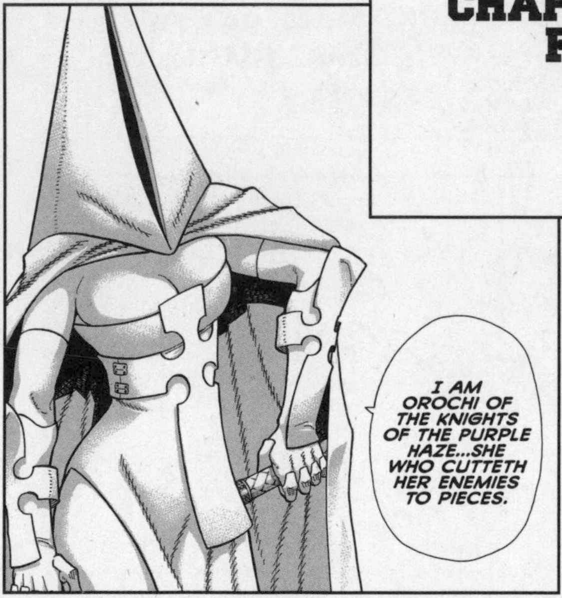
I AM OROCHI OF THE KNIGHTS OF THE PURPLE HAZE...SHE WHO CUTTETH HER ENEMIES TO PIECES.

She who cutteth her enemies to pieces, page 127

Orochi has a habit of using words and grammar that sound like an old-fashioned knight, but the correctness of her usage is often questionable.

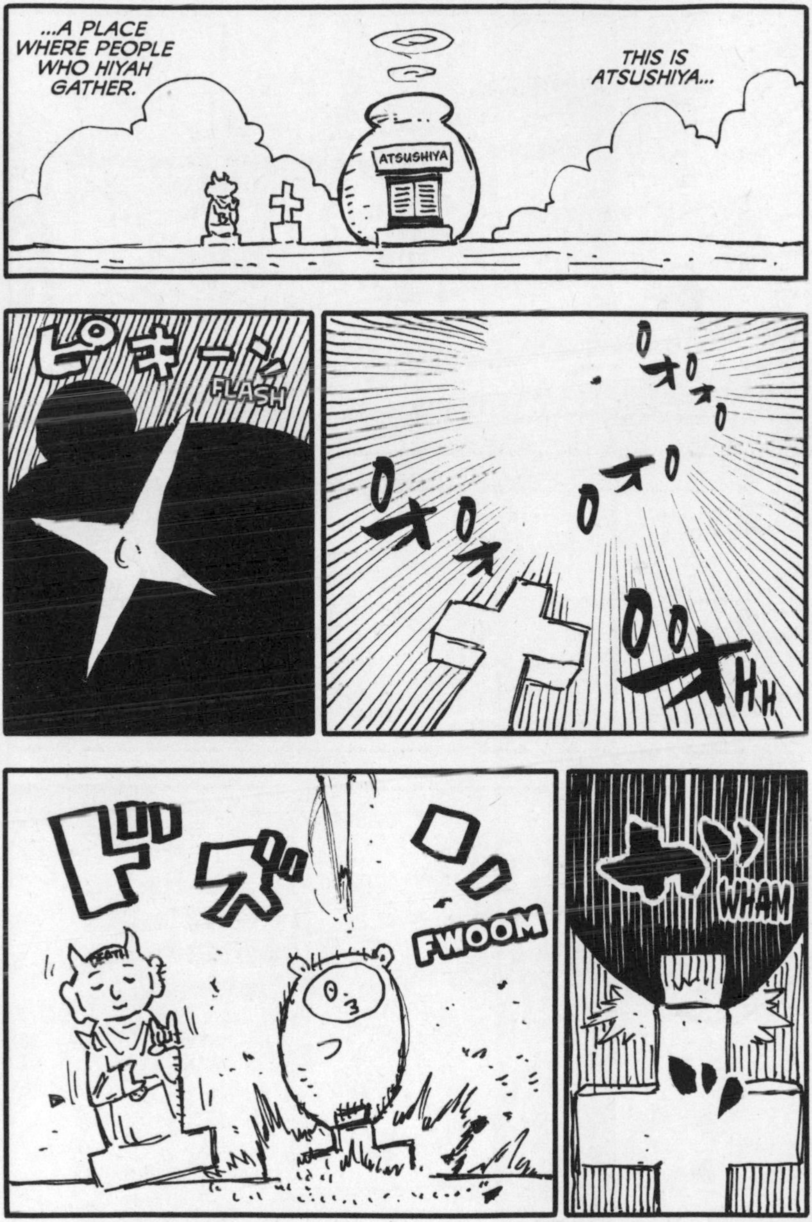
THIS IS ATSUSHIYA...
...A PLACE WHERE PEOPLE WHO HIYAH GATHER.
ATSUSHIYA
OOHH
FLASH
WHAM
FWOOM
DEATH

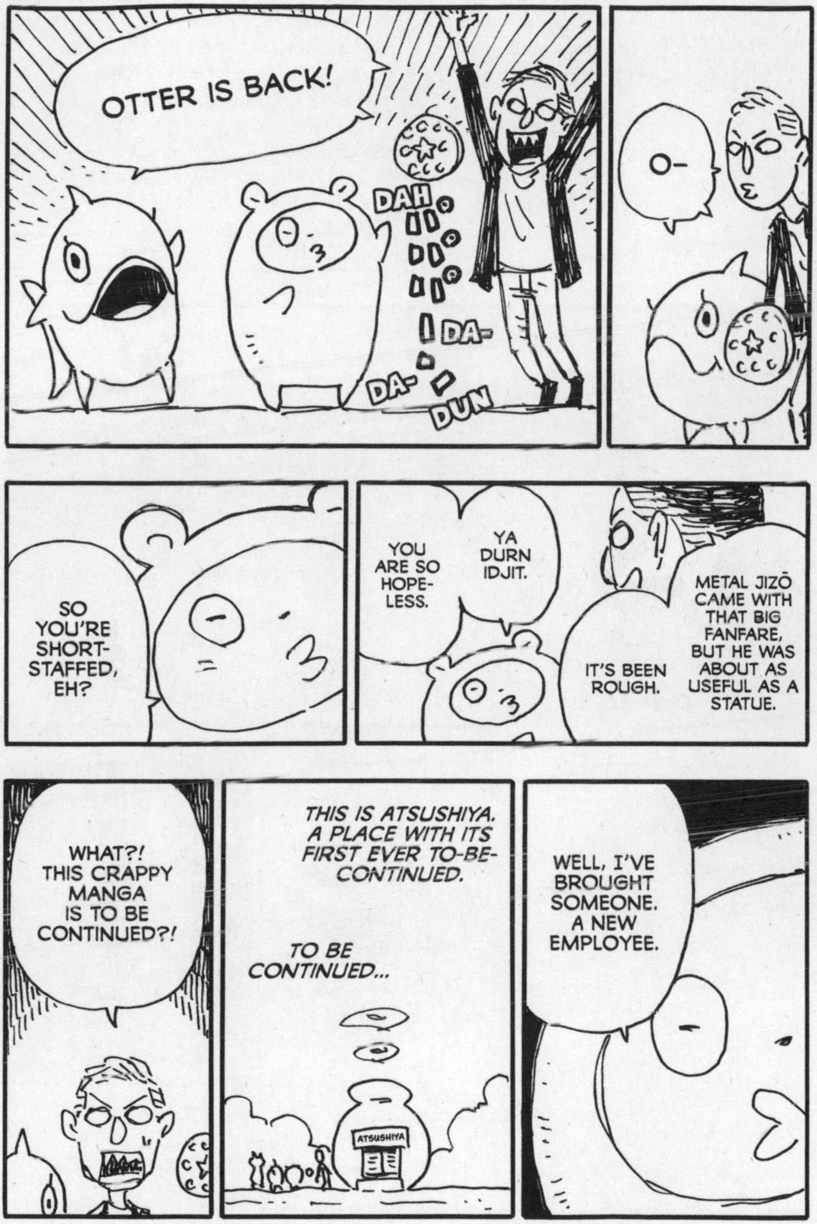
OTTER IS BACK!
DAH
DA-
DA-
DUN
METAL JIZŌ CAME WITH THAT BIG FANFARE, BUT HE WAS ABOUT AS USEFUL AS A STATUE.
IT'S BEEN ROUGH.
YA DURN IDJIT.
YOU ARE SO HOPE-LESS.
SO YOU'RE SHORT-STAFFED, EH?
WELL, I'VE BROUGHT SOMEONE. A NEW EMPLOYEE.
THIS IS ATSUSHIYA. A PLACE WITH ITS FIRST EVER TO-BE-CONTINUED.
TO BE CONTINUED...
ATSUSHIYA
WHAT?! THIS CRAPPY MANGA IS TO BE CONTINUED?!

Fire Force 18 is a work of fiction. Names, characters, places, and incidents are the products of the author's imagination or are used fictitiously. Any resemblance to actual events, locales, or persons, living or dead, is entirely coincidental.

A Kodansha Comics Trade Paperback Original
Fire Force 18 copyright © 2019 Atsushi Ohkubo
English translation copyright © 2020 Atsushi Ohkubo

All rights reserved.

Published in the United States by Kodansha Comics, an imprint of
Kodansha USA Publishing, LLC, New York.

Publication rights for this English edition arranged through
Kodansha Ltd., Tokyo.

First published in Japan in 2019 by Kodansha Ltd., Tokyo.

ISBN 978-1-63236-834-8

Printed in the United States of America.

www.kodanshacomics.com

9 8 7 6 5 4 3 2 1
Translation: Alethea Nibley & Athena Nibley
Lettering: AndWorld Design
Editing: Haruko Hashimoto
Kodansha Comics edition cover design by Phil Balsman

Publisher: Kiichiro Sugawara
Vice president of marketing & publicity: Naho Yamada

Director of publishing services: Ben Applegate
Associate director of operations: Stephen Pakula
Publishing services managing editor: Noelle Webster
Assistant production manager: Emi Lotto, Angela Zurlo